Play at the Center of the Curriculum

Second Edition

Judith Van Hoorn
University of the Pacific

Barbara Scales
University of California, Berkeley

Patricia Monighan Nourot
Sonoma State University

Keith Rodriquez Alward

Merrill,
an imprint of Prentice Hall
Upper Saddle River, New Jersey   Columbus, Ohio

Library of Congress Cataloging-in-Publication Data
Play at the center of the curriculum / Judith Van Hoorn . . . [et al.].—2nd ed.
    p.   cm.
    Includes bibliographical references and index.
    ISBN 0-13-611997-2 (pbk.)
    1. Play. 2. Early Childhood education—Curricula. 3. Child development.   I. Van
Hoorn, Judith Lieberman.
  LB1139.35.P55P57   1999
  155.4'18—dc21   98-11345
                                                                                                        CIP

Cover photo: © Stock Market, Inc.
Editor: Ann Castel Davis
Production Editor: Sheryl Glicker Langner
Photo Researcher: Sandy Lenahan
Design Coordinator: Karrie M. Converse
Text Designer: STELLARViSIONs
Cover Designer: Rod Harris
Production Manager: Laura Messerly
Electronic Text Management: Marilyn Wilson Phelps, Karen L. Bretz, Tracey B. Ward
Director of Marketing: Kevin Flanagan
Marketing Manager: Suzanne Stanton
Advertising/Marketing Coordinator: Krista Groshong

This book was set in Baskerville by Prentice Hall and was printed and bound by R. R.
Donnelley & Sons Company. The cover was printed by Phoenix Color Corp.

 © 1999, 1993 by Prentice-Hall, Inc.
Simon & Schuster/A Viacom Company
Upper Saddle River, New Jersey 07458

Photo credits: pp. 1, 21, 4659, 65, 89, 112, 135, 141, 167 by Periera Studios; pp. 5, 12,
26, 51, 63, 76, 107, 121, 175, 179, 183, 203, 207, 224, 237, 243, 263, 286, 293, 297 by
Ralph Granich; pp. 16, 37, 43, 103, 148, 151 by Todd Yarrington/Merrill; pp. 32, 99,
171, 235 by Barbara Schwartz/Merrill; p. 87 by Daniel Floss/Merrill; pp. 124, 157, 199,
209, 217, 257, 283 by Anne Vega/Merrill; p. 278 by Tom Watson/Merrill.

Printed in the United States of America

10 9 8 7 6 5 4 3 2 1

ISBN: 0-13-611997-2

Prentice-Hall International (UK) Limited, *London*
Prentice-Hall of Australia Pty. Limited, *Sydney*
Prentice-Hall of Canada, Inc., *Toronto*
Prentice-Hall Hispanoamericana, S. A., *Mexico*
Prentice-Hall of India Private Limited, *New Delhi*
Prentice-Hall of Japan, Inc., *Tokyo*
Simon & Schuster Asia Pte. Ltd., *Singapore*
Editora Prentice-Hall do Brasil, Ltda., *Rio de Janeiro*

Preface

In *Play at the Center of the Curriculum,* we create an architecture for play in the classroom. The natural link between play and development is our blueprint. Developmental theory suggests to us that play is a primary factor in the development of intelligence, personality, competencies, sense of self, and social awareness.

In spite of its importance in development, play is seldom part of the curriculum. More typically, it is used to expend energy or provide a break from classroom work for both children and teacher.

The old adage that "play is children's work" is given new meaning in this book for teachers. We demonstrate how the function of play in children's lives can be drawn upon to improve developmentally-based early childhood education.

Other works on play and education ask how play can be used to support curriculum. We take a unique position and ask how curriculum can support play. This follows from our unhesitating belief in the development and educational value in play.

As seasoned teachers, we demonstrate how to draw both the methods and the content of a successful curriculum from children's spontaneous play. We interweave anecdotes of children's play, theories of play and development, and instructional strategies that place play at the center of the curriculum. This book carefully blends theory and practice.

Each child is a developing whole—integrating competencies and skills through play. The child who is "just playing" is, in fact, blending individual needs with cultural expectations. In carefully articulating the play-centered curriculum, we more effectively support the developmental forces that advance children in their ever-broadening participation in their culture.

By combining sound theory with practical illustrations, *Play at the Center of the Curriculum* achieves a solid argument for play in formal education. Teachers and students in the field of early childhood education will find this book to be a valuable resource. This is not merely a "how to" book nor is it simply a "thought book." Rather it is a blending of each, serving the reader in a number of ways.

Play at the Center of the Curriculum is a resource for those who want to engage children in a developmental zone where both children and teachers are learning. Current and future teachers are guided in methods of supporting children's progress through play. The teacher becomes the architect and gardener of the environment, using play as both structure and nutrient.

ORGANIZATION AND STRUCTURE

The text has been written for students with varying experience and knowledge. Chapters 1–5 are designed to form foundation concepts and principles. We recommend that these are read first. Chapters 2 and 3 introduce theory and research that support our understanding of play and development. The reader is introduced to the ideas of major figures in developmental theory: Piaget, Vygotsky, Erikson, and Mead, as well as to the work of contemporary researchers. Chapters 4 and 5 bring this developmental focus back to the reality of the classroom. The teacher's role in setting the stage, actively guiding, and intervening are explored.

Chapters 6 through 10 explore the traditional curriculum concerns of early childhood education: the arts, science, mathematics, language and literacy, and socialization. Each chapter begins with an anecdote which focuses on how a potential curriculum is embedded in children's spontaneous play. The reader will find a rich palette of practical ideas for the articulation of the play-centered curriculum.

Chapter 11 looks at ways in which play, toys, and technology interact to affect the young child's life. Many practical ideas and observations are offered on the roles of computers, television, and games.

Chapter 12 focuses on the important topic of assessment and shows how, through the observation of play and the elaboration of successful curriculum, the teacher can gain a keen sense of the child's progress.

Depending on the background of students, instructors may vary the order of these chapters and draw upon some of the suggested resources to extend students' understanding. Chapters 6–12 may be assigned in an order compatible with the instructor's course structure.

Chapter 13 provides a more in-depth integration of developmental theory and play. The relationship between play and development is again addressed, with specific focus on the constructivist views of development elaborated by Piaget and Vygotsky. The role of play in intelligence, competency, personality, and sense of self are explored. Particular attention is paid to the role of work, adult models, and authority. This chapter comes later in the book because its focus is the integration between play and development and implications for practice. It will, we believe, be more meaningful after the more experientially focused chapters which precede it.

The Second Edition

In this second edition, the authors have enriched and expanded the emphasis in a number of areas, drawing upon their recent teaching and observations in classrooms as well as recent research and writing in this field. This edition includes a greater emphasis on play-centered curricula in first and second grade.

Each chapter also provides more discussion, examples, and research that shows how play-centered curricula can be inclusive, inviting programs for all children, children and families from all cultural backgrounds, as well as children with special needs. The chapters on the arts, science, mathematics, language and literacy, and socialization (Chapters 6-10) have been expanded to reflect these emphases and incorporate current work in the field.

In chapter 11, "Play, Toys and Technology," the technology section includes an expanded discussion of the developmentally appropriate use of technology, such as e-mail and digital cameras, in play-based curricula. Throughout the text there is also a greater emphasis on the theoretical work of Vygotsky and the implications for practice in a play-centered curriculum.

Anecdotes

Each chapter anchors its focus in the world of children by beginning with an anecdote related to play and education. Numerous additional classroom anecdotes and examples are provided throughout each chapter. These practical observations ground the reader in day-to-day educational experiences.

Summary and Conclusion

Each chapter ends with a summary and conclusion, giving the reader a brief review of the main points of the chapter and some practical implications.

Focusing Our Thinking

Sections at the conclusion to each chapter provide an additional aid to students' understanding. Some of these are thought exercises. Others are suggested activities that can be carried out within the context of an educational course or by individual readers.

Suggested Resources

Each chapter is rich in up-to-date references. All chapters end with several key resources that augment students' appreciation of the material and enhance course work.

ACKNOWLEDGMENTS

We gratefully acknowledge those who have shared with us their experiences, ideas, critical reviews, exemplary references, and examples from their own practice: Melinda Bachman, Lyda Beardsley, Libby Byers, Greta Campbell, Shirley Cheal, Joyce Chong, Lia Thompson-Clark, Randi Dingman, Eduardo Eizner, Buffy Frick, Patricia Fluetsch, Anita Gensler, Kristin Hope, Jackie Imbimbo, Rochelle Jacobs, Craig Jones, Richard Karsch, Marjorie Keegan, Susan Kyle, Janet Lederman, Janet Gonzalez-Mena, Gail Mon Pere, Ada Rappeport, Kitty Ritz, Kathy Rosebrook, Ann Siefert, Lisa Tabachnick, Maureen Wieser, Lucienne Wurr, and Professors Millie Almy, Elliot Turiel, Jerry Mendelson, and Edward Farrell as well as Vivian Paley. Their contributions have been practical, often inspiring, and have enriched our text.

We acknowledge the special contributions of Leni von Blanckensee, a specialist in educational technology as well as an experienced kindergarten teacher, who wrote the revised section on technology that appears in this second edition. Sara Billingslea contributed numerous suggestions and relevant references related to meeting children's special needs through play-centered curricula.

We thank the University of the Pacific for the McDaniel Grant and the Merck Foundation Grant which provided support for developing Chapters 6 and 7. Special thanks to Carly Rivers, Shiela Bradley, and Brock Kolby for their excellent work preparing the manuscript.

We are grateful for the continued support and wise counsel we received from our editor Ann Davis and Pat Grogg, her assistant. We also wish to thank the following reviewers of the manuscript who provided valuable comments and suggestions: Jane H. Bugnand, Eastern New Mexico University, Roswell; Susan Gomez, California State University, Sacramento; Lynn Lessie, Atlantic Community College (NJ); and Linda L. Reiten, University of Mary (ND). And above all, thanks to the children and their teachers who brought life to our presentation of the play-centered curriculum.

This book is dedicated to Millie Almy, beloved mentor to our study of children's play.

Contents

9   Language, Literacy, and Play   179

CHAPTER 1

Looking at
Play Through
Teachers' Eyes

With dramatic gestures, Brandon loudly sings, "Can you milk my cow?" After he and his kindergarten classmates finish the song with a rousing, "Yes, ma'am!" their teacher, Anna, calls upon Becky and Tino to figure out the date and count the days the children have been to school. (This is the 26th day.) As other children join in the counting, Brandon takes a toy car out of his pocket. He spins the wheels, turns around, and shows it to Chris. After a moment, he reaches out to touch Kara's shoelaces, whispering, "I have snaps." Then he opens and refastens the Velcro snaps on his shoes.

Anna announces that it's choice time and calls on children to leave the circle and go to the activities of their choice. Brandon sits up straight, wanting to be called on and ready to start. The moment his name is called, he heads to the housekeeping area where Chris and Andy are opening some cupboards. Brandon announces: "I'll make breakfast." (He picks up the coffee pot.) "Here's coffee." (He pretends to pour a cup and gives it to Chris.)

Mary, a new student in the class, wanders into the housekeeping area holding the pet rat. Brandon interrupts his breakfast preparation and says to Mary, "You can't bring Fluffy in here. You have to keep her near her cage."

Within a few minutes, the theme of the children's play turns from eating to firefighting. Brandon and Andy go to the block area to get some long block "hoses." They spend a few minutes there pretending to hose down several block construction "fires." Brandon knocks one down, to the angry cries of the builders, Valerie and Paul. He then transforms the block hose into a gun, which he uses to shoot at them.

As he and Andy stomp about the block area, Brandon passes Mary, still holding the rat, and says to her, "That's too tight. See, like this." He takes the rat from her, cradles it, looks it in the eyes, and pats it. "Fluffy was at my house during vacation. I got to feed her. See, she remembers me."

Brandon and Andy spend the next ten minutes building a house and a maze for Fluffy while Mary looks on. Brandon has chosen to play in the block area each day for more than a month. The boys gather five arches for a roof, partially covering a rectangular enclosure they have made by stacking blocks horizontally, using long blocks and, when there are none left, two shorter blocks placed side by side.

When he and Andy have finished building the "roof," Brandon rushes to a nearby table where Rotha and Kai are chatting and drawing. He grabs a piece of paper and hastily scribbles on the middle of it, knocking off a few templates and scissors in the process. "This is my map. This is my map for the maze" he says. Brandon then goes to his teacher for some tape to put on the maze. He points to a figure on the paper where two lines intersect and says, "See my X? That's where Fluffy gets out."

Every observation of children's play illustrates its multi-dimensional qualities. By observing Brandon's play for just a short time, we learn much about the way he is developing socially. For example, we see that Brandon is able to join Chris and Andy in their play in the housekeeping area by introducing an appropriate topic, offering to make breakfast. This observation also informs us about Brandon's developing cognitive abilities. In his play, he uses a block to symbolically represent first a hose, and then a gun. While building the house for Fluffy, Brandon demonstrates practical knowledge of equivalencies when he uses two short blocks to equal the length of one longer block. Thus, by observing Brandon's play, we witness how he applies his developing abilities in real situations.

This observation also raises some of the many questions that teachers ask about children's play. How should a teacher respond when a child plays during group instruction? How can a teacher balance spontaneous play with teacher-directed activities? Should teachers redirect children when they select the same play materials or themes day after day? Should gun play be allowed? How can play help us understand and assess children's cognitive, linguistic, social, emotional and physical development? Studying Brandon leads us to the central issue this book addresses: Why should play be at the center of the curriculum in early childhood programs?

PLAY AT THE CENTER OF A DEVELOPMENTALLY BASED CURRICULUM

Developmentally based early childhood programs place the developmental characteristics of the young child—the learner—at the center of the curriculum. This book is based on the premise that play is the central force in young children's development. Consequently, a developmentally based program is a play-centered program.

In honoring the child's play we honor the "whole child." When discussing a play-centered curriculum, we think of the child as a developing "whole" human being in whom the processes of development are integrated. Play fosters all aspects of the child's development: emotional, social, intellectual, linguistic, and physical. Play involves the integration of what children have learned rather than the linear acquisition of specific skills. This view contrasts with the idea of development as the linear acquisition of separate skills.

In promoting a play-centered curriculum, we make short- and long-term investments in development. In the short term, play creates a classroom atmosphere of cooperation, initiative, and intellectual challenge. If we look at long-term consequences, we find that play supports children's growth in broad, inclusive competencies such as self-direction and industry. These are competencies valued by both parents and educators, and ones that children will need to develop in order to function as adults in our society.

Throughout this book we emphasize how curricula in particular areas, such as language and literacy, mathematics, and the arts, can support and enrich play.

This idea contrasts with the traditional view that play enriches subject-matter competencies, and, would ask, for example, "How can pretend play help children expand their vocabulary?" Our view also contrasts with the idea of play traditionally found in the intermediate grades—play as a reward for finishing work.

This does not mean that all play is equal in our eyes. Play is fun, but it is more than fun. Its critical dimension is to provide conditions that foster children's development using their own sources of energy. In the following chapters we articulate the play-based curricula that support children's own developmental forces.

Play as a Fundamental Human Activity

Play is a human phenomenon that occurs across the life span as well as across cultures. Parents in Mexico teach their babies the clapping game "tortillas" while older children and adults play Loteria. Adolescent East Indians play soccer while younger children play hopping games accompanied by singing. Chinese toddlers clap to a verse celebrating their grandmothers, "banging the gong merrily to accompany me home," while the grandmothers, in their old age, play Mah Jong. As humans, we enjoy not only our own engagement in play, but we are often fascinated by the play of others. The entertainment and sports industries reflect the popularity of observing play.

The Power of Play in Development

What is the specific rationale for including play in school programs for young children? It is the power of play that drives development. During early childhood, play is fundamental to young children's development because it is simultaneously a facet of development and the source of energy for development.

Play is a facet of development, an expression of the child's developing personality, sense of self, intellect, social capacity and physicality. At the same time, through their play, children direct their energy to activities of their own choice. These activities stimulate further development.

The fundamental premise of this book is that play is the heart of developmentally appropriate early childhood programs and, therefore, should be at the center of every curriculum. If the young child is at the center of the curriculum, then play should be at the center of the curriculum as well, for play is the basic activity of early childhood.

Play is essential for optimal development and learning in young children. The match between the characteristics of play and the characteristics of the young child provides a synergy that drives development as no teacher-directed activity can.

Grounding Practice in Theory, Research, and the Wisdom of Practitioners

The idea of play at the center of the early childhood curriculum is grounded in work from four early childhood traditions: (1) early childhood practitioners, (2) researchers and theorists who have studied play, (3) researchers and theorists in the area of development and learning, and (4) educational historians.

Play and the wisdom of practitioners.   Historically, play has been at the center of early childhood programs (Monighan-Nourot, Scales, Van Hoorn with Almy, 1987). Early childhood educators have observed and emphasized that young children bring an energy and enthusiasm to their play that not only seems to drive development, but also seems to be an inseparable part of development. A kindergarten student building with blocks might spend an hour focused intently on this task, but might squirm when asked to sit down for ten minutes to practice writing letters of the alphabet. Using a favorite word of young children, we might ask "why?"

Play, theory and research.   Theorists and researchers who study play suggest possible reasons for its importance in the development of young children when they describe the characteristics of play. According to theorists, the distinguishing features of play include: (1) intrinsic motivation, (2) active engagement, (3) attention to means rather than ends, (4) non-literal behavior, and (5) freedom from external rules (Monighan-Nourot, et al., 1987).

When young children are actively engaged and intrinsically motivated, we observe their zest as well as their focused attention. We see them using language to communicate with others, solving problems, drawing, riding trikes, etc. Children's sense of autonomy, initiative and industry are rooted in intrinsic motivation and active engagement.

Play includes intrinsic motivation and active engagement.

Attention to means rather than ends indicates that children are less involved with achieving a goal than the process of reaching it. Young children are well aware of the grown-up things they cannot yet do. Even the competencies that are expected of them, such as waiting for a snack, sharing, cutting with scissors, and later, learning to read, add and subtract, and simple household chores, are often frustrating. In their play, children can change the goals and the ways to achieve the goals.

> This shifting among alternative patterns of means and goals appears to contribute flexibility to the child's thinking and problem solving. These new combinations may be accompanied by a sense of discovery and exhilaration. Miller (1974) borrows "galumphing," a term from Lewis Carroll's poem "Jabberwocky," to describe this. "Galumphing" with ideas lacks the smoothness and efficiency that characterize more goal-specific activity, but it is experimentation that may enhance creative thinking. Opportunities for "galumphing" are lacking in curricula that are programmed to have the child arrive at only "correct" responses. (Monighan-Nourot et al., 1987, p. 17)

Young children's play is often non-literal, pretend play, that is, not bound by rules. How is fantasy play useful to a young child learning to function in the real world? Children's symbolic development is fostered through the creation and use of symbols in pretend play as well as in hypothetical, "as if" situations. Through play, children develop boundaries of the real, the imagined, and also visions of the possible, the drive from childhood that turns the wheels of inventions.

Play, development and learning.   Support for placing play at the center of the curriculum comes from the work of theorists and researchers who have examined the role of play in development and learning. In the chapters that follow, we turn to the work of Piaget and Vygotsky for an understanding of the importance of play in cognitive development, to Erikson and Mead for an understanding of the role of play in the child's developing sense of self and social relationships, and to Vygotsky and Erikson for an understanding of how play might reflect issues of culture and society.

Play and traditions of schooling.   Writings on the history of schooling also lead us to place play at the center of the early childhood education curriculum. Historians have examined issues such as "what is worth learning" as well as the ways in which formal schools differ from informal apprenticeship structures found in less industrialized, traditional societies.

Early schools in the Middle East and Europe evolved for specific purposes, such as training scribes. Only select groups of boys in middle childhood and adolescence attended school. Later, as formal schools spread geographically, the number of students in schools grew. During the past century, the rationale for schooling changed. In today's formal schools, many activities have become separate from their applications (Cole & Cole, 1993).

During the late 1800s a greater number of adults needed to have basic competencies in numeracy and literacy while a more elite group of adults needed more technical competencies. It was also during this period and the early 1900s that children younger than seven or eight years old entered "school-like" settings. For the children of factory workers, these settings constituted "day care" institutions that had the aim of keeping children out of harm's way. For the children of the emerging, more-educated middle class, the settings were nursery schools and kindergartens that aimed to support the development of the child. Play often comprised a large part of these programs.

The gradual blending of the goals of day care, preschool, kindergarten and the primary grades has often led to increased pressure for teacher-directed curricula and programs that stress learning "academic" skills. When these models include play, the play is bent to support these skills. Teachers find that young students bring little spontaneous pleasure to learning addition facts or sight words if a didactic approach is used. Play is then viewed for its instrumental value: "What game will make memorizing these words more fun?"

As these historical perspectives of formal schooling demonstrate, teacher-directed activities are sometimes interesting for children and relate to important adult knowledge, competencies and skills. For example, children are often interested in adult daily life activities. When teacher-directed activities are appropriate to children's interests, and they are actively engaged, we then see these activities as appropriate to their development.

However, the purpose of teacher-directed curricula is not always obvious to the child, the parent, or even the teacher, as much as teachers may try to make the rationale apparent. Yet when children do not repeat teacher-directed activities in their own play, it usually means that the activities are without interest or perceived value.

These considerations of the history of formal schooling bring us back to our position that play should be at the center of the early childhood curriculum. Play-centered programs are built around the strengths of young children, rather than their weaknesses. The foundations of early childhood programs should not be grounded in accidents of history. Therefore, we see a preschool-K–1 program as firmly play-based, and complemented with daily life activities and some teacher-directed activities. We see second grade as a transitional year, with emphasis on daily life activities, complemented with play and teacher-directed activities, and third grade as a time when play and work are merged into children's extended projects, thereby integrating areas of academic learning.

Play at the Center of a Balanced Curriculum

In our view, education for children from preschool through third grade should promote the development of both the competent young child and the competent future adult. This is best accomplished by means of a balanced, play-centered program as shown in Figure 1.1.

As Figure 1.1 illustrates, play is at the center of a balanced curriculum. Daily-life activities are the critical second strata. For example, daily life activities

Figure 1.1
Play at the Center of a Balanced
Curriculum.

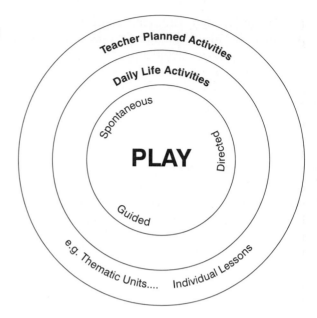

include preschoolers involved in setting the table, kindergartners involved in planting a garden, first graders involved in mailing their first letters, and second graders learning to tell time. Teacher-directed activities, thematic units as well as subject area units, constitute the third strata.

In the play-centered curriculum described in this book, there is a constant flow among these three levels. We discuss how children repeat daily life and teacher-directed activity in their play, how teachers plan daily-life activities so that they draw upon the power of play, and how teachers can use children's play to promote curricular objectives. In contrast to the traditional emphasis on how play can be used to support subject matter objectives, in this book we also emphasize how curricula in content areas can enrich and support good play.

By changing our focus from play to daily-life activities to teacher-directed activities (and always back to play), our view becomes the opposite of the traditional view. When children play, we believe they are engrossed in what most interests them. They are also practicing and developing competencies at the edge of their potential. In play, self-directed learning engages and focuses attention, and provides numerous opportunities for children to practice self control. When children are involved in daily-life activities such as cleaning up, learning to tie their shoes, learning to make their beds, etc., they are engaged in what is important in the lives of the adults around them. The purpose of daily-life activities is readily apparent, if not always enjoyable. When carrying out daily-life activities, there are procedures to learn and rules, that the society determines, to obey. This is not necessarily true of play. For example, when a child like Brandon pretends to make coffee for breakfast, he does not have to adhere to the sequence of how one really makes coffee and can choose to turn the cup of coffee into a glass of orange juice or a cup of ice cream. Play, too, has rules but children have more power to determine them.

Children's involvement in play, daily-life activities (society-directed activities) and teacher-directed activities differs when we compare the rationale for the child's activity. Children play because of their own interests. In play, there is no "one task" that is imposed upon the child by adults. There is no need for the child to utilize will power to meet adult expectations. Daily-life activities demand will power in order to accomplish tasks not of one's choosing, for self regulation. Unless teacher-directed activities are developmentally attuned to the children's level, it is difficult for children to adhere to a task. Prior to middle childhood, children have difficulty marshalling sufficient will power as they aspire to learn such adult competencies as reading or writing. In middle childhood, children become increasingly interested and able to master daily-life competencies. Historically, children living in more traditional cultures, as well as those attending formal schools, were seven or eight—the beginning of middle childhood—before such tasks were expected of them. This remains true today in many countries where educators wait until children are seven or eight before introducing formal reading or mathematics lessons.

The Play Continuum

When teachers focus on play at the center of the curriculum, they include spontaneous play, guided play, and teacher-directed play. Although these three terms appear to distinguish three separate domains of play, we view them as points along a continuum that goes from child-initiated to teacher-initiated play, as shown in Figure 1.2.

Planning the Play-Centered Curriculum

A play-centered curriculum is not a laissez faire curriculum in which anything goes. It is a curriculum that uses the power of play to foster children's development. It is an emergent curriculum in which teachers take an active role in balancing spontaneous play, guided play, directed play, and teacher-directed activities. Throughout this book, we emphasize that this balance depends on many factors, such as the developmental level and interests of the children, the culture of the families and the school. Children's school curricula must also be seen in the context of their lives. The child who goes from day care to school to an evening at home watching TV has a different need for play than the child who attends nursery school two days per week and plays outside most of the time.

Figure 1.2
The Play Continuum.

SPONTANEOUS PLAY	GUIDED PLAY	TEACHER-DIRECTED PLAY
Child-Initiated	- - - - - - - - - ▶	Teacher-Initiated

HOW TEACHERS OF YOUNG CHILDREN VIEW PLAY

In the following pages, we return to the vignette of Brandon and Anna that opened this chapter. We also draw from interviews with other preschool and primary teachers who spoke about the implementation of a play-centered curriculum.

Play Through the Eyes of Brandon's Teacher

We first consider the ways that Anna, Brandon's teacher, uses her observations of his play to gain insight into his growth and development:

ಎ Play gives Brandon opportunities to select activities of his own choosing. I am learning a lot about Brandon by watching him play. He tends to visit several areas during this 30–40 minute period, but I've noticed he often sustains a dramatic theme such as "firefighter" for a fairly long time, or returns to the same theme at several points during the day. He shows much more focused attention during this time than he does when I'm presenting a more structured lesson, like today, for example, in circle time, when I introduced counting skills.

He's definitely one of the more verbal children in our group. His social skills are improving, and he often demonstrates a caring attitude toward the other children. I noticed he was also very nurturing toward Fluffy today. He loves to help care for her. I feel this is a wonderful opportunity for him to develop his sense of responsibility, though he has been a bit possessive about her since he took her home. He's really attached to her. He's interested in learning more about rats and brought in a book from the library and copied a picture. Choice time gives him and the other children more of a chance to develop their individual interests.

He generally gets along with the other children, but he can be aggressive at times, for instance when he knocked down someone's blocks. This year he rarely got into direct physical confrontations, as he did last year in preschool. I've been keeping anecdotes on this and it seems that these aggressive acts tend to happen when he's rushed or has too many people around him. Today's episode involving using the blocks as guns certainly raised my classic question about war play: "Should I stop it?" I'm often uncertain about what to do, especially when it is such a momentary theme as it was today.

Along with my written anecdotes, I've been trying to decide what else to include in his portfolio. Today I thought about keeping the map. He was so eager to take it home that I decided to make a copy of it to save. ಎ

Anna continues:

ಎ I'm experimenting a lot with play. It's been a gradual process. Observing the children's behavior, I feel that I'm on the right track.

It's hard to believe how different my program is from the way it was only three or four years ago. I had a desk for each child and all of my "inside" time was teacher-directed, either whole class activities or centers. Now my program is definitely play-centered. I include materials to encourage literacy, math, art, and social development. Now we have work tables and a lot more open space. The first thing I did was order blocks. We haven't had blocks in a kindergarten at this school for as long as I've been here and that's twelve years. The one older kindergarten teacher here said that her old set of blocks was probably still in a district storehouse somewhere.

I also expanded the housekeeping area. In the beginning, I had a very small one, but I never really thought about it as more than a special area where kids could go when they were finished with something else. Now I see how important the playhouse is. I have had a lot of fun making it more attractive to the children who are immigrants. I included more photos of the families, pictures from ethnic calendars, dolls with ethnic clothing, and objects the children are familiar with from their own backgrounds, like rice bowls and chopsticks. The children seem to feel more at home in my classroom and can play out what they know.

Anyway, I think my kids are a lot more creative and thoughtful than when my program was more teacher-dominated. Half of the students who were in my class last year are in Kristin's class now. She told me last week that she noticed a difference. The children who were in my class are particularly eager to initiate projects and they tend to stay engrossed longer. She also sees a difference in the way they cooperate with everyone, not just their good friends, and the way they respect each others' work. ะๅ

Anna mentioned that Sarah's mother noticed a difference, too. Several years ago Anna used a very structured reading program with prereaders and worksheets. This year the children began their own journals on the first day of school. She put pads of paper and pencils in many places in the classroom to encourage writing.

Sarah's mother told Anna that she was very happy that Anna was finally teaching reading, and that Sarah was reading and writing a lot at home. Anna remarked that Sarah's sister was in her class five years ago when she was presenting formal reading lessons and having her students work in workbooks. Anna realized that this story of the two sisters didn't conclusively prove the point, but she thought that, in general, her students were now much more self-directed in reading and writing. She pointed out that, during what she calls choice time (which she used to call playtime), probably a third of the children are reading or writing at any given moment.

Anna went on to discuss the issue of choice time:

ะๅ By the way, I used to call choice time "free-activity time," and before that, "free playtime." I still haven't found a name I'm happy with. Free activity or free choice implies that children don't have freedom to choose the rest of the day, or that they can do anything they want. I began using choice time instead of playtime because I thought it was easier for parents and children to understand that important things go on during this time. But now I may change back next year because I want to emphasize to the parents that play is important. I've been joking that I want to "up play" rather than "down play" play! I want to show parents how it benefits their children.

Play often reflects daily activities.

We had our first open house last week. I put together a slide show with slides from last year and some slides from the first two weeks of school. It made a great difference for parents to see "live" examples of how play is important. As I discussed the development of self-esteem, I showed several slides of Jimmy and Andrea building a tower taller than they are. (I wish I had had a video camera for that.)

The slides also gave me a chance to talk about play and social development. I purposely selected slides that included every student in my class so each parent could get a personal message about how important play is to his/her own child's social development.

Of course, I also emphasized the ways in which children use what they've learned in academic areas, and learn more through play. I showed slides of the children building with blocks, pouring and measuring as they played "making chili" at the sand table and talked about their development of math concepts. I used slides of children writing in their journals, others scribbling on the chalkboard and one reading to another as I talked about literacy development. The slides helped parents make the connections between play and their children's development in all areas.

I worked out a way to illustrate developmental progress. There were four wonderful slides—if I may say so—showing the growth of complexity of Genette's block constructions over a two-month period last year. ❧

In this brief conversation, Brandon's teacher mentioned issues vital to the play-centered curriculum, issues that we shall return to throughout this book. She discussed the development of her program in terms of carefully observing children to understand their interests and development. She uses play anecdotes as part of her assessment program and puts play-created products, such as Brandon's map, in her students' portfolios. Anna reflected carefully on the effects of her interventions in children's play, questioning, for example, "what to do about war play" and "how to help immigrant children feel more comfortable in the classroom." She also experimented with curricular ideas such as using play to support emerging literacy and conceptual mathematics development. We discuss these ideas and provide additional examples in the subject-oriented chapters on the arts, science, mathematics, and language and literacy.

Across the country, preschool and primary teachers are re-examining the role of play in their programs. Teachers are trying to make programs more developmentally appropriate as well as more sensitive to the increasing diversity of students and families in their programs. As we wrote this book, we visited and spoke to the teachers and administrators at Brandon's school and numerous other schools to observe the variety of current practices and understandings about children's play. Our conversations with three teachers from Brandon's school exemplify the typical, yet important, ideas and concerns educators raise and which we discuss throughout this text.

Randi, a preschool teacher, emphasizes the role of play in meeting the social and emotional needs of individual children. Pat, a kindergarten teacher, raises the question "What is good play?" and the issue of assessment. Kristin, a first-grade teacher, focuses on the importance of choices in children's development. She also discusses how the play curriculum challenges students to use their developing academic skills in a comfortable environment.

❧ Randi (Preschool): Meeting the Needs of Individual Children

I think that play gives children a chance to make their own choices, their own decisions. The chances it provides for socialization also are very important. As they play, children communicate their feelings and ideas. This is especially important in my program where almost all my children have special needs. For many, English is a second language. Play gives them a chance to express themselves in a less formal and more comfortable situation than circle time, for example. Play also provides opportunities for children to use their own language fluently and to express ideas in nonverbal ways. It's important for developing their sense of self-worth.

I think that play is particularly important for children, like Brandon, whose families are having serious problems. Brandon comes from an English-speaking home and had already developed good English language abilities when he came to school. However, he was also aggressive and didn't necessarily use the vocabulary I wanted the others to learn! I noticed much progress through the year. I have enough space and materials here so that he could get what he needed. From what I hear, his outbursts are much less frequent this year than last.

Among the questions I have are: "Am I doing the best I can for my students who speak English as a second language?" It's hard for me when I can't follow the dialogue of their dramatic play. When I think about children like Brandon, I find I have questions about how to handle aggressive play. ❧

❧ Pat (Kindergarten): From Dittos and Desks to Blocks and Bubbles

I consider play anything children decide to do that's not adult-directed, like reading by themselves. If the choice is theirs, logically, they should enjoy it.

Play gives young children the time to develop language skills, get along with their peers, make choices, and be responsible. It gives me the chance to learn more about the children, see what they do, and discover what they're really interested in doing. It also gives me time to interact with each child personally.

What I want to happen, what I consider "good play" depends on the child. Yesterday I observed Marissa in what I consider good play for her. Marissa always seems to follow the other children. Yesterday, however, she was playing by herself with a small playhouse. She had selected what she herself wanted to do. She talked to herself a lot and stayed focused. This is a new behavior for her: selecting her own activity and staying with it.

I've made a commitment to write observations. I need to learn more about what to look for when I'm observing. Also, I want to ask questions to find out what children are really thinking, so they can respond without thinking "What's the right answer?" I feel as though I'm at a new stage in learning how to intervene. ❧

❧ Kristin (First Grade): Letting Children Develop at Their Own Pace

During free-choice time, my children have access to blocks, Legos and other manipulatives, art materials like paint and markers, and the housekeeping corner. It's also a time when they can dictate a story to me or a parent volunteer, or get some help from their peers in inventing the spelling of words.

I think kids need to have time to work on concepts they are developing at their own pace and by their own choice. Right now there's a lot of writing going on. Some write letters, others write whole sentences. In language, as in other areas, there is a wide range of abilities. During free-choice time, children work at a level that's comfortable for them.

During the past year I've extended the amount of play time I provide. Now I plan for at least thirty to forty minutes a day, usually in the early afternoon. When they've had enough time to make their own choices about learning, the children are much more able to focus on the social studies or science activities scheduled at the end of the day.

I'm still questioning the amount of play time that's best. I'm also constantly rearranging the environment, trying to make enough space for 31 children in this small classroom. It's hard. Another goal of mine is to discuss my program effectively with parents. Play has never been a traditional part of first-grade curriculum in our area. Parents often ask me whether we really have time to play if we are to get the children ready for second grade. 🙠

During our visits to schools we listened to the questions about play, children's development, and education—the questions that arise as educators revise or revitalize programs. These visits were fun because teachers shared so many stories. They were impressive because teachers revealed insights and raised issues. In this book we address these issues, and share stories from some of the teachers we talked to, as well as stories of our own. We create bridges between practice, research, and theory that deal with play in a playful way.

PLAY: THE CORE OF DEVELOPMENTALLY BASED PRACTICE

Some teachers with whom we spoke told us that their whole program consists of play. Others, like Kristin, are experimenting with including more play in the curriculum. Others are wondering if play is appropriate, and, if so, what kinds and how much. All are trying to answer questions about the role of play in meeting the needs of the children they teach.

"Developmentally appropriate practice" is a term used by the National Association for the Education of Young Children to describe programs grounded in child development theory and research, thereby designed to meet the developmental needs of children (Bredekamp & Copple, 1997). These are programs in which children's development in all areas is fostered through age-appropriate activities congruent with children's growth. Such programs also address the individual developmental needs of each child in the classroom.

Some of the teachers we talked to take these developmental needs into account with regard to their teaching practices. For example, in discussing her program, Rosemarie considers both typical development of 3- and 4-year-olds, as well as the particular needs of children who use English as a second language. Neil thinks about the normal growth needs of 6- and 7-year-olds, and of special needs children such as Mona, diagnosed as emotionally disturbed and mainstreamed into Neil's class for part of the day.

The growing literature on developmentally appropriate practice emphasizes the need to provide children with a meaningful curriculum to give them choices that interest and challenge, and to provide adult guidance appropriate to individual needs.

The premise of this book is that play is at the center of a developmentally appropriate curriculum. This follows from our conviction that play provides the integrative context essential to support the growth of the whole child, particularly through the preschool years and during the primary grades. This position, and the theory and research on which it is based, is discussed in chapters 2 and 3 and further developed in chapter 13.

Play supports the growth of the whole child.

The Critical Role of the Teacher in the Emergent Curriculum

If play is at the center of the early childhood curriculum, how is the curriculum developed? How does a teacher foster literacy, mathematical thinking, artistic expression, social development, self-esteem, scientific thinking, and other concepts, dispositions, and skills valued in early education?

We believe that the teacher is the key to the play-centered curriculum. This is a curriculum in constant development, an emergent, evolving curriculum. The knowledgeable teacher uses a wide repertoire of techniques to carefully orchestrate the flow from spontaneous play to guided and directed play, to more subject-oriented instruction, and back to play. This flow is in tune with and arises from the developmental needs of individual children in the class.

&. Scott introduced himself as a "third grade teacher just promoted to kindergarten." This was the first year that he had tried to "incorporate any play . . . much less make play the major part of my program." With little opportunity to visit other programs, Scott started the year feeling that he was sinking as much as he was swimming. "In my sinking mode, I went for teacher-structured activities as life rafts. They felt safe. They were like the curriculum I knew."

It took Scott most of the year to set up an environment where his students could have choices and sustained time to work through activities. Scott needed to read enough to convince himself that play was truly the cornerstone of development for young children. Then he could begin to make changes based on that conviction.

He concluded: "This has become the most intellectually challenging year for me. I am learning how to plan for play and how to use play to assess students' growth. I like the concept of an evolving curriculum but it takes patience as well as creativity to work it out each day. Things don't always work out as I had imagined.

"Because I'm an experienced teacher, I sometimes feel that I should be able to do this right away. But it doesn't work out that way. It involves a major shift in the way I'm thinking as well as in the way I structure the program: a paradigm shift."

Scott also mentioned how he felt at times when his friends from the "upper grades" came into his classroom. "I know they're thinking that I'm 'just' playing. I'm finally feeling that I can defend what I do, explain why play is so important." ❧

A play-centered curriculum needs playful teachers who enjoy being spontaneous and creative as well as reflective and analytical. This curriculum is teacher-orchestrated rather than teacher-controlled. It is not a step-by-step teacher-proof didactic curriculum. This play-centered curriculum is also very different from a laissez-faire play curriculum in which no one observes or intervenes in play, such as recess time at many schools.

SUMMARY AND CONCLUSION

This text begins with an examination of the theory and research that support a play-centered curriculum. Chapter 2 examines the development of play, drawing upon major "classical" theories as well as the work of several current theorists. Chapter 3 provides perspectives on how play supports the development of children's symbolic thought, language and literacy, logical-mathematical thinking, problem solving, imagination and creativity. Chapters 4 and 5 detail the many levels at which teachers can carefully orchestrate numerous and complex opportunities for children's play in early childhood programs. These chapters examine the many factors regarding intervention strategies, environments, materials, and timing that educators must consider in program implementation. In each chapter we discuss general guidelines as well as specific considerations and provide numerous anecdotes as illustrations. Chapters 6 through 9 focus on the relationships between play and the traditional subject areas: the arts, science, mathematics, and language and literacy.

In this text we emphasize an important question: "How do activities in academic areas support good play?" This complements the traditional question of how play fosters development in a particular area, for example, "How does play support development in math?" Each chapter emphasizes that play always remains an integrated whole—greater and far more significant than the sum of its parts.

Each subject-oriented chapter provides a particular lens through which we examine play. We discuss how play relates to the development of competencies in each area of the curriculum. We add an elementary focus to erase traditional distinctions among preschool, kindergarten, first grade, and second-grade programs.

In each chapter we discuss issues that relate to meeting the special needs of diverse populations of students and their families. An inclusive play-based cur riculum addresses issues of diversity and special needs as integral to the emergent curriculum, not as an "add-on."

In the subject-oriented chapters that follow, we provide specific explanations along with many anecdotal examples of the relationships between play and development in such particular areas as the arts (chapter 6), science (chapter 7), mathematics (chapter 8), and language and literacy (chapter 9). Chapter 10 considers relationships between play and children's socialization. Chapter 11 focuses on considerations of toys and technology in the context of young children's play.

In a play-centered, emergent curriculum, ongoing assessment is needed. Chapter 12, "Play as a Tool for Assessment," provides a multitude of examples and strategies for tracing children's learning and development through play. Lastly, chapter 13, "Conclusion: Integrating Play, Development and Practice" provides a more detailed perspective of the central importance of the play-centered curriculum in children's development, drawing upon and expanding issues discussed throughout the book.

As we have discussed, although each chapter focuses on a separate subject area, play is central to the curriculum because it integrates aspects of development, as the following example from chapter 8 on play and mathematics illustrates. Lisa and Peter are working in the "post office," wrapping packages and sending them "to the Philippines." By reading this anecdote, what can you learn about Lisa's and Peter's language and social abilities as well as their development of mathematical concepts?

Lisa:	"Do we have enough paper to wrap this package (three books)? They're for my grandma Venecia from Cebu." Peter picks up two sheets of newspaper. "We're going to have to tape these together. Wait, here's the tape. I'll hold this."
	They tape the two sheets together by cutting and sticking two short pieces of tape horizontally from one newspaper sheet to the other. They then try to cut a long piece, but the tape gets twisted. Lisa cuts four short pieces and tapes the paper together.
Lisa:	"OK, put the books down here." They wrap the books, trying to make the package smooth around the edges, a difficult task since the books are not the same size. "This is going to be expensive! I bet it weighs a ton."
	They put the package on the scale. It has numbers to indicate ounces, and a teacher-made, non-standard measurement chart with three different colors indicating three different degrees of heaviness.
Peter:	"See. It's green. That's heavy. It's going to be three dollars!" He takes the star stamps and pad and stamps three green stars at the top left of the package. "Wait. You need to put her address on it."

>   Lisa picks up a thin blue marker and slowly writes GRUM VNS-
>   ESSA 632 SEEBOO. Then she carefully selects a thick red
>   marker and draws a heart with a butterfly to the left of the
>   address.

In this episode Lisa and Peter demonstrate that they know some basic information about applications of mathematics to everyday situations. They know that one weighs a package before sending it and they have some beginning understandings of the concept of weight. Furthermore, both Lisa and Peter demonstrate that they understand that the weight of the package relates to the price of mailing it. Lisa also demonstrates that she is aware that one uses numerals to write an address. Lisa and Peter were also learning about geometry (area) as they estimated how much paper it would take to wrap their parcel. At the post office, they were able to take information about weight, prices, addresses, and area, coordinate the information, and apply it.

Observations of Lisa's play also inform us about her dramatic gains in speaking English. At the beginning of the year Lisa spoke comfortably and fluently with her family members in her native Visayan, but was hesitant to speak English with the other children. This observation indicates that Lisa has gained considerable mastery of English, with dramatic gains in sentence length and complexity, as well as vocabulary. She is now comfortable initiating and developing conversations in English with her peers.

As we watch Lisa and Peter, we notice that they are able to sustain their cooperative play for more than twenty minutes. During this time, they encounter several problems, for example, Peter notices that one piece of paper is not large enough to wrap the package. Each time, one or the other, or both, come up with a solution that the other accepts. For example, Lisa solves the problem with the tape. Their play is goal oriented, good-natured and without conflict.

Throughout this book, we take numerous anecdotes and examine them through different lenses. In the preceding episodes we used a different lens for language, socialization, and mathematics. Each time we pick up a different lens, we become more certain that the children's play contributes to their development in that particular domain. And each time we put the lens down, we see other areas of development as they emerge. We look at the complex, integrated whole of the children's dramatic and creative interactions and creations, and feel a certainty about the value of play in the development of these young human beings.

FOCUSING OUR THINKING

1. Collect a rich variety of constructive play materials such as Play-Doh, clay, toothpicks, straws, popsicle sticks, colored papers, buttons, scissors and glue, magazines, postcards, etc.

   Play with these materials for at least 15–20 minutes, if possible, in groups of three or four.

Each group, or individual, can share what they did. How does their play process relate to their thoughts? Emotions? Physical abilities? How does this experience relate to childhood experiences?

2. Begin an annotated bibliography of children's books related to play. As you develop this bibliography, include a wide variety of topics and types of books: non-fiction, fiction, poetry and picture books. In your annotations, include an explanation of how the book relates to play.

3. Gather photos, make drawings, use a time line or other representation of your life. Start as early in childhood as you can. Highlight playful childhood and adult memories. What insights do you have into the nature of the play you enjoyed or patterns of play across time?

4. Interview parents, children and teachers about their ideas of the nature of play and ask questions such as: What is play? Why is it important? What can be learned by playing?

5. What do children need to know in the 21st century? How might the qualities of thought and behavior reflected in play be useful?

SUGGESTED RESOURCES

1. Paley, V. G. (1986). *Mollie is three*. Chicago: University of Chicago Press.
2. Paley, V. G. (1997). The girl with the brown crayon. Cambridge, MA: Harvard University Press.

   Wonderful introductions to a gifted teacher and writer's careful observations of young children's play. Primary grade teachers as well as preschool teachers will find these books informative, engrossing and hard to put down.

3. Stone, S. J. (1995). Wanted: Advocates for play in the primary grades. *Young Children, 50*(6), 45–54.

   An introductory article on play addressed to primary grade teachers who want to advocate for play, rather than defend it. Stone's article introduces many of the points discussed in this text, including building a support community. Primary grade teachers may find it a good article to share with colleagues.

4. Bruner, J. S., Jolly, A., & Sylva, K. (Eds.). (1976). *Play: Its role in development and evolution*. New York: Basic Books.

   A classic book edited by one of America's most influential psychologists. This work consists of 71 essays and studies examining play within a number of disciplines, including psychology, anthropology, biology and sociology.

5. Monighan-Nourot, P. (1990). The legacy of play in American early childhood education. In E. Klugman and S. Smilansky, (Eds.), *Children's play and learning* (pp. 59–85). New York: Teachers College Press.

   This historical account of play in early childhood programs reviews ancient as well as contemporary influences on American early childhood curricula, from the eighteenth to the twentieth century.

CHAPTER 2

The Development of Play

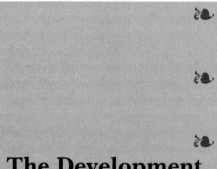

A preschool teacher hears from Andrew's parents that they fear he won't be ready for kindergarten if his major activity at school is play. Of course play is important, they acknowledge, but what about real learning like the ABCs and adding and subtracting? Won't he be at a disadvantage?

A second grade teacher incorporates activity time into each day's schedule. During this time children invent and pursue projects of their own choosing. The principal of the school visits on a day when a group of children are preparing the advertising copy for their Model 500 robot that they have built from cardboard boxes and art materials over several days' time. The principal questions the value of such playful activity in the second grade curriculum.

What answers can teachers give? Perhaps the most frequently quoted clichés are "Play is the child's way of learning" or "Play is the child's work." How does play contribute to learning? Is play related to work in some systematic manner, or is play simply evidence of the frivolity and freedom from responsibility we associate with childhood?

In order to answer these and other questions related to the role of play in curriculum for young children, we as teachers first need to formulate our ideas about the nature of play and how it develops. Although other species engage in physical or sensorimotor play, the range of play from motor play to pretend play to games with rules is a uniquely human capacity (Ellis, 1988). The development of play through these stages forms the foundation for the development of intellect, creativity and imagination, a sense of self, the resolution of feelings, and the capacity to interact with others in positive and morally sound ways. In this chapter and those that follow we view play through each of these various developmental lenses, discussing how play contributes to each in turn and to the integration of physical, social-emotional, and cognitive competencies for the whole child (Almy, 1984; Bergen, 1988; Berk & Winsler, 1995; Davidson, 1995; DeVries & Zan, 1994; Egan, 1988; Fromberg, 1992; Greenberg, 1989; Isenberg & Quisenberry, 1988; Lewis, 1995; Silvern & Chaille, 1996; Smilansky, 1968, 1990).

Play is more than a means to an end, however, even though these ends may be highly valued by educators and parents (Bruner, 1976; Jones & Reynolds, 1992; Monighan-Nourot, 1990; Sutton-Smith, 1988). Play is the source of laughter and humor, of inventiveness and beauty. It allows us to entertain possibilities and to envision the future. It helps us to persevere in our efforts and to explore the full range of our emotions. It fosters the spontaneity and joy that make us truly human. Keeping this in mind, we also invite you to consider how each lens reflects the ways development contributes to play itself as an essential aspect of human existence.

   In this chapter we look at major theories that address the development of play in childhood, and explore the levels and stages suggested by these theories. We begin by discussing the more "classic" theorists in developmental psychology whose theories about development in general are well articulated. Then we discuss research focused on play and development that we find particularly useful for teachers. We first consider Jean Piaget (1896–1980), a Swiss psychologist and biologist who set forth a comprehensive stage theory of the development of play in childhood. We then examine the work of Lev Vygotsky (1896–1934), a Russian psychologist and contemporary of Piaget whose writings were unavailable in English until relatively recently. Vygotsky and Piaget's theories share many of the same basic principles regarding play and complement one another by their differences in emphasis. George Herbert Mead (1863–1931), a sociologist who wrote about play and the developing self, is looked at next, followed by Erik Erikson (1902–1994), who theorized about the contribution of play to stages of psychosocial development. Next we turn to research by Parten regarding social participation in preschool play, and to the research of Corsaro (1985) and Paley (1981, 1984, 1992) who illuminate the role of peer culture in the socialization of young children.

   In the sections that follow, we guide your understanding of the theory and research in education that support the importance of play in the learning of young children and throughout the human life span. We address the theoretical grounding for understanding how play relates to learning and development throughout all dimensions of experience in early childhood, and help teachers formulate articulate responses to the questions of parents and colleagues regarding the role of play in classrooms for young children. We also share our insights as both teachers and researchers on how the joyful, spontaneous, and unpredictable nature of play enlivens and enriches classrooms where teachers are truly able to use play as a window for understanding the development of the children in their care.

A CONSTRUCTIVIST VIEW OF PLAY AND LEARNING

In this book we take the position clearly articulated by Piaget, Vygotsky, Mead and Erikson that development and learning occur through constructive processes. In this constructivist view, knowledge is not simply acquired by accumulating information from the environment, or even copying the behavior of others, but is based on what the individual child brings to each situation. The "schemes" or mental patterns that the child has already constructed are modified and built upon as children try to make sense of new experiences in light of what they already know. For example, four-year-old Kim explains the word "invisible" to his friend Tony when the word comes up in a story read by a parent to the two boys. "It's like you go inside visible, and then no one can see you when you're in visible!" Kim asserts, and Tony nods his head in understanding. Kim bases his explanation on what he has experienced about not being seen in the game of hide and seek; if you hide inside something, then you can't be seen.

From the constructivist view of development, what the child already knows, and his or her patterns for interpreting experience, are modified through the child's own effort and initiative. Piaget placed particular importance on the self-regulating and autonomous activity of children's play in the construction of knowledge, and it is in young children's play that we see constructivism in action. Although Piaget's work focused on the active construction of knowledge through cognitive processes, other constructivist theorists such as Vygotsky (1962) and Mead (1934) and such researchers as Corsaro (1985) have emphasized the social processes central to constructing knowledge and the essentially interactive nature of learning and development. Theorists such as Erikson (1963) have emphasized the role of play in the emotional lives of children. We first turn to Piaget's work as the foundation for constructivist theory.

PIAGET: DEVELOPMENT AND PLAY

Piaget viewed the growth of intellect or cognition as one area of development in which the role of play in constructing knowledge is most clearly articulated. We view play through this lens to illustrate basic concepts that are key to our understanding of constructivist theory.

Imagine a world in which every experience you have is new, without mental pictures of previous events in your life to help you organize your perceptions and expectations. Life would be very confusing.

Fortunately, human beings do have the means for organizing experiences so that we can make sense of the events in our lives. According to Piaget, this means of organization is intelligent adaptation. In adaptation, humans modify their environments to fit their personal needs as well as themselves in response to their environments (Cowan, 1978).

Piaget created a model of the development of thinking that incorporates each of these aspects of adaptation: changing the environment to meet one's needs and changing oneself to meet the demands of the environment. In this model, Piaget posits an interactive process between these two aspects of adaptation, which he calls assimilation and accommodation. This interaction is the source of development and learning.

In assimilation, new elements of experience are incorporated into existing structures of thought. Most importantly, these elements are not simply added to the thoughts already there, like items tacked onto a grocery list. Instead, new elements are transformed by the individual's thinking process to fit into the structure or "template" of that individual's thinking.

An example is the assimilative pattern many children develop in playing with Play-Doh or clay. Clay-like substances can be pinched, patted, molded, and rolled using patterns from previous experiences. Schemes or potential patterns of action on clay or Play-Doh are part of the repertoire of mental patterns of many young children. What happens when a child encounters "oublek," a substance made of cornstarch and water that has some of the properties of clay, but also some different ones? The child's efforts to accommodate to the differences that the new material offers cause a change in the assimilative structure that will be applied to clay-like substances in the future.

In Piaget's theory, accommodation is a complement to the assimilative, meaning-making process. Accommodation allows the structure of our thinking to change when it serves us in adapting to new experiences. Accommodation is the process through which new schemes or mental patterns for potential behavior are created, or existing patterns are stretched and changed in form in order to incorporate new information. Accommodation allows us to meet challenges presented by the environment, such as resolving the cognitive surprise generated by playing with oublek when Play-Doh was expected.

The assimilation process allows us to consolidate, generalize, and apply our current structures of thinking to new situations and materials. It allows us to make sense of our experience in light of what we already know. The accommodation process challenges us to change and adapt our mental structures in the face of new information.

According to Piaget, there is constant interaction between these processes, alternating states of tension and balance concerning what "fits" into our schemes or mental models about experience, and what doesn't fit. Awareness that a new idea or perception does not fit into our structure of thinking calls for a change in our mental models, and results in the continuing development of thought. Through the interaction of assimilation and accommodation, children balance their internal states and meet their personal needs for intelligent adaptation.

In the early childhood years assimilative and accommodative processes are constantly fluctuating. First, the mental patterns fit the new situation. Then new elements are introduced that contradict that fit. Mental structures then change to accommodate these new elements. This process of construction and expansion marks the development of children's early thinking from idiosyncratic concepts about the way the world works to more stable and predictable relationships between internal mental models and the external world. Because of the changing nature of the child's emerging concepts, young children's behavior is largely governed by play, or a predominance of assimilation. What is essential is that play and assimilation emphasize the child's interests and current structures of thinking as the source of development. In the next section we turn to the contexts in which different types of knowledge are constructed.

Three Types of Knowledge

Piaget delineated three major types of knowledge that serve as the contexts for children's development: physical, logical-mathematical, and social. In their play, children develop all three. Physical knowledge is derived from activities with objects that allow children to make generalizations about the physical properties of objects. For example, through physical manipulation in play children may discover that rocks sink and corks float, blocks stacked too

Logical-mathematical knowledge is constructed by acting on objects.

high may fall, and sand and water may be used to mold forms (Kamii & DeVries, 1993).

Logical-mathematical knowledge, or knowledge about the relationships among objects, people, and ideas, is constructed as children reflect on the relationships between actions or objects, for instance by comparing the sizes of two balls, or the relative lengths of blocks. In logical-mathematical knowledge the concepts employed by the child come not from the objects themselves but from the relationship invented by the child (Almy, 1984). These two types of knowledge, physical and logical-mathematical, are constructed through the child's own experiences. Play is an opportunity to increase those experiences (Robinson, 1996).

In contrast, social knowledge is knowledge imparted by other people and includes labels and vocabulary as well as social conventions such as proper behavior at snack or group time. This type of knowledge falls closer to the accommodative end of the continuum, relying on processes of imitation and memorization for its acquisition. However, social knowledge also depends on the mental structures created through logical-mathematical knowledge for its application. As Kamii (1982) points out, categories such as "good words" and "bad words" are derived from social experiences but it is the logical-mathematical capacity for classification that enables children to decide when a word might meet with the disapproval of adults.

In practice, physical, logical-mathematical and social knowledge are closely connected in any situation involving the education of young children, as we see in this example:

ॐ Four-year-old Enid helps Madeline, the Assistant Teacher, bring food to the snack table. "We need one cracker for each place," Madeline coaches. Enid takes the crackers from the box and places one on each plate, and looks expectantly at her teacher. "There," Madeline says. "Let's count these together—1, 2, 3, 4, 5, 6, 7." Enid counts with her teacher. "Now let's count the crackers—1, 2, 3, 4, 5, 6, 7." They count together again. Madeline asks, "How many cups will we need if we have one for every person?"

Enid carefully takes one cup at a time from the stack and places each next to a plate with a cracker on it. Two of the cups tip over as she sets them down, and as she replaces them upright, Enid looks intently at the uneven places in the table top that have pushed the empty cups off balance. She runs her hand over the table next to the remaining plates to find a smooth spot before she sets down the next cup.

Enid looks expectantly at Madeline, pointing her finger at the first cup "1, 2, 3" Enid begins, then hesitates. Madeline joins her by counting "4, 5, 6, 7," and they finish the sequence of numbers. "Seven plates, seven crackers and seven cups" summarizes her teacher, and Enid beams at her accomplishment. "Would you like to ring the bell for snack?" Madeline asks. Enid nods and goes off to accomplish this last task.

(Nourot, in press) ॐ

In this example we see Enid constructing physical knowledge about strategies for placing crackers and cups on the snack table. She learns something about balance on even and uneven surfaces. Enid also constructs logical-mathematical knowledge about the relationship of cups to surfaces and about one-to-one correspondence. Madeline helps her count using one-to-one correspondence and presents the idea of equivalent sets for the seven plates, seven crackers, seven cups. Madeline also helps her to learn social conventional knowledge about the names and sequence of numbers in English, as well as the position of cups in relation to plates. Enid uses her knowledge of the purpose of the snack bell to call her classmates to enjoy her handiwork.

Teachers' abilities to understand and support children's learning depends on their skill in identifying the types of knowledge being constructed by the child and finding appropriate strategies to enhance that new knowledge. It is too easy for teachers of all-age students to rely heavily on showing and telling as vehicles to imitation and the acquisition of social knowledge. Teachers are challenged to provide opportunities for children to construct their own learning and apply what they have learned from others through playful activity (Forman, 1994, 1996). Both kinds of learning are important—knowledge derived from inner sources and knowledge derived from outer sources—and a balance between the two is necessary for development.

Piaget: The Development of Play

Piaget's theory is intimately tied to the study of play. Many of his important works are filled with observations of his own three children at play during their first three or four years of life and of other children he observed in preschool settings in Geneva, Switzerland.

His important work *Play, Dreams and Imitation* made play a central part of his theory. Here he showed how children develop the ability to represent their world through a series of stages in which assimilation and accommodation are increasingly better coordinated with each other. Children's ability to represent their inner concerns and understandings is revealed in their play which can be seen to progress through a series of stages. As each new stage is developed, it incorporates the possibilities for play of all the previous states (Figure 2-1). In the following sections, we present a brief description of these stages. (See also chapter 13.)

Practice or Functional Play.   The first stage is termed practice or functional play by Piaget and is a major characteristic of the stage of sensorimotor intelligence. Practice or functional play is what Piaget (1962) called "a happy display of known actions" in which children repeatedly practice their schemes for actions with objects or their own bodies. It is exemplified by the play of the infant, the grasping and pulling, kicking and propelling of arms that infants engage in for the pleasure of mastering the movement. It continues as children take part in activities such as splashing water or sifting sand, honking a horn, or riding a bike. Practice or functional play remains a major form of activity throughout childhood and adulthood. How many adults doodle while talking on the phone, or enjoy the exhilaration of jogging or the body moving to music with aerobics? Opportunities for practice play remain an important source of development and pleasure throughout life and provide an essential feature of school curriculum, as we illustrate in subsequent chapters.

Figure 2.1
Piaget's Stages of the Development of Play.

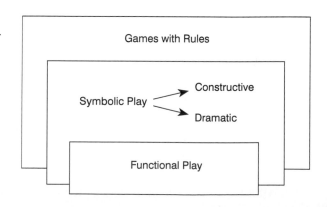

Symbolic Play.   The second stage, symbolic play, begins by 18 months of age and is a major characteristic of the stage of pre-operational intelligence (Fein, 1981; Fromberg, 1992; McCune, 1985; Rubin, Fein & Vandenberg, 1983). Symbolic play involves the use of mental representation to pretend that one object stands for another in play, or to take on a make-believe role in play. It forms a foundation of future abstract thinking and the ability to organize both work and play experiences as human beings develop. Three major forms of symbolic play are described by Piaget: constructive, dramatic, and games with rules, which demonstrate the beginnings of conceptual thought.

The first, constructive play, provides a natural link between functional play and more sophisticated forms of symbolic play. In constructive play the child uses concrete objects to create a representation of an object: blocks or Play-Doh manipulated to represent a house are typical examples. The intent in constructive play is to approach one's mental representation of the symbolized object as closely as possible. For example, three-year-old Sandy searches for just the right size and number of sticks to make five candles on her birthday cake or Josh struggles to make a peaked roof "because mine has a point on it like that."

Following closely on the heels of constructive play, and often overlapping it, comes dramatic play. This play involves the creation of imaginary roles and situations, and frequently accompanies the construction of pretend objects. But the representation is more abstract. Instead of simple object symbols, children use gesture and language to create imaginary roles and situations with complex themes, characters, and scripts. Sometimes this play is sociodramatic in nature, involving the negotiation of roles and pretend themes with others (Giffin, 1984; Goncu, 1984, 1993; Miller & Garvey, 1984; Nourot, 1996; Nicolopoulou, Scales, & Weintraub, 1994; Smilansky, 1968, 1990). At other times the play may be solitary, with characters, themes, and situations enacted by a single player. So, as Josh finishes his "peaked" garage, he may park a toy car in it and pretend that an imaginary family piles into the car for a trip to the beach. Sally may invite several children to play the part of guests at the birthday party as she enacts the role of the birthday girl. She "blows out" the stick candles and the group shares her sand birthday cake.

Both stages of symbolic play, constructive and dramatic, are intellectually and socially complicated. Their mastery sets the stage for games with rules play, which makes its appearance about the age of five or six, and continues as the predominant form of overt play throughout middle childhood, adolescence, and adulthood. Overt play is an important concept here because older children and adults continue to engage in constructive and dramatic play long after early childhood, but in a more covert manner. Dramatic and constructive play take the form of private fantasy and hypothetical thinking, and accompany the daily internal lives of adults in many of the same ways that overt dramatic play enriches the lives of young children.

The games with rules play stage involves adherence to an external set of social rules that govern play. A predominance of this type of play marks the transition from pre-operational to concrete operational thought in Piaget's theory. In this play, rules are negotiated and agreed upon by the players before the game begins. Some of these rules, such as those in games of marbles or checkers, are seen by children as handed down from God, or other authorities (Piaget, 1965d). Others are negotiated on the spot as children spontaneously invent a game, such as one with baseball cards or pebbles. The ability to negotiate and adhere to mutually-agreed-upon rules has its roots in the ad hoc negotiation of rules common to sociodramatic play at earlier stages of development (Kamii & DeVries, 1980).

VYGOTSKY: DEVELOPMENT AND PLAY

Even though Piaget was clearly of the opinion that social experience is essential for the development of rational capacities, his work largely focused on individuals rather than social interactions. Vygotsky, on the other hand, was primarily concerned with social interactions, and the historical and cultural contexts in which these interactions take place. Like Piaget, Vygotsky was a constructivist and believed that conflict and problem solving are essential features of child development. He was particularly interested in the social dynamics that support development. Vygotsky coined the term Zone of Proximal Development (ZPD) to refer to the conditions under which the child's understanding is furthered as a result of social interactions. Like Piaget, Vygotsky thought that play was essential to development. "Play is the source of development and creates the zone of proximal development." (1967, p. 16).

> Steven and Anthony are playing near the tunnel in the outdoor play yard. Steven, lying on his stomach with a face full of mock agony, moans "pretend you gave me medicine." Anthony pretends to feed him medicine, and Steven leaps up, announcing "All better." Then Anthony becomes the patient and Steven feeds him pretend medicine. They each take two turns. Then Anthony says, "I'm hungry," and they rush inside to get their lunch boxes, returning to the outdoor play area with a snack of pretzels. Steven holds up a pretzel and asks, "What letter?" "No letter," responds Anthony, and Steven takes a bite. "Now it's a B," shouts Anthony, and he bites his pretzel. "What letter?" "An O," shouts Steven. The final bite is eaten. "Now what letter?" asks Steven, holding out his empty hand. "No letter!" shouts Anthony delightedly, and they both fall on the ground laughing.

By observing children's representational play, teachers discover how new concepts, skills, and competencies emerge in the play of each child in relationship to others. In this observation of Steven and Anthony, we see how in their play they have created a zone of proximal development where their understanding of letters is further developed. This view of the zone of proximal development differs from the expert-novice model frequently studied in educational research on problem solving. Play is the source of development and creates the zone of proximal development (Nicolopoulou, 1996). What is left out in expert-novice model is the acknowledgment of play as a source of development in a zone of proximal development.

In viewing play as the source of the zone of proximal development, we focus on the collaborative construction of a pretend reality that is invented by the players and sustained by the rules they negotiate. Because relationships are of primary importance to young children, their desires to participate in imaginary worlds shared with others lead them to accept and invent new symbolic meanings, regulate their own impulses, and to collaboratively construct pretend realities. This can be observed across a wide range of early childhood settings. For example, early childhood educators and researchers working in integrated classrooms have noted that the play of children with developmental delays is more complex when they play with nondisabled peers (Smith, 1994).

Perhaps Vygotsky's most important contribution to understanding play and development is his assertion that every function in development occurs first at the social level and then at the individual level (Vygotsky, 1978). In this view, the social character of situations that promote development is of primary importance. For example, children are likely to feel more comfortable playing with familiar peers. Teachers' sensitivity to social contexts for learning and development largely governs the success of curriculum. For young children this social context is created most often through play.

Vygotksy's Levels of Symbolic Play

Vygotsky also contributed to our understanding of how play relates to levels in the development of symbolic thinking. He observed that very young children merged the meaning of objects with the objects themselves and thus could not think abstractly. In symbolic play, children use objects to represent ideas, situations and other objects. Objects that represent other objects are called "pivots." Children use pivots to anchor their mental representations of the meanings of words. For example, when Sam selects a book to represent a taco in his kitchen play, he anchors his concept of "taco-ness" with an object that opens and closes, and thus resembles a real taco in important ways. When children's representational competence grows, pivots become less necessary and meaning may be carried completely in the mind, for instance, through the use of an imaginary object. For Vygotsky the use of objects in play as support for the development of meaning-in-the-mind marks a key stage in the development of thought (Vygotsky, 1967, 1978).

Vygotsky clarified how children develop their understandings of rules. He asserted that all play has rules, and with new levels of development, rules become more explicit. In this way dramatic play, where rules are implicit, forms the foundation for games, where rules are explicit. Rules in dramatic play govern the organization of roles and behavior in play and events. For example, "Daddies shake hands like this" and "Firefighters have to hook up their hoses first." Yet the following of these rules is largely taken for granted during the dramatic play of children, until conflict among players occurs. Then children assert their versions of the rules governing characters' behavior and hypothetical events.

As children begin to articulate their ideas about rules that govern social behavior from their experiences and their family and cultural backgrounds, they also confront the ideas of others. Through these processes they develop the

In play, children distinguish their own perspective from those of others.

capacity to negotiate rules of play that are set forth before play begins. This can be particularly challenging for children with developmental delays or children with emotional disturbances. Yet basic to a play-centered curriculum are mutual understandings that throwing blocks or sand might hurt other children. In this way, children begin to understand why agreed-upon rules are essential to the functioning of society.

MEAD: PLAY AND THE DEVELOPING SENSE OF SELF

Dramatic role play in childhood contains another dimension related to, but separate from, perspective taking, abstract thinking in fantasy, and rule construction. It is through this dimension that children come to see aspects of the developing self.

Mead (1934) studied the relationship of play to the development of a sense of self. For Mead, play is the major vehicle for young children to learn to differentiate their own perspectives from those of others in their social worlds. As children take on pretend roles of others and coordinate those roles with the roles taken by their playmates, they come to view their own behavior from the perspectives of other people.

For example, Robert, playing at being a waiter in a restaurant, incorporates the perspectives of his "customers" when he asks them if they are ready to order. He then communicates with his "cook" in the kitchen and tells his customers "It will take a long time to get a burger here. Better go to McDonald's." This negotiation between the self and others also takes place outside of play scripts, as we see when Robert, his cook, and his customers have to figure out how they will put away the props and furniture for their restaurant when the teacher announces that it's clean-up time.

The Play Stage

According to Mead (1934), the preschool and primary-grade years provide the impetus and context for children to see themselves as unique human beings in relation to others. In Mead's theory, the young preschool child operates in the play stage of the development of the self, accomplishing role transformations from self to others with little elaboration or perspective. This is what Smilansky (1968) describes as the beginning stages of role play. The child simply becomes a tiger, or an astronaut, or a veterinarian, and then returns to being the self, with limited expansion of the components or complementary roles involved in the transformations. For example, three-year-old Jed announces "I'm a fireman! RRRRRRR!" and races around waving an imaginary hose. Five minutes later he becomes a puppy, barking and crawling on all fours.

In Mead's terms the child is just beginning to differentiate the "I" or spontaneous aspect of the self from the "me" or the sense of the self as a social object. In transforming himself into a puppy for example, Jed is beginning to figure out how others might view him from their perspectives. This is the stage in which children often create imaginary companions, representing the companion's viewpoint as well as that of the self. Children at this stage form the rudiments of a sense of self that include their own perspectives as well as representations of how others view them.

The Game Stage

As role play becomes more complex, children enter into what Mead called the game stage of the development of the self. In this stage the "I" aspect of self is coordinated with complex representations of the viewpoints of others about the "I." For example, five-year-old Cindy simultaneously plays the role of mother to her child who is eating breakfast, wife to her husband who is on his way to work, and ballerina to her coach who has just called her on the phone in a typical "morning in the playhouse" enactment. Not only does Cindy need to adjust her voice tone, gesture, and language to what she believes is appropriate for each role, she must imagine the complementary roles of others to each of her roles and coordinate them. All the while she uses cardboard chips to represent scrambled eggs and pours milk from a wooden block. The degree of distancing in such an enactment is impressive.

At this point, the child in the game stage of development of the self is learning to coordinate her representation of herself with the multiple perspectives that others might take with her. She can think about the various aspects of her "pretend selves" in relation to the other players. She shifts fluidly from the "I" to the "me" and considers herself a social object as well as an actor in her play.

The Generalized Other Stage

The third stage of the self defined by Mead is that of the generalized other. In this stage the child not only coordinates the "I" of the self with multiple "me's" but adopts a metacognitive stance regarding the framework within which action takes place. For example, Cindy might begin to comment on the rules of her culture that define authentic roles of mother or ballerina or accountant. Children in this stage often discuss the components of their roles with comments such as "Doctors talk like this" or "Babies walk this way." This is the stage where games with rules become of interest as children coordinate the perspectives of players with their understanding of the framework that governs the rule structure of the game. This behavior reflects the understandings children have about the social rules of our culture, as expressed in both their role behavior within the play and in their negotiations about roles outside the play.

The self at the stage of the generalized other, writes Mead, has a clear sense of the "I" and the "me" as well as the framework of social rules and expectations that monitor our behavior. According to Mead, it is this understanding that makes laws and social conventions plausible as a means of maintaining order in society.

ERIKSON: PLAY AND MASTERY OF THE INNER WORLD OF CHILDHOOD

Much of the theory regarding the role of play in the development and learning of young children is focused on the cognitive and social domains which Erikson expands to include the importance of play in the inner life of the child.

Initiative and Guilt

Erikson's theory of psychosocial development extends the work of Freud, who saw play as the expression of wish fulfillment and compensation in young children (Weber, 1984). For Erikson, the preschool and primary-grade years are characterized by the psychosocial stage, initiative and guilt, in which the child tests the expectations of himself or herself and the world (1963, 1977). The child uses play to work through past failures and present contradictions. Conflicts between archetypes of good and evil expressed in power roles such as superheroes and superheroines are common themes. Conflicts between child initiative and adult prohibitions are commonly expressed through fantasy play and stories that portray children as orphaned or separated from their parents, having to fend for themselves in the woods or at sea.

In dramatic play, preschool and kindergarten children enter into fantasies that allow them to explore their concepts of initiative and independence. In contrast to this are activities for young children that emphasize skills of learning and imitating models. Judgments of right or wrong are consistently made by adults with regard to children's processes and products, and children learn to rely on adult judgment and approval rather than their own internal resources.

  ❧ In completing a teacher-modeled project, Rebecca places the pre-cut green strip of "grass" above her name on the page and then places the "trunk" of the tree at a right angle above it. She begins to tear pieces of tissue paper for her "fall leaves." As she circulates about the classroom, her teacher pauses and says, "You've done a good job on your tree trunk, Rebecca, but your grass needs to go along the bottom edge of the paper." The teacher removes the green paper strip of grass as well as the brown trunk, placing them to match her own model. Rebecca puts her hands in her lap and stares desultorily around the room, as the teacher moves on to guide another child's activity. ❧

Both Elkind (1986, 1990) and Katz and Chard (1989) write of the effects of such judgment-laden curriculum on young children's sense of initiative. As Erikson noted, the disposition to take risks, to believe that one is a competent, capable learner, and to experiment with alternatives are undermined in such programs.

On the other hand, the child who is supported in taking initiative during this stage of development forms a firm foundation for the sense of competence and purpose that develops during middle childhood. Erikson named this next stage industry and inferiority.

Industry and Inferiority: Play and Work in Middle Childhood

During this period of development, the child's concerns center upon approval of the peer group, teachers, and the community for purposeful work, or play activities. These are more specific goals than those of the preschool or kindergarten years. The flexible goals of the initiative stage, where process takes precedence over product, evolve gradually into goal-oriented projects where children's "I can do it" attitude is expanded to include perseverance and self-evaluation.

Dewey (1971) also made this distinction between play and productive work on the one hand, and labor on the other. For Dewey, labor represents activity forced upon the child by others, with judgment and sanctions provided by others rather than the child's own intrinsic motivation for the activity. Too much labor, claim Katz and Chard (1989), leads to "damaged dispositions" of intrinsic motivation, concentration, initiative, confidence, and humor that are essential to the learning process throughout children's lives.

In all of these major theories of development, play has a major role in shaping the physical, social, emotional, and cognitive aspects of the child. Although the emphases differ in each theory, all of these theoretical perspectives underscore the centrality of play in the healthy development of the whole child as an integrated, competent and self-aware person.

RESEARCH PERSPECTIVES ON THE DEVELOPMENT OF PLAY

ટ⬥ The school day is just beginning at Gazebo Park School. Three-year-old Ben hangs around the edges of the sandbox for a long time, watching as the other children begin to take out toy vehicles and load them with sand. Finally, he picks up a truck and a shovel, kneels in the corner of the sandbox, and sings to himself as he constructs a mountain of sand.

Five-year-olds Riley, Gaelen, and Toby greet each other as they hang up their backpacks. "We're going to the magic planet today, remember?" says Riley. "Yeah, and we have to get around the Star Monster," adds Toby. "I'll be the driver." They quickly assemble seats of plastic crates and their spacecraft takes off. ટ⬥

Every day in preschools, child-care centers, kindergartens, and primary-grade classrooms, differences in the complexity of fantasy and the nature of social interaction are observed in children's play. Some differences reflect children's cultural, familial, and individual styles, others are more developmental in nature. Understanding the course of the development of play from preschool to middle childhood is essential for teachers seeking to implement a play-centered curriculum.

When teachers understand the developmental sequences and range of behaviors observed in the play of children of various ages, they are better equipped to support the play they observe. For the basis of this understanding we expand upon traditional theories of play by looking at research conducted on the development of play in preschool and primary settings.

Parten's Research on Play and Social Participation

Another useful model for looking at the development of children's play was developed by Parten in 1932. She studied the social behavior of children in a parent-cooperative preschool. Based on her observations, she hypothesized a continuum of social participation in play, ranging from onlooker behavior to solitary, parallel, and two forms of group play.

Onlooker behavior. Onlooker behavior is defined as a child watching ongoing play episodes, either because of reluctance to join, or as a way of scanning for an opening. Less sophisticated players may hang around the edge of a play scene in order to learn by observing and imitating others—at times they may be unsure how to enter a play episode. More sophisticated players use onlooker behavior to help them make choices, to decide which activity to select, or to ascertain the most effective strategy for gaining entrance into an already-established play episode. Sensitive teachers are aware of these possible functions of onlooking and use observation and intervention skillfully to determine what role, if any, he or she might take to help children make choices about their play activities. Onlooker behavior is not simply immature behavior, but, in fact, represents time for children to contemplate their actions.

Solitary play. Solitary play is defined as play alone, without overt interaction with peers. For example:

ҡ Four-year-old Hilary sits cross-legged, alone in the corner of the block area. She concentrates, wrinkling her brow, as she fits a piece of wooden train track onto the four already connected. She adds yet another piece, struggling to fit the piece evenly. ҡ

Parten found solitary play to be typical of the youngest children in her group, but more recent research has shown solitary play performs several functions, depending on the age of the child and the context of play (Monighan-Nourot, Scales, & Van Hoorn with Almy, 1987; Rubin et al., 1983). For example, solitary play may provide the context for complex dramatic play such as enacting a family drama with toy dinosaurs, or it may provide an occasion for needed respite from the demands of negotiating with others, such as solitary play with pegboards. The sensitive teacher is aware that children need opportunities for privacy and solitary play as well as opportunities for sharing and group play in the classroom.

Parallel play. Parallel play is defined as play with shared materials or physical proximity without attempts to coordinate play. Non-verbal negotiation of materials may occur but joint play themes and/or constructions are not elaborated.

Play can be solitary, parallel, or group.

For example, Joyce and Renita are playing parallel to one another with small wooden blocks and a large dollhouse. They each carry on quiet dialogues animating their characters. As one child puts down a block or a piece of dollhouse furniture, the other may pick it up, but they do not overtly acknowledge each other's play. This type of play is thought to represent the earliest, undifferentiated form of group play and teachers may often see it as a prelude to full-blown group play as children test the waters with their peers and gradually begin cooperative efforts.

Group play.   Parten differentiated two forms of group play. The first, associative play, is seen when children share and coordinate materials and space in proximity to one another, but lack true cooperation. It is similar to parallel play in its form but includes some of the elements of group cooperative play as well. For example, Frank and Mario are playing with Lego blocks at a small table. They negotiate with one another over the number of wheels they may each use out of the basket of parts, but they each continue to work on their own projects, rather than focus on a joint project.

The second form of group play, cooperative play, involves sophisticated efforts to negotiate joint play themes and constructions with peers, and is characterized by children stepping in and out of their play to establish roles or events. For example, three children playing restaurant may alternate their roles in the play as customer, cook, and waiter/waitress with comments about the plot made from outside the play, such as "Pretend the hamburger got burned."

In recent years, researchers who have used Parten's categories have included associative play within the category of group play because much inference is required on the part of the teacher observing children to distinguish between mere association and true cooperation (Rubin, Maioni, & Hornung, 1976). However, associative play may be seen as a bridge between the mere proximity of playmates represented in parallel play and full-blown cooperation and negotiation seen in cooperative play.

Research on Play and the Peer Culture

Cognitive representation, self concept and social participation are not the only aspects of children's play with objects and other people that contribute to learning and development. Corsaro and colleagues draw upon the theories of Piaget, Vygotsky and Mead to paint a picture of play as it contributes not only to the child's individual sense of self, but the creation of peer cultures among children at each level of development (Corsaro, 1985; Corsaro & Elder, 1990; Gaskins, Miller, & Corsaro, 1992). Corsaro contends that play is the primary matrix for socialization in childhood. Children's experiences as individuals are nested within a series of peer cultures that evolve at particular ages or levels of cognitive, social, emotional, and physical development. The characteristics of each peer culture are intimately connected to the integration of all levels of developing competencies and knowledge for children. From this view, the peer culture of toddlers differs from that of preschoolers, and that in turn from the peer culture of third graders, and so on through adolescence into adulthood. In their peer cultures at each level of development, children represent their interpretations of the larger culture, including the behavior of adults and older children as a compelling theme. For example, playing the role of teenager has a special allure in the peer culture of preschoolers—a view characterized by seeing teenagers as having the privileges of adulthood without the responsibilities of adult life. Young children's interpretations of the culture that surrounds them are shaped by cognitive developmental characteristics, such as young children's abilities to represent the perspectives of others, to reason about categories and sub-categories, and to use objects, gestures, and language to represent objects and ideas.

The peer culture's interpretations are also shaped by the characteristic development of the self, and the psychological and emotional concerns of a given age group. For example, in introducing a curriculum theme based on growing up, a teacher asked her preschool class of three- and four-year-olds, "How many of you have ever been a baby?" The four-year-olds eagerly waved their raised hands in affirmation, while many of the three-year-olds sat on their hands or just looked uncertain. Why?

The social construction of "babyhood" in mainstream American culture is one of vulnerability and incompetence, concepts of self that three-year-olds are typically struggling to leave behind them. On the other hand, the "baby" role in play is frequently configured as one in which the pretend baby has tremendous license to act naughty, create havoc, and control the play. One's willingness to admit to having been a baby or to pretend to be one in dramatic role play is shaped by the social construction of babyhood within the culture of preschool, and within the contexts and values of the adult culture (King, 1992; Meyers, Klein, & Genishi, 1994; Schwartzman, 1978). A good example is the use of English in superhero play by a Spanish-speaking preschooler described by Orellana (1994). She reflects on the power dimensions of language in play, and children's use of English in portraying powerful characters.

While the socially constructed meanings of objects, roles, and rules change with the developing series of peer cultures a child joins, Corsaro (1985) also notes that there are common qualities of each successive "layer" of peer culture in which children participate as they grow and develop. He delineates control and communal sharing as key elements of any peer culture, whether manifested by three-year-olds or eleven-year-olds. The matrix for expressions of control and communal sharing is peer play.

Paley (1981; 1986; 1990; 1992) in teacher research from her own classroom illuminates these themes of control and communal sharing by describing the appropriate curriculum for young children as one that includes "fantasy, friendship, and fairness" (1986). Who plays with whom, and what roles are coveted and negotiated, are of key importance in a play-centered curriculum, themes we illuminate in chapter 9, Language, Literacy and Play, and chapter 10, Play and Socialization. All the competencies of development—intellectual, social, emotional, moral, and physical—are drawn into serving this agenda: Who am I in my group of friends, and what stories can we create together?

SUMMARY AND CONCLUSION

Teachers of young children gain validation and elucidation of an interpretive approach to supporting play from the theories of Piaget, Vygotsky, Mead, and Erikson, and from the research of Parten, Corsaro and Paley. Each child in his or her classroom peer culture, shaped by family and community values and histories, plays out his or her understanding of the world in classroom play. By learning as much as one can about the sociocultural factors children bring with them to school, and by observing and listening with care and understanding, teachers enhance the learning and development of children in their care.

In our view, play is the necessary core to curriculum for young children. Play provides the teacher with cues and vehicles for assessing children and implementing curriculum goals. Most importantly, it allows children to develop to their fullest potential intellectually, socially, morally, physically, and emotionally as they learn to negotiate their developing sense of self with the demands of the group. Awareness of the possibilities inherent in play for understanding each child in the classroom opens many new doors for teachers. This awareness enhances both the professional knowledge and artistry that make teaching preschool and primary grade children a fulfilling and important profession.

T. H. White (1958), in *The Once and Future King*, tells how King Arthur is transformed into a series of creatures so that he may learn the lessons of each of their perspectives on life. In this way he might become a more sensitive and aware King. During Arthur's stint as a badger he listens to the wise, old badger's story of the Creation:

> God first created embryos for all the creatures of the earth. God called them all before Them [God is plural in this story] and gave each embryo the option of choosing specializations for parts of their bodies as they developed. Some chose to use their arms as flying machines, oars, or shovels; some chose to use their mouths as weapons, or their skins as armor or shelter. When it came Human's turn this embryo chose to remain unspecialized, relying on wisdom alone to guide it to adapt and invent as it encountered experience. God was delighted and remarked that the human alone had solved the riddle of survival in maintaining maximum flexibility for change.
>
> "Eternally undeveloped, you will always remain potential in Our image, able to see some of Our sorrows and to feel some of Our joys. We are partly sorry for you, Man, but partly hopeful. Run along then, and do your best." (White, 1958, p. 193)

And so it is in play that we make an investment to protect both the short-term and long-term futures of our children and our society. Play supports the development of specific concepts such as those needed to understand physics or our language system. It also supports more general qualities related to socialization, mastery, imagination, and flexibility of mind that help to ensure a legacy of adaptation to change and freedom to make choices. In the following chapters we begin to provide the detail of the functioning of classrooms that reflect a deep and thorough respect for children's play.

FOCUSING OUR THINKING

In activities 1–5, the same observations of children's play are analyzed from several perspectives. Therefore, before beginning these activities, you will need to complete hand-recorded observations of the play of two or three children. The children should be different ages, at least two years apart. If possible, observe them on more than one occasion.

1. Review Erikson's stages. Do you see any evidence of the development of autonomy, initiative, industry?

2. Apply Piaget's categories of functional, constructive, dramatic, and games with rules to what you observed. What differences are evident? What provisions for play in the classroom would address these differences?

3. Apply Parten's categories of onlooker, solitary, parallel, and group play. What differences do you see between age levels? What might you do as a teacher to provide for these differences in your classroom?

4. Review the material on Vygotsky's zone of proximal development. If your records include the child's play with others, look for examples of the child interacting within his/her zone of proximal development in which children seem to behave "a half a head taller." What is the nature of the social relationship that encourages children to make this stretch?

5. Which of Mead's stages (the play stage, the game stage, or the generalized other stage) would you use to describe what you see? Explain your decision.

6. This is an opportunity to engage in pretend play. Prepare and present a skit, "The Dinner Party," in which Vygotsky, Piaget, Erikson, and Mead have joined some teachers and parents at a dinner party where a discussion of play ensues.

7. Add to your annotated bibliography of children's books that relate to play. Analyze two or three books from your growing bibliography according to one of the theoretical perspectives presented in this chapter. For example, in what ways do the children in a story deal with initiative and guilt, or industry and inferiority? In what ways does the story describe their activity within their zone of proximal development?

SUGGESTED RESOURCES

1. Leong, D. & Bedrova, E. (1996). *Tools of the mind: Vygotskian approach to early childhood education.* Upper Saddle River, NJ: Merrill/Prentice Hall.

   This text provides the basic principles of Vygotsky's work and implications for American early childhood practitioners in a highly readable form.

2. Vygotsky, L. S. (1976). Play and its role in the mental development of the child. In J. S. Bruner, A. Jolly, & K. Sylva (Eds.), *Play: Its role in development and evolution* (pp. 537–544). New York: Basic Books.

   Advanced students will find that this translation of an original work by Vygotsky provides an excellent introduction to his theory. In this brief work, Vygotsky discusses the centrality of play to development.

3. Piaget, J. (1962). *Play, dreams and imitation in childhood*. New York: Norton.

   This translation of Piaget's original work on play provides advanced students with an appreciation of the scope and clarity of his observations as well as a thorough discussion of his theory of the development of play. Piaget shows how representational activity is derived from the psychological invariants of assimilation and accommodation, and relates the development of representation to the transition from preconceptual to conceptual activity.

4. Roopnarine, J. L., Johnson, J. E. & Hooper, F. H. (Eds.). (1994). *Children's play in diverse cultures*. Albany, New York: State of New York University Press.

   Explorations of children's play in eight cultures, including Taiwan, Japan, Italy, India, and the Marqueses. These studies draw upon different methodologies and illustrate frameworks from which to examine the development of play within diverse contexts. This book will be of particular interest to students and teachers working with diverse populations in the U.S. or abroad.

5. Duckworth, E. (1996). *"The having of wonderful ideas" and other essays on teaching and learning* (2d ed.). New York: Teachers College Press.

   These inspiring essays examine the learning processes of adults as well as children from a constructivist perspective. Duckworth's work captures the relationships among playfulness, curiosity, and problem solving for adults as well as children. Readers may be particularly interested in several chapters that describe teachers as learners and their "having of wonderful ideas."

CHAPTER 3

Play as the Cornerstone of Development

In chapter 2 we looked at the development of children's play as it relates to cognitive, social, moral, and emotional dimensions of childhood. We emphasized the interweaving of these aspects of development within the fabric of play, and began to elucidate the competencies that children construct through play in the years from preschool through the primary grades.

In this chapter we address in greater detail the question of how play enhances children's development, enabling them to become competent older children, adolescents, and adults. We explore in more depth the ways in which play leads development in early childhood and supports competence within the peer culture as well as academic achievements at each level of development.

Early in the history of early childhood education, teachers' views of play in school settings were dominated by philosophical approaches to play. Following the theories of Comenius, Pestalozzi, Rousseau, and Froebel, play was regarded as the natural province of childhood, and teachers believed that play in childhood was valuable in and of itself as part of respecting the vulnerable and malleable nature of children (Monighan-Nourot, 1990).

As early childhood educators became more focused on specific outcomes of educational practice, the philosophical views of play were largely replaced by more instrumental rationales for play in the curriculum for young children. Instrumental rationales focused on the future value that play accrues to children and society. The integrated nature of teaching the "whole child" was shadowed by a movement to delineate specific concepts, skills and competencies at each level of the preschool and primary curriculum. The play-centered curriculum took on a more pragmatic voice: What aspects of desirable academic knowledge are constructed through play in early childhood? (Nourot & Van Hoorn, 1991).

Research in the area of children's play followed this instrumental focus. Such research argues for the central role of play in constructing and consolidating particular knowledge, skills, and competencies in preschool and the primary grades. We begin this chapter by examining how play influences intellectual development, followed by a look at its effects on creativity and imagination, and, lastly, its influences on social and moral development.

PLAY AS THE CORNERSTONE OF INTELLECTUAL DEVELOPMENT

For both Piaget and Vygotsky, play is intimately tied to representation, that is, how the child represents the world and expresses feelings and needs. Here we look at symbolic thought, symbolic play and symbolic role playing. This discussion is refined by considering how the similarity between a symbol and what it represents (distancing) relates to development. A toy telephone is closer to representing a real telephone than is a wooden block. Additional elements of intellectual development include how children come to understand the perspectives of others, how children invent strategies for play with others (as in games with rules), and how children solve problems. We round out our focus on intellectual development with a look at language and literacy, and logical-mathematical thought.

Play and the Development of Symbolic Thought

The development of symbolic or abstract thought is one of the key aspects of intellectual development centered in the early childhood years. It is also the characteristic of early childhood play most studied by child development researchers (Fromberg, 1992; Rubin, Fein & Vandenberg, 1983), and, therefore, gives us a major lens for interpreting our observations of children at play. By symbols we mean the use of objects or gestures to represent another object or idea not present in the situation. We see these symbols in such activities as block building and the transformation of roles and situations in dramatic play. For example:

❦ Sally picks up a wooden block and holds it to her ear. She makes pushing button motions with her fingers and says, "Hello, is Mickey Mouse there?" ❦

Beginning at about the age of 18 months, the human mind has developed to the point where symbolic thought is possible, evidenced by the use of language and pretend play. From this point on, the ability to transform objects or situations, through the use of imagination, into meanings that are different from the original object or situation forms the foundation for intellectual development and communication (Athey, 1988; Fein, 1981; Fenson & Ramsey, 1980; Fromberg, 1992; Johnson, Christie, & Yawkey, 1987; McCune, 1985).

Symbolic activities rest on children's abilities to create meaning in their minds and to express that meaning through gesture (driving a pretend car), language, and intonation ("OK, honey, it's bedtime."), and objects (using sand and rocks to make a birthday cake).

Symbolic play with objects.   Researchers have studied the progression of children's abilities to transform objects into make-believe forms. Building on Vygotsky's (1967) notion that concrete objects serve to "anchor" children's early efforts with imagination and pretense, researchers have studied young children at play with objects. They have discovered that, as children's play develops, they seem able to use objects that are increasingly different in form and function from the object represented in play, building the foundation for abstract thinking (Sigel, 1993).

For example, researchers have demonstrated that younger children have more difficulty than older children in using an object that does not resemble the symbolized object; using a ball as a comb, or a tambourine as a cup requires a child to fill in the features of the imagined object with her own mental pictures. This ability to abstract the essential features of an object and to mentally represent those features are what Sigel (1993) calls representational competence.

This ability increases with development and is largely constructed through play (Jackowitz & Watson, 1980; Pederson, Rook-Green, & Elder, 1981). Some research indicates that older children may actually prefer unstructured objects such as Styrofoam chips or pebbles to real looking replicas of objects as children's capacity for symbolic representation matures (Fein, 1981; Pulaski, 1970). Presumably, when representational competence is well developed, children do

*Play with concrete materials sup-
ports children's imagination and
pretense.*

not have to interrupt their ongoing scripts of pretend play to search for an
object that closely resembles the one they wish to symbolize.

Symbolic role play.   Children also make symbolic transformations in their role
play. Research indicates that as children's capacities for representing ideas
develop, they increasingly create pretend roles and situations without the use of
costumes or props. As symbolic transformation in role play matures, children
use more subtle behaviors such as gesture and intonation to mark their transformation into make-believe roles in play (Smilansky, 1968, 1990). Teachers may
want to provide materials for costumes, such as hats, jackets, or capes for children to use in their role play. Additionally, teachers may want to model and take
note of the subtle markers, such as a tone of voice, a walk, or a gesture that children use to enter a make-believe role.

    The use of symbols is not characteristic of all play. But symbolic behavior
underlies the characteristic of pretense that we associate with the play of
preschool- and primary-aged children. It forms the foundation upon which children construct their abilities to engage in abstract thinking in literacy, mathematical reasoning, and problem solving.

Distancing in children's play.   Both Piaget's and Parten's categories of play call
for the expenditure of mental energy on the part of the child. Sigel (1993)
coined the term "symbolic distancing" to denote the degree to which a trans-

formed object represents what it is intended to symbolize. For example, if we want to find something to represent a car, a particular block might be closer in symbolic distance than another because of its shape and size, and a toy truck would be closer than a toy cow.

When children engage in symbolic transformations in their play, the use of objects which do not resemble what they symbolize calls for mental effort. This is true of the use of imaginary objects and pretend roles and situations as well. The greater the distance in the transformations, the more intellectually demanding play becomes.

The concept of distancing is particularly useful when working with young children and children with developmental delays. Some children with special needs are unable to separate reality from fantasy (Newcomer, 1993). Since symbolic distancing is a problem, most would select an object closely resembling the actual, represented object in form and function. Teachers who are aware of such considerations can support students' success in integrated classrooms by including a range of play materials.

Taking the perspectives of others.   The distancing of fantasy is not the only demand on the child's mental energy. Playing with peers requires perspectivism, or the ability to take the viewpoint of others in order to negotiate group play situations. For example, if both Sandy and Mika want to play the part of a media heroine in a dramatic play episode, the play cannot continue until a compromise is reached. Perhaps one will have a turn in the role, and then the other, or perhaps this character will now have a sister or a cousin. In any case, the continuity and stability of the players' joint creation depends on their abilities to marshal enough mental energy to mentally represent and consider the perspectives of others in negotiating their roles and the plot of their play (Black, 1989; DeVries & Zan, 1994; Giffin, 1984; Goncu, 1993; Sheldon, 1992; Trawick-Smith, 1994; Zan, 1996).

Rubin and his colleagues developed a system for combining Piaget's and Parten's levels of play (Rubin, 1980; Rubin, Maioni, & Hornung, 1976). They nested Piaget's categories of functional, constructive, dramatic, and games with rules within Parten's social categories of solitary, parallel, and group play (Figure 3.1). In their research, Rubin and his colleagues point out that play sophistica-

Figure 3.1
Stages of Cognitive Complexity of Play Nested Within Categories of Social Play.
Source: Adapted from "Free play behaviors in middle- and lower-class preschoolers: Parten & Piaget revisited" by K. Rubin, T. L. Maioni, and M. Hornung, 1976, *Child Development, 47,* pp. 414–419.

Solitary Play	Parallel Play	Group Play
functional	functional	functional
constructive	constructive	constructive
dramatic	dramatic	dramatic
games with rules	games with rules	games with rules

tion ranges from the simplest combination, solitary functional, to the most complex, group games with rules.

Although young children with emotional disturbances and developmental delays can be observed playing with their peers in integrated classrooms, they may have particular difficulties taking the perspective of their peers. According to Newcomer (1993), many cannot evaluate how their behavior affects others. Most emotionally and socially disturbed children are egocentric much of the time (van der Kooij, 1989b). For example, such children might fail to greet peers, but might become upset if peers failed to greet them. Play-based curricula provide all children numerous opportunities to engage in behaviors, such as compromising and negotiating, that foster the development of perspective taking.

Weighing the mental demands of play.   These two demands on mental effort or energy, i.e., fantasy distancing, and taking the perspectives of others, need to be carefully considered by teachers when assessing children's development through their play, as well as in planning for and intervening in play.

For example, children who are new to the group or who may be having difficulties in social negotiations with peers, need the comfort and security of a fantasy script that is not too distanced from what they know well (Black, 1989; Bretherton, 1984; Farver, 1992; Goncu, 1984). Almost everyone knows the script for playing house or blocks and trucks, or riding trikes. The less demanding the distancing demands of the play scenarios, the more attention children can devote to social negotiation with peers. This may be a particularly important issue for children with developmental delays who may have difficulties with the distancing demands of the play as well as difficulties entering the play setting. It is also a consideration for teachers of children with emotional disturbances who may respond aggressively to such frustrations.

Conversely, play with familiar peers or siblings provides an interpersonal context that is familiar and has known patterns of social interaction. The perspectivism requirements are not as rigorous as they might be with unfamiliar peers or with those quite different in age or background. In these situations of interpersonal comfort, children's mental energy is freed to engage in complicated distancing of symbolic objects and fantasy themes (King, 1992; Meyers, Klein, & Genishi, 1994; Orellana, 1994).

This concept of weighing the relative demands of fantasy and social negotiation has implications for the timing of the play curriculum. Familiar scripts and many realistic props are appropriate at the beginning of the year. More distanced themes with prop boxes that stimulate and extend thematic fantasy play are called for later in the school year as play peers become familiar and patterns of communication become more comfortable.

Weighing the social and cognitive demands of play situations also has implications for assessing and supporting the development of individual children. Some children may need the support of familiar play accessories more than others. English language learners benefit from scripts and play accessories that are familiar and offer opportunities for both repetition and expansion. Some children will naturally engage in more solitary play or parallel play as a way of meeting their own needs. Teachers who are sensitive to the group context as well as the cognitive level of children's play will be well equipped to implement the play orchestration strategies we describe in chapters 4 and 5.

Inventing strategies. Finally, let's return to games with rules. Games with rules are challenging to young children because they represent the most sophisticated levels of both social and symbolic play. They demand both distancing in terms of object transformations, role transformation situations, and the consideration of the perspectives of all players. Added to this is the dimension of the "generalized other" hypothesized by G. H. Mead (1934). In games with rules, the player is required to reflect on the relationship of all the players within the framework of the rules. For example, a Monopoly player might want to figure out who is playing fairly according to the rules and who is not, or even whom she might make an alliance with to borrow from the bank. These and similar meta-cognitive demands on the skilled games player require even further levels of distancing in order to view both social and symbolic behavior from an objective stance—and then use that information to formulate a strategy (Kamii & DeVries, 1980; Zan, 1996).

This kind of strategy-taking does not often appear until children are five or six years old. As an example, when 3-year-olds play "Duck, Duck, Goose," after the goose is tapped and named, all the children get up and run. They understand the basic rule of the game, but cannot coordinate the perspectives of different players with their own. Four-year-olds understand that only the "goose" and "it" run and that the goose must chase and catch "it." But the players chase around the circle and the "goose" inevitably fails to tag "it." At five, children begin to employ a strategy with "goose" often circling in the opposite direction in order to tag "it" before "it" can manage to run back to the empty spot.

When children begin to spontaneously invent strategies and discuss and negotiate rules before games begin, games with rules become an appropriate addition to the school curriculum. Game materials and boards may be available but children should be encouraged to build upon their understanding of how roles and rules are negotiated in dramatic play. They can be encouraged to construct their own games with rules.

In the primary grades, the playing and inventing of games with rules becomes a major component of a play-based curriculum. Children use this newly-emerging stage of play development to consolidate their understanding of rules and strategies.

Play and the Development of Language and Literacy

Much of the research on children's use of symbols has linked play to language development. Some researchers have focused on parallels between early language development and the use of symbols in play (McCune, 1985; Pellegrini & Galda, 1993; Ungerer & Sigman, 1984). Others have studied the ways in which children play with the elements of language such as with sounds or meanings. Children's exploration of sounds, arrangements of words, and meanings of words form the context for children to invent unique forms of language and to master new forms as they are acquired (Garvey, 1977; Heath, 1983, 1985; Kuczaj, 1985). Language play is ubiquitous in classrooms with young children and often occurs in the most mundane of circumstances.

   ❧ It's juice time in a preschool setting and James and Eva begin to giggle as they wait for their turns to pour juice. "You're juicy-goosey," contributes James. "You're juicly-goosely-foosley," chortles Eva, and they both dissolve in laughter. ❧

Literacy in play.   Research in the field of emergent literacy has looked at how children incorporate literacy play into their make-believe activities (Christie, 1995; Davidson, 1995; Gentile & Hoot, 1983; Isenberg & Jacob, 1988; Morrow & Rand, 1991; Neuman & Roskos, 1991; Roskos & Neuman, 1992, 1993; Schrader, 1989; Vukelich, 1990; 1991; Wolfgang & Sanders, 1981). Such play incorporates the social functions of literacy into pretend play scripts. For example, in one kindergarten classroom, children set up a bank, a store and a restaurant, all built with blocks. In order to obtain money from the bank to spend elsewhere, "tellers" in the bank asked their "customers" to pick one of the blank books from the library corner and write their names on it. After counting out paper to represent money, the teller wrote CRTO in the book, and stamped it with a rubber stamp.

In addition to understanding the social functions of print, children's schooling in the written symbols of language and mathematics requires the ability to perform symbolic transformations. For example, the ability to understand that H and K, bat and 14 are combinations of lines that represent sounds, words, and numbers is similar to the capacity to use a block to represent a truck or a telephone.

The capacity to enter the "as if" or hypothetical frame of reference in which animals talk, such as that created by E. B. White in *Charlotte's Web*, or the ability to create such a frame oneself in telling or writing a story, rests on concepts constructed in dramatic play. The ability to negotiate multiple roles and hypothetical situations in housekeeping play or to dictate and enact an episode of superheroes' adventures, calls on the same capacities in young children's symbolic thought as those needed to write a poem or a story of one's own (Christie, 1995; Davidson, 1995; Dyson, 1990; Pellegrini, De Stefano & Thompson, 1983; Sachs, Goldman & Chaille, 1984).

Children who become skilled at symbolic transformations in their play are also preparing conceptually to understand some of the subtleties of our culturally shared symbolic systems used in written language, aspects that adults take for granted, but that children find confusing. For example, in one first grade classroom, children were frequently bewildered by the arbitrary meaning assigned to symbols that look the same. The letter "C" is sometimes pronounced as a "K" such as in the word "cake," sometimes as an "S" as in "city" and sometimes as a new sound "CH" as in "chicken." This inconsistency among assigned meanings for symbols that do not change in appearance can be very confusing to a child who has not developed the concept of "multiple transformations" in his or her pretend play. For example, the idea that a rectangular block can be a car, a person, or a sandwich, depending on the context of the child's imagination prepares children to understand these differences when they begin to operate with our system of written signs and symbols. In both symbolic play and phonetic decoding the concept of one object that continues to look the same may be transformed by the mind into several different meanings is essential.

A related concept is the idea that several objects that look different may be symbolically transformed to carry the same meaning. In play, for example, you might see Sara appropriate a block, a Lego, or a toy car to represent a walkie-talkie on a spaceship. These choices depend in part on what is available and also the child's ability to abstract salient features of objects in order to use them as symbols for alternative meanings. This concept is called upon when children learn to identify symbols of written language, for example, in understanding that "A" and "a" both represent the same sound in our alphabet.

Another aspect of literacy learning lies in the experiences children have in taking alternative perspectives in their dramatic play and in sequencing events to construct play narratives. Reading comprehension, particularly with charac-

In playing with representational objects, children explore their culture.

ters, motives, and plots, also rests on alternative perspectives and sequencing events in order to create and interpret meaning (Bruner, 1986; Diaute, 1989; Roskos, 1988; Williamson & Silvern, 1990). These and other aspects of play and literacy are considered in detail in chapter 9.

Play and Logical-Mathematical Thinking

Another relationship between play and development is the construction of logical-mathematical knowledge. One expression of this is seen in the construction of cause-effect relationships through physical activities. Block building, bike riding, and sand and water play all foster the construction of relationships of action to form, gravity, centrifugal force, spatial relationships, and other concepts of physics. These cause-effect relationship experiences are essential to children's future understanding and abilities to make predictions about the physical world (Forman, 1994; Forman & Kaden, 1987; Forman & Hill, 1984; Kamii & DeVries, 1993).

In the development of logical-mathematical thinking, original experiences are more valuable than imitating adult models. When children develop their own schemes or mental patterns for organizing and interpreting meaning in the environment, they form the basis for classification abilities. Play brings children a wide array of opportunities to develop concepts based on classification, and also allows them to construct categories at their own pace (Dominick & Clark, 1996; Kamii, 1982, 1985).

For the past two weeks Marie has been working almost daily with a set of thick crayons, eight colors. Today there is something new. She chooses a large box of thin crayons, a total of 40 colors. She picks out all the crayons that have a red color and arranges them separately from crayons of orange and pink shades. As she colors a piece of scrap wood with multiple shades of red, she comments, "This is for my mom." Lily sits down next to her. Marie turns, offering a crayon. "There's more reds over here."

In this example, Marie is coordinating relationships of "more than" and "less than" and "similar" and "different." The coordination of these relationships is the beginning of classification abilities in early childhood. In fact, more mature play in preschoolers has been found by some researchers to be positively related to sophisticated classification skills (Johnson, Ershler, & Lawton, 1982; Rubin & Maioni, 1975).

Dramatic play contributes to the development of classification in another way:

Six-year-old Sam is fixing dinner for his "son" John. John says, "But I want a taco for dinner!" "O.K. I can make good tacos," notes Sam as he scans the playhouse area for a prop that exemplifies "taconess" for him. He selects a paperback cookbook from the shelf, opens it, and "stuffs" it with imaginary meat, cheese, and vegetables. "Do you want hot sauce?" he asks. John nods emphatically and Sam shakes a pencil over the "taco," pretending that it is a bottle of hot sauce.

In the above example, for each symbolic transformation Sam finds similar characteristics from objects to form the basis of his decision of what to use as a prop. Before choosing the cookbook, presumably because of its qualities of opening and enclosing that are compatible with his idea of a taco, he scans the area, rejecting the pencil and a tennis ball in favor of the book. He later uses the pencil to represent the hot sauce bottle. This selective attention to similar characteristics of objects is another concept essential to the development of categorization abilities.

Another relationship between play and logical-mathematical thinking rests on the symbolic transformations inherent in role play. The child who transforms himself or herself into a veterinarian, a puppy, or an astronaut, and each time returns to the mental concept of self, is beginning to understand reversibility in thinking, a concept encountered as children begin to learn concrete operations such as addition, subtraction, multiplication, and division. Some researchers have hypothesized that such successive mental transformations in pretend play form the foundation for the Piagetian notion of conservation (Golomb & Bonen, 1981; Golomb, Gowing, & Friedman, 1982). Conservation involves the understanding that matter does not decrease or increase with a change in its position or form just as role play involves understanding that the identity of a person remains the same when a role is taken (Forman & Kaden, 1987).

A parent discusses her four-year-old child's efforts to "conserve" identity by understanding the role play seen in a theatrical production:

🎵 A few weeks ago Hilary and I went to see a musical about Noah's Ark. I prepared him by reading Peter Spier's book *Noah's Ark*, so he would know the story. We went to a Sunday matinee, and Hilary was fascinated with the entire production: He did not miss a word! He laughed at some of the jokes but mostly he studied what was going on. Since the show Hilary has commented or asked questions about it every day. He plays out portions of the script he remembers such as Noah writing a book, but what is most interesting is his interest in the characters, their real names, and their names in the play. We went over and over the program, Hilary asking to hear the person's real name and then their role in the play. How one person can be Noah in the play, but someone else when the play is over is still puzzling to him. He asks over and over because he can't quite believe it. I guess he's still working on the concept. 🎵

Play and Problem Solving

As we see in the example above, young children persist in their efforts to make sense of new information through their play, developing the ability to entertain alternative possibilities in a given situation (Christie, 1985; Nourot, 1997, 1998; Pellegrini, 1984; Pepler & Ross, 1981). For example, the flexibility in thinking that allows one to solve a problem from a fresh perspective or use a tool in a unique way is highly valued in the literature on critical thinking (Adams, 1976).

Play contributes to this ability by allowing children to "play through" their ideas, in the same way that adults "talk through" alternatives to problems they face and imagine consequences from varying perspectives. This process also leads to the discovery of new problems or new questions to be asked as children play and think more deeply about their experience (Pepler, 1986; Sutton-Smith, 1968). This playing through of alternatives may be nonverbal, as in the first example below, or it may include verbal communication as in the second example of negotiating with peers.

&. Second graders Darren and Peter are making a sand mountain with a road around it designed for a ball to roll down. The moist sand is beginning to dry in the hot sun and pieces of the road are crumbling. They first try a "patching" job with more sand, but it is too dry to stick. When that doesn't work, they dig under the dry sand to find more of the damp sand they originally used. &.

Research on children who are popular with peers indicates that children who are flexible in their thinking frequently come up with unique alternatives for resolving disputes and suggesting compromise (Black, 1989; Elgas, Klein, Kantor, & Fernie, 1988; Hazen & Black, 1984; Howes, Unger & Matheson, 1992; Rogers & Ross, 1986; Trawick-Smith, 1988, 1992).

&. Four-year-old Mara and three-year-old Juan are playing with a hospital bed, medical props, and two dolls. They agree to have their "patients" share the toy bed, but there is only one pillow. Mara takes a blanket and folds it several times, placing it under the head of her doll. "Now we both have pillows," she concludes, and the play continues, uninterrupted by disputes. &.

Researchers who have studied children's play speculate that the conflicts and subsequent negotiations that occur as children shift from actors "in play" to directors "out of" play, force children to consider the perspectives of their play-mates. In play, children enact roles and move the storyline forward with action and dialogue. Out of play, children step out of make-believe roles to negotiate new roles, behavior appropriate to roles, and ideas for the plot of their play. If one wants play to continue, then compromises must be made (Doyle & Connolly, 1989; Giffin, 1984; Goncu, 1993; Goncu & Kessler, 1984; Kamii & DeVries, 1980; Reifel & Yeatman, 1991; Sheldon, 1992).

Play-based curricula can be beneficial for those children who are unable to resolve problems when they arise. This includes many children with emotional disturbances and children with developmental delays. Flexibility is an important dimension of problem solving. Van der Kooij (1989b) suggests that certain children with special needs lack this flexibility and react to the environment in a stereotyped way. Extended opportunities to interact with peers in play can support the development of problem solving skills. For example:

🍂 In a second grade integrated classroom, Danny and Michael are playing with small race cars. Danny has a learning disability which includes visual processing and visual discrimination deficits. As Danny pushes his car on the carpet, he says, "I want my car to go faster." Michael looks around the classroom, spots a table and says, "We can use a table 'cause it's smooth." Danny then looks around the room and exclaims, "Let's go over there," and points to an area of the classroom that is covered in shiny tile. The children take their cars to the slick surface of the tile floor and begin racing them. 🍂

Although some of the research and writing in the field of special education, like that cited above, suggests that children with special needs are unable to solve problems, this example of Danny's success in problem solving in collaboration with Michael demonstrates that it is important to observe each child's abilities in different contexts.

A related issue is the role of the teacher. Genishi and DiPaolo (1982) and Pellegrini (1984) suggest that the teacher's presence during peer play negotiations may inhibit children from solving their interpersonal problems on their own. On the other hand, researchers such as Smilansky (1968, 1990) suggest that the teacher's presence may support children's ability to work out solutions to disagreements during play. Teachers may find the issues of roles and timing especially challenging when working with children who have emotional disturbances and are aggressive when others do not play according to their wishes. In these and all interventions in play, the teacher's sensitivity and support for children's capabilities and patience for their processes is paramount (King, 1992; Schwartzman, 1978).

As we discussed in chapter 2, the idea that play leads children's development is consistent with Vygotsky's notion of the zone of proximal development (Vygotsky, 1967, 1978). He set forth the idea that children function above their normal level of ability when challenged by peers in their play. Children's desire to maintain social interaction and to encounter and coordinate perspectives other than their own contributes to the developmental stretch evident in play. Researchers studying children's play in mixed-age groups or classrooms with mainstreamed children report that younger or less sophisticated players play at higher levels of complexity when playing with older or more expert peers (Katz, Evangelou, & Hartman, 1990; Roopnarine & Johnson, 1983; Stone & Christie, 1996; Urberg & Kaplan, 1986). Children who are imaginative in their symbolic play transformations and flexible in their negotiations with peers are building concepts essential to critical thinking expertise and social problem solving.

PLAY AS THE CORNERSTONE OF IMAGINATION AND CREATIVITY

Qualities that are sometimes taken for granted when reviewing the value of play for future development are imagination and creativity. Much has been written concerning the curriculum appropriate for the 21st century. Bruner (1976) perhaps stated this dilemma best by asking: How can a system that prepares the immature for entry into the society deal with a future that is increasingly difficult to predict within a single lifetime?

One possibility is to foster adaptive, flexible, and creative thinking. According to Ellis (1988), these qualities, which represent key elements in determining the survival of our ancestors and in the future, will remain equally essential because "whenever the environment is changing it selects for playful individuals" (p. 24). Concerns about the effects of didactic teaching and skills-based curricula have led to research and writing urging educators to consider more carefully the need to foster imaginative and flexible minds (Elkind, 1986, 1990; Schweinhart, Weikart, & Larner, 1986; Singer, 1973).

Singer (1973) and Singer and Singer (1980, 1985) have written extensively about the contribution of play to the imaginative thinking of children. In the Singers' view, make-believe play is essential to the development of the capacity for internal imagery. It contributes to the development of creativity by opening children to experiences involving curiosity and the exploration of alternative situations and combinations. In addition, their research emphasizes the psychosocial benefits of imaginative play: Children who engage in much make-believe play are likely to be happier and more flexible when they encounter new situations.

Three Aspects of Imagination and Fantasy

Egan (1988) developed Vygotsky's claim that play "leads" development in early childhood. He claimed that fantasy and imagination are the appropriate content of early childhood curriculum because they highlight for teachers the passionate concerns of young children. Egan's work emphasized three major aspects of imagination and fantasy in early childhood: (1) the oral nature of the peer culture in the early years, (2) the importance of binary opposites in creating dramatic tension in play themes, and (3) the sense of wonder, magic, and joy inherent in pretend play.

The oral culture of early childhood.   Egan (1988) found the seeds of the ability to create story in the orally expressed fantasy of early childhood. As each aspect of the story told in fantasy play unfolds, its meaning is clarified and extended in relation to other aspects of the play. In solitary dramatic play these stories are told to the self, and in sociodramatic play the play's meanings are communicated and negotiated within the peer culture of the classroom (Corsaro, 1985; Dyson, 1994; Paley, 1981, 1994; Scales, Nicolopoulou, Weintraub, & Nicolopoulou, 1994).

The accompanying ability to extend knowledge of characters, situations and events from the everyday into the realm of the improbable or impossible is a primary form of logic that encompasses ambiguity and paradox and merges thought and feelings. This meaning-making through narrative forms is one of the first examples of the ordering and classification of human experience (Bruner, 1986, 1990). This early use of contradictory forms of logic in play is what Egan calls "mythic thinking," and is seen in both the fantastic series of events that children may imagine in play and in role play. For example, when four-year-old Erin pretends that she is an undersea monster she knows that she simultaneously is and is not the role that she plays. This early embrace of paradox lays the foundation for noncontradictory forms of logic that emerge in middle childhood. Egan believes that one must create and entertain a variety of possibilities before narrowing them through logical thought, and that young children's grasp of reality begins by stretching the borders of the known world into new dimensions and possibilities in play.

Bipolar opposites in play.   Researchers of children's play frequently note binary oppositions in children's play themes such as love/hate, danger/rescue, the permissible/the forbidden, big/little, good guy/bad guy, death/rebirth, and lost/found (Bettelheim, 1989; Corsaro, 1985; Egan, 1988; Garvey, 1990; Paley, 1988). These oppositional tensions help children discriminate features of their physical and social worlds, and define themselves within those worlds. The unity of thought and emotion animates their abilities to make sense of life through the stories told in dramatic play. The following example shows how children move flexibly between sense and nonsense, the physically possible and impossible, the mundane and the exotic, the safe and the threatening, and, for some, the permissible and the forbidden. Here they define the borders of their physical, cultural, social, and emotional realities.

&. Cathy and Marla are pretending to be witches, and pretend that they are taking blood from their playmates by touching their arms with a spoon, and then running back to the pot on the stove in the housekeeping area to add the imaginary blood of each victim, cackling as they stir the brew. Brian is a witch too, wearing a sparkling cape and carrying a cup with a plastic lemon in it. "This drink has poison and fingernails in it," he announces.

Cathy sends Marla to find a new victim. Marla comes back, spoon held aloft over the pot. "Yes, yes, good," encourages Cathy. Marla pretends to take some blood from one of the teachers who observes on the outskirts of the play. Marla comments to the teacher, "I have your blood and now you will be dead forever," using a high-pitched cackling voice and waving her arms majestically.

Brian holds up his cup. "But if you drink this magic potion, you can come alive again," and he offers some to Kelly, who has just joined the play. "Can I play?" Kelly asks. "Yes," agrees Cathy, "but you have to be a witch, like us." Kelly pretends to take blood from Marla, imitating the high cackling laugh she has heard Cathy use. Then Brian offers his cup to Marla, "This will turn you from a witch into a princess." She pretends to drink the princess-making potion and then the other witches try to turn her back into a witch. "No, no, drink this one." The tension between the bad witches and the good witch Brian with his magic potion continues a few more minutes until clean-up time is called. &.

The framing of ideas for character, plot, and setting through bipolar oppositions, such as the good witch/bad witch/princess, and the death and rebirth in the above anecdote also define these emerging aspects of story, even as it as clarifies children's sense of themselves. Children want passionately for play to continue despite the potential pitfalls of differing ideas about characters or events in the play. The shared understanding that comes from framing play themes and characters in binary themes such as good guy/bad guy or danger/rescue supports the shared understanding and the subsequent negotiation that allows play to flourish (Nourot, 1997, 1998).

Wonder, magic, and joy.   Although the development of logical thinking and skill in negotiating meanings with others are laudable aspects of imaginative play in early childhood, the essence of play is captured in the magical and ecstatic experiences that define creative process throughout life (Bohm, 1978; Csikzentmihayli, 1993; Egan, 1988; Nachmanovitch, 1990). The joy and wonder encompassed in imaginative play are powerful links to others and an incentive to self-regulation and perspective-taking (Lewis, 1995). The desire for this sense of wonder and joy to continue creates a powerful incentive for children to move beyond their own viewpoints to encompass the perspectives of others, a quality described in children they deem "Master Players," as children experience the power of both friendship and fantasy in their play (Jones & Reynolds, 1992; Reynolds & Jones, 1997).

PLAY AS THE CORNERSTONE OF SOCIAL-MORAL DEVELOPMENT

We have discussed some of the relationships of play to the intellectual and creative development of young children. Children use all these capacities and some new ones when they play together. Just as play forms the cornerstone of intellectual and creative development, it is also the major cornerstone for social and moral development. For example:

 In one kindergarten classroom, Jon and Rio were happily engaged in building a "ranch" out of blocks. Their intimacy was evident as they giggled and whispered to one another their plans for the fantasy occurring within the block structure. "And then pretend the bad guys can get in here," one boy said to the other. Paul watched from the sidelines and finally began to build his own structure next to Rio and Jon. "But what about me?" Paul said plaintively, as the ranch builders began to expand their construction site. "I'll tell you what," said Rio, "we'll make a line right here and you can build, too. We won't cross the line."

In this example, we see Paul learning to assert his rights, and Jon and Rio learning to understand and accommodate the perspective of a third player, without giving up their investment in keeping their ranch to themselves.

Kamii (1982, 1985) draws upon Piaget's theories of moral development (Piaget, 1965d) when she discusses autonomy and heteronomy in classrooms for young children. Moral autonomy is characterized by being governed by oneself. Moral heteronomy means being governed by others. Children who

Through interactions with play-mates, children learn to respect the perspective of others.

develop moral autonomy come to see moral values as internal guides, independent of whether they may be "caught" by a parent or a teacher. In a classroom that promotes moral autonomy, children construct beliefs about what is fair and unfair based upon their experiences with their peers. Through social-moral dilemmas that involve reciprocal interactions with their playmates, children learn to make informed choices about their behavior and practice factoring in the perspectives of others (DeVries & Zan, 1994). In the above example, Jon and Rio were able to factor in Paul's desire to play with them and still preserve their own interactive play space. They compromised, treating one another with respect and consideration.

Play and the Culture of School

Educational play always occurs within a social context and in relation to the various cultures that co-exist within the classroom and the school. The "school culture" (Heath, 1983) represents the norms of school behavior commonly accepted in our society and shaped through teacher behavior. The peer culture represents an alternative and, to some degree, a complement to the school culture in the classroom. King (1987) studied the three types of play that commonly occur in school settings: instrumental play, illicit play, and recreational play. Each is defined by the way in which the teacher responds to children's play and the context in which it occurs.

Instrumental play is sanctioned and employed by the teacher to meet goals consistent with school curriculum. Examples are blocks or games with rules that teach vocabulary or concepts, and organized motor activities. Dramatic play with roles such as parent, teacher, or astronaut is an example of another kind of instrumental play in which children explore and practice adult roles in their society. These roles may vary widely according to children's cultural backgrounds. The negotiation of the features or implicit "rules" of these adult roles provides fertile ground for children to test their mental concepts about gender and adult occupations with other children whose backgrounds may have created a different set of rules and expectations. In one preschool classroom, Nat and Katherine argue over who will fix the dinner, the mom or the dad. In Nat's home, his father is the primary caregiver and usually prepares the evening meal. In Katherine's home, her father commutes to work in a large city and her mother generally prepares the meals.

Illicit play is not sanctioned by the teacher and, in fact, may be expressly forbidden. Children engage in illicit play either behind the teacher's back or as a direct challenge to the teacher's authority. Such play is thought to provide children with a sense of mastery and autonomy within the school setting that limits the range of acceptable behavior. Examples commonly seen in early childhood settings include transforming Tinker Toys into guns when such play is prohibited, "group glee" activities, such as coughing or snapping Velcro shoes, and passing secret notes or pictures.

Recreational play is sanctioned by the teacher as a means to let off steam, but it generally occurs outside the teacher's view. Playground play at recess and free play outdoors in some preschool and kindergarten settings are examples of this type of play.

Although instrumental play in educational settings, or as Sutton-Smith (1988) calls it, "the new sacred play," is sanctioned by educators, we wish to remind ourselves and other teachers of the importance of the illicit or "festive" play. This mischievous or silly play represents another arena in which we find the social skills and concepts of young children developing.

Just as play serves an "equilibrating" or balancing force in our lives, by its paradoxical nature, play also allows us to invert reality, to throw off balance what we know to be normal or sensible. This represents the power of both nonsense and festive play (Sutton-Smith & Kelly-Byrne, 1984). One of the outcomes of this kind of play that is mischievous, rebellious, and nonsensical is the powerful social bonding that occurs among players as they jointly oppose traditional social norms and a sensible view of the world in a playful manner.

&❧ David and Brad are playing with a squirrel doll in the playhouse. David squeaks the squirrel and taps it on Brad's shoe. Brad shouts "Stop, squirrel!" "I'm not a squirrel. I'm a squirmmy!" responds David in a high-pitched voice, hopping the squirrel doll up and down. He grabs a baby doll out of Brad's hand and makes a pouring motion over his head with it. "Sh-h-h." Brad questions, "Hot coffee?" "No, hot caw-caw," David responds, laughing loudly. "Hot caw-caw!" He and Brad fall together onto the floor, laughing hysterically. ❧&

   In their evolving peer culture, children confront the differing perspectives of one another and also that of the school culture represented by the teacher. As Corsaro (1985) warns, teachers must walk a fine line between respecting children's needs to ally themselves against the constraints of adult authority (to look the other way on occasion) and their own need to provide firm and consistent limits about what is acceptable in the school setting. "Adult ideas, materials, rules, and restrictions can be seen as frames or boundaries within which features of peer culture emerge and are played out" (Corsaro, p. 289). A good example of this dilemma is the ongoing debate in early childhood education centered on the use of toy and imaginary weapons and fantasies involving violence in preschool and kindergarten settings (Carlsson-Paige & Levin, 1987, 1990).

SUMMARY AND CONCLUSION

In chapter 2 we explored the development of play as viewed by a number of theorists. In this chapter examining how play supports development, we explored some of the many ways in which play influences development and learning. Some of the material we presented is a further examination of these theories. In addition, we discussed the considerable range of research that has been conducted in this area.

   We have seen that play has a critical role in all facets of human development. These include, but are not limited to, the large domains of social, emotional and intellectual growth. With regard to some of the issues considered here, we have examined some of the specific ways that play influences symbolic thought, expressive language, literacy, perspective taking, a sense of self, social cooperation, logical-mathematical thinking, imagination, creativity, and moral reasoning. (See chapter 13 for a more general discussion of the role of play in development.) Understanding how play develops, as well as how play supports children's development, leads to the curricula strategies that will be discussed in chapters 4 and 5.

FOCUSING OUR THINKING

  1. Record several handwritten observations of children's play. In each, focus on an individual child, even when the child plays with others. Analyze the records to find examples of the following aspects of development and learning embedded in play:

     a. symbolic play with objects

     b. symbolic play with roles

     c. problem solving

     d. logical-mathematical thinking

     e. symbolic distancing

     f. pivot

     g. early literacy

     h. conservation or classification

2. Reexamine your play observations to find examples of instrumental play, illicit play, and recreational play.

3. Observe children playing in groups during a period of at least two weeks. Record examples of how children gain entry to play and how they protect their play from intrusion by others. Which strategies are the most frequent? Which seem to work the best?

4. Describe how physical, social, and logical-mathematical knowledge are interwoven in children's play behaviors. Support your description with observations you have recorded.

5. Continue to add to your annotated bibliography of children's books about play. Include at least one book that has a focus on creativity and imagination, and another that has a focus on logical-mathematical thinking.

   a. Use one or more of the strategies above (questions 1–4) to analyze a play episode in one of the books.

SUGGESTED RESOURCES

1. Paley, V. (1990). *The boy who would be a helicopter*. Cambridge, MA: Harvard University Press.

   This book recounts the case study of one child whose development is profoundly affected by his symbolic play. Paley's sensitivity to the processes inherent in play and her insights gained from careful observations of play are inspirational to teachers.

2. Fromberg, D., & Bergen, D. (Eds.). (1998). *Play from birth to twelve and beyond: Conflicts, perspectives, and meanings*. New York: Garland Publishing.

   This book explores the development of play from infancy through adulthood from a variety of perspectives, and offers both theoretical and practical lenses on the role of play in human growth, development, and education.

3. Dyson, A. H., & Genishi, C. (1994). *The need for story: Cultural diversity in classrooms and community*. Urbana, IL: National Council of Teachers of English.

   This book offers teachers essays and teacher research reports that are directly relevant to supporting children's capacity for creating story in school settings. The relationship of play to story is articulated in many chapters of the book.

4. Klugman, E. (Ed.). (1995). *Play, policy and practice*. St. Paul, MN: Red Leaf Press.

   This volume presents work from a conference on play held at Wheelock College in Boston in the summer of 1992. The conference was attended by teachers and play researchers from the United States and Israel and explored a range of issues related to play in schools and across cultural contexts.

CHAPTER 4

Orchestrating Children's Play:

Setting the Stage

🐟 🐟 🐟 🐟 🐟 🐟 🐟 🐟 🐟 🐟 🐟 🐟 🐟 🐟 🐟

In Ann's K–1 combination classroom, the environment invites play. The house-keeping area includes kitchen furniture and accessories, and a small couch and rocking chair. A girl doll with Asian features and two boy dolls, one with African American and one with Caucasian features rest in two small beds near the rocker. The children have made a VCR and a television screen from differ-ent-sized cardboard boxes. Hats and costumes are stored on shelves and hooks, doll clothes in drawers. An accessory box with props for hospital play sits open in the block area adjacent to the house, along with the ever-useful blank clip-boards with paper and pencils attached. Ann considers these staples of her play environment. She explains that a local pediatrician had visited the class the day before, and introduced children to terms and medical tools that she hoped would be recast in today's play.

🐟 🐟 🐟 🐟 🐟 🐟 🐟 🐟 🐟 🐟 🐟 🐟 🐟 🐟 🐟

Using the knowledge of theories and research that guide teachers' under-standing of the development of play presented in chapters 2 and 3 is the first step in the complex and rewarding process we call "play orchestration." Aware-ness that three-year-olds are more dependent on replica objects to sustain their play because of their emerging ability to symbolize, or that five- and six-year-olds frequently play games with rules that shift with each round gives teachers a frame of expectations for behavior and learning in a play-centered curriculum.

The next step in the orchestration process is to bridge expectations based on knowledge and understanding of development to practical strategies for sup-porting play, learning and development in settings for young children. These strategies are illuminated by an interpretive approach to teaching. In this approach, teachers always view children's behavior within the sociocultural con-text in which it occurs, noticing factors such as the social history and social hier-archy of a group of players, or the dynamics of a newcomer or an English lan-guage learner within the play (King, 1992).

We also recognize that the teacher-as-observer is not a passive party to chil-dren's play even if his or her intervention is subtle, such as enlarging the play-house to accommodate a pretend store, or adding a sieve to the water table.

We emphasize that the interpretive approach that draws upon multiple the-ories combines the best of spontaneous curriculum that emerges in teachable moments and careful planning by the teacher for children's play and learning. In play situations, teachers find that systematic observation, record keeping, reflection, and planning are essential.

Therefore, a play-centered curriculum is not made of fixed components but is emergent, finding its direction in the themes and concepts children generate in their play. For a play curriculum to be effective, the teacher must orchestrate the dynamic flow of its elements by matching play to the child's levels of func-

The play-centered curriculum is emergent.

tioning and by providing opportunities for the developmental stretch to occur for each child and for the group as a whole. In addition, the skilled teacher employs a myriad of strategies for "upping the ante" to encourage these developmental stretches. He or she must also implement strategies that foster feelings of trust and safety for children within play contexts.

PRINCIPLES GUIDING ORCHESTRATION

Four general principles guide our thinking about the ways that teachers may support play in the curriculum. Each of these principles applies across all age groups of children and in contexts that involve spontaneous play and those that involve more teacher-guided play.

Taking the Child's View

The first principle involves the teacher taking the child's view of experiences and materials in the classroom. Developmentally appropriate practice, a term coined by the National Association for the Education of Young Children (NAEYC), involves understanding age-appropriate development in young children (Bredekamp & Copple, 1997). For example, knowing that younger children are likely to need replicas of real objects in their play, while older children often prefer blocks, marbles, or other unstructured materials for their play is an example of using child development theory and research to inform practice.

Developmentally appropriate practice also involves understanding the individual development of each child. What does Raul bring to school from his home that is unique and different from the concepts and attitudes brought by Miko or Frances? How does the impending divorce of Jo Ann's parents affect her development and behavior?

In taking the child's view of experience and materials, teachers work with both of these aspects of developmentally appropriate practice: understanding the normal development of a particular age group, and understanding the life experiences in and out of school that shape meaning for each individual child.

Teacher as Keen Observer

The second principle of orchestrating play in the curriculum involves the teacher functioning as a keen observer of children's behavior. His or her observation skills are supported by designated times to circulate through the classroom, to jot anecdotal notes on peel off labels, or to sit and observe in a given area of the room. The teacher also uses observational strategies when working with a small group of children on a focused activity and takes time to write down children's observations, questions, experiments, and hypotheses as they work and play.

Seeing Meaning as It Is Constructed

Under the auspices of this third principle, the sensitive teacher recognizes that children construct meaning through many aspects of their experience. Sometimes meaning emerges as teacher and child sit together to figure out the spelling of a new word. Sometimes meaning emerges as playmates suggest a new support for a block building or a costume for a role. Children's interaction with adults and other children in classroom settings create contexts where knowledge is meaningful and elaborated.

Teacher as Stage Manager

The fourth principle involves the teacher's skill in organizing the environment. The teacher plans experiences for children, anticipating the spatial arrangements, basic materials, accessories, and time frames needed for children to construct knowledge through their play. In this role, the teacher supports play by indirectly orchestrating the physical environment and time for children's play.

In this chapter we first present some general definitions of strategies and concepts for setting the stage for play in the classroom. Chapter 5 lists more detailed descriptions of teachers' interactive orchestration strategies and examples of their uses in classrooms for preschool and primary grade children.

Our discussion of strategies for setting the stage and orchestrating children's play are applicable in full and partial inclusion settings for young children. Both federal legislation (P.L. 94-142 and P.L. 99-457) and enhanced professional awareness on the part of early childhood educators have influenced the inclusion of greater numbers of children with special needs in preschool and primary grade settings. Adaptations to the environment, careful selection of play materials, and curriculum are described extensively in the early intervention literature. A broad discussion of these issues is beyond the scope of this chapter. However, the following discussions of strategies, the illustrative anecdotes, and references are based on our belief that play "leads" development for all children, those who develop in atypical as well as more typical ways.

A CONTINUUM OF STRATEGIES

The model we present in Figure 4.1 represents orchestration strategies ranging from very indirect to very direct roles on the part of the adult. The most indirect of these strategies involve arranging and accessorizing the physical environment for play, and then planning curriculum based on observation and recording of children's play.

Setting the Stage for Play

At the indirect end of the continuum, teachers orchestrate play by setting the stage for it to occur. They first provide the physical space conducive to children's play needs. They also use their professional skills to elaborate and extend curriculum based on the children's play that they observe. Accessories for play are

Figure 4.1
Continuum of Play Orchestration Strategies.

	Setting the Stage
INDIRECT	Physical space
	Accessories
	Daily schedule
	Curriculum extensions
	Guided Play
	Artist apprentice
	Peacemaker
	Guardian of the gate
	Parallel player
	Spectator
	Participant
	Matchmaker
	Storyplayer
DIRECT	Play tutor

changed frequently as the teacher responds to the children's needs, or are readily available for children to appropriate on their own.

Preparing the Physical Space for Play

In structuring the physical environment for play, questions to consider are: How
is the space arranged, both indoors and outdoors? Is there a place for rough-
and-tumble play, an area to run and jump and chase? Are there clearly marked
spots with "soft" spaces such as pillows or soft chairs in which children may find
privacy? Are there other areas that have clear boundaries for children, such as
the housekeeping, reading, and block areas? All of these features contribute to
children's developing play complexity by fostering choice-making and the protection of ongoing play episodes.

Research on children's play environments indicates that between 30–50
square feet of usable space per child represents an ideal size for indoor environments. Spaces with less than 25 square feet per child generally lead to increases
in aggression and unfocused behavior for children (Smith & Connolly, 1980).
For teachers, crowded physical spaces promote more directive teaching and
limit opportunities for social interaction among children.

In thinking about room arrangements, teachers may want to consider both
units (the spaces arranged for children's play) and the surrounding space (the
area around a unit needed for people to move about). Space invites children to
pause and attend, to play alone or with others, to move randomly or purposefully, and to combine materials or separate them. Space generally shapes the
flow of play and communication in the classroom or outdoors (Kritchevsky,
Prescott, & Walling, 1977; Loughlin & Suina, 1982). Figures 4.2, 4.3, and 4.4
show alternative floor plans.

Considerations of the physical space are extremely important when integrating children with special needs into the classroom. According to McEvoy, Shores,
Wehby, Johnson, and Fox (1990), educators cannot assume that children with special needs will be socially integrated merely by placing them in classrooms with
nondisabled children. It is imperative for teachers to be aware of the particular
alternative learning strategies of each child (Erwin, 1993). In some cases, adaptive
equipment may be needed to promote active engagement (Hanline & Fox, 1993).
Based on this awareness, teachers can then plan environments that support the
child's development of self-initiated solitary play as well as play with peers.

Paths and boundaries.   Research on children's environments indicates that clear
boundaries between interest areas, and clear paths of movement between them,
help children to focus on their play and support their protection of interactive
space (Field, 1980; Moore, 1985; Ramsey & Reid, 1988; Vergeront, 1987, 1988).
Outdoor environments that provide linkages among play areas such as platforms,
slides, or tire nets, and multiple levels of challenge as well as diverse materials,
are most conducive to sustained play (Johnson, Christie, & Yawkey, 1987; Rivkin,
1995). Boundaries must be low enough, however, for children to view available
possibilities in the environment. Low adult-child ratios also contribute to the

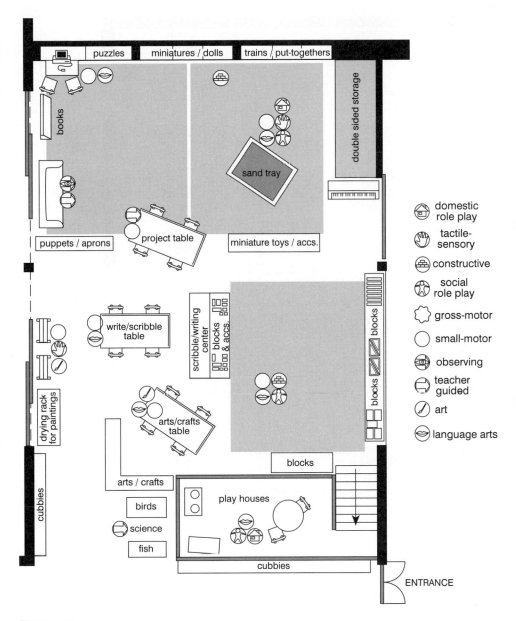

puzzles | miniatures / dolls | trains / put-togethers

books

double sided storage

sand tray

puppets / aprons

project table

miniature toys / accs.

write/scribble table

scribble/writing center

blocks & accs.

blocks

blocks

blocks

drying rack for paintings

arts/crafts table

arts / crafts

cubbies

birds

science

fish

blocks

play houses

cubbies

ENTRANCE

- domestic role play
- tactile-sensory
- constructive
- social role play
- gross-motor
- small-motor
- observing
- teacher guided
- art
- language arts

Figure 4.2
Preschool and Kindergarten Setting.

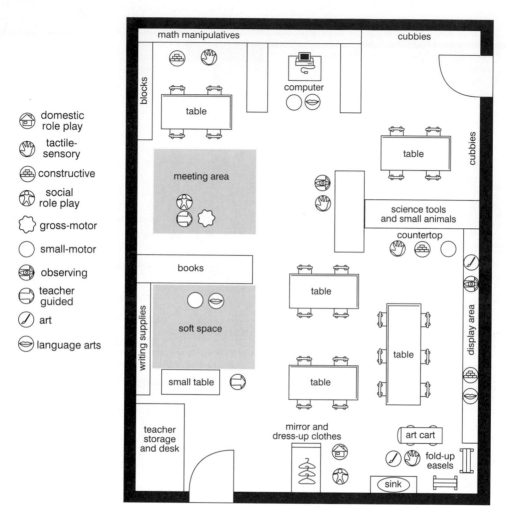

Figure 4.3
Primary Grade Setting.

maintenance of play themes, perhaps by having the mere presence of an adult nearby to act as a buffer against interlopers or distractions (Bruner, 1980).

❧ John and Sara are playing airport in the block corner. They have just painstakingly completed a control tower and runway when Andrew and Colin chase through the block area on their way outdoors to try out the magic capes they have made from yarn and paper. The block structures fall, and there are angry tears and accusations. ❧

If the pathway from the art area to the outdoors were re-routed around the block area, such events would be less likely.

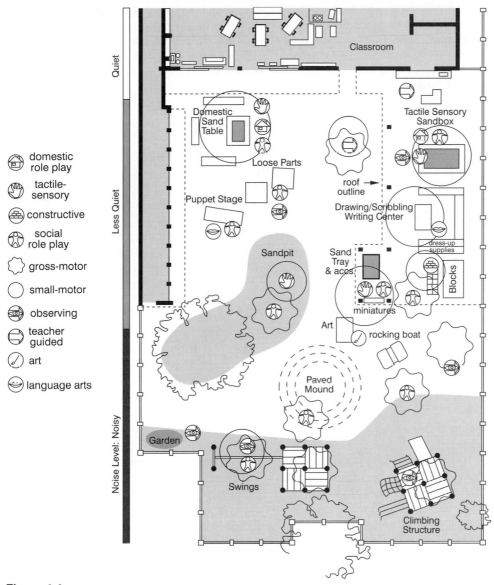

Figure 4.4
Outdoor Setting—Preschool and Primary Grade.

Quiet and noisy areas.   Another set-up strategy involves separating quiet and noisy, or private and group, activities in different parts of the setting. Activities likely to foster social interaction and busy noise are blocks, dramatic play, reading and writing corners, number activities, and climbing structures. Sand-boxes, water tables, art activities, and computers are variable: in some situations with some children, they may be conducive to social interaction; in others they may promote more parallel and solitary play than cooperative play

(Ramsey & Reid, 1988). In general, activities that encourage gross motor play, such as tricycles and outdoor climbing structures, foster more social interaction than those that encourage small motor skills, such as puzzles, table toys, miniatures, or Montessori materials. The latter materials are more likely to lead to more solitary and parallel play (Hendrickson, Strain, Trembley, & Shores, 1981).

Areas that support "social" activities are critical in classrooms practicing inclusion. Many children with special needs are deficient in the social skills necessary for appropriate development. Beckman and Kohl found that providing interactive toys leads to increased social interactions among disabled and nondisabled children (Beckman and Kohl, 1984, as cited in McEvoy et al., 1990). Similarly, Horner found that disabled children's adaptive behaviors were increased by adding large numbers of toys to a free choice setting (Horner, 1980, as cited in McEvoy et al., 1990).

Activity units that offer children privacy for playing alone or with one or two friends are created by furniture that defines the space. These "hidey-holes" for children to find respite from the group seem particularly important for children who may spend 8–10 hours a day in settings with other children (Jones, 1973). Quiet places are particularly important for some children who are easily distracted or frustrated.

෨ Hannah is a student with special needs, diagnosed as having ADHD and language delays. With the supportive teamwork of her parents, the school psychologist, and the special education teacher, Hannah has been fully integrated into Pam's first grade class. Pam finds that Hannah frequently has difficulty sustaining interactions with the other children. As part of Hannah's Individualized Education Plan, Pam and the school psychologist are attempting to assess and support her progress in social activities with peers.

In addition to interacting with peers in Pam's class, Hannah's participation in after-school day care means that she is with large groups of children for ten hours each day, from 7:30 a.m. to 5:30 p.m. Pam observes that Hannah spends quiet time each day by herself in the classroom's reading loft, looking at picture books or talking quietly to the stuffed animals. When Hannah becomes frustrated, Pam finds that she can help Hannah self-monitor her behavior by suggesting that she go to the loft or another quiet place. ෨

Soft spaces.   Soft areas in the classroom are also recommended to provide privacy and time out for children. The cozy nature of a corner with pillows and rocker, carpeting, and materials that invite sensory exploration such as sand or clay are all indicators of softness in the environment (Phyfe-Perkins, 1980; Rivkin, 1995). When children become angry or frustrated, teachers can give them a chance to retreat to a quiet, soft space by themselves, a place with no hard objects to throw or hurt themselves. Adults may need to accompany children who are, at that moment, very aggressive or have emotional disturbances.

ઠ The book corner is in a central area of the room. It is carpeted in a mellow beige tweed, which was selected both for its sturdiness and softness. The rug is bounded on one side by a piano that faces a low rose-colored couch. Several thin rectangular pillows, covered in a washable, leaf-colored velour, are available for sitting on or leaning against the piano legs during circle time. At the wall end of the rug, two birch book display stands each put five rows of picture books within easy reach of rug sitters.

(Beardsley, 1991, p. 52) ઠ

When space is limited.   In classrooms where space is at a premium, often in public school primary grade settings, teachers may be creative in the use of portable accessories or "Murphy space." For example, in one first grade classroom, where desks grouped as tables occupy a large part of the classroom, the teacher constructed easels that fold into the wall, much like a Murphy bed, that can be pulled out and set up during free playtime. He complements this with a rolling cart that includes art and carpentry materials that may be transported outdoors or to a table area.

Other teachers have decided that table space for all children to sit down at one time is not necessary in a room where the play goes on in specific areas of the classroom. For one teacher, freeing the room of large tables has enabled him to rotate the use of center areas according to the play experiences he has planned, and has left open space in the room for block play and a large dramatic play area.

Adjacent areas.   When setting up, teachers might also think about the effects of placing activity areas adjacent to one another. For example, in one teacher's classroom the dramatic play and block areas were moved next to one another. Groups of children who normally played in only one of those areas began joint fantasy play using props from the housekeeping corner to equip a "space station" under construction in the block area.

Adjacent areas also invite opportunities for the cross-fertilization of the ideas of children engaged in play even when the play areas remain distinct. For example, in one first grade classroom, ongoing play at the carpentry table adjacent to the block area prompted the construction of airplanes and helicopters to be housed at the block area airport. In a second grade classroom, a post office created to encourage letter writing soon expanded to a bank and an office on either side where children integrated literacy and mathematics concepts.

To encourage the cross-fertilization of ideas in activity areas, Griffin (1982) recommends that teachers keep a box of game parts, puzzle pieces, rocks, and miscellaneous small objects that children may use in their dramatic play. In this way, the puzzle pieces and objects associated with more structured activities are more likely to remain in their respective areas, while allowing children to appropriate flexible materials for their own uses. Heath (1983) cautions that cultural factors may affect children's understanding of the school culture's conventions for returning objects to their original storage places. For example, a child who lives in a trailer or a crowded home may have learned to store toys out of view rather than displayed on a shelf.

Accessories for play.   The provision of accessories in the environment relates to our discussion of symbolic distancing in chapter 3. For sociodramatic play, younger or less sophisticated players need more realistic props to support or scaffold their play themes and roles (Copple, Cocking, & Matthews, 1984). Their symbolic distancing skills are not well enough developed to appropriate a block or an imaginary gesture when a real-looking prop such as a toy telephone is not available. Generally, younger children (ages 2–3) prefer to have several sets of realistic props to use in their dramatic play. Multiple sets of brooms and phones, toy food and dishes, fire trucks and toy animals are necessary elements for the scaffold supporting their dramatic play. If not available, play fantasies may give way to object disputes and the symbolic distancing of roles and situations has little chance to get underway.

On the other hand, sophisticated dramatic players like to have lots of unstructured props—that is, props with limited specific use of their own available for their dramatic play. Cardboard packing, rocks, sticks, and blocks are examples of unstructured props. Such non-realistic props offer much leeway to the child to make successive transformations, for instance by using pebbles as money, food, buried treasure, and circus tickets all in the course of a single play episode (Pulaski, 1970).

School-aged children (ages 7–10) enjoy having hats and scarves available for the more formal plays they enact, and will generally use both unstructured props and imaginary ones in their play. They also use miniatures, models, and games with rules as accessories to their fantasy play.

🐾 In a second grade classroom, a group diorama representing the earth during the time of the dinosaurs is equipped with miniature dinosaurs constructed by the children. The children act out scenarios they imagine to be part of the daily lives of these creatures and construct new characters as the unit progresses. 🐾

Timing in the introduction of props is important. Replicas of real objects and props that relate to familiar scripts are appropriate at the beginning of the year, as children get to know one another. Accessory boxes that augment the familiar scripts of housekeeping or cars and trucks in the preschool and kindergarten may be introduced later in the year. Many teachers have a large selection of accessory boxes built around themes such as restaurant, office, beach trip, and camping that they introduce to correlate with curriculum themes or have available upon request by children. Accessory or prop boxes may be made from cardboard boxes, ice cream containers, or plastic bins (Myhre, 1993). Figure 4.5 provides suggestions for themes and contents for prop boxes. Some teachers offer a rotating variety of theme boxes in a designated area of the room, others periodically replace or augment equipment in the housekeeping area or outdoor climbing structure. In the primary grades, these accessory boxes are valuable as prompts for enacted plays and story writing.

Restaurant
aprons
chef's hats
menus
tablecloths
silverware
dishes
play food
chalkboard and chalk for
  "specials"
order pads and pencils
cash register
telephone

Hospital
bandages
toy medical tools (i.e. blood
  pressure cuff, syringe)
cots or mats
waiting room with magazines
white coats
medical hats
rubber gloves

Office
stapler
tape
old adding machine
copier made from cardboard box
telephones
typewriter or computer
keyboard
computer monitor made from box

Bank
tellers' windows
cash boxes
bank books
office supplies
play money

Laundromat
washers and dryers made
  from cardboard cartons
plastic or straw baskets
clothing to "wash", sort and
  fold (i.e. socks, t-shirts)
toy iron and ironing board
clothes rack and hangers
cash register or change
  machine
bulletin board and notices
magazines

Paint Store
painter hat
bucket
brushes
paper color chips in graded colors
cash register and "money"
order pads and pencils

Camping Out
sleeping bags
tent
camp cookware
flashlight
backpacks

Travel and Passport Office
toy camera
drawing and writing supplies
blank books
travel brochures
maps

Bakery
play dough
cookie sheets
oven
telephone
chalkboard for prices
cash register and cash

Figure 4.5
Some Suggested Accessory Box Themes and Contents.

Familiarity balanced with novelty.　　Children need a balance of the familiar and the novel. In addition to the traditional housekeeping props, the teacher must consider the cultural backgrounds of his students. Does the family eat with chopsticks and cook in a wok? Does the family use a barbeque? Might cherry picking baskets, beads and yarn, western hats or coal miners' hats be familiar objects in some children's homes? If we want all children to find a familiar script in the classroom, we must scaffold their symbolic behavior on what is comfortable and home-like to them (Curry, 1971).

Quiet private materials offer children opportunities for exploration before they begin to play.

Areas where materials for art and music are available open opportunities for new accessories or modifications of old ones (Bronson, 1995). In one classroom, film cans filled with rice, beans, or pebbles were placed next to the xylophone and rhythm instruments, with materials for creating individual shakers set out nearby. In another setting, a discussion of a Monet painting prompted the teacher to mix muted pastel colors and thicken the paints so that children might try the "painting in pokes" that they had noticed in the print borrowed from the public library (Beardsley, 1991).

Play materials offer alternatives.   Teachers may set up environments that encourage a particular kind of play by combining or rearranging materials. For example, setting out toothpicks with clay may encourage more social interaction than clay alone, as children link structures they build or construct birthday cakes or bridges in play that involves others.

Quiet and private materials offer children opportunities for exploration before they begin to play. In initial exploration, the focus is on "What can this object (or material) do?" After time to explore the material at hand, children begin to truly play, when the implicit question becomes, "What can I do with this object or material?" (Hutt, 1971; Wohlwill, 1984).

ஃ Sandy approaches the used adding machine that another child has just left. She pushes keys and watches the numbers print for about 10 minutes. The next day she returns and continues her exploration, systematically trying each key to note the number it produces on the tape. On the third day she invites Mark to play. "Come to my store. You can buy cookies," and she rings up a pretend purchase. ஃ

Materials that offer opportunities for exploratory and self-correcting activity include pegboards, form boards, miniatures, and picture lotto. These activities give children a relaxed time out from the mental effort of negotiating with their peers and help them restore a sense of order and control to their lives. This function seems to be age-related. McLloyd (1983) found that 3-year-olds used these materials in more solitary ways, whereas 5-year-olds engaged in more cooperative play regardless of the structure of the materials. This relates to the finding that solitary play represents an option for older children, who may be better able to verbalize their needs for privacy (Monighan-Nourot et al., 1987).

Planning the Daily Schedule

Another subtle and relatively indirect aspect of teacher orchestration of the play-filled curriculum is the daily schedule in the setting. Powerful messages are sent to children about the value of their own choices and the activities they construct for themselves by the way that teachers structure the days. This scheduling includes not only the content of the classroom, but also how much time is allotted for playful purposes.

In the most free-flowing environments, the room is arranged with activities available for children to choose (Ramsey & Reid, 1988). Furniture and materials are flexible, and the teacher floats, interacting with small groups of children more often than the entire class. Traditional nursery schools and open classrooms based on the British Infant School model are examples of this design. Teachers who use this design in their classrooms have noted that lengthening the total time for free choice activities and play increases the focus and engagement of children in their chosen activities and also encourages children to try new experiences after they have touched base with their old favorites (Paley, 1984).

In other environments, more teacher direction and less child choice is evident. Small- and large-group direct instruction alternate with free-choice time. Teachers spend more time with designated groups and less time attending to the flow in the total classroom. The pitfall of this model is that what teachers perceive as play (e.g., building an airport with blocks) may be seen by the children as labor because their choice of activities really rests with the teacher. Teachers may also miss out on important learning events when they attend to only one group.

The most structured environment leaves little time for free play. Play is regarded as recreational rather than as a vehicle for learning. Small- and large-group direct instruction characterize this design, and the teacher's attention to children's play rests primarily on concerns about safety rather than on aspects of social or intellectual development. Skills-based academic programs exemplify this model.

Teachers who are sensitive to the distinction between labor required by others and playful work selected by children in their settings will note the importance of choices for children, as well as ample time for children to elaborate and complete activities they have begun. In any activity, teachers need to ask themselves, How much of it is truly chosen by the child? Does the child have choices about where, when, how, and with whom she or he plays? How engaged are children in their play?

Extensions for Play

Setting the stage for play also includes curriculum planning. It represents the backstage versus the on-stage aspect of teaching when we focus on play as the center of the curriculum.

Play-generated curriculum.   One facet of curriculum planning is play-generated curriculum, or curriculum that emerges directly from the interests of the children. In this aspect of setting the stage for play, teachers draw upon their observations of children's interests and themes in their play to provide opportunities to extend and elaborate their learning. For example:

❧ In one first grade classroom, several of the children had participated over the weekend in a community art fair called "Art in the Park." They had all contributed their efforts to a huge wall mural on which both adults and children had painted images and experimented with color. On Monday, three of the children asked if they could have some large paper to show the other children "how you make a really big picture." The teacher set up large sheets of butcher paper and multiple containers of paint during the week. Children experimented with recipes for making paint and mixing colors. Later in the week the teacher brought in books from the library depicting murals in other communities around the world. The following week, the teacher introduced new media such as collage and group wood sculptures for the children to try. ❧

Curriculum-generated play.   This facet of curriculum planning involves a more direct role for the teacher. In planning curriculum-generated play, a teacher's observation of children's play leads her to include materials or techniques that she suspects will create a match with children's spontaneous interests. In this way, the teacher's knowledge of the content area such as science, mathematics, art, or literacy intersects with her sense of children's previous experiences and their current interests.

≥● Judy, the teacher of a second grade science program, noticed children's interests in the concept of water pressure as they experimented with dish soap bottles outdoors. She related these interests to requirements for physical science activities and the introduction of scientific terms in the state department of education's science framework. Judy placed holes in containers at different levels and set up plastic piping material with a water source, challenging the children to find out which arrangements would make the water squirt farther. She introduced terms like "pressure" in the context of their observations, mentioning that water at the bottom of a container was "heavier," and introduced the term "hypothesis" in conjunction with the "guesses" that the children made about their experiments. ≥●

≥● In a kindergarten classroom, Jennifer spent her choice time over several days creating a book she called "The Very Hungry Clowns" which consisted of clowns with butterflies in their tummies, a new one drawn for each day. Jennifer's merging of a phrase she had heard at home with the format and structure of *The Very Hungry Caterpillar* read earlier in the week were evident in her play creation. ≥●

The technique of curriculum-generated play has elements in common with the thematic curriculum design seen in many programs for preschool and primary children, and we believe it represents the best of thematic curriculum. Some thematic curriculum is based on the teacher's interests, children's families, past experiences, and resources. Truly play-centered curriculum integrates teachers' interests and concerns with those observed in children as they play (Edwards, Gandini, & Forman, 1993; Hendrick, 1997).

This continuity among families, community, and school curriculum is reflected strongly in the Reggio Emilia approach to early schooling (Edwards, 1993; Forman, 1992; Gandini, 1993, 1997; Hendrick, 1997; Rinaldi, 1993). Within this approach, the contributions of families and community and the relationships and interaction among children as they construct knowledge in small groups are all highly valued aspects of curriculum planning. Time for themes, concepts, hypotheses, and multiple representations to emerge and evolve to completion is valued. The "spiral" curriculum approach that revisits and revises representations of experience is shared by both children and teachers.

The way in which learning is documented is particularly important in the Reggio Emilia approach. Physical space supports many displays of children's representations of their experiences and thought processes. Programs for young children include an "atelier" (studio) and "atelierista" (artist in residence) whose training in the visual arts supports both teachers and children in documenting their thinking (Houck, 1997).

As noted in the theoretical foundations for play as the center of the curriculum presented in chapters 2 and 13, children's capacities to represent and to engage in reflective abstraction support the ongoing construction of knowledge. In the process of reflective abstraction, children symbolize their thoughts and feelings through a variety of media such as language, gesture, drawing, music, drama, and sculpture. The implicit relationships and understanding that children perceive as part of their developing view of the world around them become publicly as well as privately represented as they share their expressions of knowledge.

Representation that serves the process of reflective abstraction includes both multiple representation, in which an experience is symbolically represented with several media, and transformative representation in which the representations of experience and thinking are themselves represented by subsequent symbolic constructions in new media.

&. In Jackie's multi-age class of 5-, 6-, and 7-year-olds, ongoing curriculum centers on the concept of living things. A day trip to the beach was represented by small groups of children playing and working collaboratively. One group painted a mural; another made a set of flannel board pieces to tell a story; another group arranged snapshots of the trip into a book with both dictated and child-written narrative; a fourth group enacted the trip outdoors in the sandbox, creating an imaginary bus and making props for the picnic and sea creature discoveries they remembered.

Jackie and her co-teacher Peggy solicited children's drawings of their ideas about the beach before the trip, after the trip and then again as the unit was drawing to a close. They showed these "before" and "after" drawings to the children so that they could reflect on their own learning. The drawings were also placed in children's portfolios as assessment data.

"I didn't even know about the rocks and those teeny little animals before," exclaimed Jared as he compared his own before and after drawings. Jackie and Peggie also tape recorded children's comments about their representations of the beach. The tape recordings served as transformative representations as the children reflected on both the content and processes symbolized in their developing knowledge about the beach. &.

Bruner (1963) coined the term *spiral curriculum* to represent the idea that, at many stages of their development, children may grasp basic concepts, each time returning to the same ideas at a more sophisticated level of understanding. So, rather than focusing on the themes of curriculum, such as whales or dinosaurs, the teacher focuses on the concepts that might be revisited as children encounter those themes several times during their school experience. For example, the study of both whales and dinosaurs involves concepts related to comparisons—of size, of environments, of ways of living that are different from humans, and concepts of time and historical contexts. These are some of the essential concepts that emerge as children study creatures great and small, and compare them to their own perspectives and experiences. Such lessons may be revisited many times from varying perspectives and with deeper understanding as development spirals upward.

One drawback of thematic curriculum that is not directly based in children's experiences is the unsatisfactory treatment of multicultural issues in early primary education. Many teachers with good intentions address cultural diversity in a manner that has come to be known as the "tourist curriculum" (Derman-Sparks & A.B.C. Task Force, 1989). In this approach, foods, festivals, and music from cultures other than mainstream American culture are introduced once a year, often in conjunction with a holiday. Many of us as teachers have fallen into the routine of presenting out-of-context knowledge of culture, such as depicting stereotypes of American Indians at Thanksgiving or Chinese culture at Chinese New Year, without addressing the real issues of cultural diversity in our daily lives. Instead, the "anti-bias" approach advocated by Derman-Sparks and A.B.C. Task Force includes diversity as a regular aspect of the curriculum where teachers foster children's positive attitudes toward the acceptance and celebration of differences among cultures.

Consistent with this latter view, in a play-centered curriculum, aspects of the physical environment and accessories for play reflect diversity of culture, through such items as the tortilla press, yogurt maker, seaweed toaster, rice bowls and chopsticks, as well as day-time planners and briefcases that are available in Janice's kindergarten room.

In a play-centered curriculum, art, music, literature, science, and mathematics experiences reflect cultural diversity in a manner that makes it part of everyday life in the classroom, not just an infrequent glimpse of fragmented information or a song or two. For example:

ଈ In Consuelo's first grade classroom, she observed the Southeast Asian children pretending to make rice and shrimp dishes in their sand and water play. She contacted one of the parents of the children and included frequent cooking projects. The projects introduced some of these foods and the techniques used to cook them to everyone in the class and offered the Southeast Asian children foods that seemed familiar and delicious to them as part of the regular snack menu. ଈ

ଈ In a second grade classroom, the teacher incorporated literature describing the creation myths of several cultures into his curriculum on astronomy. He invited children to share stories that they might have heard from their grandparents or parents on these topics, and small groups of children illustrated these stories with murals. ଈ

Wassermann (1990) designed an interesting approach to curriculum-generated play specifically targeted at primary grade teachers. Her technique, which she calls *play, debrief, replay,* involves careful planning of the environment and materials as well as keen observation of children's activities. Her approach also calls for skilled debriefing questions that elicit children's reflections and support construction of knowledge in the particular curriculum areas embedded in children's play. For example:

ॐ Kitty introduced a unit integrating history and science to her third grade class in a rural area school. The *guided play* focused on machines for agriculture, and built on the concepts from a unit on small machines completed earlier in the year. During that unit, the class visited the county historical agricultural museum, where a docent actively engaged the children. Kitty brought the class pictures from the museum as well as real objects gathered from her own grandparents and their friends and the families of the children in the class. These objects included apple corers, flour sifters, models and pictures of tractors, huskers, and combines. One of the families brought in several looms and the parents discussed the growing and transformation of fibrous plants.

In the *play phase* of the activity, children were prompted to play with their ideas about the characteristics of the machines; spontaneous sorting and hypothesizing about their uses occurred, as well as interesting speculation about the division of labor between men and women, and the children's chores.

In the *debriefing phase*, Kitty asked each group of children to describe what they did and to draw some representation of their discussion. Each group reported on the questions she set for them: What do these machines do? How do they work? Who used them? How are they alike and different?

Hypotheses about all these topics emerged during the class discussion. Kitty invited each group to return for the *replay phase* in which they added to their drawings and wrote about their objects based on the new information they learned. ॐ

Recasting the curriculum through play.   The third curriculum strategy represents subtle orchestration on the part of the teacher and calls for finely tuned observation skills. In this strategy, the teacher provides opportunities and asks questions that encourage children to use newly constructed knowledge derived from the curriculum in their play. We return to the notion presented in chapter 2, that play is a predominance of assimilation, and represents opportunities for children to consolidate and generalize their emerging mental concepts. We see this aspect of play as extremely important. The true test of whether experiences orchestrated by the teacher help children learn a specific concept or skill, such as counting money or using a calculator, is to see it "replayed" spontaneously by children in their play.

ॐ In one first grade classroom, the teacher complemented a mathematics unit on measurement with the creation of a shoe store in the dramatic play area. She was delighted to hear children use terms like "same size" and "half an inch shorter," as they used rulers, yardsticks, and shoe measurers in their play. As part of the whole language curriculum, she facilitated the making of a shoe sale sign and sales receipt books, while children wrote about shoes they love to wear. The unit was expanded to include other stores that children knew about in their local shopping mall, and integrated literacy, mathematics, art, and social studies concepts in the play. ॐ

PLAY AND THE SCHOOL: HELPING PARENTS AND EDUCATORS VALUE PLAY IN THE LIVES OF CHILDREN

In the previous sections of this chapter, we discussed principles and strategies educators can use to orchestrate play within their classrooms. Educators who implement play-centered curricula must consider strategies that go beyond their own classrooms to foster a school and community culture that values play. Since many teachers often feel they must defend the importance of play, a significant part of implementing a play-centered curriculum is for teachers to have a network of colleagues, including parents, who support play. This network can form the basis of a purposeful community with participants who share experiences, books and articles, and arrange programs—creating a community of players.

Teachers from several schools shared attempts to involve parents and other educators in discussions about the value of play. Several tried the idea of a slide show that Anna described in the first chapter. This was a lively way to begin discussions about their programs. Seeing slides of the children engaged in different types of play made it easier for everyone to understand, particularly parents who spoke little English. It was also successful at producing a good turnout for "open house," reaching and engaging some parents who rarely came to school.

One teacher said that she explained how the children's activities shown in the slides related to their development in academic areas. A student teacher who had worked on a slide show said that she made sure that each child was included. When parents spoke with her, they spoke about what their own child did in the slide. That gave her the opportunity to discuss how that specific example of play supported development in several ways.

Shelley, a teacher-director of a parent cooperative nursery school, wrote short letters to parents. This is part of one:

"This week, with your assistance, the children and I are turning the dramatic play area into a clothing store. We have chosen a clothing store because all the children are familiar with it and will feel comfortable playing out familiar roles like salesperson and customer. We think that this theme will promote cooperative and creative dramatic play.

"'The clothing store' play promotes practice with basic vocabulary words like shirts and dresses as well as extended vocabulary such as 'accessories,' 'pleated,' 'paisley,' and so forth. This theme promotes other literate activities as children write and read signs ('boys' clothes'), receipts, and newspaper ads. Children will be working with math concepts as they figure out how to make a cash register, print money, decide what to charge for items, and write price tags, receipts, and checks. Of course, clothes always lead to discussions of sizes, especially since we have some foreign clothes with metric sizing!

We are coordinating this theme with our science program. We have been focusing on 'the seasons and change.' We have talked about what we wear in different seasons. The clothing store should give the children a chance to compare clothes worn in different seasons. This theme also coordinates with our social studies topic, 'our community.' Our clothing collection from past years includes some clothes worn by children from different cultures and countries. We have a sarong, a sari, a pair of lederhosen, and a kimono. We also have clothes worn by people in different occupations, including a medical coat and a carpenter's belt. We would appreciate it if you have other clothes to add!" 🐚

🐚 Manuel, a first grade teacher, discussed the importance of educating cross-age tutors on the value of play. He trained the fifth grade tutors for his class on how to interact with the children involved in spontaneous play. He found that this was important so that the older students understood their roles, and respected the importance of the activity. And, he stressed, it led to better public relations in the informal network of school communication. 🐚

🐚 Scott commented on his discussions with other teachers, including special education teachers, the school counselors and psychologists who worked with several children mainstreamed into his class, and administrators. He was interested to learn more about their perspectives and experiences. For example, several of them had read articles that gave them the impression that particular children were not capable of the self-direction and mastery he observed in children's play. Scott explained: "When I feel that I'm leading people to a better understanding I feel different than when I feel that I'm defending my position. When I use theoretical perspectives along with examples from my own classroom to show how play is related to developmentally appropriate practice, people begin to understand." 🐚

SUMMARY AND CONCLUSION

Teachers use knowledge of developmental theories and research when setting the stage for a play-centered curriculum. Rather than following a fixed curriculum, the teacher guides orchestration by providing opportunities for development. Guiding principles include (a) taking the child's view, (b) being a keen observer of children's behavior, (c) seeing meaning as it is constructed, (d) serving as stage manager to organize the environment, and (e) planning new curriculum.

The continuum of strategies discussed in this chapter are subtle and complex. Therefore, it is helpful if teachers work with others and think of themselves as working within their own zone of proximal development. All teachers continue to develop and refine their abilities to set the stage, prepare the physical space, plan the daily schedule, and develop curriculum-related extensions for play. In these extensions, teachers think about children's play to inspire and generate more formalized curriculum, as well as follow children's leads in recasting the curriculum through play. The chapters on the arts, science, mathematics, and language and literacy that follow will provide further consideration of these extensions.

FOCUSING OUR THINKING

1. Using either clay, found objects, blocks, or manipulatives such as Legos, build a model of a school or center environment with which you are familiar. Experiment with rearranging this environment to be more conducive to children's play, carefully attending to boundaries, pathways and the accessibility of materials. Share your models with others who have used different materials.

2. Observe children's play in a preschool or primary grade setting on at least five different days. How much time is available for play, not counting clean-up time or set-up time? In what ways do the teachers plan the environment and materials to support play? How does the teachers' curriculum connect to children's play? What ideas do you have for enhancing the playfulness of the environment?

3. Think of a prop box not included in this chapter that might be used in a preschool or primary setting. List costumes and materials that might be included. Pay attention to possibilities for literacy and mathematics tools that might enhance your theme.

SUGGESTED RESOURCES

1. Greenman, J. (1988). *Caring places, learning spaces*. Redmond, WA: Exchange Press.

   This book is a work of art, offering poetry, art, and photographs that enhance the very practical ideas for making environments for children both aesthetically pleasing and comfortable for children at play.

2. Bronson, M. B. (1995). *The right stuff for children birth to 8: Selecting play materials to support development*. Washington, DC: National Association for the Education of Young Children.

   This book contains a wealth of information on *the right stuff* and is an excellent guide for beginning as well as experienced teachers. Chapters on each age group include an overview of the children's abilities and play interests, considerations for appropriateness and special considerations. Sections on appropriate materials for each age group include social and fantasy play, exploration and mastery play, music, art, and movement, and gross motor play.

3. Wasserman, S. (1990). *Serious players in the primary classroom*. New York: Teachers College Press.

   This book presents arguments for developing a sense of "can do" in primary grade children and gives teachers specific suggestions for designing and implementing a guided play curriculum in several academic subject areas.

4. Hildebrand, V., Phenice, L. A., Gray, M. M., and Hines, R. P. (1996). *Knowing and serving diverse families*. Upper Saddle River, NJ: Merrill/Prentice Hall.

This book is based on the premise that educators should welcome diversity and acknowledge the "oneness of the entire human family." Readers will find information on laws, and discussions of what educators can do to avoid stereotyping. Chapters on African-American, Hispanic-American, Asian-American, Arab-American, Native-American Indian Families and Amish-American families as well as chapters on lifestyle variations such as stepfamilies and families with single teenage parents are included.

CHAPTER 5

Orchestrating Play:

Interactions with Children

Two children playing outdoors at kindergarten are joined by five others in and around the tunnel on the climbing structure. Casey announces to the teacher who is observing in the area, "Pretend I'm your kitty!" Carolina, Javier, Hee-Won, and Marcus chime in, designating themselves as cats, dogs, birds, and a bat. Hannah observes on the outskirts of the play, seemingly reluctant to join in, as the pretend pets cavort around the play structure and make animal sounds to their "owner." Brenda, their teacher says, "Oh dear, it's getting late, and I have to leave for my trip. Will you take care of my animals for me, Hannah?" Hannah agrees happily and Brenda moves to the outskirts of the play area, as the pretend play continues, with Hannah as the pet owner. After about 10 minutes, Brenda notices from across the yard that the pretend play seems to be disintegrating into a rough, chase and pull game. She "returns" from her trip, pets all her animals hello and then pretends to drive away in a car, waving farewell as the pretend pets respond with meows and squawks.

A large gazebo style tent has been set up in the preschool library corner today. "Wow, it looks like a circus tent," and "It must be raining here today" are among the comments made as children enter the classroom. Three-year-olds Monty, Kyle and Nils move into the tent right away. They put on pretend rain-coats and hold pretend umbrellas. Inside the tent they discuss lightning and thunder. The others squeal as one of them yells, "Watch out, it's lightning!" A pair of children join them adjacent to the tent where there is a paper fishing pond set up with magnetic fish and poles. The boys in the tent warn them to be careful abut fishing when there is lightning. Monty goes to the grocery store with his baby stroller and asks them all about their favorite foods. Kyle hunts for a toy gorilla in the block area to bring home to cook and Nils turns on a flashlight to make the "fire for cooking." Nils claims he wants to cook his own dinner (a plastic zebra from the block area) and they scuffle over the flashlight. Adam, their teacher, quietly steps in from his observation point outside the tent area and offers two other flashlights. First the children begin to "roast" their animals with their own flashlights, then Monty holds a flashlight under a low table with slats and invents a barbecue. The other flashlights are joined to "make a bigger fire" for cooking the meal.

Pam, a first grade teacher, watches as three children begin to play a board game, counting out marbles as they move to designated spaces on the game board. Peter counts whatever numbers come to mind, although he uses one-to-one correspondence as he pulls them from the barrel (1, 2, 3, 4, 7, 10). Marcia counts hers quite precisely, using the conventional number sequence, and one-to-one correspondence. Emily grabs a handful without counting, and Peter shouts, "You're cheating!" Pam asks if she may join the game and models counting in sequence and with correspondence when it is her turn. Soon Emily is imitating her strategy and Peter is attempting to master the sequence for counting from one to ten.

🐌   🐌   🐌   🐌   🐌   🐌   🐌   🐌   🐌   🐌   🐌   🐌   🐌   🐌

In each of these anecdotes we see how the teacher's ability to set up, observe, enter, and exit play with sensitivity and grace are crucial to the successful sustaining of children's play. Each teacher docs this by considering factors of age-appropriate and individual development. For example, Brenda understands that Hannah is both new to the preschool program, and her first language is one other than English. She models, then hands over a role for Hannah in the play that facilitates her participation.

Adam stays very clearly on the edges of the tent play, until he notices that the continuity is threatened by too few flashlights. His timely and subtle addition of two flashlights allows play to continue, and his quick exit to the borders

Teachers help children sustain their play by sensitively entering into their activities.

of play facilitates the children's invention of their own strategies for collaborative pretend play.

Pam knows that five- and six-year-olds are just beginning to understand games with rules, and that children's emerging abilities to use both conventional sequences and one-to-one correspondence in counting vary at this level of development.

A key role for the teacher lies in the ways he or she interacts with children as they play and think. The most important aspect of this role is the attitude that teachers maintain towards children's play. Teachers' respect for both individual and cultural variations in play themes and activities is essential, along with the cultivation of their own disposition of playfulness and humor.

PLAY AND SCAFFOLDING

The notion of "scaffolding" was developed by researchers who studied the ways in which adults support and elaborate children's early language. Just as scaffolds on a building support the new construction, adults' interventions in play assist children's attempts at effective communication (Cazden, 1983; Ninio & Bruner, 1976).

We have extended the concept of scaffolding to include the ways that teachers support and facilitate meaning-making in children's play. As we noted in chapter 4, the environment acts as a frame of reference or context for play at school. Various environmental elements scaffold for certain kinds of play. For example, the housekeeping corner supports both constructive and dramatic play as well as the use of cooperative language (Pellegrini, 1982). Small tables and chairs scaffold solitary or parallel play, and rugs and cushions scaffold opportunities for cozy sharing or privacy.

As adults, we look at an office, a restaurant, an outdoor barbecue, and know what kinds of activities and behaviors are expected. As children play in different areas of the classroom, they learn the implicit and explicit rules about what is expected, and, in effect, come to read the social and physical cues of that particular area. The environment, then, is not only "responsive," but children also respond to it by bringing their own knowledge of situations, events, people, and things of the world to bear on their understanding of what others may expect of them (Greenman, 1988; Heath, 1983).

The impact that teacher presence has on children's play is an important aspect of scaffolding. In one classroom, interaction among children at tables with toys and puzzles was considerably muted because much of the interaction was dominated by the teacher. Scaffolds became "over-built" and hence stifling as the teacher appropriated such tasks in conversation as initiating a topic, and controlling turn taking. In a contrasting setting, teachers lingered close to children's play areas doing productive work of their own such as weeding the garden or untangling a ball of yarn, remaining available but unobtrusive as children sought to negotiate turns on a rope swing (Lederman, 1992).

Acquiring skills to negotiate their own interactions is basic to children's social and communicative competence, and does not rest solely on adult modeling. Play provides the occasion for children to corroborate, question, experiment, and stretch their understandings as they actively construct knowledge of the world and their places in it.

Other examples of scaffolding include the use of music to encourage persistence at clean-up time or while on a hike. Along with scaffolding the group's efforts, songs with open-ended phrases also support children's developing abilities to hear and reproduce rhymes.

> Ted sings, "Exploring we will go, exploring we will go. We'll catch an ant and put him in our. . . . " He pauses as Sarah and Luis complete the phrase with "pants." Nessa calls out "bants" and Anthony offers "shoe." More children join in as the singing continues, "And then we'll let him go!" (Beardsley, 1991, p. 115) >

Questions that arise for most teachers are, How much scaffolding is helpful, what form should it take, and when should it be removed?

Teachers need to consider both the physical environment and the ways in which they intervene (or refrain from intervening) as integral elements of scaffolding. In the sand or water area, for example, the teacher might redirect attention from a dispute over materials by using a play voice to signal a "flood" or an "avalanche." Keen observational skills and a willingness to wait and watch as children construct their own meanings are key elements of successful scaffolding in school settings.

GUIDED PLAY

Much of what we present regarding play orchestration is dependent upon a context of spontaneous play among young children. In spontaneous play, the teacher's role is nearly invisible, just as setting the stage represents a prelude or backdrop to a drama. In guided play, the teacher's role is more directive, although these strategies, too, range along a continuum of less to more teacher direction. Guided play strategies differ slightly depending on the nature of the materials and the content area of the curriculum. For example, art play and music play may call for more guidance when new materials and techniques are introduced. The strategies listed below are appropriate for orchestrating children's exploration, sociodramatic, and constructive play in the classroom. Subsequent chapters delineate guided play strategies appropriate to specific content areas such as language and literacy, science and art. In each case, the teacher orchestrates play in all its facets—intellectual, social, physical, and emotional—by being first and foremost a keen observer.

In addition to possessing keen observational skills, the teacher who orchestrates children's play needs to learn to "dance" with the children as she facilitates their play. The first element of this dance is determining if and when she should join the children. First she needs to ask herself, Will the children benefit by my intervention or shall I simply watch?

Many teachers are uncomfortable with this notion of simple observation, since it seems at odds with cultural stereotypes of teaching as adult- directed activity (Jones & Reynolds, 1992).

One useful strategy to help teachers extend their observation skills and at the same time model representation, reflection, and recording is by taking the role of "scribe." In this role, the teacher draws or writes about children's play, and then shares her recordings of her observations with the children (Jones & Reynolds, 1992). For example:

In Gail's kindergarten classroom, Tom and Alexis have built "a machine for seeing inside your suitcase" as part of the extended thematic play unit on airports. Gail draws their construction of blocks, Play-Doh, cardboard and paper, and then invites the children to label parts and discuss their functions with their classmates at group time. Alexis points out that Gail has forgotten to draw an essential piece—a small ball of aluminum foil. "You forgot that important shiny part that makes the light go inside the suitcase," she says, and Gail adds it to the drawing, writing a label next to it.

Vivian Paley (1984, 1986, 1992, 1995, 1996, 1997) is masterful at recording children's play and then using it as a frame for group discussion.

Sally, a first-grade teacher who teaches in an ethnically diverse community with many English language learners, frequently uses this technique in her classroom. For example, Sally took handwritten anecdotal records during the candy store sociodramatic play in her classroom. She noted that Javier modeled the invention and use of pretend money for Lee, who seemed at first confused, then enthusiastically began to count his change: "1, 2, 3, 4, 5—that is five dollars!" Sally noted this in Lee's portfolio, and then used the event to launch a discussion at group time about objects that could be used as pretend money.

"We could use those plastic buttons, because they're round," suggested Frank, representing in language his thinking about a perceptual feature of both money and buttons.

"Or shells," contributed Fran.

"Or make our own dollar bills with paper," shouted Emilia enthusiastically. A plan was made to extend their play by adding a bank the following day.

What are some ways teachers can be more directly involved in children's play? The following are some orchestration roles that involve direct teacher intervention in children's play and range from the most subtle and indirect to the more active and direct. Please refer to the Continuum of Play Strategies on page 67 (Figure 4.1).

The Artist Apprentice

The most subtle of these guided play strategies is what Griffin (1982) calls the Artist Apprentice role. In this role the teacher helps to remove clutter in the physical space around an ongoing play episode, much like a set assistant in a theater.

❧ As Mark, Donelle, and Beth launch their spacecraft, land on a planet, and discover aliens, Ms. Toms, their teacher, helps to tidy the blocks when the spaceship "crashes," and the players move their play to the housekeeping corner. She provides a red scarf for their flag and a cardboard box for their control panel. ❧

In doing this, Ms. Toms helps the children to maintain their thematic focus in play. If the blocks were to become scattered, the space travel might degenerate into block throwing. Alternately, the extended theme might become sidetracked in the search for appropriate accessories to represent the flags and the control panel. In the Artist Apprentice role, the teacher does not intervene with accessories or action unless she perceives that her action is helpful to sustaining children's play. For example, earlier in this chapter we described how Adam, the teacher, interpreted the play situation involving the pretend campfire, and determined that the breakdown of play was imminent unless more flashlights became available. He quickly stepped in to provide the additional materials and backed out of the play area.

Another technique used by the Artist Apprentice is to physically protect an ongoing project and help others set up their own projects in adjacent spaces. In one preschool a plastic hoop was used to designate "in-progress" constructions in the block area, so that new players would know that someone was saving the materials to play with later (Beardsley, 1991).

The Peacemaker

The next intervention role along the direct-indirect continuum is the Peacemaker, who may help children resolve conflicts that appear in their play in several ways. First, the teacher may offer accessories that help to resolve disputes. For example, as 3-year-olds Mary and Jesse argue over a toy typewriter for their office play, the teacher might find another toy typewriter or help the children to imagine how they could use blocks to make another typewriter.

In terms of roles, teachers can help children resolve conflicts by suggesting related alternatives for disputed roles. In one kindergarten classroom, several children wanted to play the princess role in an ongoing dramatic play episode. The teacher asked if the princess might have a sister or some cousins who weren't in the movie the children had seen and the children agreed on new but related roles. These kinds of suggestions model for children the flexible thinking and hypothesizing that ideally occur in play and help them to generate solutions to role disputes on their own as teachers encourage them to invent their own alternatives.

Teachers also act in the role of the Peacemaker when they help children to invent roles that stretch their thinking beyond the need to possess disputed materials.

❧ An observer to Mrs. Paley's classroom in Chicago noticed a child standing, arms outstretched, in front of the unit blocks. No one else was able to use the blocks, as a consequence. When the children complained to Mrs. Paley, who was seated at the story dictation table, she asked, "Ben, how can they get the blocks they need?" Ben replied (after a long pause), "They have to order them!" The other children immediately picked up blocks and "telephoned" their orders to Ben. ❧

Mrs. Paley remarked later that she could see that Ben "was a character in search of a part." Her one-line query to Ben provided the scaffold for successful negotiation and maintenance of the play episode by inviting the player to stretch himself and invent a part.

The teacher may serve as an interpreter of children's motives to their peers when conflicts occur, or when children disrupt the play of others. Some children slip easily in and out of play and learn to give their fellow players "meta-messages" about their intentions. Bateson (1976) coined the term meta-communication to describe the behaviors that people use to signal play. Such behaviors include winks or smiles, laughter, play voices, or exaggerated movements. Verbal markers may be as obvious as "Let's pretend that I'm the babysitter and you're the bad baby" or as subtle as the change in voice pitch to mark the role of the "Papa Bear."

Teachers can help children interpret meanings of others signaled by such meta-communicative cues and invent explicit strategies for finding out meanings when they feel confused. Such techniques may be particularly important in helping children interpret the cues of play fighting or rough and tumble play so that the play remains a healthy and safe exercise in physical challenge rather than an escalation into violent confrontation (Aldis, 1975; Blurton-Jones, 1972; Pellegrini & Perlmutter, 1988).

Guardian of the Gate

How can the sensitive teacher help children gain entry to play without violating the rights of the players in an already-established episode or, alternatively, to judge when it may not be appropriate to interrupt?

Corsaro (1985) reported that 75 percent of the time preschool children's initial bids to enter ongoing play episodes are rejected. Young children seem to intuitively protect their shared fantasies from interruption by interlopers. After two or three attempts at entry, 50 percent of children seeking to enter others' play are successful.

How can teachers help children develop effective strategies for entry and the confidence to try again if rejected at first? Intervention strategies on the part of the teacher to monitor the gates of play parallel those for the Peacemaker role.

One way teachers can encourage children is by introducing an accessory. Griffin (1982) tells of a child who rode a trike every day around the periphery of other children's play, watching but never joining. She gave him an old camera, simply saying, "Take this with you on your travels." Other children soon noticed the camera and asked to be "photographed." Gradually, the child became included in play groups, and developed the confidence to play with others through the accessory that was uniquely his.

Sometimes teachers may suggest a new role. One teacher, seeking to help a child she had observed as an onlooker on the edge of play, asked her to help deliver a large package to the ongoing houseboat play. The "delivery people" were then invited to stay for lemonade and the onlooker child became included in the play, with her teacher there as security. In another classroom, the teacher asked a group of children who were playing camping, "What could Carl be, a

Forest Ranger?" In this way the teacher opens up possibilities for the children to negotiate new roles within their play without interfering with the integrity of the ongoing episode.

Teachers also can interpret the social context of play. Schwartzman (1976) believes that play offers teachers "sideways glances" at make-believe. First, it reflects the social status of children in the group. Children with high status often play the most powerful roles and also assign roles to their peers. Children with lower status in the group may hold that status due to unskilled attempts to enter the play of others. Play also reflects children's understanding of the peer culture in the classroom. Teachers can explain children's motives to others in terms such as, "I see Sandy really wants to join your group. She is looking for a friend to play with. Would you like to be her friend?"

Teachers may find that some children with special needs have less experience, confidence or ability when engaging in play activities. Some consistently look to adults to help them enter the play of others. This is often true of children who are unable to communicate their needs clearly. Some children with special needs may have lower status than their nondisabled peers due to the difficulties they have in entering play. In the role of Guardian of the Gate, teachers can provide the additional involvement that might be needed without increasing children's dependence on adults (Hanline & Fox, 1993). For example, a teacher might make a child's motives known in order to increase social interaction between disabled and nondisabled students.

Parallel Player

An even more active role for the teacher involves playing parallel to children. In this scenario the teacher plays next to but not with the child, using similar materials, but not interacting. The teacher might first imitate the child's behavior, such as pouring sand into a container, establishing a basis for reciprocity. Next, the teacher might introduce a variation in the play, such as using a funnel and watching to see if the child imitates the variation. In this way, reciprocity builds at a non-verbal level. In dramatic play, the teacher might use a prop in a new way, subtly extending the child's symbolic distancing, for example, by using a pretend gesture or an unstructured prop to make a telephone call within the child's view (Forman & Kuschner, 1977).

Parallel play is a strategy children frequently use for entry into ongoing play and works for teachers as well.

In Jackie's multi-age primary grade class, Ted, Martha, Elisa, and Kim were calling themselves "ocean scientists" as they played on the carpet. They were sorting, ordering, and counting seashells, discussing their criteria for classification, and speculating about which was bigger, a large flat, thin shell or a smaller round dense one. Periodically, one child would say "We're scientists doing our work," and the others would nod in agreement. Jackie sat down on the carpet with the children, first manipulating shells and informally observing and joining their discussion. She then brought out a small plastic balance scale from the shelf and began to place large shells one at a time in one bin of the balance scale and count smaller shells into the other bin, watching until it balanced. The children began observing and commenting on Jackie's actions. Jackie then began to verbally describe her own hypotheses and behavior as she manipulated the shells and the balance scale. Soon another scale was produced and the children began to play in pairs, returning to their original questions about which shells were bigger, now reframed as which ones weighed more. Jackie gradually withdrew from the play context, continuing to take anecdotal records for later inclusion in their portfolios and to support the class debriefing about choice time that would occur later in the day. 🐚

Spectator

The teacher comments from outside the play about the themes and content of play when she orchestrates play from the perspective of Spectator. In this way she indirectly coaches play from the sidelines, by taking the role of an interested spectator or a peripheral participant. For example, as Maggie and Keisha approach their teacher carrying their suitcases, the teacher might ask about their imagined travel plans, "Have you bought your tickets yet? Do you have enough suitcases?" By referencing a present context and extending it to a future event, the teacher invites the children to elaborate their play to incorporate the teacher's comment. In this way, teachers validate children's dramatic play and may subtly suggest extensions.

As with all intervention strategies, particularly those that involve a more active role for the adult, teachers must be careful to gauge the situation and determine if comments, even from outside the play frame, might disrupt the flow of children's play or introduce elements incongruent with their intentions.

Giffin (1984) developed a scheme for analyzing strategies that children use to coordinate shared meaning in their make-believe play from both outside the play frame and as players inside the frame. Some of these seem useful guidelines for adult orchestration of shared meaning in play.

As spectators outside the pretend frame, teachers can support children by implicit pretend elaboration, such as in the travel and suitcase example above. In this role the teacher is an implicit and undefined onlooker to play and may suggest extensions or clarifications that help move play forward.

Participant

In the next role, the Participant, the teacher moves from outside the pretend frame into an active role in the play, perhaps as a neighbor knocking on the door to borrow eggs, or as an ambulance driver bringing an injured person to the hospital. Once the teacher is part of the enactment of a shared script, she can indirectly communicate actions, themes and verbalizations in her role as Participant.

🐚 After the make-believe theme of an airplane trip had been established in Matt's kindergarten class, he noticed that children were boarding the pretend airplane, and just sitting in the seats. He boarded as a passenger, and asked Carlos, the flight attendant, what was on the menu for dinner. Carlos responded with "You could have pizza or fried chicken," and then began to enact the rolling of a food cart down the aisle of the pretend plane. 🐚

Another participant strategy that allows adults to enter the play space is the use of a direct or indirect comment in order to shift or extend the play in a particular way by interjecting high drama into the script. The teacher might report a warning or foretelling of an imaginary event as if it were real. "Quick, we need a nurse! Call 911," prompts Matt, as he enters his kindergartners' superhero play and encourages them to extend the make-believe play beyond the fight, die, and resurrect sequence he has observed in this play all week.

Through both underscoring and storytelling, teachers can interject verbal comments into the stream of play without disturbing the shared illusion of the pretend frame. In underscoring, the teacher might sing or use a sound effect to model the communication of pretend actions, roles or objects.

Matt speaks urgently to children playing firefighter as they have arrived at the burning house with sirens blaring and limited action. "I'll turn on the hose—sh-sh-sh-sh" (making water sounds as he mimes turning on a faucet) to douse a pretend fire.

Storytelling is a verbal strategy that allows the player (adult or child) to communicate pretend transformations using narrative forms. For example:

First grade teacher Sally shops at the pretend candy store in her classroom, elaborating the plot to extend children's problem solving as she tells her story. "It's my sister's birthday and she really likes gummy bears, do you have those? We are having a big party for ten people and we need two bears for everyone. Can you sell me enough? Also, I need a birthday card. Do you have those?"

As in the Spectator intervention, the teacher must be sensitive to cues from children and not enter into play unless it is called for. If the teacher does enter the play as a Participant, then he or she needs to play a supporting rather than starring role. Many teachers of young children enjoy engaging in play as a Participant and may have a tendency to control the flow of play without realizing they have usurped the power of the children. For example, in one preschool classroom, an over-enthusiastic parent offered to play the injured party in hospital play. She ended up directing the entire play episode, assigning roles to children and suggesting what the doctor and nurse players should say and do.

Matchmaker

In this role the teacher may deliberately set up pairs or groups of children to play with one another. He may, for example, pair a more sophisticated player with a less sophisticated player. Providing there is not too great a difference in their play styles and personalities, both children may benefit from this arrangement. Complementary emotional needs may also serve as a basis for matchmaking.

🐚 In one classroom, Sandy, whose parents were divorcing, sought out situations she felt she could control and in which she could feel power. Paul, on the other hand, distressed over the birth of a baby sister, created a baby role for himself whenever possible. These two children were a perfect match in terms of their complementary emotional needs and spent long hours in house play with Sandy as a powerful and nurturing mother to the helpless baby Paul. 🐚

Storyplayer

Vivian Paley (1981, 1986, 1990) introduced a technique for supporting children's play that structures its form, but not its content. In her approach, children dictate stories to a teacher who writes them out, to be enacted later in the school day with the class group. The text is written down exactly as it is dictated and reread in the child's language. Each author chooses the part he or she would like to play and selects who will take the parts to be enacted. The author serves as director as the teacher reads the story aloud. Elaborations of the plot are often enacted as the story unfolds in drama. Comments such as, "I forgot, the little bear does come home to his mom at the end," are sometimes added to the story's text. Props are not used to ensure that the children's imagination is exercised. In chapter 9, Language and Literacy, story playing is described in greater detail.

Play Tutor

The teacher as Play Tutor takes on the most direct role of all by re-creating the emotional security of the caregiver-infant dyad that is the source of human beings learning to play (Monighan-Nourot et al., 1987). In this context the child feels safe and is able to take risks involved in using symbols and language to represent the meaning of the concrete. The teacher models and directs children's play in this role, providing reinforcement to their efforts to symbolize and interact.

Researchers who study childhood play have been guided by the work of Smilansky (Smilansky, 1968; Smilansky & Shefatya, 1990) for many years. Smilansky focused on intervention with preschool children whose dramatic play lacked complexity. Direct tutoring may benefit those children whose play consists of repetitive one-liners imitated from television, or whose attempts to enter the play of others are awkward and intrusive. Smilansky's strategies guide teachers in their attempts to help children elaborate their play through such elements as extended role play, social interaction, verbalization, persistence, and object transformations in a process she calls sociodramatic play training. Smilansky's scheme for assessing play complexity is presented in detail in chapter 12.

Other researchers have employed a technique they call "thematic fantasy role play" (Saltz & Johnson, 1974) in which the teacher assigns roles and directs the enactment of stories read aloud to the children. This technique assigns more control to the teacher than sociodramatic training, where children form their own story lines with teacher support. It also differs from Paley's story-playing approach in its emphasis on stories authored by adults, and roles selected and directed by the teacher.

Another strategy involves both matchmaking and play tutoring. Teachers may ask children to serve as "play coaches" and help other children invent roles, pretend with objects, or join in a play episode. In many classrooms, children are given this role with regard to computer use, writing or other activities in which the status of expert encourages children in particular roles to reflect on their own thinking and communicate it to others. It adds the dimension of expert-novice to the already powerful zone of proximal development created in pretend play. Smilansky (1992) found that both the play coaches and their players benefited from this process.

Because play tutoring represents a very direct role for the adult, it must be used carefully (Christie, 1985). Children who have difficulty with symbolic play distancing and/or social play negotiations might be better served by less direct teacher strategies. For example, a multi-age setting often encourages more advanced play on the part of younger children and prosocial behavior on the part of older children, and may be a more desirable alternative than play tutoring.

CHOOSING A STRATEGY

Considerable skill and thought is required to determine which context, in combination with which child, calls for a given strategy. For example, the child who

Playful interactions with adults are just as essential as those with peers.

plays parallel functional play with blocks or sand is a likely candidate for the Parallel Player strategy. The child who hangs around the edges of play groups might benefit from an accessory or entry strategy. As a general guideline, wise teachers intervene with the most indirect strategy possible. Many teachers begin by changing the setting for play, perhaps by adding new accessories. If that doesn't work, then the teacher proceeds to increasingly more direct strategies along the continuum.

Considering Children with Special Needs

As teachers and researchers, we view children's play in a variety of early education settings. In intervening with children in their play, there are several factors to consider. We believe it is essential for teachers to keep in touch with the power of the zone of proximal development created through play. As we have discussed, all children, regardless of their current developmental capacities, stretch their competencies in play with others. For some children, playful interactions with adults are just as essential as those with peers. Smilansky's play tutoring approach and the overt modeling of pretense may be called for. For most children, however, the teacher in his role as Matchmaker and stage manager serves to support play opportunities that are productive and engaging for all.

One drawback of play in inclusive environments is that, while young children frequently empathize with their peers who have special needs, most young children are unable to take the perspective of another child and act altruistically on that understanding. For example, in one kindergarten classroom, Pauline, a child with Down's syndrome, was consistently manipulated by two of her peers into giving up her play materials in exchange for less desirable objects.

Another consideration is that children who don't have special needs sometimes feel pressured to include in their play those peers who do have special needs, and subsequently comply with adult expectations by allowing the peer in the play area, and then ignore him or her (Trawick-Smith, 1994). Conversely, peers may overdo their helpfulness by treating special needs children in a patronizing manner or by doing too much for them. For example, in a preschool classroom, four-year-olds Alkicia and Emily consistently spoke for Theresa, a communicatively handicapped child. In doing so they often squelched Theresa's efforts to communicate with others and her developing sense of initiative.

By monitoring through keen observation and sensitive orchestration as either a Spectator or Participant, the teacher may help all children find balance in their play.

Timing Is Everything: Entering and Exiting Children's Play

When teachers enter and exit children's play or shift from one strategy to another, timing is crucial. Manning and Sharp (1977) suggest guidelines for entering play. First and foremost, teachers need to observe play long enough to see if any intervention is called for or if the children are best served by the teacher in a less direct role. As part of this observation phase, the teacher has an opportunity to ascertain the themes, characters, plot, and vocabulary negotiated by the children (Reynolds & Jones, 1997). If the teacher chooses to enter the dance of interaction played out by the children, she must do it seamlessly, joining the flow of the play without disrupting its progress or integrity. Respect for children's ongoing shared make-believe is critical. Adult entry is more suitable at transition points during which children are "stepping out" of the play frame to negotiate rules about the play or ongoing themes or roles, rather than at the times when children are deeply engaged in pretend play.

Leaving the play and returning control completely to the child players is just as important as sensitive and flowing entry. Since the teacher's purpose is always to support children in their efforts to sustain and elaborate play on their own, the timing of exits is critical (Christie & Johnsen, 1989). Phasing out of play is one exit strategy that gradually returns the control of the play to children. As a participant within the play frame, a teacher might use storytelling to explain her departure or a less active role. In the example at the beginning of the chapter, Brenda exits the pretend pet play in this way, relinquishing her role to Hannah, and then returns in a less central role to monitor the play. Karen, a preschool teacher, similarly entered the train play of a group of five children with the intention of facilitating Heidi's entrance into the play.

&. Karen sees that Heidi is now engaged with others eating "lunch" in the dining car. Karen announces, "Oh good. The next stop is mine, so I'll see you next Friday on the train. She says to the engineer, "I'll be getting off at the next station." &.

Sometimes teachers may unobtrusively leave the area when children are very involved in play, as Jackie did when the children appropriated the seashell balancing activity. At other times, the teacher may speak from a different stance: "I promised some children in the block area I'd come visit their airport. I'll come back to watch you when I finish." This effectively places the teacher on the outskirts of play as a Spectator and reminds the children of her real life responsibilities as the teacher (Trawick-Smith, 1994).

BUILDING A PEACEFUL CLASSROOM

In this chapter and the preceding one, we focused on the multiple ways that teachers orchestrate children's play, both directly and indirectly. We conclude these related chapters by considering some ways in which teachers utilize orchestration strategies that promote a peaceful classroom.

Responding to Media-Based, Violent Play

Educators and families can collaborate in early childhood programs to reduce aggression and violence. Some war play or aggressive "good guy/bad guy" play is often typical for many young children in our culture. The loud noises, fast pace, and especially the thrill of the chase that have been elements of diverse forms of sociodramatic play for decades often appeal to children. The themes of good versus evil, life and death, lost and found, and danger and rescue that occur in war play and other aggressive play give children opportunities to deal with these archetypal concerns. However, as we shall discuss further in chapter 11, Play, Toys and Technology, the explicit violent details of television, movies and computer games, as well as the many toy weapons on the market today, seem to spur children on to greater heights of aggression (Carlsson-Paige & Levin, 1987, 1990). In "firing" a toy gun, for example, children may lose sight of the story line of the pretend play and end up hurting one another.

In contrast, in the "best" play derived from media, children use characters, settings, and events typical of a television program, film, or video as raw material for the creations of their own imaginations. For example,

  Ran and Marty are playing Teenage Mutant Ninja Turtle characters Leonardo and Michelangelo. They swagger around the playhouse with cardboard and tin foil swords and discuss how they will track and capture "the bad guys" by rigging traps for them in the forest (represented in the adjacent block area). "I know how to make a tent in a tree," offers Michelangelo, "so we can have a secret hideout." Leonardo elaborates, "We'll leave a map to our secret hideout so they will come there." "And then, when they smell our hamburgers cooking, they'll be hungry," proposes Michelangelo. "Yeah, and then when they get close, we'll grab 'em," continues Leonardo. They transform their swords into horses and gallop into the "woods" to pitch their tent and lay their traps.

In this example we see homemade weapons transformed into horses and a typical good guy/bad guy theme elaborated from the children's own experiences of camping out. Although the heroes are drawn from a media source, the plot and objects are of the children's own invention.

Guiding Children's Violent Play

Many teachers report that they can follow the plot of the latest violent movies or the morning's TV cartoon shows by observing children's play. However, teachers can help children to use characters, play themes, and props derived from popular media in constructive ways. Carlsson-Paige and Levin (1990) suggest several strategies for parents and teachers to cope with war play. These are easily integrated with the strategies already discussed in this chapter.

Observe play carefully.   By keeping informed about popular cartoons, videos, films, and television series, as well as toys that may be popular in the peer culture of the classroom, teachers are better able to understand the play they observe. Through close scrutiny of children's play, teachers may determine if some children are "stuck" in repetitive imitations of what they have viewed. Teachers may then orchestrate play to help children expand character roles, elaborate story lines, and use props beyond the level of simple imitation following strategies suggested in these chapters.

Look beneath the surface of play.   When teachers are sensitive to the underlying themes of play, they may suggest non-violent alternatives that appeal to children. Good guy/bad guy play encompasses themes such as danger and rescue that are central to children's socio-emotional development (Corsaro, 1985; Paley, 1990). Once the theme is identified, teachers may introduce literature with new characters and plots that elaborate these themes in new ways.

🐦 In a preschool directed by one of the authors, teachers and parents embarked upon an experiment to diminish the frequency of television-limited play that imitated cartoon violence. Noting that themes of good and evil, life and death, and lost and found dominated much of this play, the teachers and parents read various versions of *Peter Pan* and helped children make costumes and props, and act out their interpretations of the characters and events in their play. Later in the year, *The Wizard of Oz* and *Peter and the Wolf* were explored in similar ways. Children still used pretend weapons and fought and chased adversaries, but their repertoire of characters and actions for these themes was expanded. For example, after the Peter Pan theme was explored, one child noted that "turning bad guys into toads or rocks was better because if you shot them, they just came alive again." 🐦

Set limits.   Teachers may also keep children "safe" by setting limits. For some children, the appeal of war play or media-derived play is especially irresistible

Teachers may keep children safe by setting limits.

when it is violent in nature. Since the script for war play or media play is usually simple and well-known, children with limited social skills or language abilities are often drawn into the vortex. As the cast of the play grows, the level of aggression can become out of the children's control. By setting limits and carefully monitoring this play, teachers can help assure that at-risk children are protected. It is also important for teachers to understand the circumstances in children's personal lives that might be leading to an overabundance of this type of play.

Several teachers we know set these limits by banning real-looking weapons from their schools, while acknowledging children's need to do battle with imaginary ones. In this way they avoid the phenomenon of children imitating action from television with single-use weapon toys. Other teachers make a point of talking to children about alternatives for their play plots when aggressive play careens out of control, perhaps suggesting strategies for tricking bad guys instead of shooting them.

Ascertain children's purposes in play.   In considering the motives for children's aggressive play, teachers need to ask, To what degree does the play reflect the desire to be powerful in the world, and to what degree does it reflect children trying to make sense of what they have seen on the evening news or even in their own neighborhoods? Schwartzman (1976) pointed out that an important aspect of play is its "inward perspective" or the process by which children repeat experiences that are puzzling, confusing, or disturbing to them.

Tracy's home had been fire-bombed and her older brother injured. For several weeks, her kindergarten peers, in their roles as paramedics and firefighters, carried the "injured" Tracy to hospitals constructed in the block corner, under tables, and in the sand box.

Schwartzman also described the "upwards view" of playing, asserting that in play children rehearse roles and experiences they hope to have when they are older. This function of play is certainly part of the appeal behind Barbie dolls and Teenage Mutant Ninja Turtles. Still, many teachers wonder if play with toy weapons and play fighting encourages these activities as desirable goals for the future.

Promoting A Positive Peace

The previous sections have focused on reducing violence, particularly media-based violence as part of the process of building a peaceful classroom. In the classroom, just as at the international level, real peace is not merely the absence of violence.

Many of the classroom examples of play described in this book show children cooperating, learning with each other, developing friendships, and playing with peers who speak different languages, who come from diverse family configurations and ethnic backgrounds. The considerations for setting the stage discussed in chapter 4 lead to more peaceful classrooms. For example, teachers can consciously set the stage so that children will have sufficient space as well as materials that foster cooperation. Teachers should consider a time schedule that balances activities so that children do not become overly tired. Likewise, in this chapter, the strategies discussed for intervening in children's play promote children's development of the related dispositions and behaviors inherent in a peaceful classroom: empathy, prosocial behavior, and cooperation. When play is at the center of the curriculum, children are more autonomous and have multiple challenges to develop social problem-solving abilities and to take the perspective of others. Chapter 10, Play and Socialization, clearly addresses these issues, but the illustrative examples in all the chapters that follow show that cooperative, peace-promoting behaviors are always in the foreground. Placing play at the center of the curriculum provides teachers, children and parents with daily opportunities to build a peaceful classroom.

SUMMARY AND CONCLUSION

In this chapter we have discussed a number of ways that teachers may orchestrate children's play, paying careful attention to the child's perspective in all facets of play. We explained and provided examples of specific techniques for the interventions that teachers use to guide children as they play: Artist Apprentice, Peacemaker, Guardian of the Gate, Parallel Player, Spectator, Participant, Matchmaker, Storyplayer, and Play Tutor. As we indicated, choosing the right strategy involves sensitivity to individual children's needs, the culture of the classroom, and a sense of timing. These strategies, as well as the strategies involved in setting the stage, promote a peaceful classroom that fosters development. In the following chapters we offer suggestions, based on our model of indirect to direct guided play strategies, for using a thorough understanding of play to plan and support curriculum in early childhood settings.

FOCUSING OUR THINKING

1. Observe play behavior in a preschool or primary setting. Analyze your observations according to:

   How do children initiate play?

   How do children enter and exit play?

   How do they negotiate roles?

   How do adults support (or not support) play?

   How do adults extend or elaborate play?

   What ideas do you have for support, extensions or elaborations?

2. Select an area of the classroom and observe play. Try your hand at orchestrating the play from both the Spectator and Participant roles for teachers. Analyze the strategies you used to enter and to exit the children's play. Which were most successful? Why? Which were least successful? Why? What would you do differently the next time?

3. Following the guidelines in this chapter, try the technique of story play over several days' time in a preschool or primary grade classroom. What do you notice about children's dictated stories? What about their enactments? Their social relations around the experience of story play?

4. Write a children's book about play.

5. Write a brochure describing the play-centered philosophy of your school.

SUGGESTED RESOURCES

1. Singer, J., & Singer, D. (1985). *Make-believe: Games and activities to foster imaginative play in young children*. Glenview, IL: Scott, Foresman.

   A classic book for parents (and teachers) detailing games to enhance make-believe thinking and imagery.

2. Slaby, R. G., Roedell, D. A., and Hendrix, K. (1995). *Early violence prevention: Tools for teachers of young children*. Washington, DC: National Association for the Education of Young Children.

   A comprehensive, highly readable book on peace building, violence prevention, and conflict resolution recommended for all those who work in preschool and primary grade programs. The authors discuss designing the physical setting, the daily schedule, materials, and strategies for teacher intervention in children's play.

3. Jones, E., and Reynolds, G. (1992). *The play's the thing: Teachers' roles in children's play*. New York: Teachers College Press.

4. Reynolds, G. and Jones, E. (1997). *Master players: Learning from children at play*. New York: Teachers College Press.

   These are two complementary volumes. In the first, the authors describe the importance of play. Their discussions of teacher interventions provide readers of this chapter with additional information and examples.

   In their second book, the authors discuss how educators can use the concept of master play and players to observe children and support their development. They guide the reader to become more skilled in observing and analyzing children and their play through their superb, lengthy case studies.

CHAPTER 6

The Arts in the Play-Centered Curriculum

🐚 🐚 🐚 🐚 🐚 🐚 🐚 🐚 🐚 🐚 🐚 🐚 🐚 🐚 🐚

As in an opera, four-year-old Noah stands at the easel, reflects, and then declaims in song what he has playfully discovered about color:

> There is some colors which are red, blue, yellow
> There is a lot of colors
> And there is aqua, aqua,
> And there is blue, blue, there is blue, blue . . .
> and white and aqua
> There is white and aqua

Now he contemplates his palette and sings, "There is some colors," and names the primaries, "Red, blue, and yellow." He dips his brush into the blue: "And there is blue, blue, there is blue, blue," emphasizing blue perhaps because it is basic to aqua. Noah intends to create aqua and knows that one does not do that by starting with white. Finally the white is celebrated, "and white and aqua," and Noah closes softly: "There is white and aqua."

🐚 🐚 🐚 🐚 🐚 🐚 🐚 🐚 🐚 🐚 🐚 🐚 🐚 🐚 🐚

This delightful image of a child singing while painting accompanies the closing credits of Thelma Harms' film *My Art Is Me* (1969).

What does the image reveal? It reveals the creative transformations in the flow of play which lie at the heart of children's art making. It also tells a lot about what Noah knows about color, and about what he doesn't know about color—there is a bit of green in aqua. And, importantly, it demonstrates how art (Noah's painting, poetry, and song) and problem solving (his creation of aqua) are intertwined in the context of play. The creativity involved in Noah's art-making is close to the concept of intelligence, which in Piaget's view is synonymous with development (Furth, 1970). Close observation of children playing within the arts gives teachers sound content for a developmental curriculum. In this chapter, we focus specifically on what is called the visual and constructive arts, such as painting, drawing, collage and block building. However, the foregrounding of play within all the arts is the critical issue. Throughout we stress that all curricula in the arts should encompass a balance of play options. These range from opportunities to engage in directed and guided play in the arts such as often occurs at circle and project time but, more importantly, making sure there is ample time, space, and materials for spontaneous play in all mediums.

The arts, in fact, are indispensable to a successful developmental curriculum. This is because children spontaneously turn art into play, and *play is the young child's principal matrix for learning*. Indeed, the most successful curricula put art to use at every turn—and by art we mean graphic art, construction, poetry, storytelling, music, dance, and drama—so that play and the arts curriculum are indistinguishable from each other. Play for the child, and a playful attitude in the adult, can transform what is mere craft into "art."

Now, the spontaneity with which children turn art into play does not mean that specific planning for art need not take place. Such planning embraces a number of considerations:

- When should arts activities be spontaneous? When should they be guided or directed?
- What can be learned from spontaneous engagement in the arts?
- How can staff and environment encourage spontaneity? How should they provide guidance and direction?
- What materials, tools, and resources do the children need?
- What technical homework should the teacher do?

Such considerations are discussed below with particular attention to graphic art and construction but with references throughout to many of the other arts, such as music and drama.

PLANNING FOR THE ARTS IN THE PLAY-BASED CURRICULUM

❧ Donny, Alonzo, and Joe race across the yard playing superheroes. They are wearing bright capes the teacher helped them make earlier in the day. They start circling each other, incorporating the jumps and swoops they had such fun doing to music inside the classroom earlier that morning. ❧

An effective arts curriculum for young children is expressed through play, arises from within play, and is continuously modified by children to fit the circumstances of their play. Furthermore, since play occurs throughout the early childhood classroom, so too will the arts—going far beyond, for example, the "art corner" seen in many settings for young children. The issue in planning for the arts in the curriculum is not to ensure that play serves the arts (although that should occur too—Noah should discover that aqua has green in it) but, more important to this chapter, to ensure that the arts serve play. To see that it does, the teacher must, from the very outset, enter the children's world of play, and bring into that world the basic materials and props of art.

Entering the Child's World of Spontaneous Play

A teacher may enter the child's world of play by introducing a new play prop or modifying a setting at points when play falters. Sometimes the teacher does this upon her own initiative and sometimes at the children's need or request. Furthermore, sometimes she discusses or demonstrates the new prop or setting directly and sometimes she does not. Under what circumstances do these variations occur, and what, in the first place, impels the teacher to enter the spontaneous play world at all?

Since spontaneous play is often of a "pretend" nature ("I'm the mommy, you be the baby" or "Look at me, I'm a puppy"), the teacher may fear that the supportive expertise required is that of theater or drama, an arena that few feel confidently prepared to orchestrate. But what if the teacher shrinks back and merely maintains the traditional environmental supports, those familiar play props so frequently seen in dress-up or home play corners? The setting may become too static. The sensitive teacher, having observed children's play patterns closely, knows that even simple modifications in props and settings will stimulate children to initiate more elaborate pretend play. She may add to the available props an arm band with a red cross on it or a badge with "police" written on it, or a few chiffon scarves or transparent curtains. In these cases little needs to be said to the children. They are likely to pick up the indirect cues instantaneously and create scripts to integrate those props into the ongoing play. This method of indirectly shaping the context to suggest new or elaborated avenues for drama or dramatic play was utilized by British drama educator Dorothy Heathcote. Her approach is explored in detail in B. J. Wagner's *Dorothy Heathcote: Drama as a Learning Medium* (1976) and in a special edition of *Theory Into Practice* by Lux (1985).

Routines may become static in the graphic arts as well. The single easel set up in a corner of the classroom every day may get little more from the child than a perfunctory painting "for a teacher." To stimulate playful engagement and focus, the teacher might introduce novel painting tools. Sponges, for example, stimulate the creation of patterns. Rollers invite children to paint over the entire surface of the paper rather than merely working in a cramped area in the middle.

Guiding play by introducing new props or tools is frequently necessary. By demonstrating how the paintbrush can be used to apply paint to the sponge or roller rather than dipping these tools directly into paint, the teacher helps children gain greater control and mastery over their productions. By modeling these somewhat sophisticated accessories, the teacher helps children four and up create a new world of pretend. And in dramatic play, the teacher helps a child create his own superhero cape out of paper rather than pulling one from the costume box that he used when he was three. By bringing constructive art to dramatic play, the teacher engages the child anew. She will make sure that materials for drawing, cutting, and scribbling are near to hand so that accessories to complement dramatic and fantasy play can quickly be created.

Sometimes children actively engaged in dramatic play will seek the teacher's help. It may be for new props: "We need things to make a hideout!" Blankets, old sheets, pieces of carpet, and large and small blocks will serve. Or it may be for technical assistance—help, say, in designing a network of tunnels in the sand. Indeed, a young child's technical requirements can become quite elaborate. "There's buried treasure in the sand pit, we need a pirate's map," may signal the teacher to lay out a network of lagoons, walkways, bridges, and highways for the children to help construct in the sand pit, or to help devise graphics such as a skull and crossbones, DANGER, DETOUR, and other hazard signs.

On some bright sunny day we may want to trace around our shadows with the fat chalks we made by mixing plaster of Paris and powdered tempera with water in Dixie cups (remembering, of course, to pour the dry mixture into the water). Later the children will wonder about why the chalk outlines of their shadows don't fit them when they return to capture them in the late afternoon.

Are the fat chalks still at hand for use on another day (wet and rainy this time) when there are no shadows at all? The children can use them to create beautiful red and blue and violet "expressionist" stains on the wet asphalt. Maybe this is the day that Noah will discover all the necessary pigments to make aqua. Perhaps wet chalk drawing of patterns on butterfly wings cut from black paper will encourage incipient superheroes to swoop and dive more gracefully as they simultaneously acquire knowledge of the physical properties of chalk on wet paper.

Rhythm instruments, a tape recorder, old sheets, and bright scarves should be available when props and music and sound effects are needed for a puppet show or for a haunted house on Halloween. These props may demystify the spooks who sometimes scare the younger children when they visit the second-grader's haunted house in October.

The door to that house will certainly need a ghostly mural, easy to make out of black paper and the brightly colored construction paper scraps we've been saving or the wet chalk drawing technique learned when we were butterflies. Little torn scraps of paper with two holes punched for eyes make an instant little "ghost" to augment our mural. We, of course, will need to create a "really scary and spooky" tape recording for sound effects. At our Halloween party children will be sure to share with their moms and dads that the haunted house is "only pretend."

The arts, science, and play merge when children work on the skeletons they will hang in the haunted house. This artful play with bones will get its scientific accuracy from a chart from the school's encyclopedia or, better yet, from our visit to the biology department of a nearby university. Children may begin to get acquainted with their bodies: how they look and work and what's in them. There's sure to be some new as well as traditional music to go along with our study of the body.

Are black paper and a clear plastic jar on hand to make a home for the worms dug up in the moist earth the day after it rained? Tomorrow children will view worm tunnels before they create worm mazes from the large and small blocks that are stored nearby. Is this the time to start a worm compost box? Next spring this rich soil will contribute to our vegetable garden and our beginning knowledge of ecology. In this seamless world, the teacher might wonder where art leaves off and science begins.

Indeed, constructive play with blocks alone involves art and math, often replicating architecture, whose interdisciplinary richness has earned it the title of queen of the arts. Blocks are a major accessory for pretend play, creating the context for elaborate fantasies for individuals, pairs, and groups of children. Blocks serve as an important adjunct to extend play. Cardboard box houses furnished with fabric, wallpaper and rug scraps, and peopled by miniature clothes-

Blocks are a major accessory for pretend play.

pin dolls become a small city when blocks laid end to end become "Main Street." Curved units define a small park and provide other needed structures, such as a zoo for miniature animals that are likely soon to be integrated into extended play events. Here we see several guided play projects evolving and being integrated into the children's spontaneous block play, a sure validator of a play-generating curriculum. Valuable insights into the interaction of the child's developing intelligence, competence, and social awareness can be gained by teacher observations, notes, and photos of such play in block areas. (For a review of literature and new insights, see Nicolopoulou, 1991; Reifel & Yeatman, 1991.)

The Arts: Mirror of Development and Guide for Curriculum Design

Nowhere outside of spontaneous play are the dynamic elements of early childhood development, and their coordination, more richly mirrored than in children's art productions. Like archaeological remains, children's paintings, constructions, block building, assemblage and collage, recordings of songs, stories and dances can be examined and diagnosed as documents of growth and development (Griffin, 1982; Veldhuis, 1982). As such, they can be used to assess the effectiveness of both teacher and curriculum in supporting playful exploration of the arts. They can serve as the basis for designing both a relevant arts curriculum for groups of children and a learning plan for individuals.

Heidi's Horses: Documents of Change and Growth

Consider some of the drawings of horses made by one child over a period of about five years (Fein, 1984).

Heidi's drawings, in Figure 6.1, mirror her particular interests but nonetheless follow the general developmental sequence of drawing schemes reported as

2 Years: ALL OVER
SCRIBBLES

Scribbles are scrubbed on, off, and through paper.

2 Years / 6 months:

CLUSTERS

Lines are more controlled and begin to be clustered in center of paper.

3 Years :
DIRECTIONAL
MOVEMENT

Large arm movements order themselves into a circular mode around a central mark.

3 Years / 6 months:

SPIRALS

Directional movement develops to spiraling lines.

Spiraling lines separate themselves into coils.

4 Years:
THE CIRCLE

Coiling lines become deliberate circle configurations, continuous lines which start at one point and return to that point.

First Person;
Available Structures

Circle configurations are elaborated with additional circles and with lines radiating to and from their centers, creating a vertical-horizontal relationship at their intersection with the perimeter. These become representational: father, mother, dog, cat, house, birthday cake.

4 Years /2 months:
THE FIRST HORSE:
RECTILINEAR
Multiple legs

The circular formation and vertical-horizontal lines permit formation of the first horse.

Figure 6.1
Heidi's Horse.
Source: From *Heidi's Horse* by Sylvia Fein, 1984, Exelrod Press.

*Breadth and width;
Four legs spaced*

Refinement: the horse
receives four legs–only
four.

4 Years/10 months:
DEVIATIONS FROM
THE RECTILINEAR
*Slanting legs; Curved
back line*

First deviations from the
vertical-horizontal are used
for ears and legs in
opposing diagonal
directions. The new
diagonals immediately
unify head and neck and
create a new shape.

5 Years :
UNIFICATION OF
HORSE PARTS

The unification of the head
and neck is applied to
contain the whole horse
within one unbroken
outline.

5 Years/3 months:
DEVELOPMENT OF

THE UNIFIED
HORSE
Sturdy shape

Problems of leg-spacing
and length are solved.

The new diagonal
directions of line allow the
horse to run.

*Body markings: blazes
and dapples*

A learning plateau
provides time to
consolidate, and to enrich
the horse's gear and
markings.

Heidi's last major
construction before her
sixth birthday is to extend
the horse's head towards
the ground, "so he can eat."

6 Years: THE
HORSE MORE
POWERFULLY
CONSTRUCTED
*The boxy shape is
rounded*

The rigid, box shaped
horse is transformed by
fluid, calligraphic outline
into a powerful horse with
flexible stride.

Figure 6.1 *continued*

characteristic of all children (Gardner, 1973; Kellog, 1969; Lowenfeld, 1947). Heidi had many opportunities to playfully and deeply explore her own particular interest (indeed, passion) in a supportive environment that encouraged art making and allowed a free choice of subject matter. The drawings graphically illustrate that it is interest, intersecting with personality and intelligence, that fuel play and the development that results from play.

7 Years: THE
HORSE IN ACTION
Cowboys and rodeo

Heidi shifts her interest to
action-packed
performances;the elegant
single horse recedes.

As story-telling becomes
more restrained, precision
returns to the drawings,
and the rider receives
artistic attention.

8 1/2 Years: HEIDI:
SELF-PORTRAITS
Queen Heidi, the very 1st

Heidi assumes importance
second to the horse, and
appears in favorable roles.
She thinks of herself as a
horse.

8 1/2 Years: TECHNICAL
TASKS: OVERLAPPING

The rider's body turns
partially to side view.

Overlapping begins. The
horse has two legs on one
side of his body, two on
the other.

8 Years/11 months:
ADVANCES USING
OVERLAPPING
The rider in profile

Overlapping possibilities
are extended to arm and
stifle-joints.

Problems appear when the
position of the horse's
hind legs are reversed.

Two horses side-by-side

One horse overlaps another
to show that they are
standing side by side.
Figure ground relationships
have become more complex.

Children's drawings and constructions often are sent home from school with
little or no examination, even though they provide us with important information about children and about how to articulate a play-based curriculum in the
arts. Examining collections of children's work such as painting or storytelling
can provide a pivot for a better understanding of the child in parent conferences and teachers' meetings.

Staff and Environmental Support for Play in the Arts

An arts curriculum becomes established in the play-centered program through the modes of intervention described in chapters 4 and 5. In the sections that follow we illustrate in detail how the establishment of a viable arts curriculum depends critically on four specific manifestations of staff and environmental support.

First, in broad terms, it is important in the arts curriculum to provide sufficient support for a balance of spontaneous and guided play. It is also important to provide well organized but "messy" spaces for individuals and groups of children. In addition, classroom curricula should be generated from the interests and involvements demonstrated by the children themselves. Lastly, teachers need to provide sensitive support for children's efforts to integrate their experiences as they transform and recast them in spontaneous play with various arts materials and media.

In specific terms, when adequate time, space, and well-managed materials are provided—and when teachers have done their technical and conceptual homework and the appropriate balance of spontaneous and guided play is struck—engagement in the arts can be deeply explored.

Time, Space, Materials, and Teacher Know-How

Time.   In ideal programs, ample time for both spontaneous and guided play with arts materials is provided throughout the school day. A balance between the two is essential, however. Making child-structured play the only mode leads to fragmentation and chaos; but an overabundance of teacher-directed or teacher-guided activities, on the other hand, prevents children from integrating their knowledge by trying things out for themselves. A simple measure of the balance of play options can be achieved by examining the daily schedule and staffing pattern of programs to determine whether play options are sufficiently balanced and supported by adequate staff. If much of the day is devoted to teacher-led group activity, it is likely that occasions for spontaneous play are being eroded.

Space.   In well-planned programs, space is organized to encourage various configurations of children to engage in arts activities at multiple sites throughout the classroom and play yard:

- Clean, smooth work surfaces (Formica table tops and/or small Formica boards for individual work) may be set up in several areas, with seating inviting the solitary play of an individual child or the collaborative or parallel play of pairs and groups.
- Ideally these areas will be relatively quiet and protected from the flow of fast-paced play but at the same time **accessible** to and visible from active play areas.
- Expectations for the kinds of play to take place will be clearly cued by furnishings and accessories. Cues in the ways materials are presented or displayed will distinguish areas where free exploration of materials and

resources is expected, from those where teacher-guided activities or more structured projects will occur.

If monitored sensitively, both outdoor and indoor centers for drawing, scribbling, writing, dance and music making can support engagement in the arts as an end in itself. It is a social activity when two or more children invent dances and songs or draw and chat. When participation in pretend play requires the making of something—a special belt, bracelet, or helmet—it becomes an adjunct to pretend play.

Valuable guides for assessing the complexity of play spaces in general can be used to calculate the play potential of music and art-making centers (Kritchevsky, Prescott, & Walling, 1977). These guides help to achieve greater predictability in play patterns. And while management and predictability are important elements in any program, inflexible attempts to organize all aspects of arts activities lead to an inhibition and a dwindling of the child's creative expression. Conversely, too little organization in presentation and sequencing in arts activities can result in the tyranny of chaotic movement and environmental clutter. Both extremes undermine the child's chances for mastery, competence, aesthetic development and understanding.

Materials.   Open-ended arts activities and construction materials ideally complement spontaneous play, providing the raw materials, resources and accessories for the world of pretend. All the arts, including drama, song and dance, often merge with and become indistinguishable from play. Not all materials, however, need to be open-ended. For example, older children (four and up) can use templates for frequently called-upon images—stars, various animals, dinosaurs, vehicles, geometric shapes, even numerals and letters. The use of these materials should be couched, however, in an atmosphere of free exploration, creativity, and problem solving, and they should be well-balanced with an abundance of open-ended materials.

Music and rhythm instruments fall into a similar category and may need some preliminary introduction in their appropriate use in order to enhance the quality of spontaneous play with such items when they are displayed at an open center in the classroom.

At a drawing and scribbling table set up for guided play (i.e., with scissors, markers, and plastic templates set out), four-year-old Toby uses the bus template turned on its side to represent a wind-filled flag fluttering from the main mast of his ship. By tracing the curved edges of the multiple wheels of the bus, he represents the rippling fabric perfectly. Several children immediately seize upon the novel potential in the templates, creating flags for their own drawings.

In addition to the nature and use of art resources and materials, we are concerned with their presentation, accessibility, maintenance, replenishment, and imaginative selection.

Children will not spontaneously use an item if they cannot see it, if they do not have some basis for imagining its potential, or if it doesn't work. Therefore:

- Display the items at eye level. If possible, use movable shelves as well as some storage units equipped with sturdy wheels; this provides flexibility to display materials where they will be used or needed. Musical instruments, movement accessories such as scarves and headbands, and a tape recorder could be stored and displayed for use indoors or out in such a movable unit.
- Keep crayons clean, and sorted by color with the paper peeled, so a real choice of color can be made.
- Make sure that felt markers mark, that scissors cut with ease, and that masking tape is ready for use in small strips on a block or two.
- Make sure that provocative new items are available from time to time along with a continuous flow of novel "found" treasures and recyclables such as the dots from the paper punch, various stickers, or old greeting card pictures and colorful paper scraps. Even the inevitable "anonymous" easel paintings can be recycled into beautiful collage material. Cut into strips or random shapes, they provide incentive for creating new inventions and accessories for fantasy play—headbands, bracelets and belts—at spontaneous drawing and crafts tables.

The teacher's respect for the child's expression is reflected in the quality of materials and the care taken in their presentation. Sometimes the most expensive materials are not always the best. In cases of more costly materials, consider how they might possibly be obtained. For example, while newsprint or recycled computer paper may be adequate for the drawing and scribbling table, it is poor support for tempera applied with a young child's vigorous strokes. With resources parsimoniously husbanded through such activities as the recycling of crayons and diligent scrounging of paper ends from local printers, perhaps a very good quality easel paper (ideally #80) could be affordable.

Other practical pointers involve the use and display of blocks for art-making and play:

- Ideally, both large and small units should be made available in several locations where spontaneous play is anticipated. Props to support dramatic play such as miniature animals, small cars, people, and furniture should be located nearby.
- Sometimes blocks need to be loosened and placed randomly at the child's eye level in order to encourage children to make use of them. Stacking them too neatly and storing them out of the way or in the same place at all times will diminish children's expressive use. A series of large and middle size units stacked suggestively can indirectly engender play at a bank of "computers" or in the control room of a large "space ship."
- On the other hand, heaping blocks in a box or basket is not recommended, since "dumping" them out can breed chaos rather than construction, as well as an indifference to the care of the environment, especially in young children.

On another more general note, constant vigilance is needed to ensure that the children's display areas do not become usurped for teacher or project storage, or become catch-alls, thereby losing their effectiveness as a support for "choice." This is a particularly pernicious problem when there are multiple users such as occurs in the necessary rotation of a.m. and p.m. staffs or when different age groups must be served.

Teacher Know-How.   In doing their technical homework, early childhood teachers will want to equip themselves with technical information. For example: What colors make pleasing blends? How do primary and secondary colors blend? Knowing this, the teacher can set up the palette at the easel, as in Figure 6.2, so that colors that are contiguous blend pleasingly, instead of creating still another "brown."

- What are the characteristics of paint, paper, clay? The teacher will be called upon to use these media every day.
- How much starch or extender should be added to the paint? You don't want the color to look transparent, watery, and washed out. And you do want a creamy texture that flows off the brush pleasingly rather than clumping in globs.

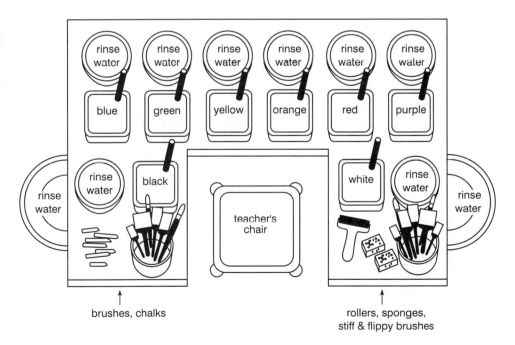

Figure 6.2
Berkeley Child Art Studio Group Palette for Painting Class.
Source: From *The Berkeley child art studio* by M. deUriarte, 1978, unpublished manuscript. Berkeley, CA.

- What kind of clay would be best for the task at hand—a low-fire white clay that takes a glaze or acrylic paint nicely when it is fired, or a rich-toned red clay that is handsome in itself when fired, but, unfortunately, may stain children's clothing if aprons are not worn?

On a less pragmatic level, teachers will want to know something about the cultural, historical, and aesthetic values not only of their own heritage, but of other cultures as well. What kinds of music or tape recorded materials are suitable for young children for use during active class time, in or out of doors? What about nap time and during the late afternoon in after school care? By gaining knowledge, sensitivity and confidence in these areas teachers may employ the power of the arts to endow children with self-esteem and enhance their aesthetic sensibilities through an appreciation of all facets of their heritage.

🍃 Jenny comes to school one day dressed in wooden shoes her Dutch aunt sent from Holland to use in dress-up play in the home corner. The next day Mikka brings a little red silk kimono. "My mommy had this from when she was a little girl in Japan." Other children in this economically and culturally diverse class want "special shoes" and "princess robes" also. What can the teacher do to further capitalize on this cultural richness? 🍃

MONITORING THE QUALITY AND CHALLENGE OF PLAY IN THE ARTS

Much of the spontaneous play in the arts found in the early childhood curriculum arises from an understanding of children's need for physical knowledge experiences. Water play, finger painting and work with play dough are examples that have a universal appeal. At least initially, children find the tactile/sensory aspects engrossing. Knowledge of the physical properties of materials is often assumed to be acquired through children's free manipulation of such media. The ease with which finger paint and play dough can be transformed through manipulation also recommends them as valuable adjuncts to fantasy and functional play. Children will frequently create songs and stories as they work with these materials.

At some point, however, the teacher must be sure to ask whether and in what ways these spontaneous tactile/sensory activities lead to more challenging experiences that advance all aspects of development. A number of questions can be raised:

- Does the activity have an educational rationale?
- Does it link up with goals for the group curriculum and/or with a learning plan for individual children?
- How much learning does it really promote, and to what extent does it support extension into pretend play with peers?

Children learn through guided play experiences.

- How can its value be assessed so that we can be sure that the curriculum, particularly for the kindergartner and older child, is a rich one?
- In mixed age groupings, are too many aspects of the curriculum overly challenging for the youngest? Or are we "dumbing down" the curriculum for the older children?

Guided and Directed Play in the Arts

We know that young children learn most effectively through play, and educational strategies often rely on guided or directed play. In the role of play tutor—for example, at the clay table—the teacher might show the children how to model basic clay shapes (as precursors to developing concepts of volume). Or, to build the child's repertoire of three-dimensional sculptural forms, she might show them how to hollow out a ball of clay to make a dinosaur's cave or to extend the hollow to make a tunnel where the hands of two friends meet, or how to make clay coils, slabs, and seriated balls. In one preschool program, Wade integrated knowledge about clay modeling when he proceeded to add "teeth" to the jaws of his hollowed out clay form. Sylvie, a second grader, using slabs of clay she had rolled out smoothly, cut and shaped a beautiful rectangular jewelry box (complete with a fitted lid) for her grandmother's birthday.

Music and Play.   In many programs, teachers present the music and movement curriculum as a directed or guided experience for the whole group as a part of each day's routine. Both new and traditional movement and music material can be introduced in such a manner. Within such a framework ethnic songs and rhythms can effectively be introduced as well. Surprisingly, one teacher discovered that the movement group became more cohesive *and* inclusive when boys were asked to pick a girl to sit beside in movement class. In this way, when paired for folk dancing routines, the option for cross gender as well as same gender dancing became possible. Within the framework of directed play, the following are some familiar possibilities:

- Call-and-response (echo) routines emphasizing playful games that train the ear to tonal and rhythmic discrimination.
- Ensemble playing of rhythm instruments with, for example, all the instruments playing the chorus of a simple tune such as "Jingle Bells," alternating with voice singing for the verses.
- Alternating a single child's improvisation on an instrument with ensemble playing and singing as in the following, where the teacher rotates turns of improvisation by placing a hat on the head of a child she selects to improvise after others sing and play:

"Bakers hat, just your size,
When it's on your head you improvise."

Similar improvisation with instruments and singing can be utilized around standard favorites with a strong and simple rhythm such as Noah's Ark. Perhaps one would alternate voice and instruments, starting first with the children singing unaccompanied at first:

"Who built the ark, Noah, Noah.
Who built the ark, Noah did."

and then continue with both voice and rhythm instruments:

"Here come the animals, two by two. If I were there I'd come along too."

This is particularly effective with various xylophone instruments accompanying the voice. If the teacher has a piano and can play, this can be an added support to maintaining the rhythm and pitch of course.

At the level of guided play, a well organized listening center for two or more children utilizing a diversity of offerings of audiotapes might be provided. These tapes can be mounted on cards with salient information written out so that the guiding teacher can point out aspects of the music to the children. For older children who are beginning to read, the cards can be filed in the listening center for use by the children directly. As many teachers know, spontaneous songs and dances are constantly created by children as they play, and these could be recorded and enjoyed at the listening center as well.

When three- and four-year-old children are empowered by being taught to use the audio recorder to preserve their musical creations, they are encouraged to reflect on what they produce. For example, in one kindergarten class, Cassandra mastered the use of the audio recorder and created this song to play for the group:

My mama went to the store, an open store.
She went to get some candy for me and milky too.
She bought some cereal, she bought some candy,
She bought everything she need for me.
I want . . . (a pause for rhythm),
I want . . . (pause again for same amount of time) candy,
I want my candy, I want my candy,
I want ta be everything I want ta be,
I want some milk and candy,
I want some milk and candy,
But I want to sock it to for me,
I want ta be my mommy.

Although much of this chapter deals with graphic and constructive play in the arts, music is an important avenue for the development of children's thinking and deserves to be carefully integrated into the curriculum. Familiar songs and games can be integrated into a more systematic, guided play framework such as that developed in the Orff-Kodaly method (Alper, 1987; Wheeler & Raebeck, 1985). The general objective of this approach is to refine the senses so that the child gains knowledge of and appreciation for various aspects of music such as rhythmic patterns and tonal discrimination. Furthermore, since the emphasis is on making and enjoying music as a group activity rather than as individual performance, the method has a positive social value and does not emphasize competitiveness.

Hans Furth (1970) echoes the Kodaly approach when he writes in *Musical Thinking* that " . . . the opportunity can be given to children to express facets of their personalities that go along with their developing intelligence in the medium of music. To play in rhythm, to control intonation and intensity of tone, to construct musical phrases over time, to symbolize all these things in musical notation, as well as to interact with others and submit one's activity to the group task—all this is part and parcel of human intelligence. It is for this reason the music teacher can justifiably rely on intrinsic motivation. His goal is musical thinking, with the accent on thinking. He is not concerned with turning every child into a professional . . . musician . . . " (pp. 140–141).

Simple "echo" routines involving rhythmic patterns of hand clapping, finger snapping, knee slapping, and other sound making, with or without rhythm instruments to accompany patterned movement or dance can be thoroughly satisfactory activities. For example, when preparing the environment, some teachers use culturally and linguistically diverse selections of tape recorded music to accompany children's dance and movement. Often parents are a rich resource that can be called upon to enhance this diversity. In one class a Chinese family provided a tape recording of popular contemporary Chinese children's songs. These became instant favorites because of their particularly catchy and appealing rhythm. In this same classroom a Russian parent interested in dance provided accessories in the form of child-sized elasticized head and waist bands decorated with bright ribbons and sequins. With these, children needed no teacher assistance to create their own brightly colored dance costumes by merely tucking a selection of brightly colored scarves into the head and waistbands. This contribution helped her Russian-speaking daughter establish early communication with other children in dance and movement. (See Chapter 9, Language, Literacy and Play.) Once such activities are launched with a small group of children, the teacher may be able to withdraw but closely monitor from a distance so that the music and movement experience can remain focused and evolve as spontaneous play without deteriorating into more random tag, rough and tumble, or chasing games.

Music can enhance the affective tone of an environment. However, musical activities that merely distract, or entertain, although possibly useful as "management strategies," cannot be justified as developmental curricula.

In guided play in the arts, care should be taken to avoid undue focus on the virtuosity of a teacher rather than the particular needs of children. Such performances may well be enjoyed by and of interest to children, but they fall into the category of directed play. As such, they should be balanced with opportunities for free improvisation with music.

In guided play teachers share children's interests and fantasies.

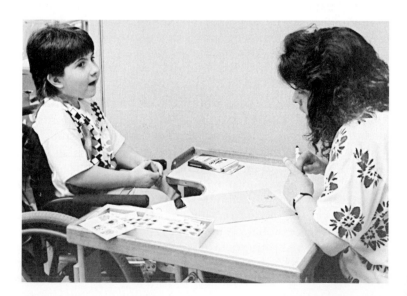

Working Within the Zone of Proximal Development. When guided/directed play in arts activities is linked in some relevant manner to children's fantasy play, or if the teacher can "play" parallel to children (as suggested in chapter 5), then such play is protected from becoming merely work disguised as play. The teacher can then stay in touch with the child's developmental needs. In this manner, the teacher participates in what Vygotsky (1967) referred to as the zone of proximal development, that area where the child experiences his own future, more advanced self through stimulation and challenge in play with an adult or more competent peer.

Consider Jerry, an active, unfocused child:

Four-year-old Jerry jumps from the jungle gym and dashes across the yard yelling, "Rocket launch! Rocket launch!" Within seconds he reaches the sand pit, jumps in, and plows through Andre's and Peter's sand towers.

Taking Jerry gently by the hand, his teacher productively redirects this explosive energy. "You seem to know a lot about rockets," she says. "How about drawing one?"

Through drawing or painting or construction with clay or blocks, she engages the child in a vivid and expressive rendering of his fantasy. The recognition Jerry may have been seeking in spontaneous play with peers may be more easily accomplished through guided, creative expression. Such expression will serve him better until linguistic ability and his competence in interacting with others advances to meet the need he feels to share his powerful fantasies.

Jerry may be helped to create some segments of a cartoon strip about rockets. When the teacher labels aspects of his vigorous but seemingly meaningless scribbles by using words in bubbles and arrows that highlight and clarify important information—"here is the launching pad, here is the rocket's nose"—Jerry is led to experience himself as a more effective communicator.

Guiding for Mastery and Competence. Guided play often provides opportunities for the teacher to closely observe and learn how the competencies, interests, and personality of a child complement or conflict with the social challenges of the group setting. For example, Lisa frequently has difficulty sharing the available supply of play dough. Learning this about Lisa's needs, the teacher might ask her to assist in the preparation of a new batch of dough to be shared with others, thereby helping Lisa to manage her needs, emotions, and impulses in the group setting. Mira has difficulty deciding what musical instrument she wants to play at circle time and becomes disruptive. When the teacher enlists her help in passing out the instruments to the children in the circle, Mira is empowered to share more readily.

However—and this point is crucial—in programs of high quality, no guided or directed circle-time activity should merely be preparation for something else. Introduction of materials is important; however, *nothing* in the early childhood arts curriculum should be simply a "dry run." Every single arts activity should make sense in the context of the children's lives at school, and each step in an art sequence should be intrinsically interesting.

Enhancing Children's Membership in the Group.   Guided play with art-making materials affords many opportunities for language use and social and cultural sharing and, again, gives the teacher an opportunity to quietly observe. Often the group project is stimulated directly by the children: "I want one like Martha has!" "So do I!" With the help of the teacher, the paper earrings that Martha just made are studied. The required materials are set up at a table so that Martha can teach the others to make earrings of their own.

In the primary grades in particular, projects that enhance group membership may sometimes be ongoing and involve long-range goals. Even so, every step toward the project goal is ideally play-centered and intrinsically satisfying. Making a group book, a class poem or quilt, a mural or decorations for a school party—all can support the child's growing ability to plan, to look forward, and to share socially. For example, in Harriett Morrison's first grade class, a group of children created a newspaper for all the members of the class. It involved several weeks of research and planning before the first and only edition was published. These first-graders also wrote "thank you" letters to the fifth graders following a drama presentation by the older group as well as letters to the principal reporting the poor quality of their pencils. These group projects also provide valuable opportunities for children to learn about and participate in the cultural richness of many of today's classrooms.

Children's Play Interests Supported in a Responsive Curriculum

Children's playful engagement in the arts frequently provide us with ideas for new curricula. This is reflected vividly in myriad ways. The monsters of one year's pretend play give way to Robin Hood the next. The prince and princesses in this year's group book become the daddy and mommy dinosaur in next year's. So, too, with the paintings and constructions any class creates: Each year the genre is different. Musical interludes can become a part of children's spontaneous story play dictation or in an "author's theatre" in later elementary school. Once introduced as a genre, children will recapitulate songs they know already, such as nursery rhymes or contemporary media songs like the Power Ranger song or "Hi Ho, Hi Ho, It's Off to Work We Go," etc., into their plays.

British drama educator Dorothy Heathcote often used child-generated songs and chants in her drama work with children (see chapter 9 for some discussion of drama as one of the literary arts). Children's guided play experience in music at one preschool led to the appropriation by novice players of formulas for achieving entrance into superhero play.

A group of four-year-old boys playing Power Rangers are blocking the entrance to the climber by two girls, Yolanda and Shani. Randall steps to the top of the slide and asserts: "I'm the red Power Ranger and nobody except Power Rangers can come."

Their teacher, taking a leaf from Paley's (1992) *You Can't Say You Can't Play,* says, "What do they have to do to play?"

Randall: "They can't."
Teacher: "You know we agreed at our meeting that we can't hit and we can't say 'you can't play.' What can they do? How do they have to act to be part of it?"

Alex steps forward and strikes a Power Ranger pose with crossed arms poised for Karate chops. "They have to do this!"

Teacher: "Randall, could the Power Rangers have a meeting with Yolanda and Shani and teach them what to do? They know the Power Ranger song."

Yolanda begins to sing the song the boys taught at music earlier in the day.
    The teacher says: " . . . could they come up and guard the back platform?" (The climber has multiple platforms.)
    Randall replies "OK, but I am guarding the slide and Alex is guarding the pole." Yolanda and Shani clamber up the slide.

Children also create their own curricula. Guided activities in which peers exchange and share experiences through paintings and drawings are a case in point. Mikka originates "rainbow belts" for "rainbow power rangers," and the Power Ranger group becomes gender inclusive. In another class, children seize upon Toby's bus-on-its-side template to create flags of their own, thereby making Toby's problem-solving experience theirs.

Integration of Children's Experiences and Feelings Through Play in the Arts

Spontaneous play allowed Noah to integrate his new knowledge about colors—he used this growing grasp of color to start creating aqua. Such integration and recasting of experience and the application of knowledge in new contexts can occur also in guided play.
    Consider Jason:

Jason's only painting for the monthly art show revealed much: His intense interest in depicting trains and the intersecting lines of railroad tracks revealed the cognitive and representational competence of a five-year-old and related to his new and spontaneous interest in writing his name and making signs to designate areas of play for himself and his four-year-old friend, Wesley.
    In this particular classroom, a problem arose when Wesley, as a young four-year-old, did not share Jason's interest or capabilities in writing. Wesley felt left out, and his mother asked the preschool teacher not to stress writing.

As we can see, life in the zone of proximal development is not always fun, nor does it always flow smoothly, but it certainly challenges children.

Distressing experiences, such as mom's too abrupt departure, or the birth of a new baby brother, may also be relieved and integrated through expression in art or play activities at school. For example, Lonnie, a formerly abused child currently healing in his adoptive home, needed to include multiple masking tape "band-aids" in the many self-portraits he produced.

A Balanced Arts Curriculum

Throughout this book and in this chapter we stress the need to balance curriculum offerings across the continuum of directed, guided and spontaneous play. When play is at the center, the arts as well as other options will be carefully examined to ensure that the balance between spontaneous and guided or directed play is optimal for the group served. Table 6.1 provides a generous, but by no means exhaustive, listing of some basic arts activities, showing their positions along the play intervention continuum.

In determining the appropriate balance of arts activities, we must always consider:

1. The particular needs and developmental levels of individuals and groups served.
2. Length of the program day.
3. Number of staff.
4. Quality and size of physical environment.

Some individuals and groups will need more structure and fewer options, or more complexity with an increase in guided or even directed play; others will need less complexity with more opportunity for spontaneous play. In each case, we can select from the basics to create a menu of activities that enhances potential for play.

SUMMARY AND CONCLUSION

In this chapter we have based our rationale for an arts curriculum in early childhood on the following premises:

Children learn best through play and are incapable until middle childhood of performing work in the adult sense. (This issue is discussed more fully in chapter 13, and in Alward, 1995.)

A curriculum in the arts for early childhood both at the preschool level and in the early elementary grades finds its center in the necessity for children to play. It encompasses not only graphic arts, but drama, music, dance, movement and all forms of constructive play. It should be a play-generating curricula in which children's autonomy and interest are supported by their experiences in the arts. We have suggested that an arts curriculum can take several forms, being orchestrated along a continuum that supports both guided and spontaneous play.

However, the effectiveness of an early childhood arts program can be measured by the degree to which we observe that children are able to enter into sustained, effective, self-directed play. Is guided or directed art the only form we see? Do we see knowledge gained in guided arts activities being integrated as it is reapplied in spontaneous play? In sum, the major question to ask is: What is the quality and quantity of children's spontaneous play within the arts curriculum?

An important task for the teacher is to balance the options for kinds of play in the arts program. By ensuring the child's independent choices in play, the teacher is assured of both supporting development *and* engaging the child's *interest* and authentic expression.

In conclusion, when teachers find the source for their curricula in play, they link it to child development and discover its validation. In the following section, suggestions are made for compiling children's work for assessment. The child's development is revealed most vividly through such documents. When teachers share these compilations with a child, they can grow in self esteem through witnessing their own advancing competence.

FOCUSING OUR THINKING

1. Collect self-portraits drawn or painted by children at two intervals, fall and spring, for comparison and contrast in development. As a curriculum extension, ask children to tell what they like about each child and write what is said under the child's portrait for an acknowledging class display.

2. Collect a monthly sample of each child's painting for an art show in the classroom. Use the selection of each child's work as a topic for a staff meeting at the end or beginning of each month. Be sure to send notes home to parents to notice the new show each month. Use the collection of paintings to graphically illustrate development in parent conferences.

3. Tape-record and collect children's spontaneous songs over a period of time to further study children's developing aesthetic sensibility and their growth in musical thinking.

4. Provide journals and/or booklets for each child to draw and scribble in and then for them to either dictate or write their own stories. Compile these for a ready form of assessment of the child's development of fluency and creativity in dramatic and language arts.

5. On a small format, invite children to draw the members of their family. They might also draw pictures in a similar format of all their teachers or classmates. Some things to note and interpret will be features such as the varying sizes of figures and how they are rendered.

Activity	Spontaneous Play	Guided Play	Directed Play
Drawing and scribbling	Free use of markers, pencils, chalk, crayons, scissors, punches, assorted papers.	Teacher sets up environment. Little monitoring required.	
Collage	Selecting and arranging.	Teacher sets up environment. Children learn from each other.	Help with cutting and pasting initially.
Painting Tempera	Free application of paint to paper. Free to select "content"	Teacher sets up environment. Monitors from a distance until rituals learned.	
Easel	Free application of paint to paper. Free to select "content"	Monitors from distance	
At table	Free experiment from primaries plus black and white	Monitors from a distance once rituals learned re obtaining a supply of clean water and paper, etc. Teacher available to discuss work.	Sets up environment and introduces materials and palette.
Group palette	Free experiment and free content	Teacher discusses application, choices children make (see diagram Figure 6-2).	Sets up environment and presents palette and guides selections of paint and brushes.
Water color and crayons	Same as above	Monitors from distance	Introduction to materials.
Clay	Free expression with ample amount of clay	Monitors from a distance—teaches further skills only as interest arises from work.	Teaches initial skills, i.e., use of cutting wire to obtain clay, use of slip and powdered clay; models rolling out a slab, making a ball, (snakes), etc.
Play-doh	Free exploration with or without tools	Sets up environment. Monitors from distance. Prepares dough of good consistency. Presents different types.	

Table 6.1
Traditional Arts Activities.

Printmaking (Relief)	Free selection of materials—never self-directed.	Guidance in making plate. Teacher presents appropriate materials.	Inking and printing of plate.
Silk screen	Selecting elements from torn or cut paper	Guidance in placement to insure registration on paper.	Inking and printing
Wood gluing	Can be self-directed once skills learned and area for use set.	Presentation of materials	Guidance initially in gluing
Woodworking	Can be self-directed for one or two, once skills learned and appropriate area for use established. Seen as possible adjunct to spontaneous play.	Usually necessary to have teacher guidance or close monitoring.	Skills in use of tools taught; hammer, nails, vise, chisel, screwdriver, handsaw, etc.
Special events; holidays, t-shirts, or group works such as murals, quilts, greeting cards, invitations, decorations, calendars	Various steps can be intrinsically interesting and often may be incorporated into play.	Some steps can be monitored from distance	Teacher has goal. Presented in a sequence. Sequence and goal clearly presented.
Diagnostic self-portraits Collage	Children construct. Interpretation of how to do it left up to child.	Monitors from distance. Replenishes materials.	Teacher provides elements and describes activity. Eyes, ears, mouth, nose, egg shape for head.
Drawing (from mirror or free)	Same	Children may be provided with a life-size cutout of a head and shoulder shape	Teacher describes activity.
Whole body painting	Same	Sets up materials.	Teacher describes activity.

Activity	Spontaneous Play	Guided Play	Directed Play
Music and instrument—teacher modeling	Not spontaneous play	Guides, as in finger plays, simple songs, rhythmic patterns	Teacher directs
Music and instrument—improvisation	Children improvise. Open center.	Musical environment—Teacher monitors, may model some music or instrument ability.	
Story telling and dictation	Content usually open—not spontaneous play—may influence later sociodramatic or private play.	Teacher available one on one—or for small group doing one story or poetry. May probe for narrative elements.	Variously directed, various goals. Takes dictation or gives direct assistance to writers. May aid invented spelling or simple sounds as warranted.
Drama conventions such as use of a "play" voice.	Can be used to facilitate spontaneous play	Teacher monitors when it is for *understanding*. Helps children reflect and take perspective without disrupting play.	Teacher-directed play when *production* becomes the goal.
Story playing	Spontaneous play interpretations of roles, events, or stories	Teacher reads text and guides story playing.	Teacher writes dictated story play or assists child to do so.

SUGGESTED RESOURCES

1. Alper, C. D. (1987). Early childhood music education. In C. Seefeldt (Ed.), *The early childhood curriculum: A review of current research* (pp. 211–236). New York: Teacher's College Press.

   Good survey of research on music education and play. Gives brief description of Orff-Kodaly method.

2. Dyson, A. H. (1989). *Multiple worlds of child writers: Friends learning to write.* New York and London: Teachers College Press.

   Enchantingly written book demonstrates the role that drawing and scribbling plays as a precursor to narrative construction and writing.

3. Dyson, A. H. (1993). *Social worlds of children learning to write in an urban primary school.* New York and London: Teachers College Press, Columbia University.

   Dyson has long stressed the vivid connection between children's drawings and their oral and written composing and the impact such activities can have on their social worlds. The portraits of children presented in rich detail in this work demonstrate the power of the arts to transform relationships, lives and classrooms. An inspiring "must read."

4. Furth, H. G. (1970). *Piaget for Teachers.* Upper Saddle River, NJ: Prentice Hall.

   See Letter 10, Creative Thinking, and Letter 11, Musical Thinking. This classic work provides a developmental rationale for the inclusion of the arts that is still valid for today's constructivist classroom.

5. Goodnow, J. (1977). *Children drawing.* Cambridge, MA: Harvard University Press.

   One of several good surveys of the stages of children's drawings.

6. Ho, W. C. (Ed.). (1989). *Yani: The brush of innocence.* New York: Hudson Hills Press.

   Excellent discussion of the development of a gifted child. Beautiful and extensive illustrations. Demonstrates that developmental stages are universal but can be infinitely varied within stage.

7. Piaget, J., & Inhelder, B. (1967). The treatment of elementary spatial relationships in drawing pictorial space. In *The child's construction of space* (Ch. II, pp. 44–79). New York: Norton.

   A basic but rather technical chapter. Provides teachers with an opportunity to read a primary source. The children's interviews that are included in the chapter nicely illuminate the more theoretical portions.

8. Heathcote, D. & Herbert, P. (1985, Summer). A drama of learning: Mantle of the expert. In D. G. Lux (Ed.), *Theory Into Practice, 24*(3), pp. 173–180. Columbus, OH: Ohio State University.

   This article, as well as a number of others in this edition of TIP, give a fuller picture of how Heathcote's approach can be articulated in the classroom.

9. Dillon, D. (1988, January). *Language Arts, 65*(1). Urbana, IL: NCTE.

   The theme of this edition is drama as a learning medium. Articles by Ross (pp. 41–44) and Wagner (pp. 46–55) discuss Heathcote's work at length.

CHAPTER 7

Science in the Play-Centered Curriculum

🐚 🐚 🐚 🐚 🐚 🐚 🐚 🐚 🐚 🐚 🐚 🐚 🐚 🐚

Rosa is playing with a boat at the water table under the shade tree. She slowly pushes the boat down and looks as the drops of water gradually fill it. She watches it sink, whispering, "Come up now!" She lifts it up. She collects small rocks and bark chips from the base of the tree and fills the boat with six large bark chips. "Here you go—Toot! Toot!" She adds three rocks and the boat slowly begins to take on water. Quickly, she piles on two more rocks and the boat sinks. The rocks go down with the ship but the bark chips come floating to the top. "Pop! Pop!" Rosa pushes one of the chips down again and watches as it pops up as soon as she lets it go.

🐚 🐚 🐚 🐚 🐚 🐚 🐚 🐚 🐚 🐚 🐚 🐚 🐚 🐚

Play at the center of the curriculum integrates science as well as language, art, mathematics, and social studies. And, just as with these disciplines, it takes the trained eye of the educator to see the science processes, concepts and content that the children are involved with as they play.

Children are engaged in scientific processes whenever they are observing, comparing, and exploring. We often find young children experimenting with objects even though this is not the formal, analytical process of the scientist or older student. Let's take a brief look at Rosa's water play—an example of a typical activity in early childhood education programs.

We notice that three-year-old Rosa is exploring the concepts of floating and sinking. At first she pushes the boat down slowly and watches the water enter the boat drop by drop. When the boat is almost full it sinks quickly, listing a bit to the right side. Later, when Rosa adds the bark chips and rocks, she selects the chips first and appears to notice that the boat lowers in the water only slightly. At this point she adds the three rocks and watches as the water begins to come in. She appears to be trying to make the boat sink. She picks up two rocks and puts them both in. The boat sinks. As the bark chips float to the top, she imitates the popping sound they make as they break the surface of the water.

How does this child's activity relate to science? When Rosa carefully pushes the boat down, she is investigating what will happen, a scientific process. She observes the water enter the boat. Observing is another basic scientific process. If Rosa notices that the rocks sank but the bark chips floated, she would be "comparing" bark chips and rock with respect to sinking. Comparing is another scientific process. Notice that all these scientific processes relate to her own actions and her understandings of the way things work.

In addition to the scientific processes that emerge in her play, Rosa is also involved in learning scientific concepts such as cause and effect. Another scientific concept, or "big idea in science," that Rosa is investigating is the difference in the properties of objects. Some, like water, are liquid. Others, such as the rocks and bark, are solid. Rosa does not yet understand that systems that are heavier than their equal volume of water will sink while those that are lighter will float. However, through activities such as this, she develops a beginning understanding of weight, an important scientific concept.

Rosa is also learning more about the content of science, factual knowledge. For example, she notices that the bark chips float and make a popping sound as they break the surface of the water. She might notice other properties of the bark chips, their specific color, shape and size. As we shall discuss, scientific processes, concepts and content are all key aspects of appropriate science curriculum for young children (e.g., Benchmarks for Science Literacy, American Association for the Advancement of Science, 1993).

But why should an early childhood education curriculum emphasize science? Young children need to learn about the physical as well as the social world. In this way, science is a natural and necessary part of the process of development. Children's attempts to learn about the world and their understanding of the world, of how things work, can be thought of as their science curriculum. Science is an integral part of the traditional curriculum that centers on play. However, many early childhood educators lack the background in science to identify the many aspects of science that the children are involved in, from activities like making melted cheese sandwiches to making art collages.

The focus of this chapter is different from the focus of most books on science activities for young children. These books usually suggest ways for teachers to set up structured science activities. The teacher's role usually includes organizing materials specific to those activities, setting up this special environment, and carrying out particular activities. These activities are the ones that teachers usually think of when asked to describe their science curriculum. The teachers we talked to described experimenting with food coloring and water, growing seeds and sorting autumn leaves, activities they found in books on science education for young children. Some of these are excellent. Examples are included in an annotated bibliography at the end of this chapter.

While we agree that these are developmentally appropriate activities and very typical of those found in the science resource books we recommend, they are not necessarily part of children's play nor are they necessarily based upon children's own expressed interests. In that sense, they represent only a small range of the science curriculum. They are good examples of teacher-planned activities. To design a program with play at the center, we must highlight activities that children initiate through their own exploration and play.

One purpose of this chapter is to demonstrate how science is already integrated into the play-centered curriculum. Teachers can then identify it and also help parents, other staff, and administrators see how rich the traditional play curriculum is in the area of science. Considering play as the core of the curriculum, we will then go on to discuss how teachers can extend the investigation of ideas and processes that arise within the context of children's play.

This chapter begins with a tour of the environment of a typical early childhood program, analyzing how different indoor and outdoor areas offer numerous opportunities for children to be involved in science. We then provide an introduction to the nature of science education. We discuss ways in which teachers can extend the themes that children use in their own unstructured play to more structured activities that involve the children with science concepts, content, and processes. The chapter concludes with an analysis of the ways in which teachers can integrate other science curricula with a play-based program. We use the continuum of intervention frameworks presented in chapters 4 and 5.

SCIENTISTS TOUR THE KINDERGARTEN

The integrated play curriculum is the basis for a developmentally appropriate science program for young children. As young children play, they are involved in many things that scientists would identify as "learning about science." If a scientist toured your program, what would she find? This is what happened when several science professors toured a local kindergarten program. Marilyn is a biologist, Bob is a chemist, and Toni is a physicist. Although they made these observations in a particular kindergarten class, they could have made similar observations while visiting any play-centered preschool or primary program.

Outdoor Area

Marilyn: I'm amazed at how much goes on in such a short time. I've seen a lot of activity related to the rain we had yesterday. Jerry was watching a snail move along the side of the sandbox. He commented on the silvery trail the snail made and then discovered the many trails already made all over the wooden side of the sandbox. He's involved in the scientific process of observing. He and Alicia organized a "snail race" with three snails. The road was the slide. They were watching the different speeds the snails traveled. In science, "comparing" is also a fundamental process. I was surprised that the children pointed out that the snails crawled up at an angle. Many adults wouldn't have discovered all that information about snail behavior.

Bob: Yes, I was also surprised at what I saw happening without any formal instruction. The sand in the sandbox is pretty wet and several youngsters were making "cakes." There was a lot of investigating going on to find out what they called the best batter, just the right amount of moisture to hold the shape in their cake pans. They had all kinds of ideas on how to improve the "batter" including adding more water, more coarse sand, and mixing the sand with Play-Doh. Through the scientific process of experimenting, they were learning about the properties of materials. Several of the children worked on this for thirty minutes, about half a high school chemistry lab period. Their attention span and absorption in their activity impressed me.

While the children continued to play, Marilyn, Bob, and Toni pointed out many things they considered involvement with science concepts, processes, and content. For example, Soshi was trying to learn to pump on the swings. As she tried to figure out how the rhythmic rocking of her body would make the swing go higher, she was involved in learning more about cause and effect. Lisa and Peter were "fishing" in a puddle and found the Loch Ness monster, a giant worm with many "rings" that the children called armor rings in their dramatic play. Learning about the particular characteristics of living organisms is important content in the field of biology.

The Block Area

Toni: This looks like "pre-architecture." I'm impressed with the children's understanding and use of shapes. Look at this repetition of triangular blocks here and the interesting example of symmetry there, an important concept in both science and mathematics.

Marilyn: It's been a long time since I've been in a kindergarten class. This is terrific! Look at how Luis concentrates as he places that block on the tower. And how the children are experimenting, trying to figure out if the longer block or the two shorter blocks will work better . . . and how they try again . . . and, of course, look at the fun they're having.

Toni: I wonder if he will be able to figure out a way to make that block tower stand. . . .

Marilyn: Yes, he just learned about the idea of buttressing . . . another important concept . . . and now, I bet, he's going to use it again over there. . . .

They all fall silent for a moment, watching April and Tanisha build roads for small cars. The children use a block for an arch and several triangles to make a bridge. Tanisha puts a car at the top of the bridge and lets it roll down. April repeats this, experimenting by giving the car an extra push: "Sooo fast!"

Art Area

Marilyn: I'm not sure whether I would have considered these art activities play before I saw this. I'm still not sure. That little girl looks so serious as she selects the "right" collage materials and places them in the "right" places. Is that play?

Bob: What do you call it when you're involved in a project in the lab, so involved that you don't realize that it's time to go home for dinner? Is it work? It often feels like play to me. I'm having a great time. Perhaps neither is the right word. Is there a word that shows that you think of something as challenging and fun, and that you will work very hard on it?

Toni: Good point. Certainly, there is a lot of play and science going on right here. Take a look at that clay table. What strikes me immediately is the way the children explore the properties of the materials. That "food" made out of Play-Doh is not nearly as clearly defined as the food made out of plasticine. The kids have investigated the properties of these different kinds of clay and the limits of what one can do with the clay. Which clay is harder or softer? Which is smooth? I noticed that that boy discovered that the bridge he made with the Play-Doh doesn't take much stress. The plasticine had more of the tensile properties he needed in a building material.

Marilyn: I'm enjoying watching that girl, Marcia, mix fingerpaints. She's trying to make a shade of green that matches the color of the paper. And she's quite meticulous about it. Look how she adds such a small drop of white. She's involved in the processes of observing, of comparing, and of experimenting. She's also learned a lot about concepts relating to shades of color.

Bob: Look at Monie. She's transforming those pieces of cardboard packing materials in interesting ways: painting them, squashing them, putting glitter on them. The longer we stay here, the more interesting it becomes for me because I'm beginning to see so many scientific dimensions to these activities.

SCIENCE IN THE EARLY CHILDHOOD INTEGRATED CURRICULUM

The visiting scientists observed Soshi, Jeffrey, and Alicia and the other children pursuing a variety of their own interests through play. In fact, in some of their activities, we see a curiosity about concepts that are milestones in the evolution of science itself: the laws of floating, the relationship of time, distance and velocity, the physics of the buttress. These interests and the activities that they stimulate are common among children. How can our observations of young children's natural interests as expressed through play lead us to the formation of a balanced science curriculum?

The Goal of Early Childhood Science Education

If we analyze the nature of science, we recognize that central to all scientific inquiry and discovery are certain dispositions: curiosity, a drive to experiment, and a desire to critically assess the validity of answers. We believe the goal of science education for early childhood education is to encourage and support these dispositions.

This is our rationale for seeing play as the core of the early childhood science education program. Children's spontaneous play informs us as to children's own interests, what they are curious about, and how they attempt to solve problems. We believe that a developmentally appropriate science program is based on the similarities between scientists involved in science and of children involved in play—an interest and the energy to pursue that interest. In addition,

Play fosters children's curiousity about the world.

we find that in both science and play the interest is often social, shared by others or provoked by the social context.

Therefore, to infuse the early childhood program with the spirit of scientific inquiry, we need to acknowledge the vitality of the children's scientific interests as shown through their play and incorporate these interests, and the social energy that accompanies them, into the curriculum.

This approach to early childhood science education addresses what we believe is the basic weakness of the traditional K–12 science curriculum. Many of the students in the United States graduate with a low level of science literacy. Their lack of interest and ability seems especially dismal when one considers that our nation has contributed so much to scientific development and has prospered so much from its applications. As educators, we are being asked to produce students who will continue to make contributions, yet most science curriculum programs are seriously flawed by their focus on science facts and routines. What these curricula lack is that which is central to scientific endeavor, the joy of finding out.

The child who asks why certain yellow flowers appear in some places in a spring meadow and not in others is a naturalist, whereas the child who dutifully colors a ditto "spring flowers" is doing something unrelated to the process of science. What separates the two children is that one has put forward a problem to be solved, which at its core is scientific and, for the moment, thereby has declared herself a scientist. The second child has formulated an entirely different problem, which is how to succeed in the lesson plan. In a play-centered curriculum, young children are not studying science or a body of facts about nature, but rather are scientists learning to pursue problems of interest and to judge the adequacy of answers.

In order for children to participate in science education, teachers must respect them as emergent scientists. We can encourage all children to see themselves as members of the community of science.

In addition, as the scientists observed on their visit to the kindergarten, both boys and girls are curious and eager to learn about the physical world. Early childhood educators can play a critical role in providing equal support for girls and boys, for children from all backgrounds, to define themselves as competent scientific investigators. National associations of scientists and science educators, such as the American Association for the Advancement of Science and the National Science Teachers Association underscore the importance of focusing on equity issues in science education.

We can show young children that their scientific interests and curiosities, their attempts at understanding, their gradual growth and spurts of insight, deserve our attention and respect. This is our role as early childhood science educators. If this sense of community with science is not established in the early years, the prospects of attracting these children to science in adolescence and young adulthood are diminished. It is in these later years and not before that children become capable of participating in the more rigorous forms of scientific inquiry which we recognize more clearly as scientific thought.

For decades, the American Association for the Advancement of Science has sponsored the work of scientists, science educators and classroom teachers in an effort to foster programs that ensured that all students would become literate in science, math and technology. *Benchmarks for Science Literacy* is the report of the Association's Project 2061 (1993). How is scientific literacy for children in kindergarten through grade 2 described?

> From their very first day in school, students should be actively engaged in learning to view the world scientifically. That means encouraging them to ask questions about nature and to seek answers, collect things, count and measure things, make qualitative observations, organize collections and observations, discuss findings, etc. Getting into the spirit of science and liking science are what count most. Awareness of the scientific world view can come later. (p. 10)

To develop an appropriate science curriculum, we draw upon what we know about the nature of science and the development of children. In analyzing the scientists' comments as they observed the kindergarten program, we see that they discussed scientific processes, content, and concepts as well as dispositions such as curiosity. These are the very points made by the American Association for the Advancement of Science, in Project 2061 (1993), and in science education texts for teachers such as those by Althouse (1988), Cliatt and Shaw (1992), Harlan and Rivkin (1996), Holt (1977), and Kellough (1996). As teachers, we can analyze the scientific nature of children's activities by asking ourselves: What scientific processes are involved? What scientific concepts are the children developing? What is the scientific content of their activity?

The Nature of Science

The following is a typical definition of science: a study that deals with an area of facts or truths which are arranged systematically and demonstrate the operation of general laws.

Many early childhood educators and parents of young children recall memorizing a definition such as this one. Many remember lists of facts painfully memorized in science classes, or formulas written but not understood. Science education in the past three decades has changed significantly, and there is an emphasis on the importance of helping students gain competence in the processes of science, through scientific activities as well as scientific concepts— the "big" ideas in science. Scientific content, the facts, is still a basic part of science education, but as Project 2061 (1993) and others emphasize, unlike the science taught in previous decades, learning scientific facts is not the primary goal.

Scientific processes, concepts and content.   In the early childhood years, *scientific processes* are the ways children seek answers to their questions. Young children can engage in various science processes by observing, describing, comparing, questioning, problem solving, thinking about data, recording information, and interpreting the results.

Marilyn noted that Jerry observed how the snail moved along the side of the sandbox and described the silvery trail the snail made. When Jerry and Alicia organized a snail race, they compared the movement of several snails. Toni watched Jerry's attempts to ride the trike with the wagon attached. She commented on the trial-and-error manner in which Jerry tried to find a good way to attach the wagon.

In a first grade class, six-year-old Mark and seven-year-old Gilian observed that earthworms had rings and some of them had a thickening near the front end. They compared several earthworms and found that both small and large worms had a lot of rings, but that "only the bigger ones have a lump near the front." They wanted to find out what the lump was and if the older worms, like trees, had more rings. With their teacher's help, they found the answer to their question about the lump in a high school biology text drawing of a worm. There was no information in the text on the number of rings, so they went back and counted. To do this, they found that they needed a magnifying lens because one worm was quite tiny and it was difficult to count its rings. Learning to use the tools of science is an important aspect of the development of science process competencies. Mark and Gilian drew pictures of the worm, involving themselves in the scientific process of recording information.

The work of Piaget and others demonstrates that young children do not carry out scientific processes such as experimenting in the same way that adults do (Piaget, 1965). For example, children may experiment with yellow and blue paint to create a particular shade of green, but their experimentation will not be systematic. Rather than adding a bit more blue and mixing it well, they may add different amounts of different colors. Young children may try different ways to use a set of weights to balance a balance beam, but their efforts are trial-and-error, rather than planned and comprehensive.

Young children are capable of using many scientific processes. They are often careful observers and hone that ability when they examine the rings on a worm or the legs of a beetle. They are eager to engage in communicating, another scientific process. Young children can compare objects, they can organize information, and they can record their data through drawings, photos, or videotapes (Holt, 1990).

Scientific concepts are organizing principles of "what we know." "Cylindrical," "green," and "hard" are examples of concepts that we can apply in many content areas. For example, Ibrahim knows that green is a property that can refer to different objects: the tomato leaf, the harder tomatoes, as well as the paint at the easel. Many basic concepts young children develop relate to the properties of objects. They learn to describe objects in terms of such properties as color, shape, size, and weight. As children grow older they are able to understand more abstract, relational concepts such as ideas about motion, light and shadows, changes, and relative position. Children learn science concepts best when they encounter the same concept in different content areas.

ع. Leah is learning about the concept of "causality" (cause and effect). She adds another block to the tower and the tower falls. She gives a toy car a greater push and its speed increases. She leaves a crayon in the sun and it melts. ع.

During their brief tour, the scientists observed the children dealing with a great many scientific concepts. Jennifer and April were learning about concepts of distance and velocity, while Luis was learning about the concept of buttressing.

Science content refers to the subject of our attention, the "subject matter." Many science books and textbooks are science-content oriented. For example, a book on insects might include sections with facts about leafhoppers and aphids, dragonflies, mayflies, moths, and butterflies. A book on pond life might include sections on plants such as algae, fungi, and vascular plants as well as animals such as one-celled animals, worms, arthropods, mollusks, fish, amphibians, reptiles, birds, and mammals. It is useful for young children to learn factual information to better understand their own environments. From a sociocultural perspective, this is one important way for them to become competent adults.

However, many traditional science education programs emphasize the memorization of such content materials with little regard for the reason to learn those facts. This is particularly inappropriate when the content is not related to the individual child's world. For example, second graders in Texas might be expected to learn the names of insects of the northwest or the names of five kinds of rocks found in the Sierras, even though they might never see them in their own environment, unlike children in Oregon.

In a balanced science curriculum, children learn science content within an organized framework of scientific concepts, and through their involvement in the processes of science. In a balanced science curriculum that is play-centered, the particular scientific content, concepts, and processes that children explore at any moment are expressions of the children's own curiosity, interest, and creativity.

If we analyze the scientists' observations at the kindergarten in terms of science content, we find that some children were finding out about worms, some about sand, some about blocks, and some about different collage materials. Content variety is important. It is critical, however, for children to have the chance to return to favorite activities again and again. As children work with the same objects over an extended period, they enjoy their growing mastery of specialized science content.

❧ At four, Ibrahim has learned a lot about the tomatoes in the small garden outside his day care center. He knows that there are yellow tomatoes as well as red. He can identify several varieties of cherry tomatoes and beefsteak tomatoes. He can also distinguish a tomato leaf by its shape, texture, and fragrance. He knows when the tomatoes are ripe and how to pick them carefully. ❧

The Nature of the Child

To promote a developmentally appropriate science education program, teachers must be knowledgeable about both the nature of science and the nature of the development of the children they teach. What are the interests shown by four-year-old Lex and seven-year-old Rory? How can we describe their way of understanding the world around them?

The child's level of development.   In chapter 2, we briefly introduced basic principles of constructivist developmental theories. Other aspects of these theories are discussed in greater depth in chapter 13. In developing an early childhood education science curriculum, teachers find constructivist theories helpful in explaining children's responses, their ways of interpreting their observations and experiences.

A close look at children's level of cognitive development leads us to understand why young children will not be able to comprehend many scientific concepts despite any well-intentioned instruction. One of the authors observed a teacher's frustration when teaching a lesson on gravity to 4-year-olds:

❧ Catherine dropped seven or eight objects. She explained to the children that the objects fell because there was a force of attraction between the earth and the object. She told them that the objects in a space ship float around. After this demonstration and explanation, Catherine asked the children to explain why the objects fell when she dropped them. Their replies: "They like to." "They're attractive." "It gets pushed down." "It's falling." "Is it lunch time?" ❧

Children's thinking about basic science concepts is very different from the thinking of adults. Mature scientific thinking involves the ability to analyze, to form hypotheses, and to make inferences and deductions. Young children are not able to do this. As the above example illustrates, children's thinking is egocentric, perception bound, and often magical.

For example, in *The Child's Conception of Physical Causality*, Piaget (1965b) describes children's growing understanding of shadows. He found that young children believed that the objects themselves produced the shadows, e.g., that the shadow next to a book was like a substance coming from the book. Little by little, children came to understand that there was a relationship between the shadow and the source of light. Not until most children were in middle childhood did they understand that the shadow is an absence of light and that the light is being blocked by the object.

Science learning and social contexts.   Children's development in science learning is also influenced by their social and cultural environments. In some cultures, children have many experiences that support the development of particular scientific processes, concepts and content. Parents and teachers in urban areas might focus on providing children with explorations with different types of building blocks. Many children build cityscapes—apartment buildings, offices, factories and freeways. In contrast, the parents and teachers of children who live on farms may stress content such as plants and animals, concepts such as the life cycle, and observational processes such as observing whether plants are ready for harvest.

Children's understandings usually develop faster in subject areas in which they have greater experience with the physical world. These are also areas of knowledge in which they have greater experience with the social world, as important adults and peers share social knowledge with them. With time for further maturation and more interactions with the physical and social world, young children's manner of thinking changes. We need to build our science programs around children's present ways of thinking and provide the experiences that will foster future development.

Although play-centered curricula draw upon and reflect children's social contexts, it is critical that we not limit our expectations and curricula to these contexts. This principle is particularly important in science. The majority of Americans today live in urban areas. In cities and suburbs, and particularly in unsafe areas, we need to ask: How can we help urban children, their families, and ourselves to develop a sense of place, an appreciation and ease with the outdoors, and a feeling of wonder about life?

Jaelitza, a teacher in a rural day care center and school, reflects on outdoor adventures in her article, "Insect Love: A Field Journal" published in *Young Children* (1996):

Teacher Neil found a Promethia moth, a nocturnal moth, which had attached itself to a bottle in the pony shed. Brought into the light, it did not fly away, and so we were able to observe it very closely. Matt and Levi were very interested. Neil showed us its picture in the field guide and went on to answer the two boys' questions by referring to the moth as well as the text of the guide.

Matt and Levi were interested in our new field-study materials—bug "houses" and a new magnifying glass. They were ready to set out immediately, and I followed. Turning over logs that demarcate the tepee garden patch, we found a ready supply of sow bugs, immature snails, worms, ants and spiders. . . . 🐛

Jaelitza (personal communication, 1996) and other teachers and naturalists express the concern that few of today's children have opportunities to develop a deep connection to the land, a sense of geographical place, through sustained opportunities to play outdoors in fields, woods, beaches, and even empty city lots.

This need for place is beautifully expressed in Nabhan and Trimble's (1994) *The Geography of Childhood*. Similarly, in the article, *How nature shapes childhood: Personality, play, and a sense of place,* Nixon (1997) reflects on the wisdom of naturalists and conservationists such as Pyle, Louv, and Nabhan, who have written about the need for children to have extended time in which to play and explore in their natural environments. Nixon introduces Pyle's compelling concept of the "extinction of experience" and discusses Louv's insight that today, just when more children are developing greater awareness, knowledge, and feelings about protecting the global environment, fewer children are having unstructured and direct experiences with nature in their local environments.

The child's interests. Observation of individual children's spontaneous play is central to discovering their interests. These interests are the children's bridge between play and science and home. As teachers committed to equality of opportunity, it is particularly important for us to consider the ways in which children's interests can lead all children to participate in science (Browne, 1991).

🐛 Bee loves to observe the silkworms. She feeds them mulberry leaves, has arranged her own box, and is keeping a daily journal with descriptions and pictures. Her teacher discovers that Bee's grandmother comes from Laos and knows how to spin the silk from the cocoons into thread. Bee, her grandmother, and her teacher work together to plan a series of activities that are both multicultural and scientific. 🐛

🐛 In her kindergarten, Alia has built a treasure box. First, her teacher has the children draw a representation of their carpentry project. With some adult help, Alia carefully measures and cuts the wood. She learns about sanding, first using coarse, then finer sandpaper. This activity is part of the ongoing science program that promotes equity for all children, rather than a one time "antibias lesson." 🐛

In the next section, we discuss how teachers can use different intervention strategies to extend children's development and interests.

EXTENDING THE SCIENCE CURRICULUM

How can we, as teachers, extend the science processes, concepts and content that children deal with in their own unstructured play? How can we decide when to intervene and when not to? What best supports children's learning?

Play offers children opportunities to explore scientific artifacts.

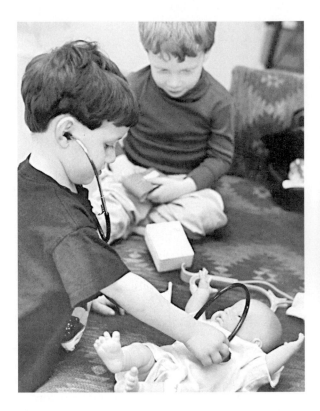

In chapters 4 and 5, we discussed principles that guide orchestration and presented a continuum of intervention strategies. When thinking about enriching the science curriculum, we can think about strategies at all points along the continuum. In this section, we discuss strategies and their implications for extending children's involvement with science. When we recognize the key role of play in development, we plan the curriculum by focusing first on providing an environment rich in possibilities for spontaneous play. We then think about teacher-planned interventions. This contrasts with science programs that typically begin with particular activities and then consider opportunities for children to explore and create.

Developing an Environment for Exploration of the Physical World Through Spontaneous Play

The basis for a play-centered curriculum is a well-planned environment. As described in the tour of the kindergarten, the traditional preschool and kindergarten environment allows for multiple opportunities for spontaneous play. Developing an environment that is rich in opportunities for children is a great challenge for teachers. In a well-planned environment, children have the chance to work with a wide variety of materials in a great variety of ways. Different types of paints, clays, collage materials, blocks in different shapes and sizes, sand

and water, climbing structures, plants, and animals are some of the materials found in play-centered programs.

The play-centered environment is flexible and the physical space can be rearranged as interests change. If a group of children is interested in working with large blocks, the teacher may decide to extend the space allotted for block activities as well as provide additional materials. We observed children in one class making an impressive collection of blocks with milk cartons of different sizes fitted together. One fortunate class in a rural area had new possibilities open up when Russell's father brought in a truckload of coarse sand from the river and the parent group built a sand and gravel pit. The children became more involved in large vehicle construction play. In an inner-city, multi-grade primary classroom, Allegra's mother helped the children build several shadow boxes that they used for light experiments during choice time.

Encouraging Further Exploration of the Environment

After initially developing the environment, teachers then observe children in their spontaneous play in order to modify the environment so that children can extend their play. Like a dance, this involves the teachers themselves in a creative and playful process. Let us take another look at some of the activities that occurred on the scientists' tour of the kindergarten to see how a teacher might add materials to allow children to extend their observations and experimentations. Jerry and Alicia were very interested in snails. What would they do if their teacher turned over a shovelful of soil to expose worms, sow bugs, and larvae?

Other children were using blocks to build towers. What would happen if the teacher took this opportunity to introduce blocks of additional shapes? Perhaps a set of table blocks, such as pattern blocks, would lead to greater interest in different types of constructions.

Rosa's teacher observed that Rosa continued to play at the water table for several days, experimenting with boats and cargo. Based on these observations, her teacher decided to place a box with an assortment of objects near the water table. She included objects of different sizes and materials such as metal, wood, plastic, and cork. She also added some large wooden objects that floated and small metal objects that sank. Rosa's teacher understood that she was providing new curricula opportunities for all the children as well as individualizing the curriculum for Rosa.

Marcia's teacher thought that Marcia's play with fingerpaints might be extended with the provision of multiple media such as tempera paints and watercolors to allow her to compare the properties of each. The availability of wide and narrow brushes fostered her experimentation with different types of brush strokes.

By extending the environment in this way, teachers also can support the extension of the children's interests by introducing similar materials. As these vignettes illustrate, interventions in the children's environment involve the teacher in a very creative process. The teacher observes the children, follows their lead, thinks of the many materials that might be added, and selects one or more to add in a non-obtrusive way. This is an ongoing process of matching and extending.

Interacting with Children in Their Play

Taking the child's-eye view in science education often takes the form of wordless communication. A teacher's smile, returned to a child's questioning glance, is non-verbal communication. In the context of the child's attempt to balance one more block on a tower of blocks, it is a scientific conversation: "Yes. This is a science laboratory where we experiment with stacking blocks." "You're right. When you do it that way they fall over." "I share your sense of surprise."

In guided play, teachers also may decide to play parallel or side by side with children. If you enjoy exploring and playing with blocks or with sand or collage materials, your own sense of interest, wonder, and focused involvement through your spontaneous play will be communicated. As long as your own explorations and play involve you in experimenting and discovering new ways to do things or the enjoyment of familiar patterns, you will avoid the trap of producing static models that children might copy. Some questions come to mind: How can you build a twin connecting tower with table blocks? Can you build a tunnel under the sand pyramid you just constructed? What are different arrangements that you can make with collage materials? Enjoy the creative process of seeing how many directions there are to take in a given situation.

Play-Generated Curriculum

ক্ষ Sarah, Dean and Nellan expressed an interest in worms. They played "Loch Ness monster" for several days. John, their second grade teacher, saw this as an opportunity to introduce different science experiences involving worms. He brought several large pieces of paper outside on the patio, put several worms on them, and suggested that, if they wanted to, the children could draw the worms. When this proved a popular activity, John asked the children to find other worm-like animals. Within a week, there was an exciting collection of caterpillars, several kinds of worms, as well as insect larvae which Nellan brought in. This lead to a conversation between Nellan and the other children about the sequence of the insect life cycle. It also led to a visit by a pet snake and his fifth grade owner. This was followed by discussions of similarities and differences in body parts and movement. ক্ষ

ক্ষ The children in Shelley's preschool program had been playing in the snow for weeks. Shelley first extended these activities by bringing snow and icicles inside in containers so that the children could watch and discuss the melting process in greater detail. She then put water in an ice tray and took the tray out of the freezer throughout the morning so that the children could observe the changes. This led to a week-long observation of the melting of a fifty pound block of ice that Shelley purchased from an ice company and placed in a baby bathtub. ক্ষ

ক্ষ One teacher in a school-age day-care program enjoyed the enthusiasm that the children brought to their play with light and shadows. She extended this play by showing them how to outline each other's shadows with chalk on the walkway. This lead to the question: "How long and how short does your shadow get?" In follow-up activities, they outlined their shadows on butcher paper several times during the day. The children and staff had fun generating many researchable questions, for example: "Can you shake your shadow hand with someone else's?" "Can you make your shadow stand on someone else's shadow shoulders?" The children's continued interest in shadows lead the teacher to collect additional resource materials. 🐌

In our choice of science-related activities, we, as teachers, reflect our own social and cultural values as well as our personal interests. For example, when John asked the children to collect other worm-like animals, he thought about his state's science frameworks that included a focus on living things and the life cycle for the primary level. In the state where Shelley lives, the physical science strand of the state frameworks includes "states of matter" as an important concept. These are both examples of ways in which teachers expand upon those aspects of the children's spontaneous play that are recognized by society as relevant to science learning.

Curriculum-Generated Play

In a play-centered curriculum, teachers constantly explore the ways in which the curriculum can lead to play. The connection is often seamless.

A second–third grade combination class was working on the Full Option Science Study (FOSS Newsletter, 1995) unit on batteries and bulbs, a topic that can be adapted for students at different developmental levels and grades. During the FOSS unit, the children continued to explore the materials available during

Exploration leads to spontaneous play and teacher-directed activities.

choice time. This is a typical example of curriculum-generated play. Teachers often find that children's interest continues after the unit or theme is completed. In this classroom, children continued to play with batteries and bulbs throughout the year. By the end of the year, many students were able to make systems of far greater complexity than those that were made when the unit was taught.

A first–second grade teacher described her first year's experience with a FOSS unit on Balance and Motion with a class that included a blind student, Emma-Lee. This description illustrates the many possibilities for curriculum-generated play that appropriate curriculum can generate.

‮ She balanced the cardboard crayfish, the arch, and the triangle right along with everybody else. She couldn't see the tops spin, but she could handle the tops ahead of time and listen to the motion on her desktop, and then stop the tops with her hands. Making rollers was fun. I think she really enjoyed the surprise when the cup or the wheel apparatus she and her partner made rolled into her hands. (FOSS Newsletter, 1995) ‮

After participating in this teacher-guided lesson, Emma-Lee and her classmates might spend many hours discovering more about the concepts of balance and motion.

A teacher-planned science program can be an integral part of a play-centered program. However, it is critical to carefully evaluate the program's philosophy, format and specific activities. The following principles are useful guides for evaluating curriculum-generated play to assess whether entire programs or specific activities complement a play-centered curriculum.

1.   Think about those science-related activities that you enjoy so that your students will observe your curiosity, your sense of wonder.

Marilyn found that she enjoyed carpentry activities. One year, she and a group of parents built an outdoor dramatic play space and involved the students in measuring, sanding, and painting the structure. The following year she brought in a collection of different types of woods and different grades of sandpaper so that the students could experiment with the qualities of the wood and sandpaper.

2.   Evaluate the purpose of exploration in teacher-planned curricula.

Within the context of a play-based curriculum, exploration leads to both open-ended, spontaneous play, as well as to more structured, teacher-directed activities. In contrast, in more didactic curricula, exploration is included merely so that the children won't "fool around with the materials" in the subsequent, highly structured activities.

3.   Emphasize activities that promote open-ended exploration and discovery as complements to spontaneous and guided play.

Primary teachers in particular often experience pressure to teach specific concepts and content. Trawick-Smith (1994) discusses ways teachers can reframe more didactic lessons so that children can explore and discover concepts and information themselves. Similarly, in *Serious Players in the Classroom,* Wasserman (1990) describes how teachers can plan thematic science units so that children have opportunities to replay concepts and content they have already encountered in more structured lessons.

4. Emphasize science units or themes that promote in-depth engagement and understanding.

The National Science Teachers Association (NSTA) and the American Association for the Advancement of Science (AAAS) underscore the importance of focusing on in-depth understanding rather than the topic-a-day approach to science. In keeping with this, they further recommend that students return to reconsider concepts and content during different years in the elementary school.

A first–second grade teacher found several teachers guides for units on light and shadow. She took several ideas and adapted them for her class, and also brought in resource books from the library. By chance she discovered that a high school art class was making Indonesian puppets and putting on a shadow play. The play, presented in her room, proved a high point of the year and the inspiration for additional dramatic play that incorporated further experimenting with light and shadows.

Italian educators and parents who have developed the Reggio Emilia approach to education experiment in their curricula with the many ways that children can bring greater depth to their examination of experiences such as a broad jump event or a butterfly project. This approach also exemplifies how an emergent curriculum is dependent on teachers' close observations of and conversations with children (Edwards, Gandini & Forman, 1993; Hendrick, 1997).

5. Select units that include science processes, concepts and content that the children can relate to their everyday lives. The National Science Education Standards adopted by the National Research Council recommend that the central strategy for teaching science is the exploration of "authentic questions" (National Academy of Science, 1995, p. 30). Furthermore, these standards emphasize the investigation of authentic questions such as those encountered in daily life situations when considering issues of equity and access for all students: "The diversity of students' needs, experiences and backgrounds requires that teachers and schools support varied, high quality opportunities for all students to learn science" (p. 4).

6. Select units that naturallly lead back to spontaneous play and an integrated curriculum. The FOSS unit on balance and motion is an excellent example because children become engaged in further developing concepts that they have explored in previous play.

7. Enrich children's experiences through field trips. Children's museums and exploratoriums, with their hands-on activities, provide wonderful experiences for the fortunate schools and families in their areas.

ᘒ Rotha's bilingual second grade class visited a nearby children's museum. During the next few days, several children set up their own exhibits and experiments in class. When Rotha saw that the children remained engaged and that the class museum evolved further during the next few weeks, he suggested that they open the class museum to other classes. Not only was the museum highly popular with the preschool through first graders, but the upper grade students enjoyed it as well. Rotha noticed that some of the students who were limited in their English proficiency, and who were sometimes hesitant to speak English for that reason, became gregarious and talkative. Talking about their projects with many children in several classes in an actual situation gave them the chance to practice their language skills in a more authentic way than through a language drill. ᘒ

8. Further support science literacy by surrounding children with science resource media. There are many science books for children with photos or accurate illustrations. Science films and videos abound. Nature films and videos are especially plentiful. In an environment that is rich in science resources, children and teachers continually extend their knowledge of the physical world and their opportunities for exploring it.

Recasting the Curriculum in Play

When curricula are appropriate for the development and interests of the students, students constantly recast the curriculum in their play. Of course, children do not separate their play by subject matter areas. Therefore, as they recast the curriculum in their play, children are integrating the curriculum as well.

For example, we might see that the children who delight in making different systems of batteries and bulbs expand upon this in their shadow play. They might use these lights in creating a tent for dramatic play.

SUMMARY AND CONCLUSION

As early childhood educators integrate the curricula with children's spontaneous play as the focal point, they begin to see the great extent to which children's activities involve science processes, concepts and content. Young children are curious about the natural world. They are interested in finding out about their physical environment, finding out about how things work. A program based upon their interests therefore includes a great emphasis on science. Like the scientists who toured the kindergarten, teachers begin to "see science" and also see opportunities for additional science activities everywhere.

Teachers can begin with an environment that invites children to explore their physical world through spontaneous play. Further exploration is encouraged through the addition of materials and through supportive teacher-child interaction. Drawing upon the children's expressed interests, teachers can introduce science activities related to children's play. Appropriate teacher-directed activities can be introduced that complement play-centered activities and lead back to play.

The early childhood years provide a rich and perhaps critical opportunity to draw the natural power and direction of children's reasoning into the community of science. If we incorporate these interests and energies into the early childhood education classroom, we will have fostered the steps toward raising a scientifically literate generation.

FOCUSING OUR THINKING

1. If a scientist toured your program (or a program with which you are familiar) what would he or she find? Draw a simple map of the environment and identify five or more opportunities for learning science concepts, content, and/or processes for each area.

2. In one anecdote in the chapter, Jerry and Alicia were watching snails.

   a. If you were their teacher, how could you intervene to encourage "further exploration of the materials based upon the children's spontaneous play"?

   b. How could you introduce "additional science activities or materials related to the children's own spontaneous play"?

3. Using an example from your state's science framework or guide for second or third grade, list the opportunities teachers can provide for children to recast this curriculum through play.

4. Increase your own observational abilities: Select a leaf that you find aesthetically pleasing. Observe it closely. What are its properties or attributes? Can you make a list including more than 25 properties? (e.g., "translucent," "smooth.")

5. Add new references to your annotated bibliography of children's books. Include both non-fiction and fiction books that relate to science and play.

SUGGESTED RESOURCES

1. Hill, D. M. (1977). *Mud, sand, and water.* Washington, DC: National Association for the Education of Young Children.

   This book is a classic among preschool educators, and includes many appropriate suggestions for using these child-proven materials with primary grade children as well. For students and teachers who have had few encounters with mud, sand, and water in their own educational experience, we recommend this book as another source of activities to "focus our thinking."

2. Holt, B. G. (1990). *Science with young children.* Washington, DC: National Association for the Education of Young Children.

   A general introduction for educators who want to enrich their program. The author emphasizes the importance of supporting children's curiosity about their world and helping them to remain concerned about all life.

3. Cliatt, M. J. P. and Shaw, J. M. (1992). *Helping children explore science: A sourcebook for teachers of young children*. Upper Saddle River, NJ: Merrill/Prentice Hall.

    One of the few sourcebooks written expressly for early childhood educators. This book helps teachers prepare and maintain an environment rich in possibilities to explore science. Appropriate activities are also suggested.

4. Nickelsburg, J. (1976). *Nature activities for early childhood*. Menlo Park, CA: Addison Wesley.

    The numerous projects included reflect children's interests as well as the richness of nature. A rainy day, butterflies and moths, looking at feathers, keeping a canary, earthworms, and bare twigs are typical examples. This special book conveys the author's sense of curiosity and love of nature on every page.

5. Kellough, R. D. (1996) *Integrating mathematics and science for kindergarten and primary children*. Upper Saddle River, NJ: Merrill/Prentice Hall.

    A comprehensive science and mathematics text that presents basic concepts and processes and numerous examples of instructional activities.

6. *Young Children*

    For the past decade, this monthly journal published by the National Association for the Education of Young Children (NAEYC) has included numerous articles on science each year. Many articles include examples of science in play-centered curricula in preschool through second grade.

7. Full Option Science System (FOSS) units for K–3 are distributed by Delta Education, Inc., Hudson, NH.

    The FOSS curricula materials provide opportunities for children to explore and discover as well as chances for teachers to take the lead in introducing scientific processes, concepts and content. Many of the units involve materials and activities that are naturals for curriculum-generated play, such as batteries and bulbs, wheeled constructions and tops.

8. Nabhan, G. P., and Trimble, S. (1994). *The geography of childhood: Why children need wild places*. Boston: Beacon Press.

    Nabhan and Trimble are respected contemporary natural history writers who are recognized for their beautiful prose and insightful reflections. This is a collection of essays in which they reflect on their own childhood experiences, their children's experiences, and the experiences of the world's children. Their descriptions of the work of others who have written about the environment and children will inspire readers to follow up on this vital topic.

CHAPTER **8**

Mathematics in the Play-Centered Curriculum

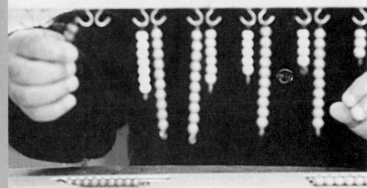

The blocks have arrived! After weeks of anticipation, the students in Virginia's first grade class get their first opportunity to create with blocks. Some of the 27 children have never played with unit blocks before. Until this year, there were no blocks in the school's three kindergarten classes. Virginia is the first of the first grade teachers in the school to use them.

Chhoun runs to the blocks purposefully. He builds a two-tiered structure and divides it into symmetrical sections. Several towers add an interesting touch of asymmetry (Figure 8.1). In front of the structure he builds four small, separate constructions that look like animals. He groups three to his right and a single one to his left.

Leah and Becky work together to build a castle (Figure 8.2). It has a triangular base, so that one looks into the structure as if looking onto a stage. They also emphasize asymmetry by adding a second tier on one side.

Virginia was surprised at the children's skillfulness in block building and their sense of design. When discussing their work, she emphasized their sense of balance and symmetry, and how they "decorated" the more regular, symmetrical structures with small shapes to make them a bit asymmetrical. She pointed out that the limited number of blocks available sometimes led to exchanges in which children discussed issues of fairness concerning numbers of blocks each child could take. Chil-

Figure 8.1

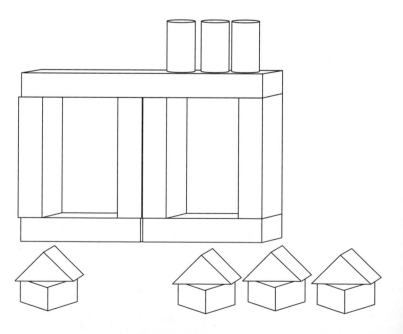

Figure 8.2

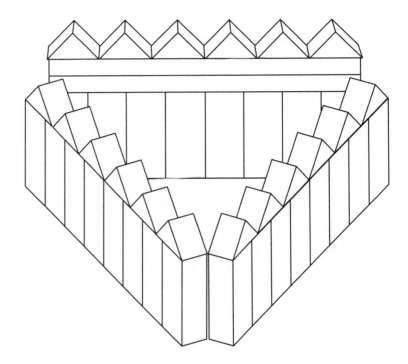

dren traded one longer block for two shorter blocks. They counted the total number of blocks different children had. They searched for particular triangular or cylindrical blocks to complete their structure or provide greater stability.

As Virginia's comments indicate, block play provides opportunities for children to consolidate and extend their mathematical thinking. In constructing with blocks, children deal with relationships involving the major areas basic to mathematics during the early childhood years, for example, space (geometry) and quantity (number). Blocks have always been a favorite play material of young children. Blocks have long been recognized by early childhood educators and researchers for their appropriateness in supporting the development of mathematical abilities within a playful context fostering the development of the whole child (Hirsch, 1977; Reifel & Yeatman, 1991).

MATHEMATICS EDUCATION AND YOUNG CHILDREN

Our approach to math education parallels our approach to education in all the content areas: developmentally appropriate programs are based on an understanding of mathematics, and of children's development and interests.

The Nature of Mathematics

Before turning to a discussion of mathematics education and young children, we begin with a brief discussion of the nature of mathematics. Mathematics involves all three types of knowledge that Piaget described: physical knowledge, social knowledge, and logical-mathematical knowledge. Mathematical thinking involves physical knowledge because we use mathematics to describe relationships in the real world, e.g., these tomatoes weigh three pounds and cost $1.29 per pound. Mathematical thinking also involves social knowledge, information we learn directly from others. English-speaking children learn the number name "seven" while French-speaking children learn the number name "sept."

The basis of mathematics is logical-mathematical thinking because problems that involve mathematics require solutions based on logical thinking. Logical mathematical thinking is a key dimension of thought for children's development. This type of thought involves the logical relationships that our mind constructs rather than the information our senses observe (physical knowledge) or that we obtain from others (social knowledge). Each of us constructs for ourselves the mathematical concepts we know. In this way, children reinvent for themselves what adults and older peers in their social environment already know (Kamii with DeClark, 1985). When we think "mathematically," we use our logical abilities to solve problems.

Logical-mathematical thought is the foundation of our understanding of many aspects of the physical world: How many floor tiles will we need to cover the kitchen? How many miles per gallon does our car get? Throughout childhood, children's grasp of relationships involving mathematical concepts develops. Children, too, grapple with problems requiring applications of logical-mathematical thought. How many sheets of paper do we need so that there will be enough for each student in the class to have four? How many forks do we need to set a table with four places? Logical relationships are at the heart of all mathematical thinking, all everyday problem solving.

What do we mean by logical-mathematical thought? We know that Sally is taller than Marie. We know that Marie is taller than Melody. Even if we have never seen Sally and Melody together, we know that Sally is taller than Melody. We are certain. We understand the relationship of Sally's height and Melody's height as a logical relationship that "must be." As adult thinkers, we are certain of our answer without seeing the physical evidence. We do not have to see Sally, Marie and Melody standing next to each other. Young children have not yet constructed this logical way of thinking about problems involving height, or volume, or area, or even ideas that seem as simple to us as the idea of number.

The Development of Operational Knowledge

As logical-mathematical thinking develops, it is by middle childhood capable of producing what Piaget called operational thought or operational knowledge. As adults, we know that the number of objects in a collection remains the same even though the objects may be rearranged. *This is the conservation of number.* We know that two equal length paths rearranged to look different are equally long if they are composed of the same number of units (e.g., the same number of inches). *This is the conservation of length.* We know that if we do not add or subtract mass, the weight of an object is conserved even if we change its shape. *This is the conservation of weight.*

Each of these conservations requires the knowledge of an underlying concept of a unit and, in turn, each conservation is a unit, since a unit is a conserved amount, a "constant." The concept of a unit requires the ability to coordinate a series of classes such that a class of units (e.g., the class of "five units") is coordinated with other classes which are both more and less than it (e.g., the class of "four units" and the class of "six units"). This coordination of classes and series is talked about in more general terms as the coordination of part-whole relationships or inclusion relationships where a part is included in the whole.

The development of operational thought grows through the ability to coordinate part-whole relationships. That is, schemes for assembling (combining) parts into wholes and disassembling (separating) wholes into parts make up the mental activity which, when coordinated in reversible systems, yields the conservation of objects and their quantitative properties (units).

Logical operations are also necessary for true concepts. True concepts are ones that are conserved or remain valid through the process of social interactions where issues of agreement and disagreement are faced. For example, it is possible for two children with operational understanding to come to agreement when two different forms of the same concept are presented. Saying that "all mothers are women," for instance, is equivalent to saying that "some women are mothers." The concepts of "mothers" and "women" remain conserved even though they appear in different linguistic forms. The conservation of objects and ideas depends upon the logical and reversible coordination of inclusion schemes. This reversible coordination is referred to as "operational knowledge."

Piaget used the theory of *operational knowledge* to study a large array of children's thinking. Studies of number, classification, seriation, geometry, space, conservation, causality, probability and chance, and time-movement-speed are some of the more familiar areas of investigation (Piaget, 1965a, 1969a, 1971; Piaget and Inhelder, 1967, 1975; Piaget, Inhelder & Szeminska, 1960). Piaget provided ample evidence that the development of children's thinking is closely tied to a developing coordination of inclusion relations.

In a simplified way we can see that a number (16) is included in other numbers (17) and is also a product of other numbers (15 plus 1). A class (the class of women) is included in other classes (the class of people) and is made up from other classes (the class of women with children and the class of women without children). A position in a series (fourth) is included in other positions (fifth) and is made up from other positions (second and third). A position in space (point *a* is in front of point *b*) is contained in other positions (in front of *c,* which is behind *b*) and is itself composed of other positions (behind a point that we can call *q,* which is in front of *a, b,* and *c*). This same is true of geometry, causality, conservations, measurement, time, speed, distance, and motion. In each of these areas, systematic concepts are dependent upon the composing or de-composing of wholes into parts and the reintegration of parts into wholes or, in other words, the coordination of inclusion relations.

The basic development of these relations is most clearly revealed in studies of children's classification and seriation activity. Piaget relegated the development of logical-mathematical thought to these two areas and saw the other areas of development, such as number, space, geometry, etc., as the product of these basic logical developments (Inhelder & Piaget, 1964).

In classification, for example, classes can be combined to yield new classes, and the new classes can be separated into the original sub-classes; a group of yellow wooden beads could be mentally combined with the blue wooden beads and thought of as wooden and, at the same time, as yellow and blue. This coordination of classes is the hallmark of operational thought because it allows us to clearly see the reversible coordination of part-whole relationships. It also clearly illustrates how the child can conceive of the same referent (yellow beads) as simultaneously existing in separate yet interrelated states (the class of yellow and the class of wooden). That is, an object is a member of a number of classes at the same time, just as a particular idea is part of a number of separate ideas.

Likewise, elements in a series can be combined to yield new elements. Series can be de-composed as well as composed just as in the case of classes. An element in a series can, at the same time, be both "more than" and "less than" other elements in the series. For example, "fourth" is less than "fifth" but more than "third." Before a child's logical mathematical thought has reached the reversible coordination of inclusion relations (part-whole relations), the child will not be capable of true conceptual understanding or systematic logical-mathematical reasoning.

Assessing Children's Development of Mathematical Thinking

The development of logical-mathematical thinking occurs from infancy to early childhood to middle childhood to adolescence and into adulthood. When early childhood educators and other adults attempt to rush the processes of development, young children's lack of a firm foundation can lead to frustration, not only in preschool and the primary grades but later on as well. The development of basic concepts such as number sense takes time. Children often show that they have informal knowledge and can use informal strategies. This forms the basis of more complete conceptual mastery. Ginsburg, Klein and Starkey (1997) provide a comprehensive review of the research on the development of mathematical thinking in young children, including the development of informal understandings.

However, it is often difficult for teachers to assess the child's understanding of mathematical reasoning, both what they know and what they can do with the support of others. For example, Amy is a student in Leni's first grade class. How does Amy understand the concept of number? On dittos, she can draw the numeral "9" under the circle with nine ducks. When Leni asks her to show with her fingers how many nine is, Amy counts on her fingers from one to nine and holds up nine fingers. At first glance it seems that "nineness" is an idea that Amy understands. Leni now follows one of Piaget's assessment procedures (Piaget, 1965a) to see whether Amy has developed the mental ability to understand conservation of number. When a child understands that a given number of objects may be rearranged and that a change in the arrangement does not result in a

Figure 8.3

change in number, the child is able to conserve number. The ability to conserve is fundamental to a true understanding of number.

🔖 Leni places a pile of pennies on the table in front of Amy. Leni selects nine pennies and places them in a row. She asks Amy to take pennies from the pile and to make a row for herself that will have the same amount as Leni's row. Amy does this easily (Figure 8.3). 🔖

🔖 Next Leni moves the pennies in her row so that they are close together. Her row is now shorter than Amy's row, as Figure 8.4 shows. She asks Amy if they both have the same amount of pennies or whether she has more or Amy has more.

Amy replies without hesitation: "I have more pennies because my row is longer." 🔖

Although she can count and recognize the numerals used in mathematical recording, Amy does not truly understand the basic concept of number. Young children like Amy rely on their perceptions, on how things look. Amy might be able to tell that when four pennies are rearranged, there are still four pennies. But when the number is too large to grasp perceptually, she becomes confused. When nine pennies are rearranged, she looks at the two groups to determine which group looks bigger. Answers to problems involving logic are not "out

Figure 8.4

there" in the physical world through better observation. Amy must use logic to construct the answer that rearranging the pennies does not change the total number of pennies.

Some children, in a transitional phase between what Piaget referred to as preoperational and concrete operational reasoning, realize that counting the objects is a strategy for solving the conservation of number problem. These children respond that there is the same number in each line because "both have nine." However, a complete understanding of number comes only when children no longer need to count or check the appearance of the rows, when they understand the logical relationship that "must be so." In time, Amy will master the concept that "the number nine" refers to a relationship among objects that remains stable even when the arrangement of the nine objects changes.

Children's abilities to understand these logical relationships between objects develop during the primary grades as children progress from the pre-operational stage to the concrete operational stage. A few children will understand concepts such as conservation of number and length in preschool; many more in kindergarten and first grade; and most children will understand by second grade.

Mathematics Education Based on the Nature of Mathematics, Children's Development, and Children's Interests

If mathematics education is based on an understanding of mathematics and of children's development and interests, which programs are appropriate for early childhood settings? The National Council of Teachers of Mathematics (NCTM, 1989) proposes that basic goals of mathematics education include (1) students becoming confident of their mathematical abilities and (2) students becoming competent mathematical problem solvers.

What is the role of play in a quality mathematics program? We think that daily life situations and play are the cornerstones of mathematics education in early childhood. A mathematics program centered on daily life situations and play can be a vital dimension of partnerships with parents, particularly since most parents recognize the importance of children's developing competencies in mathematics. Teachers and parents can share examples of how daily life situations and play can foster play and mathematical thinking at school and at home.

Daily life situations are one cornerstone of a mathematics education program in that they provide opportunities for children to informally develop mathematical understandings within the context of their own lives and the lives of people in their community. This now classical principle of John Dewey is emphasized by many math educators. As children encounter and try to solve problems in daily life that involve logical-mathematical thinking, they realize that as their understanding grows, they will become better at solving problems that matter to them, not simply problems on a worksheet.

Young children are intrigued by the problem of wanting to make twice as many muffins as the recipe calls for, or putting eleven raisins in each. How should we encourage them to do that? If four children order a book that costs one dollar and fifty cents, how do they know whether they have the right amount of money from each child?

Lillian Katz and Sylvia Chard's book *Engaging Children's Minds* (1989) includes a wonderful example of a class project focusing on a building being constructed in the neighborhood. A project such as this can involve children in model and map making, the measurement of the site, children's own construction projects with blocks and Legos as well as carpentry involving measurement of length and area. Through such experiences, children come to regard math as something that "happens in your head," rather than the mindless repetition of drills and worksheets.

Play is the other cornerstone of mathematics education. Like daily life, play situations provide numerous activities for children to use their emerging logical-mathematical abilities. Some play situations are children's own reconstructions of events in daily life: setting the table in the housekeeping area so that everyone will have one of each utensil, or making Play-Doh hamburgers that are "just as big" so no one will complain. The children in Peg's kindergarten class have begun to play "gas station," discussing quantities of gas and payment of cash as an extension of play with trikes and wagons.

Play has two characteristics not always found in daily life situations that have further advantages. First, play is flexible. Situations from everyday life may sometimes have a single solution, but problems encountered in play more often have many possible solutions.

Second, play involves children in problems of their own choosing. Children select both the content and the level of difficulty. Three-year-old Raoul has spent several days working on a multi-tiered Lego building. Four-year-old Miriam discovered yesterday that she could make smaller triangles within the larger triangles she constructed on a geoboard. Today she is using colored rubber bands and four geoboards combined to make a square and is "going to town on triangles," Mrs. Ward, a participating parent reports. Miriam's play with the pattern boards illustrates how she integrates and extends her mathematical understanding through play.

≥ In Susan's kindergarten class, some children carefully count out stamps, "take money and make change." They write numerals in the receipt book complete with carbon paper. In contrast, other children simply take the letters, stamp them, and put them in the box. ≥

Games with rules are one form of play that Kamii, DeVries, and others strongly recommend as experiences that encourage the use of logical-mathematical thinking. *Young Children Reinvent Arithmetic* (1985) provides an account of how Constance Kamii, a constructivist theorist and researcher, and Georgia DeClark, a first grade teacher and researcher, developed a first grade math curriculum based solely on group games and situations from everyday life. It includes a chapter by DeClark that chronicles her change from a teacher who relied on direct instruction and worksheets to one who advocates a game-centered curriculum. *Group Games in Early Education* by Kamii and DeVries (1980) also includes descriptions of games and suggestions for appropriate implementation.

Children's Interests

Throughout the book, we have discussed children's interests in the play materials found in traditional early education programs, such as clay, blocks, dramatic play props, sand, water, games, and paints. Another area of interest reflected in children's play is their interest in the adult world, in learning about and understanding the things that adults do. This is shown when they play house, store, or "going to the office." It is also shown when they pretend to read because they are in a literate environment. Similarly, their interest in numbers is shown when they use calculators when playing store or telephones and computers when playing office, thus reflecting their life in a number-literate environment.

SOME BASIC MATHEMATICAL CONCEPTS AND EXAMPLES OF HOW THEY ARE SUPPORTED IN CHILDREN'S SPONTANEOUS PLAY

Through play, children construct understandings of many basic mathematical concepts. In the following sections, we discuss some of the mathematical concepts that begin to develop during early childhood and provide illustrations of how typical spontaneous play activities help children develop, consolidate and extend their understanding of these concepts. Subsequent sections in this chapter focus on how teacher-guided interventions in play as well as teacher-directed mathematics activities can complement spontaneous play activities in order to provide a well-balanced mathematics curriculum.

Spatial Relationships

We begin with concepts that involve spatial relationships. These form a foundation from which more sophisticated geometric concepts can develop as children grow. Basic geometrical concepts are just as fundamental to children's understanding of the world as numerical concepts. As we observe children's interactions with their surroundings, we find that even infants' movements provide experiences with explorations of space and shapes. In fact, more of young children's experiences involve spatial relationships than numerical relationships; yet most adults—and mathematics texts—emphasize numerical concepts.

Young children often explore and play with their spatial environment. As infants, they crawl around and over furniture. Later, they construct mazes with pillows or obstacle courses with chairs. They roll down hills, down slick slides and bean bag chairs. They play with their bodies' shapes as they dance, their round fluid movements becoming linear and staccato. Perhaps this is the first awareness of spatial relationships, awareness of one's own body and its environment. As adults, we see that this fundamental exploration and play involves basic concepts of spatial relationships. These include proximity, enclosed versus open space, vertical versus horizontal movements, and numerous shapes.

Playing "post office" reflects children's lives in a number-literate environment.

Proximity.   Proximity refers to the closeness or separation between objects. When one object is near another, we can say that it is in close proximity.

🙢 Janet paints a tree right next to the house she has just finished painting. She paints grass around it so that the green fills in the space between the tree and the house. In one spot, the tree almost touches the house. After mistakenly painting a small section of the house green, Janet selects a narrower brush and carefully traces around the area between the house and the tree. Through this activity, she is learning about the proximity of the tree to the house. 🙢

Vertical and horizontal.   When something is vertical, it is perpendicular (upright) to the ground or another reference point. When something is horizontal, it is parallel to the ground or another reference point.

🙢 Tomas uses red and blue pegs to make four horizontal rows of alternating colors across the pegboard. He then makes a brilliant strip of yellow pegs that run vertically to the bottom of the pegboard. 🙢

Shapes.   The concept of shape refers to the form of an object. Children frequently have experiences that involve regular shapes such as triangles, circles, and squares. These shapes are called *Euclidean shapes*.

🐚 Nick and Emma stretch rubber bands across the nails of a geoboard, making hexagons and octagons. Noticing the students' interest, their teacher introduces more advanced pattern cards for the geoboard and suggests that they try making their own cards as well. 🐚

🐚 Eight-year-old Brendt has a keen eye for symmetry and yet experiences developmental delays in many areas. He has spent several days cutting squares and triangles of various colors and sizes, using large, beginners' scissors. He carefully places them on the large mosaic he is constructing, exploring the relationships between shapes and sizes by superimposing the triangles on the squares. 🐚

Children also have numerous experiences with irregular or *non-Euclidean shapes*. For example, two-year-old Peggie delights in squeezing the light green Play-Doh through her fingers. She then opens her hand and looks at the Play-Doh form in her palm. It certainly is an irregular, though very interesting, shape!

Relationships Involving Quantity

"Five little monkeys jumping on the bed. . . . " When people think about math, they generally think about relationships involving quantity. How many monkeys were jumping? What is the value of X if six X equals thirty? How high will the temperature be today?

In early childhood, children begin to develop an understanding of the many ways in which we take measure of our world. When we describe aspects of the physical world, we often use concepts that indicate how much there is (e.g., "That's too much milk.") or how many there are (e.g., "Six glasses of milk!").

Continuous quantities.   Continuous quantities refer to those objects whose amounts we don't count, like "a lot of milk" and "a little rice." Although preschool and kindergarten programs have traditionally included materials that foster the exploration of continuous quantities, such as sand, clay, water and even mud (Hill, 1977), primary grade teachers as well are recognizing the value of providing these special materials that playful people of all ages enjoy.

🐚 Steve takes big handfuls of Play-Doh to make giant hamburgers. He rolls out two large circular forms, and declaims, "These buns are still too small," and places the hamburger inside. 🐚

Discrete quantities.   These are the objects whose amounts we count, like "seven cookies" or "three grains of rice." Discrete quantities are also called non-continuous quantities.

🐚 Laurie, Sandra, and Marie are exploring a collection of shells. They divide the collection into three sets of 26 shells each. They then begin to classify their sets, demonstrating their understanding of the relationships between the numbers in the supraordinate and subordinate classes. 🐚

Estimation.   When children estimate they form a judgment of the approximate quantity. They will use this process throughout life, both to make preliminary judgments and to assess how reasonable an answer might be. For example, a fifth grader estimates that 31 times 33 is about 900. Therefore, if she gets the answer 10,230, she would know that there was an error in her calculation. In play-centered curricula, children have many opportunities to develop estimation abilities.

🐚 Sandra says that they need two big blocks. But Melinda finds only small ones and returns to Sandra with an armful of five small blocks. 🐚

Quantifiers.   When children are learning to deal with quantities, initial concepts include "some," "fewer," "all," and "none."

🐚 Bradley selects all the red pegs. When none are left in the tray, he asks Cheryl if she has any red ones. "No," she answers, "none of these are red." 🐚

Equalities and inequalities.   At a young age, children develop the ability to make judgments as to whether two objects or groups are equal or unequal. Indeed, some children seem to spend much of their time focused on whether they have the same quantity of whatever it is that their classmates have!

🐚 *Steve:*   "You took more red [Play-Doh] than me."
   Karen: "Well, I'm the grandma so I get more."   🐚

Seriation.   After children are able to sort objects by one property, for example, a blue color, they learn to order the objects according to "how much" of that property the objects have, for example, light blue to dark blue.

🐚 A second grade teacher has worked with the children to create flannel board cutouts of dolls of four different sizes, each having backpacks and objects that fit in the backpacks of corresponding sizes. Some children are intrigued by these multiple seriation problems and create others of their own. 🐚

   Young children's construction of concepts involving quantity develops over several years. Before children can truly understand number concepts, they begin to understand the concepts of one-to-one correspondence. They learn number names and learn to count by rote. They learn the numerals that represent number concepts. They also begin to understand the difference between ordinal and cardinal numbers.

One-to-one correspondence.   We begin with two sets of objects, such as paper dolls and paper umbrellas. If we place one umbrella next to each doll we have established one-to-one correspondence between the objects in the set of dolls and the objects in the set of umbrellas.

🐦 Craig and Karen establish one-to-one correspondence between the four dolls in their chairs and the quantity of plates and utensils. Tomas has placed the red and blue pegs in one-to-one correspondence in two horizontal rows. As she makes her Play-Doh rings, Laurie places one on each finger. 🐦

Number names.   Number names are the names we use (in our language) to represent the number concepts.

🐦 Maria tells Jason, "I got three, three buttons." Later, in playing in the housekeeping area, she talks to Rosa in Spanish, "Tengo tres, tres botones." 🐦

Rote counting.   Children first develop the skill to say the names of numbers in correct order without understanding the meaning of the number concepts or, consequently, the importance of the order. In rote counting, the order of numbers has no special significance, like the order of letter names when chanting "a, b, c, d. . . . "

🐦 While filling a jar with cupfuls of water, Jeremy counts "five, six and seven, eight." (But the words do not correspond to the actions of either filling or pouring the cup.) 🐦

Numerals.   Numerals refer to the notation or symbols we use to represent the number concept. The same number concept is represented by "15" and "XV."

🐦 Jeffrey sits outside next to the compact pile of weeds pulled from the garden. He bends a stem into different configurations, exclaiming, "It's a 7. . . . Look, now I put a foot on it and it's a 2!" 🐦

🐦 One of the girls in Kristin's first grade class is seated at a desk, working by herself. She draws a picture of a woman with a bubble caption above her head. In the bubble she has printed the numerals in order from 1 to 21. When she notices Kristin looking at the picture she explains that "she's counting in the picture." Then she begins to draw another picture of a counting lady. 🐦

Ordinal numbers.   Ordinal numbers indicate the place order of the object such as the "third child in line." They answer the question "Which one?"

🐦 Alvin looks at the line forming behind him for turns on the new scooter. "I'm first!" he announces. 🐦

Cardinal numbers.   Cardinal numbers indicate the quantity of the set. They answer the question "How many?"

🍃 Mary turns over a Candy Land card: "I've got two yellows." 🍃

🍃 Two girls in Shelley's kindergarten class are playing with a flannel board. There are a dozen flannel pieces for the story. The girls divide them evenly before beginning to make up their own story. They put out one piece for each girl until they both have six. 🍃

Number concepts.   When children truly develop concepts of number, they understand the relationships among numbers, for example, eight is "bigger" than seven. They also understand that a set of objects may be rearranged without changing the number of objects in the set.

🍃 *Tomas:*   "I need three red ones to fill this line."
    Karen: "We don't have three. We just have two."   🍃

🍃 Aimee is building a tower with the 1-inch-square blocks, alternating stories of three and two blocks. Aimee's teacher comes over and asks, "How many layers do you have?" After they count together, Aimee excitedly says, "It's a pattern . . . two . . . three. . . . " as she points to each of the layers. 🍃

Mathematics and Problem Solving

Most of the examples listed above also involve problem solving. In building a symmetrical design with attribute blocks, Ricky adds a green triangle and a yel-

Manipulative materials allow children to explore logical relations between sets.

low hexagon to the right side and then must decide what to add to the left side. Tuan tries to glue a big piece of wood on top of several smaller ones. After the pile falls over several times, Tuan tries putting a larger piece on the bottom, and finds that it works. Lisa and Peter, busy wrapping packages at the post office, are involved in estimating how much paper they need to cover the package and fig- uring out how to solve the problem of having sheets of paper that are too small.

Although problem solving is basic to mathematics, most mathematics curric- ula present children with prefabricated problems. The problems that children face in their spontaneous play and everyday life situations are their own prob- lems. Perhaps it is their "ownership" of these problems that contributes to the extraordinary competencies Vygotsky noted in children's play and lead him to hypothesize that play leads development (see chapter 2).

ORCHESTRATING PLAY IN MATHEMATICS

The general guidelines for setting up the physical environment and developing time schedules presented in chapter 4 apply to our specific concerns about set- ting up an environment that fosters the development of logical-mathematical thinking.

Setting the Stage

How is the physical space arranged? Is there room for children to work on block constructions without constant interruptions from others in a crowded space? Should we put the small wood table near the water table so children can have a place for their assortment of measuring cups and containers?

Are there sufficient materials basic to the support of play that can involve dealing with shapes and number concepts? For example, are there blocks of all kinds? Is there an adequate quantity of differently shaped unit blocks for the creation of diverse structures? Are there several kinds of table blocks such as pattern blocks, attribute blocks, and Lego blocks?

What other materials are available that lend themselves to play and explo- rations of shapes and number? Different types of clay provide opportunities for children to explore non-Euclidean shapes. Pattern boards, tangrams, and pat- tern blocks give children experiences with Euclidean shapes that they can also use to sort. The multitudes of peg-type manipulatives give children chances to think about quantity as well as patterns.

The sandbox and the water table are sometimes neglected areas with cast-off materials and odd containers. Although it is useful to have containers of differ- ent shapes, it is also important to provide graduated sets. A measuring set with a quart pitcher, a pint pitcher, a cup pitcher and a half-cup pitcher gives children a chance to explore equivalencies.

Time considerations are important here as in all considerations of play. How long do children have to work uninterrupted? What are the rules about leaving a Lego construction overnight? What about Cindy, a student with special needs who tends to need closer supervision after 15 minutes in the block area? And if

Jonny has been working intently on his Lego construction for 20 minutes, must he stop because it is his turn to make an apple snack that looks like a turtle?

Accessorizing: Transforming the Environment to Extend and Enrich Play

𝒳 Virginia observed that block play had settled into a routine after five weeks. At the beginning, she enjoyed the great variety of construction. Now she wondered whether things had gotten into a rut. Day after day, block play involved building ramps and racing. The same boys tended to play in the same groups with the same repetitive themes. When car racing first came into vogue, there were several girls involved, and the ramps had become more complex each day. This was no longer the case. 𝒳

Rather than intervene directly through out-of-play suggestions or through entering and redirecting the play, Virginia decided to experiment with accessories placed near the blocks. She placed a box of toy people and animals on the block shelves. This brought several children, including several girls, back to the block area. New themes evolved. The castle-like structures that had been built during the first few days re-emerged. And the car races seemed more complex, with drivers and teams.

𝒳 Pat decided to use an explicit approach with her kindergartners. Three of the children riding trikes had appropriated a hose to play gas station. Pat asked them what other things a gas station had and what they could use. Within a few days, the drivers were busy adding measured oil, checking tire pressure, pumping gallons of gas, and waxing the chrome. 𝒳

Accessorizing is a playful activity for teachers as well as for children. All parts of the environment can be further enriched to stimulate mathematical thinking. This not only helps children acquire mathematical abilities within a meaningful context but also helps them apply their skills and abilities in numerous situations. What can we add to the housekeeping area? Are there measuring spoons, food cans of different sizes, silverware settings for six or eight? Dramatic play accessory boxes can be assembled easily. What is needed to play store? Post office? Bank? Office?

Play-Generated Curricula

Children's play in a rich environment leads to curricular innovations that are more challenging and sophisticated than most traditional curricula. Martine is building a *pyramid* of cubes. Stevie needs another *cylindrical* block. Many standard preschool and primary curricula include identifying and naming the basic two-dimensional Euclidean shapes: triangle, circle, square, and rectangle. But as experienced block builders, sand castlers, and artists, children have the background to support a much more sophisticated mathematical vocabulary. Furthermore, as the above examples illustrate, they have a real need to use the terms in their daily activities.

Ideas for numerous activities and extended curriculum units related to mathematics arise through careful observation and reflection on children's play. After discovering that the "car racers" were fascinated with measuring, Virginia developed a unit on measurement. She introduced a measured roadway for cars, which she marked with colored paper. She then removed the paper and introduced nonstandard units such as popsicle sticks, knots on a string, and Unifix cubes, along with standard measuring units such as rulers, yardsticks, and the popular tape measure. Based on her observations of children's play and her knowledge of children's interests, she included activities that reflected children's fascination with the minuscule and the gigantic, from sprouting seeds to measuring the length of the playground. Many children spontaneously wrote about measuring in their journals, reflecting their interest in numeracy as well as literacy.

ဆ Pat decided to extend her kindergartners' gas station play by including the gas station in her social studies curriculum that centered on "our neighbors." The children discussed their own experiences at gas stations. Many had significant experiences involving cars that they wanted to share—cars breaking down and being fixed, getting stuck on the highway with flat tires, tales of stolen cars, and accidents. These were important communications and the storytellers received serious attention and sympathy from their classmates. The children then drew and wrote about these experiences in their journals. Pat then arranged for a tour of the local gas station. The children saw where the big gas truck pumped the gas into the underground tanks and found out how many gallons were in the tank. The mechanic showed them how he raised a car to check the brakes and how he used a funnel when he added oil. The mechanic also visited the class and showed some of the tools he used. ဆ

ဆ Randi used children's play experiences with patterns to lead into a series of planned activities. She found that several of her preschoolers delighted in making repetitive patterns with colored pegs. She extended this into several organized pattern activities for interested children. These included copying patterns, weaving, and patterned rhythmic clapping activities. ဆ

Curriculum-Generated Play

Children consolidate and extend the experiences they have in their math education program through their spontaneous play. Teachers can consciously create bridges from the mathematics program to play activities. In addition to providing an environment with the basics for rich play, accessories can be chosen to relate to specific aspects of math curriculum goals defined by the teacher, the district, or the state department of education. As in all other subject areas, teachers can promote curricula-generated play by making materials from mathematics activities available during choice time, as well as by assuring that a wide variety of materials are available during this time.

*Teachers can create bridges
from teacher-initiated activities to
play.*

&· Souvanna has been working with her second and third grade students to put together several boxes with materials for playing store. They decided on a post office, a grocery store, and a computer store kit. Souvanna makes sure that there are multiple opportunities for students to practice adding, subtracting and multiplication by including scales, timers, calculators, and student-made pads of sales slips. &·

&· According to her district's kindergarten math curriculum, Marilyn is expected to teach rote counting and recognition of numerals from 1–20. She also decides to experiment with turning the dramatic play area into a store. In addition to a balance scale, she is lucky enough to obtain an old hanging scale. She includes a Bates stamp with numbers that the children can rotate and change. She has several hand calculators and an old adding machine borrowed from a third grade teacher. She also includes tubs of small objects, like Unifix cubes, that can be sold. She is delighted to find that she now has a use for out-of-date coupons and the weekly ads from local supermarkets. The pictures and the numbers make the messages understandable for kindergartners. The store is now open for business! On opening day, workers and customers discover that Marilyn has forgotten an important component: they need money. This leads to a group project of making bills and coins. &·

SUMMARY AND CONCLUSION

Marilyn's and Souvanna's curriculum development flows from formal math curriculum to guided and spontaneous play and back to the development of math curricula activities related to play. This flow is characteristic of integrated and appropriate early childhood education mathematics curricula. When early childhood environments provide opportunities for play with blocks, and materials such as clay, sand, and water, children develop and consolidate mathematical concepts as they play. We can observe activities in which children deal with spatial concepts such as proximity, symmetry, Euclidean, and non-Euclidean shapes; with concepts of measurement such as area, volume, and weight; and with relationships involving classification, seriation, and quantity.

Children think "mathematically" as they use their developing logical abilities to solve the real problems that confront them in play. In solving their own problems, children develop an appreciation for the usefulness of mathematics.

Teachers can then extend play activities into the more formal curriculum. In mathematics education programs that are based on play, we find children who bring energy, joy, and imagination to their own relationships with mathematics.

FOCUSING OUR THINKING

1. Use clay or pieces of yarn to illustrate the concepts that involve spatial relations, for example, proximity, ordering, symmetry, non-Euclidean shapes, and so on.

2. Think of one kind of store that might be set up for dramatic play. Make a list of the materials or props you could provide to foster children's play that involves mathematical thinking. For each type of material, identify several pretend scenes that might arise. Are there materials that might be added to reflect greater cultural diversity or meet children's individual needs?

3. a. Write a 15-minute observation of children playing with blocks. Analyze the observation to determine which mathematical concepts discussed in the chapter were evident in the children's constructions.

   b. Observe the block play of preschool or kindergarten children and second or third grade children. Discuss some similarities and differences across grades and ages.

4. a. Analyze a teacher-initiated, mathematics-related activity and suggest multiple ways in which children could recast this particular activity in their play.

   b. Write an observation of a child's spontaneous play activity and suggest ways in which a teacher could generate curriculum based upon that child's interests.

5. Add to your annotated bibliography of children's books by including some of the many books on play and mathematics.

SELECTED RESOURCES

1. Althouse, R. (1994) *Investigating mathematics with young children*. New York: Teachers College Press.

   Althouse suggests strategies for helping children connect mathematics to daily life. These activities involve students in exploring themselves and their environments, for example, ourselves, our day, our room, our shapes in the classroom, our houses, our city, our playground, etc.

2. Baroody, A. J. (1987). *Children's mathematical thinking: A developmental framework for preschool, primary, and special education teachers*. New York: Teachers College Press.

   This book provides teachers with information needed to understand mathematical concepts more thoroughly as well as an understanding of how children learn mathematics. Baroody discusses the transitions from informal mathematics to the formal mathematics of the intermediate grades.

3. Hirsch, E. S. (1996). *The block book* (3rd ed.). Washington, DC: National Association for the Education of Young Children.

   Teachers have valued this book for several decades. *The Block Book* explains how teachers working with children in preschool through the upper elementary grades can use the many different types of blocks to support development. This updated edition presents the many ways that blocks relate to all areas of the curriculum, including math.

4. Kamii, C. K., with DeClark, G. (1985). *Young children reinvent arithmetic: Implications of Piaget's theory*. New York: Teachers College Press.

   Kamii, a researcher, and DeClark, a classroom teacher, provide insights into early mathematics learning and teaching based on their collaborative research in DeClark's classroom. This book provides a detailed analysis of the ways in which children construct mathematical knowledge through math games and daily life activities.

5. *Teaching Young Children Mathematics* (published by the National Council of Teachers of Mathematics) and *Young Children* (published by the National Association for the Education of Young Children) include numerous articles on teaching mathematics in an integrated curriculum, involving play, the arts, literature, reading and writing, social studies, and daily life activities.

CHAPTER 9

Language, Literacy, and Play

At Patrick's school, "story playing" is a regular activity. Children have the option each day to dictate a "story play" to a teacher. Later it will be enacted by their friends during circle time. Three-year-old Patrick has attended his school for only two weeks. Prior to coming here, he attended a small play group. He has not yet made friends with anyone. He spends most of his time near his teachers, where he has frequently observed the story play dictation but has not yet dictated a story play of his own.

An important breakthrough happens when Patrick quietly tells the teacher he has a story to tell. His first story dictated, he is assured it will be enacted at circle time.

At circle time Patrick is invited to the "stage" (a taped rectangle on the rug). He shyly steps forward. Patrick's story is about "I have lots of friends." Patrick has picked himself to be one of his friends. He has also picked "Margaret" and "Barbara" (two teachers) to be his friends. His teacher begins to read Patrick's story.

Teacher:	"Now, listen to what Patrick's story said. I have THOSE friends. Who wants to be THOSE friends? If Patrick points to you, come right on the stage. All right, Patrick, pick someone who has a hand raised. All right, Sophia, you were picked. Who else? Patrick, look around, here are some more people."

With the teacher's active assistance, Patrick chooses Mary, Ian, and Catherine.

Teacher:	"Good! All right, now, those are THOSE friends. Now the last part of Patrick's story is 'I have THESE friends.' If you want to be THESE friends, raise your hand and Patrick will pick. Patrick, would you like to pick Kelly? You want Felix to be one of THESE friends? All right, Felix, you're one of THESE friends."

Patrick then picks Nathan, who comes on stage and then follows with Jessica, Sam, and Patrick.

Teacher:	"Now, Patrick, you've got THOSE friends and THESE friends. Lots of friends. Do you want your friends to do something while they are on the stage?"
Patrick:	"Yes."
Teacher:	"What would you like them to do?"
Patrick:	(looking at the piano just outside the circle) "Play piano."
Teacher:	"Play the piano? All right, all of you sit down and pretend you're playing the piano. Because that's what THESE friends and THOSE friends do. Good! All of Patrick's friends are piano players. Good!"

What an important day for 3-year-old Patrick! Not only has his story launched him as a member of a community of "storytellers," it has established him as a person who, having started with only two friends, his teachers, now has many new friends, his peers. For sure, Patrick will be chosen to have a "part" in the plays of others.

This example of how play motivates the development of language and literacy and how these literate behaviors in turn enhance play is but one of many that could be taken from early childhood classrooms using play-based curricula. Patrick's story-playing is a guided-play situation in which the teacher's presence, comments, and questions serve to scaffold learning as children convey meaning to themselves and others through oral and written language forms.

In this chapter we take the position that play provides the motivating context for the "literate behaviors" that precede the development of more specific literacy skills (Heath & Mangiola, 1991). Literate behaviors are the numerous forms of expression, both verbal and nonverbal, that fulfill the fundamental purpose of communicating the child's needs, interests, and desires. For the young child, the larger purposes of language provide the motivation and framework for later literacy development. Taking a broad sociocultural perspective derived from Vygotsky, we see language and literacy arising from the collective resources of the classroom, not just in a dyadic mentoring relationship with the teacher wherein the tendency might be, as noted by Nicolopoulou (1996), to "... dissolve the individual in his or her sociocultural context" (p. 376).

With this orientation in mind, we first consider how play and literate behavior support one another and then how a play-based curriculum for the development of literate behavior differs from more traditional approaches that emphasize the direct teaching of isolated literacy skills. Special attention is paid to balancing spontaneous and guided play and to several particularly exciting "authoring" activities: sociodramatic play, story dictation, story playing, and narrative construction in journals and booklets.

PLAY AND LITERATE BEHAVIOR: A NATURAL PARTNERSHIP

In play-based programs, verbal and nonverbal communication through gesture, action, talk and written symbols supports play everywhere from the library corner and the language arts center to the sand table and the dress-up corner. This opportunity to communicate allows children to establish a theme in play and a role for themselves in that play. Signs, even when not legible to everyone, can label things and designate a territory. Communication, via words, numbers, letters, and names, is needed to mark turns or to catalogue and graph things or, more importantly, to convey ideas. Through play, literate behaviors develop most readily. Here are some of the ways the developmental thrust of play and literate behavior serve each other:

1. Play provides a motivating context for literate behavior as children communicate through language to themselves in solitary play and to their peers in social play. Noah is talking to himself at the easel—"Now there is blue,

blue, and now white"—thus schooling himself in the creation of a new color. Or, as Maria says to Juan, "I know what to do to help make a tunnel! You have to dig another hole."

2.   Language and communicative actions allow children to create and share imaginary worlds and participate in the beginnings of narratives. Lizzy, whose mother was ill, wants to play hospital so she can be a doctor who cures someone. She needs to communicate and use language in order to get the play going, attract other actors, and carry out the theme.

3.   Language makes collaboration in play with others possible and facilitates the development of "friendship." Patrick had just two friends before he dictated his "I have lots of friends" story, but a whole classroom of buddies thereafter.

4.   Language in collaborative activities with others enhances the complexity of play by deepening, lengthening, and diversifying play forms. Lizzy's hospital starts with one ward but expands as the children pursue the theme over many weeks to include a "chief of staff" and everything from an operating room to an eye clinic, a pharmacy, and an ambulance unit.

5.   Through her interest in the class's story-play activity, Russian-speaking Masha communicated her desire to play with others and rapidly acquired English skills in this motivating context.

6.   Language in play enables children to share and exchange their knowledge about literacy skills. For example, in the social context of one first grade classroom, which we will discuss more fully later, children are encouraged to spontaneously exchange ideas and share what they know about writing during their regular "Booklet Writing Time." In this way not only the teacher, but classmates as well, are resources for language learning.

Thus, literate behavior, as developed in play and expressed through play, introduces children to language as the medium through which all humans construct a personal identity and participate in the social forms of their culture.

Communication as a Prerequisite for Play with Others

In spontaneous play with peers, children recast their knowledge of the world in terms that are compatible with their interests, competencies, and levels of cognitive, social and affective development. Play in the home corner is not simply a copy of what "mommies and daddies" do, nor is such play merely the children's attempt to repeat stories they have heard read to them or have seen on television.

Spontaneously created play narratives are occasions for children to share and develop a sense of "topic" and "sequence," the basic elements of written texts. In such collaborative literate behaviors, a topic and an ordered sequence are coordinated with play partners, thereby successfully maintaining the "narrative" thread of a cohesive interaction.

In play, children recast their knowledge of the world in new ways.

&. Jelani, playing at a sand tray, initiates the topic of "saving freezing bunnies" by hiding several miniature bunnies in a "safe sand mountain." Cody stays "on topic" when he follows by sprinkling dry sand over the mount, exclaiming, "It's raining, it's raining." He has both successfully followed with an appropriate sequence of activity and expanded the initial topic. &.

In the above vignette, Jelani and Cody verbally coordinated their constructive and dramatic play. Nonverbal expression, however, also contributes to and often provides the communication needed for shared spontaneous action sequences. Tag, chase, or superhero games immediately come to mind. One child sounds the theme music from Batman and, in short order, others take up the theme, and a highly coordinated activity of swooping or "flying" gets underway.

Other nonverbal initiation of topic and sequencing actions occur in settings such as the home play corner, where props have a familiar function for many of the children. For example, when Josh brought the laundry basket to Amanda, who had just picked up the iron and ironing board, he was "on topic." When

Ethan entered the play and began wielding a plastic carrot like a sword, he was clearly off topic and not in synchrony with the ongoing interaction.

Alert teachers will find that often it is these nonverbal aspects of play communication that help them make decisions about intervention strategies. Ethan may need to be guided:

&. "Ethan, in kitchens, carrots don't cut; they are cut. Can you help us by being a carrot cutter? Good. First you cut it, then cook it, then we can eat it!" &

Play as a Form of Communication

Long before acquiring verbal competency, young children are able to convey their needs and desires, likes and dislikes, understandings, competence and knowledge. They do this through gesture and expression and through choice of objects and activity, in both solitary and interactive play. For example, Matthew, a speech-impaired child, indicates his interest in entering Greg and François's play by the nonverbal act of kicking a tire near their play space. In response to Matthew's nonverbal overture for entry into play, the teacher might move in closer to this spontaneous play and assist the potential play-partners in finding a role for Matthew.

Thus, play constitutes its own language. The wise teacher monitors this language closely, finding in it much of the source of the play-based curriculum.

FOSTERING LITERATE BEHAVIORS

The Value of the Play-Based Curriculum

In contrast to some approaches, which stress "drill and practice" and the acquisition of isolated skills such as rote practicing of letter formation or memorization of phonics rules, play-based language arts programs do not foreground the honing of isolated skills unnecessarily. If we attempt to teach such "skills" before children have shown through their interest and motivation in spontaneous attempts to use language in playful engagement, or through dictation of a text or attempts at writing a text themselves, we turn the natural process of language learning upside down. While they often play at letter formation, young children do not use or learn a word's component sounds before they articulate the word—they do not practice the "d," "o," and "g" sounds before saying "dog"— and they do not start with more simple sentences before expressing complex emotions or desires. It is through nonverbal communication—gesture, interaction, expression—that children initially communicate desire or pain. Only after using language in these ways do they come to consider adult norms (Heath & Mongiola, 1991).

Contrary to traditional views, the *direction of the learning process* is not necessarily linear and progressive. Research tells us that for some children it may be curvilinear or cyclical, and even sometimes regressive, only to spiral out again later (Heath & Mangiola, 1991).

• In guided-play activities, Nathan dictated many stories, all of which revolved around the Beatles and seemed to be attempts to mimic adult fiction he had heard. As he became more integrated into the peer-group culture of the school, his stories began to have greater personal impact. At this point, teachers noted that his previously long-winded and convoluted narrative style seemed to "regress" to a more age-appropriate level. The urgency of Nathan's need to express something meaningful to his peers took precedence over literacy skills that were not well established. When Nathan's narratives were intended to *communicate*, they were a model of economy and directness. •

Despite some earlier notions, the *rate of learning* does not always proceed at an incremental rate. It may be marked by "quantum transformations"—great leaps in progress and "periods of latency," that is, stretches when there appears to be no progress at all (Heath & Mangiola, 1991). Learning for young children is determined largely by what the child wants to know and when he or she needs to know it. To illustrate this point, we look at the development of an accurate concept of gender in children's storytelling efforts.

The three-year-old child typically begins story constructions with fuzzy, gender-undifferentiated bunnies and cuddly creatures and, upon approaching four, introduces more seemingly gender stereotypic characters as he or she advances to greater narrative competence. Often the four-year-old child may begin repetitively to relate gender-stereotypic stories derived from the media and peer culture. Familiar media-derived heroes and princesses seem to be taking over the classroom (Nicolopoulou & Scales, 1990). This period of seeming stagnation and creative impoverishment actually serves to mark the child's membership in his or her peer group. It is followed, at ages five and six, by a spurt of more creative and elaborate narrative, encompassing and interweaving this same stereotypic material with material based on personal interest and family experiences and expectations (Nourot, Henry, & Scales, 1990). In preschool and elementary classrooms the opportunity to "play" freely with the possible social ambiguities of thematic choices in narratives provides occasion for classroom dialogue. As Dyson (1993, 1997), Paley (1995, 1997) and others have noted, these dialogues are often centered around issues of power, fairness, gender, ethnicity and culture. Such dialogue provides not only a motivating context for the growth of language and literacy; it can also provide the context for the development of more accurate notions of a social self within a social world. The impetus for literacy and social development is augmented by honoring children's authoring and by providing many opportunities to play at story construction during well-defined periods of the day. Children will actively seek the skills they need from all the social and literacy related resources of the classroom and beyond when their storytelling and story writing is foregrounded.

While the diversity of many classrooms is a rich resource, Heath and Mangiola (1991) remind us that agents and settings of language learning are not limited to teachers and schools. When children have opportunities for spontaneous

Once there was a
lady who lived
in a house and
didn't have anything
to eat.

Figure 9.1
Angela's Drawings.

play in early childhood classrooms, they generate a curriculum that integrates all their experience and knowledge and that is, therefore, naturally relevant to both their cultural and personal lives. This natural relevance promotes development.

This is poignantly revealed by the case of Angela, who illustrated her traumatic story of poverty and homelessness, then dictated its text to a teacher she trusted (Figure 9.1, pages 186–189). Angela's story reveals not only the sadness of her life outside school, but also her need to communicate her special story. It demonstrates the efficacy of the play-based curriculum to meet that need. Furthermore, the story's wording—"Once there was" and "The End"—reveals that Angela is beginning to grasp the social conventions surrounding the literate activity of storytelling. For homeless Angela, "school" learning was intertwined with other more basic learnings of mere survival.

How the Play-Based Literacy Curriculum Serves Children of All Cultures and Languages

Today's classroom is richly peopled with children of African American, Native American, Hispanic, Asian, and European backgrounds. These children may bring to school markedly different cultures, languages, or ways of handling the English lan-

guage. Traditionally, educators have attempted to ignore sociocultural differences in the classroom. But differences arising from the uniqueness of race, culture, gender, and lifestyle can be used in the service of education. In attempting to attain equity by neutralizing our classrooms we fail to notice that children of different backgrounds bring rich variety to play patterns and language (Genishi & Dyson, 1984).

Books of traditional stories from different cultures, tapes of songs in different languages, and ethnic dress-up clothes and eating utensils help all children learn that there are different ways to live and communicate. In one particularly diverse classroom, centers and materials were labeled (with the help of parents) in English, Russian and Chinese to reflect the various cultures and languages of the students. In classrooms where all cultures are recognized and accepted, all children feel valued.

🍂 Tom's mother and Portuguese grandmother visit his first grade class. His grandmother reads a folktale from a well-illustrated book while Tom's mother translates. Later that morning in directed play, the three of them teach all the children a Portuguese hand clapping game that is accompanied by a simple rhyme. For the next week, the class practices together. After that, it becomes part of the students' repertoire of hand clapping games. 🍂

This woman has a home and doesn't

have any soap, so she had to buy some to wash her dress.

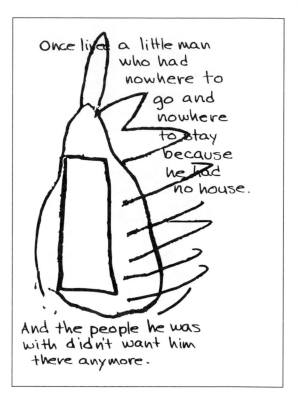

Once lived a little man who had nowhere to go and nowhere to stay because he had no house.

And the people he was with didn't want him there anymore.

Figure 9.1   *continued*

It is in the play-based environment that opportunities for second language acquisition are paramount. In contrast to traditional settings where adults often control the language spoken, the play-based program exposes children to the full range of their peers' language abilities. It is particularly important to involve native speakers who can extend children's opportunities to use their primary language as well as learn English. Bilingual teachers, aides, parents, volunteers, and cross-age tutors can all support a program that is language varied for all students.

Play encourages limited English speakers to develop their own language competence for its strategic value in social relations. This frequently occurs in interactions involving few or no words as shown in the following examples:

Sylvie, newly arrived from France, is playing at the water table, pouring water back and forth between two cups. Sarah, standing next to her, is pouring water into the water wheel. Sylvie watches, then wordlessly begins to take turns.

Mauricio walks over and picks up a stop sign in the trike area. He steps up to the line painted on the blacktop and orders, "Stop!" to Chris and Sarah. Chris stops, but Sarah rides on. Mauricio runs after her calling, "Stop. I'm the police. You stop!"

Everything was stolen and there was nothing left.

The End.

🐚 Consuela has vivid feelings about the rainbow she has just drawn. She gestures to her teacher to write "Rainbow" on it, and that label becomes one of the first words she learns to recognize. Later that month, she paints another rainbow and tells her teacher, "Write 'I love rainbows.'" 🐚

In this last example, note that play elicits emotions, and emotions beg for expression. Consuela now understands the communicative potential of art and words. Both types of expression allow Consuela to share her feelings about rainbows with others.

In the following, more lengthy, anecdote drawn from records of story plays created by an immigrant child, we document her acquisition of a second language as well as her integration into the play culture of an American preschool classroom.

🐚 Having recently arrived from Russia, Masha spoke little or no English on entering a preschool program in the fall of the year. She had attended preschool in Russia and was very accomplished in dance, movement and gymnastics as well as drawing, painting and crafts. At the school, Masha contented herself with these pursuits for most of the fall and winter, rarely going outside to the play yard. In these activities she received a great deal of acknowledgment from her teachers, and much time was spent near them at the drawing table. At circle time she was very attentive when children's story plays were enacted. Despite this interest, Masha had laboriously dictated only one story in October, near the beginning of the school year. The text of her first story resembles a Haiku poem. This is what Masha dictated:

> "My head and my eye.
> My veil . . . white.
> And play veil.
> Someone pull my veil and play."

In her limited English she has tried to recapture the excitement of whirling with colorful scarves in dancing with the other children.

After this first attempt, Masha did not dictate any stories for many months. But she had begun to make friends at the drawing table, where she was also near a teacher most of the school day. Finally, early in April, Masha rushed to her favorite teacher in the school, announcing urgently that she had a play to write, her first since October. It was a pivotal story that reflected her social development at the time. In her story we hear a poised four-and-a-half-year-old obliquely announcing that she is now ready to enter the world of her peers fully. She symbolically bids her teacher and mentor (and the drawing table as well) a gracious farewell. Tactfully, she honors her teacher by giving the only character in this play the teacher's name. Listen to Masha's story.

"Once upon a time there was a little girl named Janet. And she so much liked to draw pictures, beautiful pictures. And she stopped drawing beautiful pictures and then she started to climb up the tree. And that's the end."

Now the stories began to come fast and furious. She dictated nineteen stories between April and the first of July. They vividly reflected her advancing development through the expression of her changing social motivations and her acquisition of greater and greater fluency in English as well as a grasp of the peer culture. First to appear was the familiar character of Cinderella, which she also knew in Russian. Soon other Disney-inspired figures began to enter—Pocahontas and Captain John Smith. She made sure that there were many roles so that all her new friends could participate; sometimes she multiplied the characters so that no one was left out. In order to have parts for everyone, some stories involved two Cinderellas and several others had multiple characters named Pocahontas, distinguished as "a big one" and "a little one". She wrote several stories about "Fly Horses" and, much to the teacher's consternation, many little horses began "flying" about the play yard as the Fly Horse theme daily became more integrated into the peer culture. Masha, despite admonitions to slow down, kept flying. She had moved from the schoolroom and made the whole school her own and she was not about to stop flying at this point.

The following story dictated in May is about Pocahontas. It demonstrates Masha's mastery of English over a very short period of time. While only a little over a month has passed since the story about "Janet," note how she has grown not only in her fluency in the use of English, but in her use of literacy conventions as well. In terms of social development, she displays a well-developed sense of herself as a participating member of the peer group as she integrates and reproduces themes of her life in a new school in a new culture.

"Once upon a time there came little Pocahontas. And then another big Pocahontas come and she picked little Pocahontas up in her arms. And then there came the Mico, and the two little kids. And then there came a Flit with Mico together and then they started to play. And then John Smith came and Pocahontas with the little. They were both scared of John Smith because they didn't know him. And then the little kids come and Pocahontas' father too. And then the little kids started to play with the father. And then big Pocahontas come to the grandma tree in the forest and there was around water and the two Pocahontas started to swim in the little boat and then the little tiny bird, she scared of the grandma tree and little Pocahontas she go 'mama, mama help me.' And then mommy she did not come. The Ghost come and then the good ghost come and the ghost said he said, 'I'm a ghost this only a costume.' That's the end."

Casting for this story included everyone in the story circle.

By June, a few months before kindergarten, Masha's stories began to express her growing awareness of herself as ultimately becoming independent not only from her teachers, but also from her parents. Listen to Masha reflect on growing up.

"Once upon time there was a little baby with her mother. And then the mother said to her little child, 'Look, child, there's your father who's coming.' The father, he come and he showed the little child a toy. And the little child grew up into a grown-up girl and that's the end."

But the ending of childhood carries a bit of anguish for Masha, which is expressed in her very next story, also dictated in June. Masha related a brief tale about two friends whose parents die while the friends "play hide and seek. . . . And then they were sad for a long time they didn't see their family and their family was dead." Possibly the consideration of independence from her family was a bit too frightening for Masha, and she modified the ending of her story by saying: " . . . and then they come alive again. They said 'hello, we missed you, we didn't be dead, we was only sleeping.'"

Masha's stories are a vivid record of one child's growth in language acquisition and social integration and reveal, in a minor way, how her personal play theme (Fly Horses) was integrated into the culture of her American classroom.

(Scales, 1997, pp. 2–5) ❧

HONORING THE IMPORTANCE OF LITERATE BEHAVIORS

A group of fast-paced four-year-old superheroes were stimulated to elaborate their play when their teacher suggested they draw pictures showing the features of their characters' costumes. Each child excitedly drew his or her character, and the teacher then labeled each character's essential items of apparel—one character, for example, wore a belt with an "M." As "superhero experts," the children used their language skills to give the teacher the information she needed to label their characters accurately.

Had the children been older, the teacher might have asked for their help in spelling, and some of the children could have rendered their own labels or created cartoon books about the adventures of the famous turtles. Language would certainly be used to verify and dispute the details of the pictures and the order of the story's sequences. Other media could be harnessed as well—an audiotape narrating the project with speech and music. All these types of communication—writing, drawing, oral expression, and the use of different media—serve as stepping stones to more developed literacy concepts.

Writing and Graphics

Writing is critical in helping young children grasp the concept of "story" or "narrative," and the perspective this implies (see, for example, Dyson, 1989). Writing, in turn, occurs as part of a social context. It often emerges from the shared verbalizations surrounding scribbling, drawing, labeling, letter writing or dictating that lead to the child's first understanding of the requirements of written communication. Whether the subject that is shared with friends is superhero lore (what are they wearing, who did what to whom first?) or other media-derived fantasy creatures (what color is this one's hair or attire?), the child comes to grasp the relationships of an author to a text and a text to a reader.

Subsequently, children will come to understand that stories follow specific narrative conventions (such as "once upon a time" or "the end"), and will use such conventions appropriately as they become storytellers for themselves and others. Just as Angela began her story by marking new episodes with "Once there was . . . " and closed with "The End," eventually she will learn to mark sequences within her story, first by using the simple device of "and then," later by linking events causally ("because," "and so") as she encounters the need to explain her sequencing.

Children can be encouraged to send notes to each other by making a mailbox for intraclass mail out of a sturdy twelve-section beverage box. (If there are more than twelve children in a class, more boxes may be used.) The box is laid on its side, exposing twelve mail slots, each labeled with a child's name. Bookmaking and publishing would be encouraged in such a center by setting out a few pages of paper stapled together or with holes punched to receive yarn ties. In one class, an autograph book proved a successful activity for all when one child introduced the idea (Koons, 1991). More high-tech activities for older children in primary school can involve computer journals and E-mail (See chapter 11).

Another exciting possibility involves journal writing, wherein the child creates a written and/or drawn record of his or her experiences. The writing itself may be done by the child independently or with the teacher's help or may be dictated to the teacher. Journals can be prepared by adding pages to a construction paper cover or using binders with fairly sturdy paper, unlined for the younger children, possibly with lines for older beginning writers.

LANGUAGE AND LITERACY LEARNING IN
AN EARLY ELEMENTARY CLASSROOM:
THE MOTIVATING POWER OF PLAY

Erikson noted that elementary school age children become interested in mastery and the need to prove themselves. By first grade they are more ready to participate in the lives of adults, and in coming to terms with the social expectations of teachers and parents. To illustrate how play can provide motivation for language and literacy learning in the more formal context of elementary school classrooms, we very briefly share some observations of a teacher of a first grade language and literacy program.

Parents of children involved in whole language programs sometimes question how children progress from the drawing, scribbling, dictation, pretend writing and invented spelling that we know so well from preschool, to the ultimately necessary formal conventions of literacy. To answer these questions about elementary school as a context for play and learning, we examine an important element of a very effective curriculum developed by a first grade teacher whose school is located in a large urban area (Scales, 1997).

Many of the literacy activities we will be describing will be familiar to you. Harriet, the first grade teacher in the following anecdote, is not a radical innovator (spelling tests are given, for example). She views herself, her classroom environment, and all her students as the major resources in a sociocultural context that enhances language and literacy learning. Importantly, she is wise enough to provide ample time for children to integrate their emerging knowledge through playful engagement with the social resources of this classroom. The motivation and practice necessary to acquire skills in letter-sound recognition, rules for capitalization, punctuation, and dictionary spelling augmenting children's invented spelling is provided primarily through the children's spontaneous act of writing about things that interest them rather than through unattached repetition. This respect for "authoring" in many forms manifests itself in the centrality of a small group activity called "Booklet Writing Time," where Harriet and trained parent volunteers support children in guided play surrounding writing and drawing. After Booklet Writing Time, opportunity is provided for children to take the "author's" chair to read or tell the class about what they have written or drawn. Sometimes Harriet points out special features she notices, such as asking them to "listen to Michelle's story and when we get to the point where people are talking, put your hand up, and when they stop, put your hand down. That's called 'dialogue.' Doesn't it make this piece of writing more interesting?"

After lunch, a period of spontaneous play again offers opportunities to write and draw, and numerous pieces are produced by the children during this time. These may be as simple as a block builder's sign saying, "Don't shake the table," or a "Kwyot plas" if that is necessary. Or they may be as complex as the letter to the principal written by Emilie and Vanessa requesting better "pensiels" (Figure 9.2). Some groups may create more extended pieces, such as a play or a class newspaper.

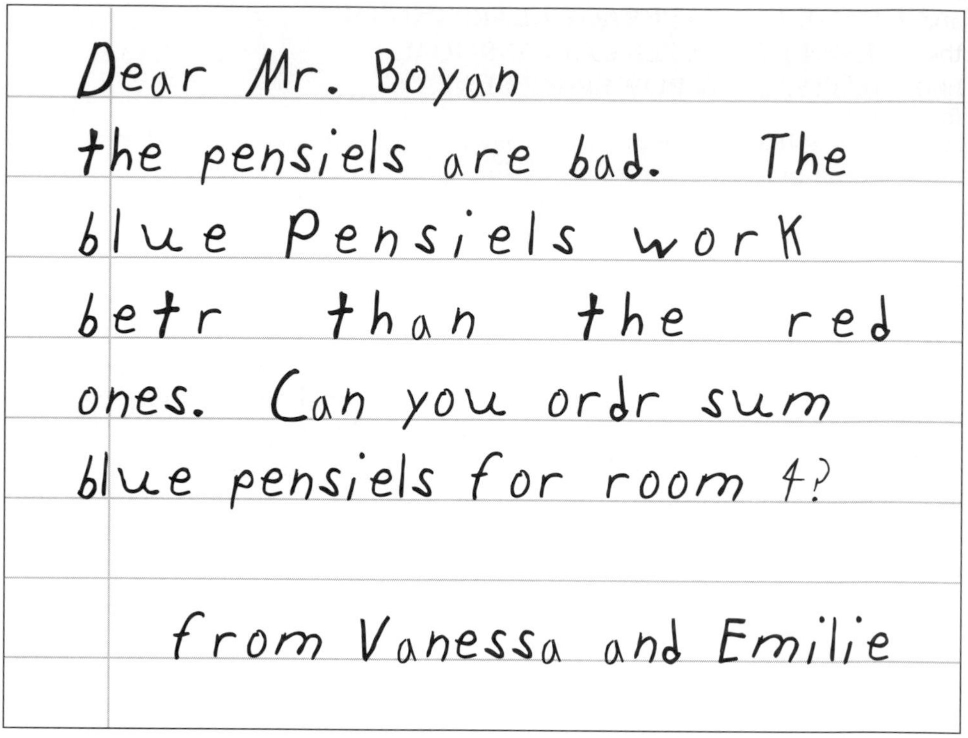

> Dear Mr. Boyan
> the pensiels are bad.   The
> blue Pensiels work
> betr   than   the   red
> ones. Can you ordr sum
> blue pensiels for room 4?
>
>   from Vanessa and Emilie

Figure 9.2
Emilie and Vanessa's letter to the Principal.

During these spontaneous and guided play periods, the generative power of play provides the motivation for children's authoring. Like the ephemeral quality of play itself, the creative flow of writing is fleeting, not to be interrupted by premature corrections of "form." In this classroom, neither the teacher nor parent volunteers spell words for children, but encourage them to try to figure out for themselves how words should look. Later, children are guided to learn correct form as individual development dictates. Here is an observation from this classroom:

It is Booklet Writing Time, and Jomar invites his teacher to look at his booklets. He has filled the pages of several. Each entry is dated and he and his teacher start with the earliest. A vivid illustration accompanies this first story: "THiS Is MY SPAS-MANHEEIZFLIEEN."

Pointing to the word "THiS," Jomar's teacher Harriet comments, "I noticed you changed "THiS." How did you know the dictionary spelling? Jomar murmurs, "I learned it and I changed it." "Right, it was a spelling word and you went back and fixed it," his teacher responds.

Carefully drawing a line with a ruler well below Jomar's writing and illustration, she says to Jomar, "Let's do some dictionary spelling because you already know a lot about dictionary spelling." She carefully copies the first word of Jomar's story and then comments enthusiastically that "Is" is also spelled "just right too, except would we put an 'I' like that there?" Jomar has used a capital "I." "No, we would dot it," Jomar replies. His teacher carefully writes "is" with a lower case "i" after "This." Harriet and Jomar read through his story, and Jomar is invited to point to the three words in his story he would like to be able to spell the "dictionary" way.

Jomar points to SPASMANHEEISFLIEEN and they discuss the "soft" sound of "c" in spaceman, and Jomar is invited to spell along as his teacher writes "spaceman." Later she comments, "You remember, we have just learned about 'ing' endings," and Jomar is guided in his dictionary spelling of "flying." As they proceed through his story, she demonstrates that a "two finger space" is a good rule for separating words from each other. (Morrison & Grossman, 1985) 🐝

If you remember, Jomar's teacher talked not about his most recent piece of writing, where he may still be integrating recently acquired knowledge, but about one of his earliest efforts. In this way Jomar comfortably appropriates formal skills he has already nearly acquired in the context of his own writing. In the process of "proofing" his earliest efforts at "authoring," Jomar becomes what Harriet likes to call a witness to his own growth and development. As Michelle, one of Harriet's other students, reflects on her own growth as an author, she exclaims: "At first you couldn't even read what I wrote!" In this classroom, Michelle knew she was an author before she knew how to write (Morrison, 1985). Whereas younger children like Masha acted out their reflections in dictated story plays, older children are more able to put them into words.

In Harriet's first grade classroom, the children's frequent engagement in writing during their spontaneous play periods is a testament to play's value as a catalyst in their appropriation and integration of the resources of a rich sociocultural context. The varied pieces of writing children produce in this first grade classroom as well as the story plays created by preschoolers provide documents through which the children can observe their own personal progress as authors or playwrights and become "witnesses to their own development."

How the Multimedia Extends Meanings of Literacy

The wealth of different media available today argues against narrowly defining literacy as the acquisition of specific reading skills. Consider the range of possibilities. Oral storytelling stimulates the imagination of the listener and contributes to reading as a habit. Books, of course, contribute to knowledge of literature and, if illustrated, appreciation for art.

Audiotapes and radio contribute strongly to imagination and may influence speech ability and comprehension. Movies, videos, and television, today's principal storytellers, contribute to the child's imagination, speech, and ability to listen and comprehend, as well as to an appreciation of music and art. *Interactive computers* may make the broadest contribution across all areas, from imagination to potential for control of the medium and creativity in its use (Brown, 1986). (See chapter 11.)

DYNAMIC APPROACHES TO PROMOTING
LITERATE BEHAVIOR THROUGH PLAY

Young children spontaneously initiate sociodramatic play. In the case of three-year-olds this may occur more frequently in home play areas (as in "playing house"). In the case of four- and five-year-olds, sociodramatic play may occur more often in open areas with themes of superheroes and princesses.

Careful observation of the cadence of children's speech and gestures reveals when sociodramatic play is coordinated and cohesive, if the children know who is taking part and who is not, and what the play is about (Cook-Gumperz & Scales, 1982, 1996; Scales & Cook-Gumperz, 1993). A well-coordinated play scenario is, in a sense, a story the children are telling with an agreed-upon theme and cast of characters.

The sensitive teacher can enhance the development of this literate behavior by responding to, or even helping to establish, a sociodramatic play interaction. He will want to avoid dominating the dramatic play with his power as a grownup, but, on the other hand, abdicating his educative responsibility must also be avoided. In other words, a balance must be struck between spontaneous and guided play.

Using Drama Techniques to Enhance Sociodramatic Play

One way to support more complex sociodramatic play is for the teacher to enter into what English drama educator Dorothy Heathcote called "role" within children's sociodramatic play (Bolton, 1985; Buege and Stewig, 1994; Wagner, 1976, 1990). Heathcote developed an extensive repertoire of drama techniques for the classroom emphasizing strategies that enable children to create and elaborate roles in spontaneously created dramas that center around historical or social themes. One example is a drama that might be developed centered around the needs of zookeepers concerned with animal caretaking at a zoo. One can envision the many roles that could be generated from that scenario. Other scenarios she developed involved sudden changes due to technological advances: how does one fishing village confront the loss of their livelihood when a neighboring village upstream begins fishing with large nets instead of the old traditional ways? On another occasion, Heathcote worked with older elementary school children in developing a drama involving a funeral home (the children's idea). A historical drama also developed around prisoners of war in World War II (Three Looms Waiting).

Drama themes are generated from the children's suggestions and with minimal props and direction. Children playfully elaborate these dramas from their own knowledge and understanding. These methods have been particularly successful with elementary school-age children. Heathcote suggests that in initial fragile phases of the establishment of a drama interaction (or a play interaction), the teacher's interventions must be subtle. By taking a role that enables the teacher to speak indirectly about the unfolding play or drama, its context can be supported as well as shaped. One teacher adapted Heathcote's drama methods to intervene in preschool children's spontaneous play. In the following hypothetical example, the teacher, speaking as if she were a member of the hospital governing board whose office was located "upstairs," has taken a role that allows her to withdraw from direct involvement once the play interaction is under way (Scales, 1970). The teacher might wish to remain indirectly available via a pretend telephone or intercom, thereby being able to return to help negotiate any breakdown in the interaction or expand upon a child-generated "problem." The teacher intervened in the following way when she decided that shooting play was getting out of hand in the playground of her school:

The teacher, adapting Heathcote's drama methods to a spontaneous play scenario, picked up a portable phone (made of a nearby unit block), and called out, "We need a mobile ambulance unit to handle the wounded in the play yard!" In this manner, she temporarily stepped into the play frame by taking a "role" in order to quickly and indirectly reshape the context of the children's play. Following this intervention, the play took a more positive turn when many of the gunslingers stored their arms in the "armory" the teacher had created under the climber in order to enlist in the "medical units." Particular favorites were "Pharmacy" and "Intensive Care" scenarios, where children could prepare vials and bottles of brightly colored medications, dispense pills, bandages and splints, and monitor IV's made of plastic tubing, funnels, and colored water.

This *expansion of the theme* from random shooting play to hospital play engaged many more players. The theme of the play changed again on another occasion, when the teacher merely gave the children armbands marked with a red cross. Less mature players could now be included, and the older children could and did assume more complex roles in an elaborated play theme that entailed greater interactive challenge.

The teacher should also *shift responsibility for advancing the play to the children* at a later time. The teacher, who in the earlier example was only member of the "hospital governing board," might now appear to be "helpless" to know what to do next or to know who is in charge. In this way, the teacher can subtly shift her "teacher power" and authority to invent over to the children (Heathcote & Herbert, 1985). In the hospital drama, the teacher turned to Jason, addressing him as a colleague:

"Jason, have you been 'certified' by the governing board of the hospital to serve as its 'director'?" "Yes," he replied. "Have you appointed your 'chief of staff'?" "Yes." And with the seriousness of "role" modeled by his teacher, Jason chose Juan. The two of them paired up to dispatch the various emergency units to save victims from a fire on the large climber. The "member of the hospital board" disappeared to set up a "disaster control center" with several toy phones.

Jason and Juan were left to negotiate who would drive the emergency truck, who would carry the fire hoses, and who would bring the victims back on stretchers (small aluminum ladders with blankets and four aides).

Avoiding some pitfalls.   The teacher in a "role" must not forget that it will always be necessary to *return to being the teacher*—signaling this shift in relationships by a change of voice or posture—for it is inevitable that the children will have to go home, no matter how much fun they are having. Shoes and socks and jackets and sweaters must be found and projects stored and the school tidied for tomorrow. Hence, whatever part in the play the teacher creates for himself, it must allow movement in and out of a role. And, again, the teacher's role should never be a central one; it should only be one that allows him to be available when needed to support, guide, and sustain the play, but never to direct or dominate.

Moreover, in assuming his "role" in play, the teacher must *communicate clearly that the drama is part of the world of pretend*, the world in which things are only make-believe. Otherwise, the children may become confused about the reality of their play.

Consider the teacher who failed to do this. After spending several days with a child participating in constructing a robot out of cardboard boxes, tape, and wires, she was shocked when, on completion of the robot, her partner demanded that she "plug it in!" It is impossible to describe the look of disappointment on the child's face when told, "It's only make-believe." One can only speculate that the child's confusion arose because he thought he had entered the powerful world of adults, where things "really" happen, whereas the teacher felt she had entered the child's world of make-believe, where all things are possible because they are only pretend. The teacher had much to learn from this episode.

Story Dictation and Story Playing

Do you remember Patrick, the three-year-old who dictated the story "I have lots of friends"? By encouraging a child to dictate stories to be acted out later by classmates, the teacher provides an outlet for the child's deeply felt needs—in Patrick's case, the need for friends. Furthermore, because of the urgency of the child's desire to communicate those needs, and because of the autonomy allowed by virtue of the *child* being the one to choose the subject, story, and players, the teacher establishes fertile ground for the development of literate behaviors.

The story dictation/story play curriculum, articulated largely by Vivian Gussin Paley (1981, 1986), recalls Sylvia Ashton-Warner's (1963) discovery that reading is easily mastered if the words to be learned are autonomously chosen by the child (for these are the words that have personal and emotional impact for the child). It is a literacy and play curriculum that lends itself to applications in pre-kindergarten, kindergarten, and elementary classrooms, allowing opportunities for children to move from dictating story plays to eventually writing their own creative texts.

The following are a few examples from the stories dictated to teachers in one school over the course of several years. In these teachers' classrooms, the story dictation and story play curriculum are quite simple. The opportunity to dictate a story is offered every day. A record of who has dictated and who has not is kept so that all may have a turn. Some first and many second grade children write their own stories and read them or enact them for their classmates (Dyson, 1997; Scales, 1997).

In comfortable play spaces children share and exchange their knowledge of language and literacy.

Minimizing the addition of props to enhance children's use of their imagination, the stories are "acted out" by the child-author and others whom she or he selects. For children not yet reading in preschool and kindergarten, the story may be read by the teacher and the acting spontaneously performed with a bit of minimal direction from the child-author and the teacher. A record of these stories, along with field notes on the dramatization, is kept in the portfolio of each child.

Laronda.   Laronda came from a large, hard-working and strict family where pretense was frowned upon. She differed from her peers in class who were, for the most part, offspring of university-based, academically oriented families. She dictated a number of story plays during her second year at preschool when she was four. An enthusiastic story teller, she quickly grasped the conventions of storytelling and story playing.

Laronda was popular with her classmates, and her stories mention many of her friends by name. In content, the stories are tied to themes and activities of her home life, the world of work, and the domestic comings and goings of an extended family. Laronda's stories rarely mention "play" as an activity and incorporate few fantasy elements. Here are five stories as they were presented chronologically over the course of the school year.

Jack had a sister. Amy ate dinner. After that her mother bought a chair. (November)

Once upon a time there was a party. David met a lion. He had a sister, her name was Lizzi. Then she painted a picture for her grandma. The End. (January)

Once there was a sister, and there was a pretty girl. The pretty girl got lost. Then their boyfriends caught them. Then they went home to eat dinner. After that they went over to their grandma's house. And then their daddy came home. Then their mother went to work. Then the sister had a cold. That's it. (February)

Once there was a bear. It got in the bed and fell asleep. Then there was a pretty girl who came home. Then when she came home she saw a bear in her bed. Then he died. Then she took him out and put it on the street. Then the mother came home. Then she cooked the dinner. Then she ate it all up. (March)

First there was a bear. And he hurt himself by falling on some wood. Then he played with his dollies. Then his sisters come home. Then mom came home with the baby. Mom found some broken glass in her kitchen. Then dad came home and ate dinner. Then their Grandma came home from work. Then they all went to bed. In the morning one of his sisters woke up and went to school. His other sister woke up and went to the store. The End. (April) &

From her field notes on other children's plays, the teacher noted that Laronda was frequently called upon by other children to play the role of "Queen" but never the "Princess." This, despite the fact that in some of her own stories Laronda created a "princess" role for herself, although one who "left because she had to cook." Apparently the children recognized something "adult" about Laronda's pragmatic world. There are few parties there. There are domestic chores to be performed, there is work to "go to" and "come home from."

Other children in this mostly middle-class group placed themselves at the center of the worlds they created, often being taken to the park to "play," whereas the voice of Laronda was part of a choir of family voices. The teacher wondered about the impact of Laronda's group-oriented culture that discouraged too much focus on the self, play, and imaginative expression. How much of Laronda's intellectual energy in her future schooling might be spent on managing and bridging the two disparate worlds?

Jason.   Jason, a kindergartner, is the only child of an adult-dominated household. His parents are adamantly opposed to gun play and vigilantly monitor his television viewing to minimize his exposure to violence.

During the year, Jason ambivalently and somewhat cautiously attempted to establish himself as a member of the peer group, particularly with a group of the more vigorous boys in the class. The first of his last two stories he dictated shocked his parents:

& Once upon a time there was a dragon and he went home. And he went to his friend's house. And then he went to another friend's house. And then he saw a horse. And then he saw another horse and killed the horses. And then he went back home. And then he saw ten hundred million horses and killed them. And then he saw some people and he killed them. And then he saw everything that's alive in the whole wide world and he saw all his friends and he killed them. ❧

Building the dramatic momentum of this chronicle of devastation, Jason's dragon goes to "New York," where "he killed everything else." He then goes to school and kills his teachers, all his friends and the people at school, and "knocked down all the trees of the whole school."

Finally " . . . he knocked down the whole world and the whole sky and every plant. The End."

When Jason's alarmed mother queried him about this play, he turned to her with twinkling eyes and said, "I *was* a dragon, you know." This did not surprise the teacher, who had already seen in Jason's previous stories a little dragon shyly trying to show its face. She sensed that this story was Jason's declaration of independence. It unleashed the full power of his imagination as well as his ability to express latent aggression in a literate, creative way.

Here is Jason's next (and final) kindergarten story:

❧ Once upon a time there was a Ghostbuster. And then the Ghostbuster went to his friend's house and instead of his friend there was a dragon. And then the dragon said, "Bye, bye. I don't want to play with you. I'm going to the park!" And the dragon went to the park and he got to the park and then when he was at the park he went on the swing. And then a girl came and she said, "What are you doing here?" And then the girl played on the slide. And then the dragon played on the slide. And the girl played on the swing. And then a spider came and then a spider found a web. And they both said, "How are you doing?" (Stage direction: one says it first and then the other.)

And then the dragon went home and he drank some tea. And when he was done he went to bed. And the robbers came in and they looked around and then they went out. And then the little girl played a little more and went home and ate dinner and went to bed. And when she went to sleep some robbers came in, and they looked around, and they stole everything that she had. And they went out. And they all woke up in the morning and ate their breakfast. And they all went to the park and had a party. (Stage direction: All the characters hold hands and begin their singing.) The End. ❧

Here we see a competent and vigorous six-year-old very much in command of the story writing conventions he has acquired. He uses a formulaic opening, "Once upon a time," and while most of the occurrences are physical, one represents a mental event: Jason indicates expectation when, in the second sequence, he says, "instead of his friend there was a dragon." Jason supplies stage directions to clarify and expand the story and presents a mixture of popular media characters (Ghostbuster, robbers), fairy tale characters (dragon, spider), and others, all using direct speech and reciprocal conversation. Sentences are complex and include subordinate clauses, such as "when she went to sleep."

Using these conventions with style and poise, Jason constructs a story that successfully integrates the strands of his life (e.g., going to bed or to places like a friend's house, the park) and incorporates expectations derived from his family and teachers (you eat dinner, then go to bed; the girl and dragon take turns on the slide). In the style of many traditional tales, all of his characters, good and bad, end up as friends—they all go to the park and have a party. The story ends with the friends taking hands in a musical number.

Furthermore, by including such details as Ghostbusters and robbers, Jason also incorporates the demands of the peer culture. He has now established himself as not only his own "person," but as a full fledged "member."

The story dictation activity of the preschool evolves naturally into journal and booklet writing activities in the later elementary years. The motivating power of this activity is augmented by the social opportunity to share stories from an "author's chair," as in Harriet Morrison's class mentioned earlier in the chapter, or in a third-grade classroom's "author's theatre" described so powerfully by Anne Dyson (1995).

BALANCED OPPORTUNITIES FOR SPONTANEOUS AND GUIDED PLAY SUPPORT LITERACY

Spontaneous sociodramatic play and guided play through story dictation/story playing and writing are by no means the only literacy activities to be emphasized in the play-based curriculum. Literate behaviors are best supported by a wide range of diverse classroom resources and activities that are well balanced on a continuum from spontaneous to guided play. Careful consideration of time, space, materials, and staff provides a planning context for achieving diversity and balance.

First, does the program permit sufficient *time* for literate behavior in play? The pattern of the day should allow for long, uninterrupted periods of spontaneous play in all centers. If children are rushed and the day is chopped up with teacher-directed "inside time," "group time," "sharing time," "snack time"—that is, with too much teacher choice and teacher voice—the children will have little opportunity to integrate and contextualize their play themes through literate behaviors.

Is there enough *space* for literate behavior in play? Work tables, writing centers, and play areas should be spacious enough to accommodate communication and be set up in such a way that the children can establish face-to-face engagement and visually share materials (i.e., draw on materials that serve as a source for a topic such as miniature toys, etc.), or comfortably share and exchange their knowledge of language and literacy with each other, as in Harriet's Booklet Writing Time.

Materials for language and literacy play include all kinds of writing and printed materials, including books, catalogues, tablets, clipboards, Post-It notes and, of course, ample amounts of attractively displayed and maintained supplies of paper, crayons, and markers. Books, paper, and writing materials should be not only in the reading or writing center, but also in the dress-up and home play corners, near the outdoor climber, in the block play area and next to the fish bowl (to record the daily development of the cluster of baby snails!). With the

A young author selects "characters" to enact the story play he has dictated.

teacher's help, items can be labeled, directional arrows drawn, and symbols and signs made to identify activities and projects.

In promoting literate behaviors, the staff should know when and how to imaginatively join, but not "take over," the children's play, as well as when and how to withdraw. The teacher can help the children elaborate their play themes through language, from simple guidance involving help with the construction of a treasure map or the "S" on a Superman cape, to making signs for streets, "Dalmatians" or "Lost Boys Only," the bus stop, airport, or house numbers for the cardboard box homes of miniature clothespin dolls.

SUMMARY AND CONCLUSION

A play-based language arts curriculum arises from a context that honors the purposes of children's communication before it stresses isolated strategies for literacy learning. In a play environment that is rich in print and language, literate behaviors are developed and elaborated through the many occasions provided for children to communicate and use talk to exchange their knowledge of language and literacy in the motivating context of play.

Literate behaviors, particularly in pretend and sociodramatic play and story telling, are seen as precursors to a grasp of the concept of "story" or "narrative" and the necessary perspective taking this implies. Such understanding emerges through play as, together, children talk, draw, and share their early attempts to write. Through ample opportunities in guided and spontaneous play children become the authors and readers of their own stories. They become motivated to begin to learn dictionary ways to spell words, acquire letter and sound recognition, utilize upper- and lower-case letter forms appropriately, as well as master the rules for capitalization and punctuation. Reading widely and writing in many forms, along with learning about the work of writers, leads to an understanding of the many genres of authoring. Teachers and parents and the wider community, along with the classroom environment and the children's classmates, all serve as powerful resources for literacy and language learning.

Language arts activities, such as story dictation and story writing in the play-based curriculum, will reflect the intersection of children's social understandings, cognitive development, and literacy skills. Recall how in one classroom the story play activity acted as both a catalyst for learning and a mirror of development in the case of a Russian-speaking child. Happily, in her case, advances in second language learning, socialization and literacy moved as an integrated whole. Other patterns might emerge in other situations. These advances are not necessarily linear or progressive, but may be curvilinear or cyclical or even regressive. The rate of learning may move in spurts determined by children's wants and needs.

While the classroom that is rich in language and literacy is a powerful resource for children, sources, agents and settings for language learning, however, are not limited to teachers and schools. In many contemporary classrooms, children's classmates and their worlds beyond school are also resources that provide a broad sociocultural context. Through a play-based language arts curriculum we tap into the richness of the full range of diverse cultures and languages in our classrooms and communities.

FOCUSING OUR THINKING

1. Observe and record an episode of sociodramatic play in the home play or block area. How do the children express their desires and interests and establish a topic? If other children entered the play after the topic was established, how did they communicate that they were "on topic"? Are there shifts of topic? If so, which child or children change the topic and how is this communicated?

2. If there is a bilingual child in the class, discretely make three or four observations of the child's play for ten-minute periods during the course of a week. What opportunities do these play situations provide for primary language and second language learning? Contrast the child's use of language in play situations with that in teacher-structured lessons.

3. Consider the case of Laronda. If you were her teacher the following year, what would you learn about her if these stories were included in her records?

4. Date all entries in journals children write. Use these to assess development of language and literacy skills but also, more importantly, so children can witness their own growth. They are also a valuable component of any assessment process for parents and administrators.

SUGGESTED RESOURCES

1. Cook-Gumperz, J. (Ed.). (1986). *The social construction of literacy*. New York: Cambridge University Press.

   This book provides a social perspective on the acquisition of literacy and discusses how it has been used as a measure of the success of both individuals and social groups.

2. Dyson, A. H. (1997). *Writing superheroes: Contemporary childhood, popular culture, and classroom literacy*. New York & London: Teachers College Press, Columbia University.

   Another equally valuable and more recent contribution by Dyson. Here she continues her examination of peer cultures in urban elementary classrooms. Especially useful and inspiring for teachers working in ethnically and culturally diverse schools.

3. Genishi, C., & Dyson, A. H. (1984). *Language assessment in the early years*. Norwood, NJ: Ablex Publishing Corporation.

   A classic work that will assist parents, teachers and caregivers in developing ways to foster and assess children's spoken and written language. It has an excellent section on second language learning and takes a sociolinguistic and developmental perspective covering preschool to ages six to eight. It is well grounded in both research and practice.

4. Graves, D. H. (1983). *Writing: Teachers and children at work*. Exeter, NH: Heinemann.

   This book uses data collected on the development of writing over a three-year period. It documents children's writing progress and is particularly helpful in assessing that progress.

5. Heath, S. B. (1983). *Ways with words: Language, life, and work in communities and classrooms*. New York: Cambridge University Press.

   Provides a sound ethnographic view of the influence of culture and communication on literacy learning and schooling.

6. Scales, B., Almy, M., Nicolopoulou, A., & Ervin-Tripp, S. (Eds.). (1991). *Play and the social context of development in early care and education*. Part II: Language, literacy and the social worlds of children (pp. 75–86). New York: Teachers College Press.

   Brief articles in this section consider various perspectives on how recent research has affected practice in language arts teaching in early childhood education.

CHAPTER **10**

Play and Socialization

207

Andrew lopsidedly heads out the door of his preschool classroom with his mother's large leather briefcase slung over one shoulder. Despite being encumbered by the briefcase, he insists upon carrying it wherever he goes. His destination today is the swing at the rear of the play yard. He has recently become willing to set the briefcase on a bench nearby when he uses the swing. However, if anyone goes near it, stormy protests can be expected.

Andrew is three years and one month old and a newcomer to this four-hour program. He started school here when he was two years and eleven months old. Separation from his mother, when it came time for leave-taking, has been quite difficult. To ease Andrew's adjustment to school, his teacher invited his mother to remain at school until a reasonably amicable separation could be achieved. Andrew's mother, on leave from her part-time job at the time, was able to accommodate his need. Since Andrew played happily while his mother was present, she anticipated this interval would be brief. The interval, however, began to stretch into weeks rather than days, and his mother's leave from her job was nearly over. Andrew, even if engaged, continued to insist on leaving with his mother. Finally, Andrew's mother and his teacher devised a strategy they believed might allay his anxiety: mother was to leave her large leather briefcase on the bench near the door as a reminder that she would be returning at some pre-determined time. First, she stayed away until "snack time," then she was to return at "story time," and so on for longer periods of time each day.

Andrew's mother was always meticulous about returning at these clearly bracketed times in the preschool day, and eventually Andrew was able to stay for the full four hours of the program. Not without a catch, however; the briefcase must stay behind to insure mother's return. It was many weeks before Andrew allowed the briefcase to be safely tucked away by his teacher into his cubby, and not until the second half of the school year that it did not come to school with Andrew at all.

SAYING GOODBYE TO PARENTS

Separation from parents is a major milestone for children, and both theory and research on this subject suggest that the character of this achievement is an important indicator of secure or insecure attachment to the parental figure. Teachers know that the initial transition from home to school is important to both the child's comfort and success in school (Balaban, 1985). Attachment theorists assert that when unusual conflict and/or anxiety surrounds separation from the parent, the child may develop significant other problems in relating to others. These problems may cloud the child's comfort and adjustment to school routines as well as impact the child's success in relations with peers in play.

Much of the research on attachment has been conducted in what has been called the "strange situation" in a laboratory setting (Ainsworth, Bell & Stayton, 1974). A very recent, naturalistic study looked at patterns in separation on entrance to preschool and then observed the same children's attempts to enter into play with other children (Tribble, 1996). Preliminary findings from this study indicate, not surprisingly, that children classified as insecurely attached (i.e., had difficulty separating or rejoining a parent) also had subsequent difficulties in persevering in and/or varying their attempts to initiate in spontaneous peer play. Teachers find they need to be particularly supportive of such children's efforts to interact with others. In these cases the modeling of entry strategies such as those recommended by Smilansky and others (Smilansky, 1968; Trawick-Smith, 1994) may be warranted.

The ability to initiate in play with peers will be referred to frequently in this chapter as one of the major indicators of a needed social competency for effective play. Consider the following incident as an example of the multilayered complexity of play in mixed age and culturally diverse settings.

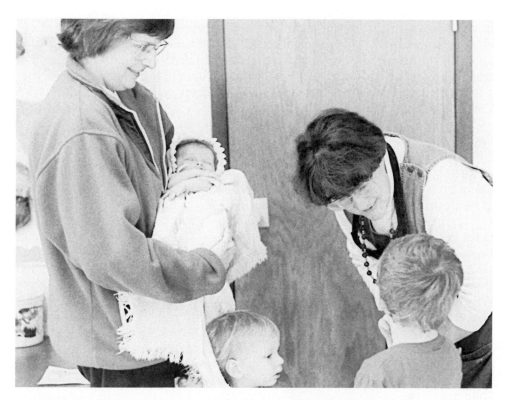

A comfortable transition from home is important to a child's school success.

"Little Dragon"

  Sometime after a successful celebration of the Chinese New Year and the children's astounding creation of a dragon, three-year-old Christopher began emulating the actions of a dragon. He rigidly strode through the play yard, imaginatively breathing fire while stalking some of the older boys in the class.

At about the same time, Christopher's mother noted that she had begun receiving an unusual number of "Ouch Reports" for Christopher. She wondered what was going on. As a Chinese American, was it possible that he was becoming a target of abuse by the "rough" older boys in the class? Christopher's descriptions of events in the "Ouch Reports" generally indicated it was often Alex, the oldest, largest and most popular child in the program, who had chased him (Alkon, Genevo, Kaiser, Tschann, Chesney & Boyce, 1994) (see Figure 10.1).

Following this, the teacher surveyed the "Ouch Reports" and, sure enough, found that Christopher did have a few more reports of bumps, falls and scrapes than other children his age. She also noted that, in general, the younger children had a somewhat higher proportion of reports of such minor injuries. The implications of these findings were discussed in a staff meeting in relation to Christopher. Teachers were also able to make reference to the set of ongoing observations on this particular child that had been compiled. While in the early days of the program Christopher had spent most of his time in the near vicinity of his early morning teacher, now he had begun to spend more time in the active outdoor play areas of the school. In their observations and anecdotes, teachers noted that when Christopher pretended to be a "dragon," the older boys chased him with cries such as "Here comes the bad guy!" Teachers' attempts to reason with Christopher and the older boys about the pattern in their play would temporarily end the chasing by the four-year-old boys. Three-year-old Christopher, however, always tearfully but implacably insisted that he wished to continue to be a "dragon." He seemed to have little interest in integrating himself by taking on a character from the play scenarios of the older boys. The moment the teacher's attention was averted, he would again approach the group as a "dragon," with the expected consequences being repeated.

Christopher seemed enchanted with his ability to obtain the attention of the older boys. When conflict arose or when he fell while fleeing from the "superheroes," he seemed developmentally unable to comprehend the teacher's admonitions about the consequences of this entry strategy and was unable to understand the need to thematically coordinate his play with others.

Luckily, around the time of spring break, a new child of about Christopher's age was admitted to the program. *His* favorite play persona was Tyrannosaurus Rex. Not surprisingly, the two formed a union and soon became the magnet for a small, but fairly cohesive, group of younger children who were granted a special dragon territory on one of the smaller play structures where they could rant and rage powerfully but still be protected from forays by "superheroes" in search of "bad guys."

University of Califormia   Child Care Services

OUCH REPORT

Child's Name: ___John Doe___   Teacher's Name: _Jane Doe/Teacher_

Today's Date: _7_/_25_/_97_ Time of Accident _4_:_40_   a.m/(p.m.)

Location of Event: Far yard

Contributing Factors: "I hurt myself right on the leg.
                       I was being chased and I bumped."

Type of Injury: Location of Injury:

__ Cut
_✓_ Scrape
__ Bump or Bruise
__ Mouth injury
__ Crush injury
__ Human Bite
__ Insect bite/sting
__ Injury by foreign object
   (splinter, sand in eye etc.)
__ Hair pulled
__ Other

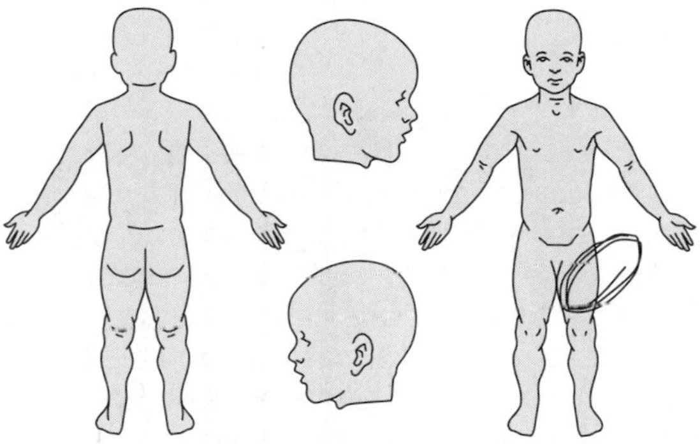

Type of Treatment Given: Recommended Follow-up:

— Cleaned injured site
_✓_ ice pack applied   He seems great - he was
__ bandaid or dressing applied a little shaken by
_✓_ Child rested or laid down   hurting himself.
_✓_ given comfort
__ antiseptic applied
__ Other

                    Head Teacher (initial/date)   BJS

Figure 10.1
Source: Adapted by University of California Head Teacher Rebecca Tracy for classroom use.

DIVERSITY CREATES CHALLENGES FOR TEACHERS

In culturally diverse classrooms, in mixed-age groups, and/or in classrooms with a policy of including children with physical impairments, the open play setting can represent quite a challenge. Younger or particularly immature children in mixed-age classrooms may have difficulty interacting because they are unable to comprehend the intentions of others such as is required in a fast-paced, open play setting. They may have difficulty in coordinating their movements with others, even to go down a slide safely, for example, or in determining the trajectory of a ball, trike or wagon, or in understanding the effect they may arouse when they approach others as a "big scary" dinosaur, a dragon, a robot, or a powerful superhero.

Some of these diverse factors may have been a barrier to the successful inclusion in play of a child with a speech impairment in the vignette that follows. In the move toward "inclusion," play-based classroom teachers must be realistic both about the goals they set for all the children, including those with special needs, and the potential of available resources to implement them.

Matthew

❧ Matthew, a child (age six years and five months) with a severe speech impairment, has entered the sand play area where two active boys, Greg, an adopted child (five years and one month), and François, a child of African American heritage (four years and nine months), have, after a lengthy and tenuous negotiation, established a play interaction. They are making "quicksand" by pouring water and sprinkling dry sand into an area of the sand pit where a trench has been dug by the teacher. Matthew has jumped to a mound nearby and stands opposite Greg, looking down into the "quicksand."

As they face each other across the trench, Matthew attempts to enter the play not by speaking, but by kicking a tire embedded in the sand above the trench. Greg jumps across the trench, pushing Matthew into the sand. ❧

A major way that children develop socially is through play with other children. How might Matthew's teachers respond in this situation? This chapter focuses on the teacher's role in thinking about and guiding the children's socialization. We show how careful observation of children's talk and interactive behavior is one of our best guides to determining children's social and communicative competence. Many of the illustrations presented in this chapter are drawn from teacher anecdotes and teacher research. They raise many questions, show some of the dilemmas teachers face, and suggest some answers.

We return to Matthew's encounter with François and Greg. Matthew, the speech-impaired child referred to above, is a large, slow-moving child who has begun to attempt to play and interact more frequently with other children. Previously, he relied solely upon the teachers to interpret his needs. His teachers, however, still closely monitor his play with peers because of his rather limited physical skills (Scales, 1989, 1996). In this, Matthew resembles many children with special needs who rely greatly on adults to provide them with support in the interpretation of their needs. (Erwin, 1993; Newcomer, 1993). The manner in which Matthew attempts to enter the play between Greg and François (by kicking a tire as an initiating act) is somewhat typical of other children with special needs. According to van der Kooij (1989b), some children with special needs respond to their environment in a single way, either nonverbally or verbally, which makes it difficult for them to enter play situations.

"Quicksand"

The following excerpt from a longer text indicates what happens when Matthew attempts to enter the play with Greg and François:

Greg:	Take this, Matthew.	Greg jumps to a mound near Matthew and shoves him over.
Matthew:	(unclear utterance)	Matthew picks up a handful of sand and throws it at Greg.
Greg:	Take this.	Greg shoves Matthew again and jumps over trench.
François:	Ya! Ha!	François returns to the sand pit.
Greg:	[Help me], François.	
Greg:	Get him.	The two boys begin to attempt to push Matthew into the trench.
François:	Hi ya!	
Greg:	Push him over. Shove	Both boys are pulling Matthew.
François:	Are we pushin' him in the quicksand?	
Greg:	No, push him right down here.	Greg points to center of trench.
François:	Now you come here, Matthew, I've got something to show you.	François stands up, moves to Matthew.
Matthew:	I know what you're going to do. I saw it.	(Matthew's speech is understandable as he points to François.)
François:	Come! Help me lift big boy up. Fat mouth.	Both boys tug at Matthew.

At the beginning of the above sequence, shortly after Greg pushes Matthew, two teachers intervene. One attempts to encourage Matthew to use his language to tell Greg his objections to being pushed into the sand. A second teacher moves to assist and redirect Greg. She first acknowledges the good aspects of what Greg and François have made together, but also warns that it might need "special attention" because it could be "dangerous." Thus, she signals the boys that they can expect closer monitoring from teachers. Despite this warning, the two boys continue to attempt to push Matthew down into the sand.

Again, a teacher arrives to alter the direction the play has taken. "Are you playing the game with them, Matthew?" he asks. Without waiting for Matthew to respond, Greg and François chime in. They define the game as one that involves " . . . tryin' to push him [Matthew] down there." They say that Matthew has said "Yes," he wishes to play. At this point Matthew speaks up relatively clearly to say, "No," he does not wish to play.

When the boys persist in attempting to push Matthew into the "quicksand," the teacher again restrains them and informs them that if they continue, they will have to leave the sand pit: " . . . I say again there's no throwing sand here. I wouldn't let sand get in your eyes." Following this warning, Greg and François resume their play around the theme of making "quicksand."

Somewhat later Matthew makes another attempt to enter the play with Greg and François. This time he has a modest success when he relatively clearly assures the two boys, "I know what we can do, put sand on top." Having affirmed the theme of the play, he is not bothered further and sits quietly nearby, observing the pit of "quicksand."

		François leaves to obtain more water.
		François returns to sand area with more water.
Greg:	Quicksand. You know how we did that before. OK, put the water all over.	
François:	Put it where?	
Greg:	Right up there.	
François:	Oh right, right. That makes chocolate milk.	François pours water, making a froth in the sand.
Greg:	Yes. You remember, that will make quicksand.	
Matthew:	I know what we can do.	Sitting on mound above trench watching Greg and François.
François:	What?	
Matthew:	[. . . put sand on top.]	
François:	You're right, Matthew.	
Greg:	Then when people walk here, they'll sink in.	
François:	I'm gonna go get some more water.	
Greg:	[and go in quicksand]	
Greg:	Kaboom!	

The teacher in this anecdote was in something of a dilemma about how to intervene in order to modify this "play curriculum." Greg and François, two difficult and not very effective communicators, had just established a fragile interaction. Should he interrupt it by attempting, probably unsuccessfully, to help Matthew enter the play? Matthew, on the recommendation of his speech therapist, had been retained in the preschool program for an additional year. The teacher wondered if he should protect or encourage Matthew to enter this fast-paced, rough and tumble play with two unpredictable partners. In this anecdote we see how Matthew was largely unsuccessful in establishing cohesive play with Greg and François. They persisted in trying to push Matthew in "the pit" until two teachers intervened. At this time, Matthew verbalized that he did not wish to play in this way with them. However, the boys continued to throw sand at Matthew. This example points to the social difficulties that disabled children may have with their peers during play.

In this episode involving three children—a speech-impaired child, a child who was culturally different from his classmates, and an adopted child who often acted out aggressively—we see that it is not always easy to know precisely how to support play.

TRADITIONAL RESEARCH AND PRACTICE

In the past, teachers who turned to research with questions related to play and socialization found relatively few answers. Researchers were sometimes even uncertain that play was really taking place. They were not always able to identify its boundaries. This made it difficult to determine who was playing "what and with whom." So complex was the phenomenon for researchers that one compared play to "cotton candy," a substance that seems to vanish as soon as it is touched.

Meanwhile, many early childhood teachers continued to believe in the value of play in the socialization of children. Perhaps intuitively they felt that, comparable to the simple paper cones used to support cotton candy, the use of delicate, unobtrusive supports in early childhood classrooms could loft play to its place in nurturing children's social development.

In keeping with this metaphor, teachers often hesitate to intervene directly into children's play. Smilansky's (1968) recommendation for intervention to support elaborated dramatic play is one notable exception. The view that the child learns best when self-directed has largely prevailed, despite Smilansky's findings about the value of elaborated play for later academic learning. More recently, Paley (1992), in a work entitled "You Can't Say You Can't Play," has also recommended a socially responsible, albeit sensitive, form of intervention.

Teachers, however, have long been aware that the nature of children's play and social interaction is related to the physical environment of the school setting. In order to lend more rigor to the manipulation of settings for play, they have employed various checklists and rating scales to assess environmental features such as boundaries and links between areas, as well as level of play complexity (Harms & Clifford, 1980; Kritchevsky, Prescott & Walling, 1977). These methods verify the presence or absence of desired features in classrooms and play yards. However, such methods do not reveal *how* settings or features of settings *in themselves* might act to generate social and cooperative behavior. These issues have only recently begun to be studied in detail (Dyson, 1997; Cook-Gumperz & Cansaro, 1977; Reifel, & Yeitman, 1991; Tribble, 1996; Woods & Scales, 1995).

In the 1980s and early 1990s, as researchers began to collaborate more closely with teachers, and as some teachers began to do their own research, our knowledge of the value of play in socialization increased. Teachers now have more than their experience and knowledge of children to guide them (Cochran & Lytle, 1993; Cook-Gumperz & Scales, 1996; Corsaro, 1997; Erickson, 1993; Scales, 1996).

Currently, researchers are also focusing on play and socialization within special education and integrated classrooms (Erwin, 1993; Hanline & Fox, 1993; Hartmann & Rollett, 1994; McEvoy, Shores, Wehby, Johnson, & Fox, 1990; Ostrosky, Kaiser, & Odom, 1993). Young children with special needs have exhibited an increase in socialization skills after interacting with peers in a play environment. Researchers have found that children with severe disabilities in integrated sites spent more time in activities with their classmates than in unoccupied behavior, which broadened their base of social support (Erwin, 1993). This is especially important, since many children with special needs are lacking in social competence. Play in inclusive settings may have the potential to enhance social competence for these children.

CURRENT PRACTICE ILLUMINATED BY RESEARCH

Recent naturalistic observational studies looking at peer play and communication in early childhood have shown how children develop the skills to monitor the varying social contexts they encounter. Studies also have shown how school practice constrains or complements the development of essential features of social competence (Cook-Gumperz & Corsaro, 1977; Cook-Gumperz, Corsaro & Streeck, 1986; Corsaro, 1985, 1997; Corsaro & Schwartz, 1991). For example, some recent research has brought to light the complex issues involved in the gender socialization of boys and girls (Goodwin, 1990; Nicolopoulou, Scales & Weintraub, 1994; Scales & Cook-Gumperz, 1993).

Differences in Boys' and Girls' Play and Socialization

Paley (1984), a teacher and writer, examined the differences in the play of preschool boys and girls. She found that when time for spontaneous play was lengthened, boys became more willing to engage in quiet table activities more typically favored by girls.

A year-long study of children's narratives by Nicolopoulou and Scales (1990) found that preschool boys' and girls' stories differed in both content and form. In their stories, boys were inclined to pile powerful or violent images one upon another, with little apparent order or sequence. Girls, on the other hand, tied their stories to the rhythm of the home. For example, babies get up and have breakfast, go to the park, come home, and go to bed.

For girls, the family romance was paramount, with marriage, the arrival, losing, or finding of babies frequent themes. Relationships of mother, father, sister, and baby were often depicted. Boys, on the other hand, rarely spoke of any relationship other than that of a "friend," a friend with whom they more than likely battled as a culminating feature of their stories. These gender differences emerged quite early and persisted despite teachers' efforts to broaden the repertoires of both boys and girls.

"Tough Guys"

The following anecdote, drawn from a recent article in *Advances in Early Education and Day Care* (Scales, 1996), reveals a hidden gender-related social hierarchy in the allocation of roles in children's storytelling.

🐚 Imagine a scene near the end of the day at a university based preschool. Twenty-eight children are seated around a "square" taped on the carpet. This is "the stage" where they will enact the stories they dictated to a teacher earlier in the day. At this particular moment, however, the proceedings have stalled: the child-author's original choice of an actor for the part of a blue Power Ranger has refused the role. The children are becoming restless and inattentive. The teacher, hoping to get things moving again, whispers a suggestion: "Why don't you pick Max? He really wants a part in your play!" "Oh no," responds the author, "He can't be it! It has to be one of the tough guys."

Suddenly, a previously unseen aspect of the social life of this classroom has become transparent. We knew that for the girls, "Princess" roles were highly prized tokens of social favor, argued for and parceled out in play and story-acting. Now a once hidden social hierarchy in the boys' world had opened as well. 🐚

When stories such as this and the power relationships they reveal are merely suppressed in "gender-neutral" classrooms, they go unnoted as a hidden cur-

In play, boys and girls strive to reconcile old conventions with new ones.

riculum. However, through story playing in preschool and what Anne Haas Dyson (1995) has called an "author's theatre" in the elementary classroom, such power relationships can become accessible for negotiation and dialogue about who "gets in" and who "gets left out," who owns which social roles and who has power in the play life of the classroom (see also Scales, 1996).

As teachers and researchers are aware, not only do the themes and characteristics of boys' and girls' stories differ, but so, too, does their willingness to engage in play usually associated with members of the opposite sex. Garvey and Berndt (1977) found that boys were reluctant to play roles of a specific female character such as "mom," or even assume roles that are commonly associated with females, such as preparing food.

A similar reluctance was evident in the story-play observations of two of the authors. Preschool boys refused to allow girls to play "male" roles such as "bad guys" except by "default" when no one else will take such roles. Even as early as kindergarten, boys refused to play "prince" roles typically found in the girls' stories.

Paley (1984) recommends that teachers respect children's role choices as important parts of children's self-concepts. In addition to Paley's work, further observation, reflection, and sharing by teachers about their classrooms can contribute to greater understanding of this critical issue.

Children's Negotiations Create a Dynamic Context for Play

Working closely with teachers, Corsaro, a sociologist, and his colleague, Cook-Gumperz (1986), studied the ways children negotiate and achieve their own self-generated social objectives in play through their conversations. Cook-Gumperz, Corsaro, and Streeck (1996) found that play interactions are both shaped by and, in themselves, shape children's understanding of the social and environmental expectations of situations.

In a recent article, Scales (1997) noted that in studying the ways children communicate with each other in play and with their teachers as they dictate stories to be heard by their peers, we find that children's lives in preschool are embedded in a particular social context whose impact cannot be ignored without neglecting children's interest, self-direction, and motivation. The social work that children engage in as they play has been largely unexamined by practitioners whose valuing of play has its roots in early childhood's psycho-dynamic and constructivist heritage. Constructivists such as Piaget and Vygotsky have had an important impact on our view of children's development. Both researchers and teachers have been stimulated by Vygotsky's reference to the "zone of proximal development." Many recent articles, however, have taken a too narrow interpretation of the "zone of proximal development" and failed to note that Vygotsky also asserted that *play* is the *source* of development and *creates* the zone of proximal development. In a play-based curriculum, teachers have a potent opportunity to observe how, as children insert elements from the larger culture into their play world, they are forced to make sense of both their real and fantasy worlds (Nicolopoulou, 1996). To illustrate this point, consider the following anecdote, where the play roles that four elementary-age children set for themselves will lead them in developing social competency.

Newspapers

❧ At mid-year, six-year-olds Clay, Zoe, Randall and Michelle have decided they will use their daily activity period to make a class newspaper. In this language- and literacy-rich classroom they have had many opportunities to examine and play with different kinds of writing, such as letters, articles, books, lists, signs and so on. A large block of time is allocated on most days for drawing and composing texts for their writing booklets. Children are encouraged to write about anything that interests them and to invent the words they need themselves or ask for help from each other, a teacher, or parent assistant. These sessions are noisy, playful and productive. Sharing and discussion of these texts with the class from an "Author's Chair" occurs on most days as well. There are also, of course, opportunities on a daily basis when their teacher wisely helps them develop traditional competencies in handwriting, spelling and letter sounds. So Zoe, Clay, Randall, and Michelle did not come to their play project uninformed.

Their interest in the newspaper project extended over many weeks and involved much research and many revisions, additions, and reviews both by their teacher and their classmates. News articles as well as jokes and cartoons were collected and included in the final comprehensive version. While only one "edition" was "published," every child in the classroom received a copy. The "letters to the editor" column spurred two other students to write a letter to the principal complaining about the school "pensiels" and included suggestions for changes. (See chapter 9 for a discussion of this elementary classroom.)

In this elementary classroom, this daily activity time, where children have ample choices of things to do, provides a "zone of proximal development" or what Newman, Griffin and Cole (1989) would call the "construction zone," where interaction among peers and their teachers in sharing varying interests, concerns, knowledge and competencies provides the *source* of development for many. Their teacher feels this "play period" provides a real test of how well the children are adapting to the "learning plan" she has for each child. Through both structured and spontaneous opportunities to play with varied writing materials and formats, children are "learning to write and writing to learn" (Morrison, 1985). ❧

In the play that occurs in the free interaction among peers involved in the activity period, children are provided with an opportunity to experience the "give and take," or reciprocity, that is a salient feature of effective social play, where shared needs, interests and competencies can be mediated. Alward (1995) noted that this reciprocity also provides the context for moral, social and ethical development as well. "This reciprocity is rarely achieved between children and adults, but in play it is the rule rather than the exception" (pp. 1–2).

Although reciprocity is a salient feature of effective social play, many young children with special needs do not demonstrate this skill (Newcomer, 1993). Many are unable to incorporate another peer into shared play. According to Newcomer, some may be overly inhibited and "extremely wary of play situations" tending to rely on adults. On the other hand, children with too few inhibitions may be reluctant to delay gratification of their impulses (Newcomer, 1993; van der Kooij, 1989). Van der Kooij (1989) and Newcomer (1993) noted that these children often become angry and aggressive when their peers do not follow their suggestions. Because reciprocity may be problematic in children who have special needs, teachers must be especially aware of play situations that involve these children and encourage them to share in interactions with their peers.

PLAY PROVIDES A BRIDGE BETWEEN THEORY AND PRACTICE

We have discussed some of the ways in which our examination of children's play interactions and storytelling provide a bridge between theory and practice. As demonstrated in the anecdotes and cases we present, our broad constructivist view of child development does not confine us to relying on any single, rigid theoretical approach. Classical Piagetian theory can serve us well in the study of individuals, but we also look to Vygotsky when examining how the social dynamics of the classroom intersect with individual development.

Rather than taking a top-down approach—that is, bringing only a selected theory to bear—teachers may find greater explanatory power in analyzing their own records and observations. This has been described earlier as an interpretive approach (see chapter 2). Such an approach looks closely at specific play interaction, and takes an insider's view rather than the detached one of an outsider (Cochran-Smith & Lytle, 1993; Corsaro, 1992, 1997; Gaskins, Miller & Corsaro, 1997). This stance relies on observations and reports of informed "insiders" such as teachers themselves. It bases its explanations on evidence from detailed and systematic observation and analysis of actual events that have transpired in real situations, such as a teacher's classroom or play yard. It grounds these explanations in contexts well known to participants. By this means, findings can be corroborated and discrepant cases identified and explained (Erickson, 1993).

The value of an interpretive approach is demonstrated by the "tough guy" anecdote cited earlier in this chapter. Remember that the child author first resisted letting Max play the role of a Power Ranger, saying he was not a "tough guy." He changed his mind, however, when it was suggested that Max could pretend to be a tough guy. This event could be analyzed from a number of perspectives. A classical Piagetian point of view might suggest the class of actors pretending to be Power Rangers could be analyzed to consist of both tough and non-tough guys (that is, in terms of class inclusions and coordinations), or in terms of children's understanding of pretense (even non-tough guys could act tough), or the same person could be both tough and non-tough as an actor (an example of conservation and identity). Other theoretical approaches can also shed light on the complex issues involved in this child-playwright's seemingly simple decision that another child, not of the "tough guy" group, could "pretend" to be a tough guy in order to take part in the play. Developmental issues such as classification and the ability to conserve certainly were involved. But these analyses do not account for all of the child's reasoning, and do not account for his agency and motivation. Here an interpretive perspective, with its sociocultural orientation, broadens constructivist thinking to provide further explanatory power (Scales, 1996).

From a sociocultural perspective, the context of the story-acting activity presented the child with a conflict and an ambiguity that needed resolving, and the teacher, as mentor, helped him find a solution within the collaborative construction of the "play." At the individual level, from a Piagetian perspective, it might be considered to be a disequilibrating situation that helped the child advance to a higher level of thinking. With respect to the social dynamics of the classroom, this is the kind of negotiation of power roles that Dyson (1995) refers to in her work on urban classrooms. When teachers take an interpretive approach, they discover that children actively contribute "to their own socialization and a sense of themselves as a social entity," and "to the production and reproduction of what has been called the children's culture" (Gaskins, Miller & Corsaro, 1993, 1997).

Dyson (1995) and Dyson & Genishi (1994), in discussing ethnographic and linguistic research on children's narratives in inner city elementary classrooms, noted that individual children assume the voices of others, both past and present, as they use the linguistic forms they have appropriated from teachers, parents, and peers to construct a text. Dyson also found, however, that when addressing present-day events, such as the ambiguity surrounding gender, the text is, in and of itself, transformative. That is, it transforms the child's perception of both the past and the future. For example, when today's child uses a past expression of gender (e.g., "Princess"), she is not merely miming in some frozen way an outmoded social attitude. Rather, because the old-fashioned expression is now embedded in the very different social context of today's world, it brings about change or transforms by giving rise to ambiguities the child must resolve through dialogue with others. If we merely drive gender expressions underground as a hidden curriculum, we fail to provide any occasion for this transformative mediation to occur as the child struggles to reconcile the tension between gender conventions of the past and emerging ones of the present (Dyson, 1995).

Teachers Take a Research Stance

Teachers can take a research stance by systematically observing play communication to see how the classroom social environment is being "read" by children. For example, the teachers' observation of the interactive strategies of the three children in our "quicksand" episode gave them important information about how to guide their interactions and later modify the environment to support more players.

The interactive strategies that children utilize provide clues to their ability to understand the views of others. Children's situational strategies also reveal how they coordinate or synchronize actions and speech to conform to their understanding of the situation. Such behaviors are essential to prosocial behavior or cooperation with others. Children can be provided with opportunities to learn needed skills at "turn-taking" in play interactions with peers. The notion of taking turns may arise in play at the swings on the playground, or when a child puts his name or mark on a waiting list for a turn at the water table. The wise adult makes sure the child gets a turn; children need to be able to trust the "marks" on those lists.

The notion of turn-taking is especially important for children who have difficulty cooperating with peers. For example, in general, "one will observe the mutual influence of individuals upon each other" (van der Kooij, 1989, pp. 328–329). However, with regard to some special needs children, "egocentrism" may block such mutuality" (ibid.). Opportunities to practice skills such as turn-taking are important for these children so they may learn to interact effectively in play with other children (van der Kooij, 1989b).

In most early childhood classrooms, turns at games can start quite early if only "pairs" play at first. If groups are not too large or too formally structured, the understanding of a conversational turn can be demonstrated in talk at circle-time. Small games, such as lotto, and familiar songs, can contribute as well. And, of course, children need to be given ample opportunity to practice their skills at turn-taking in spontaneous play.

Central to this approach to understanding children's socialization is the notion that the play context is dynamic. As they play, children develop their understanding of the unfolding activity (Cook-Gumperz & Gumperz, 1982). For example, when negotiating a theme such as "home play," children come to understand what kinds of behavior are acceptable. To successfully enter into play one must be "on topic."

Research tells us that to maintain social cooperation, children, like adults, constantly signal their mutual understanding of unfolding play themes. Mutual understanding is signaled when children initiate a play episode or topic (Corsaro, 1979, 1997; Gumperz & Cook-Gumperz, 1982). Play partners will often be observed to affirm with a "right" when a topic is changed, "We're making soup, right?" "Right!" "And it'll have alphabets, OK?" "OK!"

In order for the negotiations of further features of the play to proceed, the child who initiates an idea must have an affirmation. This is usually expressed in a co-player's "right" or an "OK." However, affirmation also can take a nonverbal form. For example, a co-player may express uptake of a theme of cooking by an appropriate gesture, such as beginning to stir a bowl of "sand soup."

Most of the observational material cited in this chapter has been drawn from preschool and/or early elementary settings for 3- to 6-year-olds. The basic methods used in analyzing the material have been derived from studies of adult conversational strategies and are applicable at any age.

STUDYING THE CONTEXT OF CHILDREN'S SOCIAL INTERACTIONS

Cook-Gumperz and Corsaro (1977) analyzed four episodes that were drawn from a preschool classroom. In this section we discuss and contrast these episodes in order to demonstrate how the social and ecological cues of settings influence children's play and socialization.

The first episode involved two children, Rita and Bill, playing husband and wife in the play house. It demonstrates how little negotiation is required to establish play themes in the home play center since children bring what the researchers call conventionalized expectations to home play centers.

For Rita and Bill, the most difficult portion of their interaction involved their attempt to ward off the incursion of two unruly "kitties" who attempt to enter the playhouse. Corsaro and Cook-Gumperz note that once a play episode is under way, children are very protective of their interactive space.

Knowing that children's interactions are fragile, the teacher will respect ongoing interactions by helping potential intruders such as the "kitties" become established at a site nearby or involved with others who are not already engaged. In this case, Rita and Bill handled the problem themselves by dismissing the "kitties" to the "backyard."

In the second episode, an open setting, a small four-sided sand tray provided cues for more inventive play themes. It challenged children's use of their linguistic and communicative skills to create a unique collective play fantasy. At the sand tray, three children developed a highly coordinated play fantasy. It opened with a "rainstorm." Then a small sand mound was elaborated into a "home for freezing bunnies." The players coordinated the changes of theme and did so again as the sand mound became a final safe haven from "lightning" in a "B . . . I . . . G steel home."

In contrast to the first episode, the children at the indoor sand tray were required creatively to structure their activity as it emerged. They could not rely on conventional expectations. Rather, they had to depend on their own communication to collectively create and sustain the order of their talk about their spontaneous and novel fantasy.

While the home play corner is ideal for the neophyte communicator, more open settings (such as a sand tray with miniatures) are also needed to provide challenge for older children. At such sites children stretch their communicative strategies as they cue each other to the meaning of unfolding play events. Such strategies include some of the following:

1. Using special linguistic cues to signify the fantasy (i.e., taking the role of the bunnies);

2. Using repetition to acknowledge some feature of a previous utterance (such as echoing and repeating key words and phrases like "freezing," "rain," and "lightning");

3. Tying new material to previous thematic content. For example, using the word "and" plus a phrase containing new material allows an opening for another child to interact. In one episode, a child named Sabrina said, "I'll take the baby to the store." Her friend Sarah employed the device of "tying" to insert her own idea by adding, " . . . and the big sister will drive the car; and I'll be the big sister."

4. Using ongoing verbal description of behavior as it occurs. For example, saying "Help, we're in the forest, and it's beginning to rain," while visually manipulating miniature toys.

By clearly defining play zones, teachers facilitate cohesion in interactive play.

Play Settings That Constrain Peer Talk and Interaction

Cook-Gumperz and Corsaro analyzed a third episode which occurred at a work table. The teacher attempted to engage the children in a guided-play activity involving the creation of pictures with paint-filled squirt bottles. The teacher inhibited the children's language use and development of interactive skills because she did most of the talking, controlled the flow of talk, and initiated most topics. With a greater awareness of the importance of the need for children to exercise their interactive skills, teachers might consider how they can include plenty of opportunity for self-directed talk among peers at the project table. In this way, teachers can attain their instructional goals in guided play while maintaining the value that comes through peer talk.

In a fourth episode, the setting also constrained interaction. It involved what Corsaro and Cook-Gumperz refer to as an *undefined* context. Here conflict and confusion in play resulted from the ambiguous cues that the teacher had inadvertently set up. Children did not know whether they were at a teacher-dominated site or a child-dominated site.

In the school where this episode occurred, the researchers observed that work tables usually cued "school" kinds of behaviors. In contrast, play in the home corner or at the sand tray was much less constrained by teacher models, and peer talk flowed freely.

On the day that this episode was observed, a teacher had casually placed a work table near the home play corner, inadvertently confusing cues for play behavior. Three children were seated at the table. However, there was a singular lack of coordination in their short-lived play interaction. Two were playing "teacher" and one was playing "police." The informed teacher alters contexts with cautious awareness of possible unforeseen consequences. While, on occasion, mixing environmental cues can produce interesting and positive transformations in children's play, it may also result in disaster.

Solitary and Parallel Play Re-examined

We can sometimes be misled about children's social skills when we classify play solely on the basis of what we hear in their play. Children do not place speech in the foreground of their communication. Instead, they use all modalities of communication, such as gesture, rhythm, and intonation, to achieve their interactive goals.

Three children, Andrea (age three years and two months), Celine (age three years and four months), and Peter (age three years and four months), were playing with pots and pans at an outdoor sand table. Andrea and Celine were busy chatting about what the "baby" would eat for breakfast, while Peter silently stirred a bowl of sand nearby.

Pam, their teacher, observed their play and assessed Peter's silent engagement as an example of solitary or perhaps parallel play. However, her later analysis of a videotape recording of this episode provided evidence for Peter's more active participation in the group interaction.

During this episode, Pam had been casually observing nearby. Though close at hand, she failed to take note of the role that Peter had been assigned. Only at the end of the episode was she made aware that she and Peter had been filling the roles of "baby" and "baby-sitter," respectively. This was revealed to her at the end of the episode when Andrea, the "mommy," emphatically pointed her finger and said to Pam: "Baby, you—I'm goin' out to the woods." Then gesturing toward Peter, Andrea said: "You stay here with the baby-sitter."

Later, when shown the videotape of the episode, Peter confirmed his knowledge of his role. However, he seemed disinterested in informing Pam exactly how or when he became the "baby-sitter." Presumably for him it was an obvious "given" (Scales & Webster, 1976).

Whether Peter's play was solitary, parallel, or collaborative was not easily determined. However, close analysis of the videotape revealed that even without speech Peter was a significant participant in this interactive play.

For the older child, language plays a more important role than it did for these three-year-olds. Older children do not rely to such an extent on environmental cues to guide understanding. With their increasing linguistic ability they are able to detach play from its situational context. Should play be disrupted, older children are more capable of reestablishing it and also able to maintain interactive play across various sites through use of language alone (Scales, 1987).

Initiating and Sustaining Play Interactions

In this chapter we have attempted to show that initiating or entering play is a complex matter and involves more than mimicking adult formulas such as, "Hello, may I play with you?" Such an opening would probably be greeted with a resounding "No," particularly among four-, five-, and six-year-olds. Within the children's culture, distinctive forms of communication are constructed.

Research shows that children develop their own particular strategies for making an entrance into an already established play episode. One successful tactic children use involves circling about the site of the play event until the players make an overture to them (Corsaro, 1979).

Teachers (again in the role of gatekeeper), noting a child's desire to enter a play episode, can assist by helping the newcomer find an activity or role that complements the play event. The teacher might also set the newcomer up nearby with similar props.

It should be noted that many children with special needs do not have strategies for making an entrance into already established play. Many are "passive observers rather than active participants" (Newcomer, 1993, p. 462). Once again, teachers should be aware of these students' difficulties and assist in facilitating their participation.

Spatial Arrangement Supports Interactive Play

An example of a unique solution to a gatekeeping problem occurred when two girls barred the entrance of a third to the play house. The teacher's repeated suggestions of possible roles for the entering child had been rejected again and again.

Squabbling and howling continued for some time until one of the rejecting pair had a marvelous idea: the newcomer could be the "door." This role eminently suited Mia, the newcomer, who on other occasions often took the role of gatekeeper, excluding others herself. She immediately took a posture that barred the entrance with widespread arms and legs.

At the environmental level teachers facilitate cohesive interactive play by defining various zones in the classroom and play yard. Dividers and other spatial markings or arrangements protect interactive space so that players are not easily distracted or play is disrupted. An example of this is seen when teachers arrange the environment so that block building or other floor play does not occur in the middle of pathways.

Teachers can establish spaces that bring children into proximity to each other, like around a rectangular sand tray or table. Then, for example, if two children are playing and a third enters, a side of the table can accommodate the newcomer. The visual array of toys shared by all informs the entering child about the play theme in progress and suggests a possible role to be taken up. Such rectangular spaces also help establish "face engagement" for those along the sides. In this case, the basics of communication (e.g., face engagement) are ensured as well as a shared understanding of the content or theme of the unfolding play (Goffman, 1974).

Such configurations provide what some architects call "defensible space" (Cook-Gumperz, Gates, Scales & Sanders, 1976). Each child has a territory (his side of the table) so that entry into interaction with another in this situation places everybody on an equal footing. Such a space also provides for two pairs of children playing side by side in parallel play. This opens up the possibility that the play of two pairs may become socially more coordinated as a foursome.

The environmental component is also critically important in early childhood special education classrooms and in classrooms that operate with a policy of inclusion. McWilliam and Bailey (as cited in Erwin, 1993) suggest that engagement of children with special needs can be especially influenced by the following: physical arrangement of the classroom, the appropriateness of materials and activities, and the interactions of the people in the environment.

Children Grant Warrants for Play

Sometimes play seems to be established around action alone, as in the game of tag. However, close observation reveals that even such seemingly simple play involves what Cook-Gumperz (1977) calls the granting of a "warrant." Think of a warrant as permission to establish a new play theme.

A typical example of the granting of a warrant occurred in connection with the quicksand segment we presented earlier in this chapter. Greg and François agreed that an area in the sandpit was quicksand. However, François, seeing that the water poured into the sand created a froth, pronounced it "chocolate milk." This constituted an attempt to get a warrant for a new theme. This elaboration was rejected by Greg, who said, "You remember, we're makin' quicksand." François affirmed by a cheery "Oh, right, right," and the previous warrant was reestablished.

Negotiations around the *granting of warrants* go on continuously in children's interactions. These warrants provide a thread to link sequences of activities. When a warrant has been granted, close observation of the play interaction reveals this as a *focal point* where all communicative modes, both verbal and nonverbal, converge. Teachers can observe that children's rhythm and posture, gesture and action, are well coordinated. These focal points are evidence that a warrant has been successfully established or, put another way, that a mutually satisfactory interaction is taking place.

On further observation, teachers will also note sequences of maximal divergence or *transition points*. At these times the children do not share a mutual understanding of the context and, therefore, have different views about the ongoing interaction. This lack of mutual understanding will even be evident in the children's body language and posture which will also not be coordinated.

In the following segment of the quicksand interaction, because the event consists largely of rough and tumble play, most of the transition points involve a teacher intervention. Two of the boys, François and Greg, seem to wish to engage in rough and tumble play and play fighting (they are laughing). As noted in the segment presented earlier in this chapter, the third child, Matthew, does not. (This is signaled by the fact that he is not laughing.)

At such transition points, teachers may wish to intervene as peacemakers to clarify and reorient the players to a mutually acceptable focus. However, if teachers are not observing closely, they may sometimes intervene at the wrong point or make an irrelevant suggestion, thereby actually disrupting rather than supporting the interaction. Even a teacher's well-meaning reinforcing behavior, such as registering approval of children's cooperative play, sometimes serves only to disrupt the play and distract players.

"Quicksand" Revisited

We return now to an earlier segment of the "quicksand" episode. Our purpose here is to consider in detail the initiating and sustaining of play. In this segment we also learn about some of the problems that can arise in multi-dialectical play interactions. François, a child of African American heritage, speaks Black English as well as standard English and a form of English used by TV heroes as well. Unfortunately, most of François's teachers speak only standard English. His play partner, Greg, uses standard English as well as a form of English used by TV heroes.

At the beginning of the episode, Greg is in the center of the sand pit at the intersection of the three pathways that had been dug previously. Greg stationed himself there as soon as he arrived at the beginning of the school day. Only three interactions occur in the sand on this day, and all involve the negotiation of a warrant with Greg in order to gain access to the sand pit.

In environmental terms, an obvious feature of this particular sand "curriculum" is that the physical setup of the sand pit constrained play because the arrangement gave dominion over a large area to only one child. It also limited the possibilities for what types of play could go on. The steep slopes and narrow passages of the pathways invited very close physical contact. They tended to generate virtually a single possibility: rough and tumble play.

❧ First attempt to establish a warrant for play
François enters the sand pit and addresses Greg with "Hi ya, Greg." Greg responds, "Hi ya, François." Then Greg jumps to a mound of sand near Greg as the episode begins: ❧

François:	Let's see what time it is. Oh, yeah, it's time for one by two by two.	Speaks rapidly, using style, rhythm, and tone of Black English.
Greg:	No. No.	
François:	OK—well one by two by two, one by two, by two—ooda do da doo, one by two by two—me and my two by two—one by two by two—one by two by two is over.	François wrestles with Greg. both boys are laughing.
Greg:	OK, François.	
François:	OK, Fatso.	François moves away.

Greg:	Here you go. Take this!	Throws a handful of sand at François.
François:	Take, take this—take this, Greg.	Throws sand.
Greg:	Ah—you missed me.	Teacher moves closer.
François:	Now . . .	Picks up sand to throw.
Greg:	(laughs)	Runs down trench toward upper right exit.
François:	Gotcha—get you in the middle of the leg.	Throws sand.

In this sequence, François has attempted to establish a warrant with Greg for a play fighting game called "one by two by two." François, the African American child, addresses Greg in what, because of rhythm and intonation and other features, is recognized by linguists as Black English (Labov, 1972).

As the two children tussle about in the sand, François continues to address Greg in a kind of rhythmic song-like manner, saying: "Oh, I'm gonna catch you." Sand is by now flying about. The teacher begins to monitor more closely. As the children begin to throw sand at each other, the teacher moves in to intervene. The sand throwing, though a prohibited activity, is well coordinated, and is not in itself a transition point. However, as a prohibited activity, the teacher cannot permit it. A transition that disrupts this interaction occurs when the teacher is required to enter.

❧ Second attempt to establish a warrant
François falls into the trench. Greg moves over and they tussle and toss sand about. ❧

François:	Oh, oh, my goo goo.	
François:	Why—I'll get rid of your shirt if you do that again. I'll take your shirt off and I'll tear your shirt right off. That's the first thing I'd do.	
		Greg moves on mound above trench; turns to look at François.
François:	Tear you [inaudible] come back.	Two children, Greg and François, tussle about in the sand.
Greg:	(laughs)	

In this second attempt to establish a warrant, François again has used intimate Black English, addressing his friend as if Greg were a member of François's culture. The attempt ends with the boys tussling in the sand and the predictable entrance of the teacher.

At this point, Greg's complaint to the teacher, "I don't wanta play this," constitutes a rejection of François's second bid for a warrant for play. At this transition point, the teacher attempts to help the children find a more suitable focus.

🐚 Third attempt to establish a warrant
Speaking in deeper tones and switching to a TV hero voice, François stands on the mound above Greg and initiates another warrant. 🐚

François:	I'm at the cliff of the mountain.	François takes a new posture on the mound, speaks in a new tone, like a media hero.
Greg:	You won't get me, François.	Greg moves from François and the intersection.
François:	You won't get me either. Try to tear me apart.	François moves out upper left exit. Greg follows.
Greg:	Take this then.	Greg returns to sand pit, passing through toward Teacher.
François:	[Try to start . . . fight]	
Greg:	(laughs)	Greg runs around periphery of sand pit with François in pursuit.

This warrant is more to Greg's liking, and a well-coordinated game of tag is launched. The warrant attempt has succeeded. The play interaction, though primarily gross motor in nature at this point, is well coordinated and cohesive.

The episode just described is particularly noteworthy because one of the children speaks both Black and standard English as well as TV English and shifts from one to the other midway through the episode. We see here that there is a greater demand in this setting for the African American child to adapt his linguistic style to his play partner's speech style. François's initial overtures to establish a play warrant by utilizing Black English were not successful (Labov, 1972).

However, because he is multi-dialectical, François switched first to a form of TV English and then to standard English. Teachers analyzing these data do not consider it an accident that when he employed the alternative strategy of changing dialects to initiate his next two play warrants, François was successful. One was a game of tag and the other centered around the theme of "making quicksand." Not unpredictably, as we noted in the beginning of this chapter, François and Greg, the now cohesive pair, later tried to exclude Matthew. As Corsaro (1997) has noted, children often will vigorously resist the entry of others in their play, fearing the disruption and breakup that such entry often inflicts on their fragile interactions.

The challenge in this play for Greg, François, and Matthew was to find a common language. Two boys were successful and established a warrant for cohesive play; a third, Matthew, was not. Situations such as this provide an interesting challenge to the skills of teachers in creating a supportive play environment that responds to the diverse social needs of all children.

SUMMARY AND CONCLUSION

This chapter assumes that a major way children develop socially is through the exercise of their communicative skills in pretend play with peers. Adult modeling of verbal skills and interactive strategies is not enough. The child's application of given strategies is not only developmentally determined, but also requires the child to interpret the *situated* character of meaning in unfolding play events. When teachers take over this interactive work, they rob children of opportunities to develop their own strategies. This makes close observation by teachers a critical factor in providing relevant support, particularly for mixed-age and/or inclusive groups or in bi-dialectical, bilingual, or bi-cultural play settings.

Such observation allows teachers to:

1.   Examine play through its communicative features to assess how contexts interact with social expectations to influence children's play;

2.   Make and test judgments about the effectiveness of play settings; and

3.   Utilize their knowledge of the classroom context with its interplay of environmental and social expectations to create new curricula for play and socialization. A genuine play curriculum can respond to children's special needs or individual interests as well as lend support to diverse cultural, linguistic and developmental needs and competencies.

Categories of play, such as parallel, solitary, or collaborative, have served us well over the years, as has our psycho-dynamic and constructivist theoretical heritage. This heritage has been augmented by new technologies, analytic methods, and the fresh theoretical orientation of the sociocultural school of Vygotsky. The recent publication of some previously unnoticed writings of Piaget on the role of social factors in the development of children's reasoning provides us with the means to help integrate various strands of constructivist thinking (Alward, 1997b; DeVries, 1997; Piaget & Smith, 1995). This lends a new perspective to our analysis of the social context of play events and deepens our understanding of traditional categories of play and socialization. We are now able to obtain better and more relevant information on how and when to intervene to help mediate gender, cultural, linguistic, or individual differences that may constrain the child's effective participation in play with peers. Teachers also are able to demonstrate how children's communication in play is an important mechanism that helps them become socialized. In practical terms we can design and implement curricula that support socialization in more relevant ways. Through observation and analysis of play in its sociocultural context, our strategies can relate to local and antecedent conditions, such as problems with separation, individual and special needs of particular children, and the diversity of classrooms and play situations.

FOCUSING OUR THINKING

1. Role-play episodes of play drawn from contrasting ecological settings in your own classroom. Examine how language varies in different settings. Is one setting more demanding of children's interactive skills? What kinds of knowledge do children need to sustain play at various settings in your school?

2. Role-play gender stereotypic play events. What kinds of themes are typical for each? Where does each most commonly occur? What are some things teachers do or need to do to the environment and social expectations in order to make it possible for children to play effectively in mixed-gender groups in their classroom?

3. Collect accident or "ouch" reports and analyze them for information on who, what, where and when accidents in your play yard occur. Summarize your data for discussion with co-teachers and administrators.

4. In mixed-age classrooms, departing members of the class can cause a sense of loss in a formerly equilibrated social milieu. By providing opportunities for children to view photos or make drawings of departed classmates, the group's disquietude may be alleviated.

SUGGESTED RESOURCES

1. Corsaro, W. (1997). *The sociology of childhood*. Thousand Oaks, CA, London & New Delhi: Pine Forge Press.

   A new work on cross-cultural aspects of interactive play and interpretive research.

2. Corsaro, W. (1979). "We're friends, right?" Children's use of access rituals in a nursery school. *Language in Society, 8*, 315–336.

   Drawing on ethnographic research in nursery schools, Corsaro demonstrates particular strategies children employ to accomplish their social goals, such as entering into play with peers.

3. Nicolopoulou, A. (1997). Worldmaking and identity formation in children's narrative play-acting. In Brian D. Cox & Cynthia Lightfoot, (Eds.) *Sociogenetic perspectives on internalization* (pp. 157–187). Mahwah, NJ: Lawrence Erlbaum Associates.

   Like Paley, Nicolopoulou notes that when children create their own narratives social, developmental and gender issues intersect in ways that can be thought provoking for the teacher. (See Cook-Gumperz & Scales, 1996; Dyson, 1997; and Goodwin, 1990.)

4. Paley, V. G. (1981). *Wally's stories*. Cambridge, MA: Harvard University Press.

   Paley traces the social integration of a newcomer to her classroom through observation and interpretation of the child's play and storytelling.

5. Paley, V. G. (1984). *Boys and girls: Superheroes in the doll corner*. Chicago: University of Chicago Press.

   In "real-life" stories drawn from introspection about her own classroom, Paley brings new insights to our grasp of differences in the play patterns of boys and girls.

6. Paley, V. G. (1996). *You can't say you can't play*. Cambridge, MA: Harvard University Press.

   This work gives teachers an inspiring new approach to play intervention and helps them challenge children to think of ways to avoid the exclusion inherent in saying, "You can't play."

7. Trawick-Smith, J. (1994). *Interactions in the classroom: Facilitating play in the early years.* New York, Oxford, Singapore, Sydney: Maxwell Macmillan International.

Excellent anecdotal reports on children's interactions in play. Gives authentic and insightful observations of many facets of the play-based curriculum.

CHAPTER **11** ❧

Play, Toys, and Technology

🐋 🐋 🐋 🐋 🐋 🐋 🐋 🐋 🐋 🐋 🐋 🐋 🐋 🐋

Maxwell, Akemi, and Duane are playing spaceship using the housekeeping area and part of the block area. They have appropriated blocks to construct seats for their spaceship and a pilot's cockpit, using a cardboard box on which they have painted pretend dials and knobs as the control panel. Next to the seating area they have incorporated the playhouse kitchen.

Maxwell is making "space food" with the toy microwave. "Dinner in five minutes, everyone!" he calls. "Just a minute," says Akemi. "I have to check where we are going." She runs over to the computer that sits on a table near the block area, and turns it on, revealing a blank screen. Duane joins her and they peer intently at the computer screen. "It's the Enterprise," warns Duane. "It's coming closer."

🐋 🐋 🐋 🐋 🐋 🐋 🐋 🐋 🐋 🐋 🐋 🐋 🐋 🐋

Toys are the concrete objects that children use to fashion their experiences with sensorimotor play, constructive play, dramatic play, and games with rules. As we see in the example above, children use toys such as blocks and cardboard to construct settings and tools for their pretend play. They use replicas of objects from the adult world such as microwave ovens and dishes to carry out their pretend scripts. Children may even use computers, either as they were designed to be used, or as accessories to their own dramatic purposes, representing the social uses of technology in their play.

But the toys themselves are not the only ingredient of children's play. We also need to examine the cultural contexts and social interactions that surround the use of toys and technology. In the example above, Duane, Akemi, and Maxwell have created a scenario drawn from their viewing of space theme videos and television programming. They use their knowledge about how computers might be used on a spaceflight to incorporate their classroom computer into their play as a prop. They also use information from their daily lives regarding the preparation and social conventions of dinnertime.

In this chapter we look at both toys and the use of technological media that influence children's play. We invite you to consider how both the objects themselves and the social contexts in which children and adults use those objects shape children's play in early childhood settings.

TYPES OF TOYS

The category of toys is large and composed of many sub-categories. There are purely sensorimotor toys which give rise to repetitive activity and the joy of making things happen with an object. Bouncing balls, shaking rattles, spinning tops, rocking horses, and monkey bars are a few familiar examples. There are representational toys that look like other objects in the culture or in nature. Miniatures of animals, toy vehicles, houses, utensils, furniture, and dolls are familiar exam-

Children use blocks to construct
settings for pretend play.

ples. There are construction toys that can be manipulated and used to create new objects. Blocks, Legos, Bristle blocks, and Tinkertoys are examples seen in classrooms for young children. There are locomotion toys such as tricycles, bicycles, skateboards, scooters, and wagons (Hewitt & Roomet, 1979).

Toys affect development in profound and sometimes subtle ways. For one thing, toys orchestrate both individual and social activity. Toys have a "logic-of-action" that suggests how the toy is to be used. For example, a toy telephone suggests or "cues" particular forms of motor, representational, and social behavior.

Some toys are specific in their cues. Legos and pattern blocks cue children for constructive play; action figures, dolls, stuffed animals, and toy vehicles cue for dramatic play; and game boards suggest games with rules. Toys also cue teachers for specific play expectations. The toys that teachers designate as "math manipulatives" might include collections of miniature animals, vehicles, or furniture for children to arrange in sets and thus construct logical-mathematical relationships. Manipulatives might also include pattern blocks or Cuisenaire rods for similar purposes. In the case of miniature objects, experience with logical-mathematical thinking is linked to children's dramatic play accessories. In the case of patterning materials, these relationships are linked to constructive play.

Another common "teacher category" for classroom toys is motor toys. Pegboards, pattern boards, and puzzles aid in developing fine motor coordination, whereas trikes, scooters, swings, and climbers help children develop large muscle skills.

Other toys or materials for play in the classroom are raw materials for art and construction. Sand, water, paint, mud, Play-Doh, and collage materials fall into this category.

No matter how adults classify toys and raw materials for play, the key point is that children will use toys in their play in ways that suit their own agendas, not necessarily those of adults. The essential question is "How does the child see the play potential of a given toy or material?"

Along these lines, Griffin (1982) suggests that teachers categorize toys by the effects they have on children's inner feelings and social interactions rather than by the intellectual concepts and skills the toys are thought to develop. Some toys suggest active group play, such as blocks, housekeeping toys, and art materials. Others, such as pegboards, puzzles, miniature animals, and books, cue for quiet, solitary play. Griffin notes that toys that are self-correcting in nature such as bead strings and pegboards are soothing to children because they give children an opportunity to create order and control in their physical environments. They are calming in the same way that gardening might be for adults. Many of Montessori's self-correcting toys have this appeal for young children (Montessori, 1936).

Toys such as miniatures and books in a solitary context encourage flights of imagination without the burden of negotiating pretend play with others. Children can use miniatures to represent emotionally laden experiences, thus allowing them to process confusing or troubling experiences at a more comfortable distance (Oaklander, 1978). For example,

≥⬥ Sean had trouble separating from his mother at the start of the preschool day. Each day for the first few weeks of school, after a tearful good-bye, Sean took out the tiny family dolls and a small plastic playhouse. "Bye Mommy," he said as he walked the little boy doll into the house. "I love you," he whispered, as he put the Mommy doll into a toy car and "drove" it away. He then brought the Mommy doll back to the house, and said, "It's time to go home now. Did you have a good day?" as he put the Mommy and little boy into the car. ⬥

This kind of play allows children to project their feelings onto toys without having to play just one role. It allows them to control the situation from the outside. Accordingly, Griffin (1982) suggests that classrooms have an ample supply of toys that are potentially "charged" for children: baby bottles and high chairs, spiders, dragons, capes, magic wands, and hats.

Griffin (1982) also recommends raw materials that appeal to children's senses such as sand, water, mud, fingerpaint, glue, and collage materials. These are also important vehicles for helping children to establish emotional equilibrium in their play.

TOYS AND DEVELOPMENT

As development proceeds, children's primary uses of toys change. The best toys for young children have the quality of "play-ability" that allows children to adapt the toy to their individual needs and stages of development over an extended period of time. Blocks are a good example of a toy with high play-ability. A two-year-old may experiment with stacking and falling blocks, repeating the process over and over in sensorimotor play. A three-to-seven-year-old child might use the blocks to construct objects she has seen ("This is the dolphin pool at Marine World") or as a prop in dramatic play (a telephone or walkie-talkie). Finally, blocks might serve as the pieces for a game with rules, as children stand blocks on end and "bowl" them down with a pitched tennis ball, giving points for each "hit."

In addition to providing toys with high play-ability, teachers may also want to provide toys that meet specific needs at particular developmental stages. For example, the process of symbolic distancing described in chapter 3 calls for sensitivity on the part of the teacher to provide toys that are a good match of structure to the child's developing symbolic concepts. Structure is the degree to which a toy or other object resembles the object that the child is symbolizing. For example, in order to scaffold their play scripts, two- and three-year-olds may require high structure in their toys, such as replicas of tools, vehicles or housekeeping accessories. Play may easily break down in disputes over who gets to talk on the toy telephone or use the toy fire engine, so teachers may want to have multiple sets of realistic toys available.

As we discussed in chapters 2 and 3, older children, four- to eight-year-olds, are more likely to use "unstructured" toys such as blocks, marbles, or sticks in their play. The representational abilities of older children have developed to the point that meaning exists in their own imaginations rather than depending primarily on the characteristics of the objects themselves. For example, an older child may appropriate a block to stand for a sandwich, a helicopter, a wallet, and a cup of coffee all within the course of a single play episode.

Teachers who carefully observe children's sociodramatic play can ascertain the levels of symbolic distancing in both role play and in play with objects. Then teachers can provide an array of toys ranging from structured replicas to unstructured objects for children to use.

Toys that Limit Development

The issue of toy structure also relates to the profusion of electronic and "do everything" toys on the market. In order to develop abstract concepts and the capacity for imagination, young children need opportunities to apply their own meanings and actions to toys. Toys that have only one use do not provide children with the flexibility they need to use the toys in alternative ways. An action figure whose role or behavior is narrowly defined by the toy's features or a doll whose body movements and talk are produced by the machine inside stifles children's emerging imaginations. Such toys can interfere with the development of distancing strategies that underlie abstract thinking. These one-use-only toys make millions of dollars for toy manufacturers but they are not conducive to children's play development. In fact, the limiting characteristics of some toys not only affect the development of cognition and imagination for young children, but also limit development in other areas. For example, some of the highly detailed toy weapons available for children suggest only violent play, and some of the media character dolls are packaged to persuade children that each character performs only one role or function in play, often a gender-stereotyped role (Carlsson-Paige & Levin, 1990; Levin, 1998).

GAMES WITH RULES

As children move from early childhood into middle childhood, games with rules become increasingly evident in their play. Board games and games of motor skill, such as jump rope, soccer, hopscotch, and tetherball, have long dominated games with rules for children in primary grades. Most adults have vivid childhood memories of ball and rope games, clapping and chanting games played spontaneously on their school playgrounds or neighborhood streets.

Some games with rules such as hopscotch or tic-tac-toe require no special equipment and can be played in a variety of settings. Others, such as jump rope or soccer, require some purchased materials. In contemporary society we have an increasing variety of commercial toys in the category of games with rules. These range from traditional board games such as *Candy Land* or *Monopoly* to video and computer games with rules. These games have in many ways supplanted the pervasive outdoor motor games of earlier decades and replaced them with games that rely on visual acuity and fine motor coordination to carry out winning moves.

Planning for Development in Game Play

Whatever the form, board game, computer game, or playground game, teachers need to be sensitive to the cognitive leap represented by children's entry into the play stage of games with rules.

In dramatic play, children construct the cognitive and social basis for their emerging understanding of the nature of rules. In the dramatic play of preoperational thought, children's fantasies are explicit and frequently articulated: "Let's pretend that it's raining today so we had to get our umbrellas" or "You have to be the big sister that's going to the store." Rules of dramatic play are implicit and are negotiated as the fantasy unfolds. Comments such as "Puppies sound like this," or "Cowboys run this way," accompany children's verbalization and enactments of fantasy story lines.

As children enter into the play stage of games with rules, usually beginning about the age of six, the relationship of rules to fantasy shifts (Nicolopoulou, 1991). Now the fantasy becomes implicit or taken for granted by the players, such as the "as if" frame of reference for *Candy Land* or *Monopoly*. The rules are explicit, formulated by the manufacturer, and are often further negotiated by the players before the play begins. Verbal discussion shifts from "Let's pretend . . . " to "The rule says. . . . "

Games need to honor this developmental progression. Games with rules marketed for preschool and kindergarten children need to be used with caution and sensitivity by teachers. Board games and sports equipment have their place in the early childhood classroom, but should not be used in place of the more appropriate constructive and dramatic play materials for this age group. Instead, sensitive teachers will encourage children who use balls and bats, jump ropes, board games, and computer programs to create their own rules and construct their own understandings of winning and losing (Kamii & DeVries, 1980).

Selecting Appropriate Games for Young Children

Understanding the development of play is only one aspect of selecting appropriate games for young children. Other features of game design are important when choosing games for children to play in early childhood classrooms.

Malone (1983) designates three critical characteristics of game play. Although he focuses on the computer medium, many of these characteristics also apply to board games and motor skill games that children enjoy.

The first of these qualities is challenge. For challenge to be effective, the goal of the game should be obvious to children and the outcome uncertain. Goals that engage the child with personal meaning are most effective. In a board game such as *Bingo*, children delight in covering squares with the appropriate shape or animal, with the winner having the opportunity to shout "Bingo!" In computer software, these goals might include such activities as creating a birthday card for Grandma in "Writing Table" in *Bailey's Book House* or a design with *LOGO*. These kinds of goals are more interesting than simply keeping count of correct answers to problems.

Materials for games and games themselves continue to challenge individual play and are adaptable to children with varying abilities when degrees of challenge are built in. Card games, for example, offer many possibilities for levels of challenge, from the simple matching of *Concentration* to the classifying and counting of *Go Fish*. In computer programs for young children, such as the patterning activity *Bing and Boing* in *Millie's Math House*, levels might be selected by the player or determined by the computer, based on the child's performance.

Fantasy is the second criterion for motivating game play. Children's entry into an "as if" frame of reference for their play provides the context for mental play with rules and strategies. Malone distinguishes between "extrinsic" fantasy games and "intrinsic" fantasy games. In extrinsic fantasy, the player pursues a fantasy goal such as landing on the moon by spinning a spinner, or avoids a fantasy catastrophe such as crashing a boat by earning points for correct answers to problems posed by the computer. For example, spelling words, answering addition facts, or matching letters to objects with the correct beginning sound results in progress toward the fantasy goal, much like throwing dice moves one along in a board game.

Intrinsic fantasies are linked to the problem-solving goals of the game. Children become more successful in their play as they create better strategies, rather than relying on luck or improved eye-hand coordination. The long-time favorite *Monopoly* is a good example of a board game with intrinsic fantasy. In the computer game *Gertrude's Secrets*, children discover Gertrude the duck's secret treasures by negotiating her through maps of rooms depicted on the screen. An example for older children is the pursuit and apprehension of Carmen Sandiego and her band of thieves through information gleaned from the player/detective's crime database in *Where in the World Is Carmen Sandiego?*

Fantasy is also implicit in children's art and design programs, such as *Etch A Sketch*, *Facemaker* or *Fantavision*, in which players create their own animated faces or drawings, or in computer software such as *Playroom* or *Inigo's Dream*, where children enter layers of fantasy environments and actions by clicking a computer mouse on computer screen objects.

Malone's third criterion for effective games is curiosity. Curiosity may be fostered in the exploratory phase of play in which children experiment with light, sound, and movement to see what patterns are created by their actions. Curiosity also arises about how to resolve a paradox or discrepancy in the logic of a game, such as how to find Carmen Sandiego fleeing with her stolen goods to an unknown destination.

One important element of curiosity is that the novelty or discrepancy represented must be moderate for the child. It should be unique enough to arouse interest, but familiar enough for the player to resolve the discrepancy on her own. A related aspect of curiosity is that the complexity factors unfold slowly, allowing players to incorporate new strategies into their play before being enticed, and perhaps overwhelmed, by even more novelty. In *Millie's Math House*, the game *Mousehouse* allows children to build structures on the screen using blueprints of increasing complexity or to invent their own plans.

"BOY TOYS" AND "GIRL TOYS"

Teachers across the country report marked differences in the play of boys and girls in their classrooms and discuss the possible influences of "boy toys" and "girl toys," particularly those that represent media characters. Boys battle and vanquish bad guys. They rescue and escape, climb and fall, pursue and are pursued. Girls are most frequently engaged in domestic play themes and nurturing roles, and create situations where they must be rescued (Gould, 1972; Sutton-Smith & Rosenberg, 1971).

Boys dramatize these themes using toy weapons, vehicles, and He-Man and GI Joe dolls. Girls are more likely to select Barbie dolls, My Little Pony, Pocahontas, house accessories, and toy cosmetics. Has it always been like this? Yes and no. Before the 1960s and 1970s, toys were very stereotyped regarding the adult occupations of men and women. Boys might play at being firemen or doctors, girls mothers or nurses. Both boys and girls, however, participated in the active adventures of riding the range as Dale Evans joined the ranks of Hopalong Cassidy and the Lone Ranger as adventurers.

In the 1970s there were concerted efforts by parents and educators to diminish the gender stereotypes promoted in children's literature, television, film, and toys. These efforts were somewhat successful as girls, particularly, began to cross gender lines in their play (Liss, 1986). It became more acceptable for boys to be sensitive and nurturing and for girls to be assertive and independent. But in the 1980s much of this ground was lost as deregulation of commercials shown during children's programming allowed toy manufacturers to specifically target children's interest in conforming to social perceptions of gender identity in order to sell more toys (Shapiro, 1990).

Developing Gender Identity

A major developmental milestone for preschool, kindergarten, and primary grade children is the establishment of a positive gender identity, feeling good about oneself as a boy or a girl in our society. With their emerging concepts of classification in full sail, children eagerly classify information from their parents, teachers, peers, and the popular media into categories of "boy behavior" and "girl behavior." In our culture many behaviors are "boy-or-girl" behaviors. In the same way the "good guy/bad guy" distinctions appeal to children because of their concrete qualities, children look for the concrete indicators for gender classification, such as haircuts or clothing, as well. Once an object or a behavior has been classified as boy-like or girl-like, then the reasoning continues. "If I am a boy I must do boy-like things and play with boy's toys," or "If I am a girl I must behave as girls do and own girls' toys."

Educators have expressed concerns about the gender stereotyping of computer play.

Gender stereotyping limits the range of experiences that children have in their play and the concepts and skills development associated with those experiences. For example,

🔖 Leslie, a K–1 teacher, has purposely selected a wide range of play materials for her classroom. "I want both boys and girls to develop fine motor skills, such as the cutting, pasting, and using a paintbrush that accompany art play," she comments. "I want both genders to develop large motor skills in climbing, running, sliding, and riding. A wide range of toys helps both the boys and the girls in my group to develop spatial reasoning and the bodily kinesthetic intelligence associated with constructive play. Building a spaceship of Legos or a fort of blocks enhances these experiences for all children. To encourage this, we as teachers need to consciously arrange for children to move beyond stereotyped conventions of what boys and girls do and try new activities." 🔖

Educators have expressed concerns about the gender stereotyping of computer play (Clements, 1987). Many teachers fear that, like mechanical toys in the past, computers will become part of the "boys' toys" category and avoided by girls. Not only does stereotyping limit the developmental opportunities of young children but it also sets the stage for limiting imagination opportunities and children's ideas about what they might like to do when they grow up (Halliday & McNaughton, 1982).

TOYS AND THE MARKETPLACE

In considering both developmental stages of play and the structure of children's games, teachers inform themselves about what play materials are most appropriate for their classrooms. By doing so, teachers may ameliorate the fact that children and parents, as well as teachers, are continually under siege from the toy industry to purchase toys and games that may not be in the best interests of children or appropriate to the development of their imaginative play concepts. Issues such as gender bias and toy safety arise when we consider children as consumers of commercially produced toys and games.

Toy Safety

One of the most compelling issues related to toys and marketing is the question of the safety of toys for young children. Each year hundreds of children are injured while playing with commercial toys. Toy manufacturers have become increasingly sensitive to consumer concerns, probably as the result of prolonged and expensive litigation. Government regulation of toy safety standards has increased with both the Hazardous Substance Act of 1973 and the Consumer Product Safety Act of 1978. These standards include the important requirement that toy manufacturers clearly label products with age appropriateness. This means that toys containing tiny pieces or sharp edges must be clearly labeled to warn adults that they are not designed for children under the age of three. Toys that are electrical in nature, and thus present a potential hazard of burning children, must be labeled as hazardous for children eight and younger.

Consumer publications inform parents and teachers about toy safety issues. (See Suggested Resources at the end of this chapter.) The magazine *Child Health Alert,* in the February and May 1991 issues, reviewed recent efforts to regulate toxins in children's art supplies, citing the *Center for Safety in the Arts* as a good source of current lists of materials recommended to be free of chemical toxicity for young children.

The Toy Manufacturers of America, in conjunction with the United States Consumer Product Safety Commission, developed and published guidelines for guarding against potential accidents involving toys. These guidelines include:

1.   Select toys that are appropriate for children's interests and stages of development. This includes avoiding toys with long strings or small parts for infants and toddlers. "Choke tubes" are available to measure the size of pieces in toys that are suspected of being dangerous.

2.   Read labels on packaging carefully and dispose of packing material (such as plastic wrappers) that might be dangerous to children. Choose toys with non-toxic paints and flame-retardant fabrics.

3.   Keep toys clean and in good repair. Store toys for older children out of sight and reach from those at earlier developmental stages.

4.   Supervise the play of children, particularly very young children, to see that they do not use toys in ways that are dangerous to their health or safety.

Not all products are screened under consumer safety guidelines. Parents, teachers, and other professionals who work with children and families must still be vigilant. Many products available by mail from overseas do not meet these standards. Toys that children acquire from someone's attic may be in poor repair or have pieces missing that make them potentially hazardous.

Playground safety.   Another issue is playground safety. While space limitations do not allow us to treat this topic in depth, we have recommended several resources useful for planning safe, outdoor play areas that have high play-ability. One of the most "user friendly" of these resources is the manual on playground safety written by Jambor and Palmer (1991). These authors offer both general guidelines and specific criteria in checklist form.

They discuss three general principles for school playground safety. First, enclosures that shelter play environments should have no visual barriers so that children may be adequately supervised and protected from hazards outside the play area. Second, adequate space is needed to safely accommodate children using equipment on their own. The authors include guidelines for space surrounding slides, swings, and climbing structures. Third, play surfaces must minimize the impacts of children's falls. In general, Jambor and Palmer recommend that more resilient surfaces (such as grass or packed dirt in comparison to cement or asphalt) are less likely to contribute to injury when children fall.

MEDIA-BASED PLAY

In chapter 5 we presented another dilemma teachers face at this time in history, the link between play and audiovisual programming. The most obvious culprit here is television, although commercial videotapes and computer software have become problematic as well.

Television and Children's Play

Critics of television for young children have long argued that television viewing deadens children's imaginations and social interaction skills in two ways. First, the process of television viewing puts the young child in a passive role, absorbing the products of others' imaginations in full color and sound, rather than stimulating the child's own imagination. Second, if children weren't watching television, then they would be playing. And in that play they would develop their own symbolic concepts, extend their capacities for problem solving and creativity, and increase their abilities to negotiate and cooperate with others (Winn, 1977).

Critics of television have also argued that the stereotyped and often violent content of children's programming is detrimental to their play and future development. The media influence on children's play takes several forms, one of which involves the characters and plots that children create for their play narratives. This influence is particularly insidious because young children are just learning to develop their sense of story. Bruner (1986) describes character and action as the first "landscapes" of the human capacity for narrative. When these formative landscapes are filled with violent and destructive characters and action, they may have pervasive and long-lasting effects on development.

Although characters such as Luke Skywalker and Princess Leia from the Star Wars trilogy or Robin Hood represent positive forces, they repeatedly resolve conflicts through violent actions. Characters such as Darth Vader represent villains that may help children define their understanding and resolution of good and evil, but again, the resolution of evil influences is achieved by violence. Children watch these characters enthusiastically kill and injure others. Because young children are very literal in their thinking, they understand that "this is how we do things." The battles that ensue between the positive and negative forces in Robin Hood, the Teenage Mutant Ninja Turtles films, or Ghostbusters and their slimy adversaries influence children's emerging beliefs about the manner in which good vanquishes evil. Unfortunately, most media examples convey the message that violence is acceptable as long as the motive is good.

Fortunately, positive role models are also available and illustrate alternative possibilities (Greenfield, 1984). Mr. Rogers, Barney, and Bert and Ernie on Sesame Street are all characters whose attraction for young children rests on their warmth, humor, and caring behavior. They resolve conflicts without violence. Teachers need to talk to children about the personalities and powers of their heroes and heroines and help them to imagine non-violent alternatives to resolving conflicts between good and evil.

Let's consider action, the second "landscape" in Bruner's model for the structure of narrative. In this aspect of narrative, children construct plots and themes for their play. At worst, the action in television/video-derived play is limited and repetitive as well as violent. Children imitate with great insistence to detail the characters, events, and actions they have seen. This limited play is often accompanied and exacerbated by commercial accessories that have explicit detail and cue children to use them in only prescribed ways.

Talk to children about the media and their play.   Although there are limited federal regulations on children's programming, teachers should alert parents and discuss with children the television toy commercials they see. Young children do not have a well-developed sense of what is fantasy and what is reality, particularly when confronted with the special effects of audiovisual media. Nor do they have the life experience or self-reflective concepts needed to make wise consumer choices.

Questions such as "Will it last?" "How much would I use it?" and "Am I being manipulated by commercials?" need to be discussed with children to counteract the effects of toy and media exploitation. One first grade teacher found her daily sharing time to be a good avenue for consumer education. She helped children to discuss the features of toys they liked and to focus on the play alternatives for a particular vehicle, action figure, or doll rather than on their plans to collect them just for the sake of collecting.

Advocate for good children's programming.   Most young children spend hours watching television each day. The previous limitations on the length, type, and number of commercials during children's programming that were present in the 1960s and 1970s were suspended by government actions in the 1980s. This deregulation has resulted in a rash of television commercials disguised as children's cartoons, whose major purpose is to convince children that they can't "play" the themes they see on television without purchasing all the toys. Each character in the line of toys such as GI Joe, He-Man, or My Little Pony has specific features so that children are led to believe they have to own the complete set (Carlsson-Paige & Levin, 1990). In addition to talking to children, teachers can advocate for good programming for children by actively supporting the efforts of such organizations as Action for Children's Television and informing parents about their efforts.

COMPUTER PLAY AND YOUNG CHILDREN

We have discussed the topic of computer play throughout this chapter, taking the view that computers in classrooms for young children should be treated much like any other toy or material for children's play. In fact, this was the view of computers set forth by Seymour Papert (1980), creator of LOGO, in his now classic work *Mindstorms*. In discussing the potential for the graphics program LOGO to influence education, Papert referred to computers as "powerful objects to think with" and predicted that they would revolutionize classroom practices.

But this view was not easily embraced by early childhood educators (Clements, 1985). When computers were first introduced into the educational marketplace, many educators were skeptical of the value they would have for young children's play. Early critics of computers for young children such as Barnes and Hill (1983) and Cuffaro (1984) seriously questioned whether the abstract medium of computer graphics was appropriate for young children. Along with others, they also expressed fears that the computer did not foster active exploration and play in the same ways that toys such as blocks, Legos, tricycles, sand, paint, and water play might. They feared that the direct experiences that come through children's play with real objects and are so central that the foundation for logical-mathematical thinking would be "short-circuited" by the abstract quality of computer images. Another pervasive fear was that computer play put the machine in control of the child rather than the child in control of the machine.

Now that computers are being used in most early childhood classrooms, many educators, including Papert (Papert, 1993; Porter, 1991), acknowledge that the educational revolution once predicted has not occurred. Nor have computers harmed development, as the early critics predicted. Rather, teachers tend to design computer activities and choose software that reflects their own instructional strategies. Teachers who emphasize drills tend to use computers for this purpose which Taylor (1980) labeled the "computer as tutor." This genre of computer play activities for children resembles "animated workbooks" in which the computer presents skill-oriented tasks, such as matching shapes, letters, or numbers, and encourages the child based on the child's performance. But many of these skills such as vocabulary for directionality (above, below, right, left) seem to be more appropriately learned in the context of active play with concrete objects. As Cuffaro (1984) puts it, "The question here is not 'Why use a microcomputer?' but rather, 'Why use workbooks, animated or not, with young children?'" (p. 5).

In contrast to the "computer-as-tutor" approach of animated workbooks, teachers who value play tend to choose "computer-as-tool" and the "computer-as-tutee" types of software which offer children more opportunities to control computer play (Taylor, 1980).

Tool Software

A variety of software is available for young children that provides the same "tools" that adults use, but with more child-friendly user interfaces. As young children begin to read and write, they can use some adult software such as e-mail programs quite successfully as well. Art/graphics programs, word processing, and multimedia programs that combine the child's written words with images, sound and sometimes animation, are readily available.

Children use these programs in the context of their play to create and illustrate stories, make books, greeting cards, and gifts of their creative work, or, in the same way as "real" drawings or paintings, to express their artistic inclinations. Whether children use multimedia programs to integrate images with words, or use graphics programs alone, it is important to apply the same standards as with "real" art materials. Children should always be encouraged to create original artwork rather than relying on clip art or electronic coloring books.

Older children can make wonderful mentors and role models when they assist with computer play in the early childhood classroom.

⬥ Maria is a fifth grade mentor who helps in Andrea's kindergarten computer center twice a week. On this day, Joshua has been playing with a graphics program. He has made a line drawing of a bunny and Maria has taught him how to fill in the area with different colors. After several minutes, Josh frowns. "I don't want this bunny for my story. I want *that* bunny," he says, pointing to the painting he had made earlier. Maria, who recently learned to use a scanner for her own work, asks the teacher if she can take Joshua to the school library to scan his painting. Later, he dictates his story using the scanned image of his bunny. When Joshua's writing is printed with his scanned drawings, the result looks much like a printed book. ⬥

While educators should focus their attention on the processes of children's play, not their products, it is also important to think about both process and product from the child's view. Some researchers have found that young children's self-esteem increases more over time in classrooms with computers than in classrooms without them (Haugland, 1996; Clements, Nastasi & Swaminathan (1993), in Haugland, 1996). Haugland and Wright believe that children feel more competent and important when they use computers because they view computers as "adult machines."

E-mail is a wonderful communication tool for children's play. The speed of sending and receiving e-mail makes it especially exciting for children who have a hard time waiting for a response by "snail-mail." Teachers often find that children write more, write in greater detail, and correct their writing more when they use computers to write for a real audience as in using e-mail (Bernhardt, 1997).

⬥ In Nancy's first grade class, students have same-age e-mail buddies at another school, adult e-mail buddies through a corporate partnership, and fifth grade buddies at their own school. The children have partners in their class and, together, they write to their e-mail buddies. Nancy finds that the children not only benefit by helping each other, but enjoy the social aspect of composing written language together.

When the computer sounds to signify that a new e-mail message has arrived, a child rushes to the computer and announces that Lily and Brian have e-mail. They head for the computer and find a message from their adult e-mail buddy. The children love getting mail, and want to write back right away. In response to their question, their buddy has written about her pets and asks, "Do you have any pets?"

Twenty minutes later, Brian and Lily send off the following message:

I have a gol fis. My gol fis is bubbles.
I have a dog. My dog is very ol.

Do you like gol fis?
Do you like hres?
Do you like cows?
Do you have a cow?

Nancy finds that the students write differently to their different buddies. They write quickly and informally to their same-age buddies. They try very hard to correct mistakes when they write to their adult buddies. Since their fifth grade buddies come to class to read to them, they usually write with a purpose, asking for a particular book or commenting on a book that has been read. Although participating in e-mail is always a matter of choice, most children rush to answer their messages and wait with expectation for a response. 🐌

Guiding Play with Computers as Tools

Teachers can guide children's play with computers by scaffolding its use as children explore its features and begin to use it for their own imaginative ends. For example, Cochran-Smith, Kahn, and Paris (1990) note that word processing can serve to free children's imaginations from the constraints imposed by handwriting. The five- and six-year-olds they studied were often sidetracked from the goal of creating text by difficulties in handwriting. Their attention would shift from the story line to the production of letter forms.

Word processing freed children to compose more connected text. They were able to use their mental energy to compose story lines and construct concepts about letter-sound relationships in invented spelling. The formation of letters no longer claimed the lion's share of their attention. The teacher helped children to review what they had written and to plan more complex texts by asking questions such as "How did the mom feel about that?" The teachers also helped children to coordinate their invented spelling with finding letters on the keyboard. (See chapter 9 for a further discussion of acquisition of literacy skills.)

This guidance in shifting focus among the various tasks of writing composition, taking the perspective of one's audience, and transcription serves as an example of children and teachers working within what Vygotsky called the "zone of proximal development." It helps children to construct patterns of their own and will eventually lead them to coordinate independently all aspects of the writing process.

Computer Simulations, Games, and Books

"Tutee" software for young children also offers opportunities to control play with the computer. Some of these are simulations in which children enter as characters into the play and control characters' actions on the screen. Others allow children to manipulate objects in interesting ways. One program, for example, allows children to create buildings and towns, and then change their perspective gradually, as if they were able to fly overhead like a bird. Other forms of computer programming software, such as LOGO, were developed especially for young children. In these types of software, children encounter challenging problems to solve that are built into the software design. Forman (1994) believes that when children use computer simulations to augment real materials such as blocks, the program's ability to replay the previous actions allows children to reflect on and improve their problem-solving strategies.

The availability of interactive books, generally on CD-ROMs, is another popular form of "tutee" software. A quality interactive book first begins with a good story worth reading again and again. Children control the story by clicking on objects to begin animations, hearing the story in different languages, turning off the "reader" altogether, and, in some cases, choosing alternative events and endings. While some interactive books are available on the Internet, at this time, the pictures generally "load" very slowly even with fast Internet connections.

While computer simulations, games and books are attractive to children and offer many opportunities to develop problem-solving strategies and creative thinking, teachers need to be diligent in applying the same criteria in their selection as with other books or games (i.e., gender equity, non-violent content, sensitive awareness to culture and ethnicity, child-centered and developmentally appropriate, etc.).

Integrating Technology

Teachers increasingly view computers as simply another valuable part of the young child's environment, rather than as a panacea for all learning or a threat to social play (Clements, 1987; Haugland & Shade, 1988). From this view, the ways that the computer fits into the culture of the classroom and children's play within that culture become the important issues to consider.

For example, the social context and manner in which children come to use computers as objects for play determine their comfort level with this aspect of technology in their lives. When computers are used to serve children's own imaginative purposes, this process is enhanced. Play with computers fosters attitudes of competence and flexibility. It humanizes the machine through a playful stance rather than allowing the machine to dehumanize the child in situations where only the machine has the "right" answers and the child must struggle to produce them (Jungck, 1990).

Recognizing that appropriate use of technology fosters learning and self-esteem in young children, the National Association for the Education of Young Children (NAEYC) developed a position on technology in 1996. The NAEYC recommends that educators:

- apply the principles of developmentally appropriate practices (Bredekamp, 1987) in choosing and using technology.
- integrate technology as one of many options available to children in the learning environment.
- be conscious of promoting equal access to technology to all children, including children with special needs.
- take responsibility for avoiding software that includes stereotypes or violence, especially if the violence is controlled by the child. Software selec-

tion, like selection of other materials, should reflect the diversity of today's world.

- take responsibility for working with parents in choosing appropriate software.
- use technology in their own professional development, such as using e-mail as a tool to collaborate with other educators and to access educational resources on the Internet.

We agree with these recommendations, and also emphasize the following: teachers should encourage children to play with technology in ways that are open-ended, allowing children to determine the outcome of their play.

To help teachers choose instructional activities that are technology based, von Blanckensee (1997) designed the following scale, *Choosing Technology-based Activities for Young Children, Ages 3-7*. (See Table 11–1.) These include activities that use audio recorders, cameras, video recorders, computer simulations, games and books and e-mail. This rating scale includes three issues for teachers to consider when evaluating the appropriateness of an activity: (1) content/method, (2) technology design issues, and (3) computer software design issues. The items used for ratings help teachers assure that they use technology in ways that reflect individual needs, promote gender equity and respect cultural diversity.

Choosing Computer Software

Because new software is constantly becoming available and existing software is constantly being upgraded, we have avoided recommending specific software in this book. Rather, teachers need a framework for judging software themselves and/or access to software reviews that share their point of view. The above rating scale provides an excellent framework for considering the many issues involved in selecting software which we have mentioned throughout this section. The scale takes into consideration technical and interface design, issues of diversity, equity, and non-violent content, and whether the software supports constructivist learning in ways that are age appropriate.

Teachers may also turn to ratings of software based on criteria that are in keeping with NAEYC guidelines. The Haugland/Shade Developmental Scale (Haugland, 1997), revised in 1996, is well known and has been used to evaluate a wide range of current software. (Evaluations of children's software based on this scale are available through The Kids Project, Center for Child Studies, Southeastern Missouri State University.)

Other sources of information about high quality software are state departments of education. Many states provide a variety of resources on the Internet, accessible to teachers anywhere. For example, the Internet site of the California Instructional Technology Clearinghouse has a searchable database of software for grades K–12, rated by teachers (http://clearinghouse.k12.ca.us). Much of the software rated "exceptional" at the kindergarten and first grade level is also appropriate for preschool classes. Additional information may also be available through county offices of education or local school districts. When choosing soft-

Table 11.1
Choosing Technology-based Activities for Young Children.

Ratings: 0= poor   1= adequate   2= good   3= excellent
Teachers may want to redesign or avoid activities which are poor on any criteria.

Content/method

The activity supports learning objectives which are developmentally appropriate and consistent with the curriculum. The activity:

- relates to the child's direct experiences.
- is integrated into the curriculum through connections to other hands-on activities which support the same learning objectives.
- is interesting and challenging to students at a wide range of ability and skill levels.
- is open-ended, allowing children to learn through their own playful investigation.
- supports language development either directly, through interactive use by children in groups, or through extensions of the activity.
- is appropriate to children with varied learning styles.
- can involve two or more children working cooperatively.
- positively addresses or is sensitive to issues of multiculturalism.
- positively addresses or is sensitive to issues of gender equity.
- positively addresses or is sensitive to issues of individual differences.
- has non-violent content, in the case of computer games and simulations.

Technology Design Issues:

- The child can learn to physically operate the technology independently.
- The technology is safe for the age level intended.
- The technology is chosen and set up to minimize the risk of breakage.
- The technology can be adapted, if necessary, for students with special needs.

Computer Software Design Issues:

- The menu is uncluttered, and uses picture clues with words for menu choices.
- The child can navigate through the software easily, go back to the main menu, or exit the software at any time.
- The program provides help. The child can escape and/or get help at any time.
- The design is attractive to children: it may include colorful graphics, sound, animation.
- The program can be used in more than one language.
- The program can be used by students with special needs.
- Children can print and save their work.

Source: Copyright 1997 by Leni von Blanckensee. Reprinted by permission.

ware rated by others, teachers will want to make sure that the criteria used for rating is philosophically consistent with a play-centered curriculum.

Structuring the Physical Space

If computers are to be used as a tool for children's play, they must be part of the classroom rather than isolated in a computer lab. Physical placement in the room becomes an important consideration. First, there are health and safety issues for both the children and the computers. The computer needs to be placed near a grounded electrical outlet, away from water, other potential spills, and food. A surge protector is recommended to protect the hardware and to provide additional outlet space if necessary. The computer center also needs to be far enough away from very rigorous physical activity to avoid potential accidents. When positioning the computer, avoid places where direct sunlight creates glare on the screen.

A second consideration is creating an optimal environment for children's play. We suggest a table large enough for two to three children to work together, with space on both sides of the computer for children to place materials related to their computer play. A printer should also be connected to the computer so that children can keep the products of their play.

SUMMARY AND CONCLUSION

In this chapter we have looked at toys and games for young children and explored some of the issues that confront educators when selecting materials for children's play. We have looked at cognitive and social development as reflected in children's play materials, and have discussed issues of gender stereotyping and toy safety. We have considered the effects of media-based play on children's development, and outlined strategies that teachers might use to control the influences of popular media culture on the play in their classrooms.

Finally, we have looked at the influences of technology on children's play in early childhood classrooms, and explored some of the interactions we see in materials for play and the social contexts in which play occurs. Like book literacy, computer literacy occurs in a social context, nested in the culture of the classroom, the school, the community, and the society at large. The same might be said of "television literacy" or "video literacy" in that by expressing literacy in any medium we exercise the skills and knowledge that are approved by others in the social contexts we value (Emihovich, 1990; Greenfield, 1984).

These literacies are in turn affected by what children bring to school from home as well as what they experience in their classrooms (Genishi & Strand, 1990). Perhaps "toy literacy" is stretching the concept, but socially approved ownership and behaviors with toys are of great importance in the peer culture of young children. Toy ownership and familiarity with scripts from TV, video, or books are the "cultural capital" of the peer culture in classrooms for young children. In this sense, cultural capital represents the knowledge and skills that give some children status with their peers, such as knowing the plot of Robin Hood, or the latest media superhero toys, or understanding the strategies needed to succeed at a computer game (Emihovich, 1990; Gumperz & Cook-Gumperz, 1982). For example,

&. Nate, a kindergartner whose fine and gross motor skills were poor, who spoke with a lisp, and was difficult to understand, was not a popular play companion in his classroom. Learning to use several computer programs made him the expert to whom other children came for advice and helped him to carve out a niche of competence for himself within the classroom culture. &.

We see toy and computer literacies in this broad view as "an encounter between thought and reality, between desire and possibility, that takes place in the symbolic realm and thereby vastly multiplies human capacity to process, analyze, criticize and reinvent experience" (Easton, 1980, cited in Emihovich, 1990, p. 230). From this perspective, all toys in the classroom—from the blocks to the computer, from lotto games to Robin Hood—contribute to children's emerging literacy in our culture as they find ways to express themselves and ask them to communicate with others through play.

FOCUSING OUR THINKING

1. Evaluate a board game or a computer software program for children ages three through eight using the criteria identified by Malone: challenge, fantasy, and curiosity. Play the game with several children of different ages and tell why they think the game is fun.

2. Visit a toy store and write a review of several toys you find there. Carefully read the labels and descriptions on the boxes and evaluate the toys for safety and gender bias.

3. Interview several children ages three through eight about television shows and toys they see advertised on television. Ask them to describe their favorite television shows or videos and talk to them about commercials on television. What differences do you see in the attitudes of children of different ages?

4. Observe one or two children engaged in an activity that uses computer technology. Use the rating scale presented in Table 11–1 to assess the content, the technology design issues and the software design issues.

SUGGESTED RESOURCES

1. Carlsson-Paige, N., & Levin, D. E. (1990). *Who's calling the shots? How to respond effectively to children's fascination with war play and war toys*. Santa Cruz, CA: New Society Publishers.

    A well-written and conceptually rich book for both parents and teachers concerned with media-based play. The authors offer many practical solutions and real-life examples.

2. Levin, D. E. (1998). *Remote control childhood: Combatting the hazards of media culture.* Washington, DC: National Association for the Education of Young Children.

   In this comprehensive resource for teachers, Levin presents research findings and anecdotes that illuminate the pervasive influence of popular media on children's play. She offers concrete strategies for counteracting the effects of media violence in classrooms and for working with families and advocating on behalf of young children.

3. Clements, D. (1985). *Computers in early and primary education.* Upper Saddle River, NJ: Prentice Hall.

   A comprehensive resource for teachers using computers with young children. The author discusses computer software in a range of curriculum areas and suggests guidelines for setting up computers in classrooms and selecting appropriate software.

4. Jambor, T., & Palmer, S. D. (1991). *Playground safety manual.* Birmingham, AL: American Academy of Pediatrics.

   A concise and practical guide to promoting safety on children's playgrounds. The authors offer checklists and resources for planning for outdoor play spaces that reduce the risk of injury to children.

5. Mitchell, P. (Ed.). (1991). *Child health alert: A monthly survey of current developments affecting child health.* Newton Highlands, MA: Child Health Alert.

   This newsletter is a valuable resource on children's health and safety issues, as well as television programming and nutritional issues, that concern educators of young children.

6. Wright, J. L. and Shade, D. D. (Eds.). (1994). *Young children: Active learners in a technological age.* Washington, DC: National Association for the Education of Young Children.

   This book provides both a summary of research and practical suggestions for teachers on using computers with young children. Chapters are written by many of the major contributors to the field.

CHAPTER **12**

Play as a Tool for Assessment

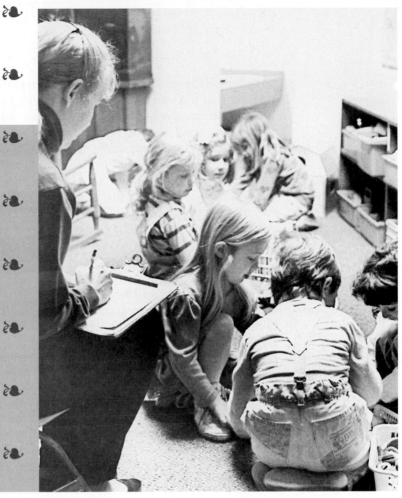

257

🐸 🐸 🐸 🐸 🐸 🐸 🐸 🐸 🐸 🐸 🐸 🐸 🐸 🐸 🐸

In Kathy's kindergarten classroom, four children have set up a "bank." They have stacked two rows of large hollow wooden blocks to form a counter and built chairs for themselves out of smaller blocks. Additional small blocks on the countertop form windows and have the "teller's" names taped to them. Pat, an adult visitor to the classroom, walks up to the teller's window. Shawna, one of the tellers, asks Pat if she brought her bank book. When Pat responds "No, I don't have one," Shawna directs Pat to the basket of small blank paper books that Kathy makes available in the classroom. "Write your name on it," Shawna tells Pat, and Pat prints her name on the front. "P-a-t," Shawna says as she touches each letter, and then remarks that her grandmother's name is Pat too. "Does she spell it like this?" Pat asks. "I don't know," replies Shawna, "I'll ask her."

Returning to her place behind the bank counter, Shawna takes the bank book and opens it to the first page. She carefully writes "CRTO," and then asks Pat how much money she wants. Pat says, "Fifty dollars." "I can't count that much, you know," says Shawna, "How about ten?" Pat agrees and Shawna takes out a piece of 8 × 11 white paper, folds it in half and makes a series of horizontal cuts. She then cuts the paper down the middle and counts out ten pieces of paper. She writes a "1" on each "bill" and counts them out carefully on the counter in front of Pat. "Here you go," Shawna says as she uses a rubber date stamp and a stamp pad available for children's play to stamp the bank book. "Just come back when you run outta dollars."

🐸 🐸 🐸 🐸 🐸 🐸 🐸 🐸 🐸 🐸 🐸 🐸 🐸 🐸 🐸

ASSESSING DEVELOPMENT THROUGH PLAY AT THE "BANK"

Later that day Kathy, the teacher, discusses the dramatic and constructive play at the bank with Pat, who teaches kindergarten in a neighboring school. She talks about the ways in which Shawna's play yields information about her developing concepts and skills in literacy, mathematics, and social studies as well as her social and emotional development.

Kathy has taken Polaroid photographs of the bank in its various stages of construction over two days of free play periods. Both Pat and Kathy are impressed with the complexity of the block representation of the bank environment. Kathy's anecdotal records indicate that the children who built the structure discussed and negotiated their experiences of how banks look. They used spatial reasoning and part-whole relationships to select blocks for the counter, the chairs, small blocks for the name plaques, and long rectangular blocks for the teller's windows. Her notes indicate that Shawna was one of the children who persisted with the project over several days' time, while two other children lost interest after the first day. Shawna and her "new" best friend Emily continued the project and directed the creation of the tellers' roles, which they were eager to play.

The tellers have each written their names and fastened them to the "name plaques," using a social form of literacy they have observed in banks and, at the same time, practicing their own renditions of their names.

Kathy and Pat discuss the conversation about Pat's name, and how Shawna spontaneously identified each letter. "Shawna is still working on the idea that some names are spelled the same way every time—probably because not all the adults who work in this classroom know how to spell her version of 'Shawna,'" Kathy informs Pat.

Another example of how Shawna is working on the consistency of letters to spell words is shown in her careful writing of "CRTO" in the bank book. Apparently there was quite a bit of negotiation when the bank "opened" before the children agreed on "the thing you hafta write in the book." Emily's mother works in a bank and had apparently used the term "credit to" in talking about accounts. Emily was quite emphatic that this was the proper term and used her invented spelling concepts to create the notation "CRTO." The date stamp is another form of social literacy that children have observed in the real world.

ᘒ "Shawna's awareness of the limitations of her counting amazed me," said Pat. "I thought of offering to help her count to 50 and then realized she had already come up with her own, better alternative. I also wondered how she learned to cut paper that way." ᘓ

Kathy explained that weeks earlier they had experimented with paper folding and cutting in order to make shapes for valentines. Shawna was apparently replaying this skill and applying it in a new situation. Kathy and Pat agreed that Shawna's writing of a "1" on each bill and then counting them out carefully for the customer not only showed Shawna's counting skills, but also informally contributed to the concept of place value she will construct in the future.

Kathy is interested in Shawna's progress as an individual and as part of her kindergarten group. Kathy uses information from her assessments of children to plan curricula for her classroom and to monitor the learning that has taken place through the activities she has implemented.

Play is a natural "piece" of the assessment "pie" because it offers perspectives on children's progress in all areas of development as they are spontaneously integrated into daily experience. Ongoing observation of spontaneous play such as the "bank" is an ideal complement to assessments made during guided play with specific goals and to more direct measures of children's achievement in subject-centered activities.

ASSESSING AGE-APPROPRIATE DEVELOPMENT

These examples from Kathy's classroom illustrate age-appropriate development for five- and six-year-olds in the areas of emergent literacy and mathematical concepts. This framework for viewing development, according to the National Association for the Education of Young Children (Bredekamp & Copple, 1997;

National Association for the Education of Young Children & National Association of Early Childhood Specialists in State Departments of Education, 1991) includes the teacher's knowledge of the typical stages of development for children in a given age range on a variety of skills and concepts. Kathy showed Pat Shawna's assessment portfolio which contained handwritten observations, called "anecdotal records," of Shawna's spontaneous and guided play since the first week of school. They compared Shawna's rendition of her name with well-formed letters and adequate spacing in March to the shakily written backwards "s" followed by a series of curved lines that Kathy had placed in Shawna's portfolio in early October.

Pat and Kathy looked at Shawna's early attempts at spelling words other than her name, beginning with the pictures and letters on a shopping list made in the playhouse in November, and then random letters in December and January. Her most recent writing, like the "CRTO" (Credit to) at the bank showed attempts to use some beginning and ending consonant sounds. "I lk wtrmln" (I like watermelon) is Shawna's recent contribution to a class book about favorite letters of the alphabet.

In the area of geometric and spatial reasoning, Kathy collected snapshots of Shawna's block structures, some built along with peers and others individually. Kathy also showed Pat an observation form on which she records anecdotal records of children's spontaneous and guided play, and then marked the context for the observations on a matrix in the upper right-hand corner (Figure 12.1).

"You can see that Shawna enjoys block building from this," remarks Pat. "Yes," says Kathy and points out an anecdotal observation, taken in October, in which Shawna staked out her territory in the block corner by standing up to a group of boys who were trying to take all the blocks for their airport project. "Shawna's been almost single-handedly responsible for the block corner being well integrated with both boys and girls," laughed Kathy. She points to the anecdotal record where she had recorded Shawna's assertion to the boys that "girls need the blocks too!"

Kathy has also assessed Shawna in mathematics play. She shows Pat her notes from earlier months of the school year when she informally questioned Shawna regarding her understanding of counting and one-to-one-correspondence.

One situation was in the playhouse, where Shawna was setting the table for "breakfast" for four stuffed animals. She had each animal sitting at a chair at the table and was passing out napkins. She took the napkins one at a time from the playhouse cupboard and placed each at an animal's place, walking across the playhouse each time. She went through the same process with spoons and cups until each diner had a place setting. After discussing Shawna's breakfast guests and the menu with her, Kathy asked Shawna how many of each—napkins, spoons, and cups—there were. Shawna counted each set aloud, "1-2-3-4." "Four and four and four," she said, smiling, "for my four friends."

Name: Shawna E.	Year Group: '92 Kgn	SOCIAL CONTEXTS				
LEARNING CONTEXTS		pair	small group	child with adult	small/large group with adult	solitary play
collaborative reading & writing activities				9/12	10/24	
play, dramatic play, drama & storying		9/22				11/4
environmental studies						
maths investigations						
design, construction, craft & art projects			11/17			
outdoor play						
science play						
blocks			10/15			

Play stages

Functional (sensorimotor) play: repeated actions for pleasure, such as pouring sand or riding a trike. **(FP)**

Constructive play: play with intent to build something that represents an object in real or imaginary world. **(CP)**

Dramatic play: play involving make-believe objects, roles, and situations represented by gesture and/or language. **(DP)**

Games with rules: play with rules that are set forth or negotiated before play begins. **(GP)**

Dates	Observations and their contexts
9/12	CP Writing card to mother—asks to spell "I love you."
9/22	DP Play with Emily—they set up office with telephone message pad and typewriter made of blocks; elaborate episode, lasts 15 minutes
10/15	DP Defends block use—"girls need blocks too!" She builds a house, while boys nearby build an airport and ask for her blocks.
11/4	GP Sets up Candyland game and moves pieces on board as she talks to herself. Seems very focused.

Figure 12.1

Play Observation Diary.

Source: Adapted from *The primary language record,* by M. Barrs, S. Ellis, H. Hester, and A. Thomas, 1988. © ILEA/Center for Language in Primary Education. Published in the U.S.A. by Heinemann Educational Books, Inc.

Later, in January, Kathy's notes showed that Shawna had set the table for her snack group of six children. She had carefully counted the number of places aloud, then gathered sets of six napkins and six cups and placed one of each at each setting. "Sometime in those three months Shawna learned to count and mentally match equivalent sets instead of doing it one at a time," remarked Kathy. "In October, when I discovered that many of the children were just beginning to construct the idea of one-to-one correspondence, I planned a series of guided play activities where I set up materials like straws and cups and brushes and paintboxes. I asked children to help me set the places for children to work, and found out how they were thinking about counting and correspondence. My observations of play helped me plan a curriculum that was a good match for children's needs and also see how successful my ideas were."

Kathy also had collected samples of Shawna's cutting projects over the course of the school year. Shawna's early attempts at using scissors were characterized by cutting straight short lines, and then tearing the paper with the scissors the rest of the way. Kathy recalled guiding Shawna's hand to show her how to close the blades of the scissors on each cut and how Shawna and a group of friends spent most of their time for nearly two weeks in November making collages for people from magazines and paper scraps.

After that, Shawna's cutting showed smooth edges and control over different shapes. By February, her creations at the valentine table and her subsequent use of folding to make multiple sets of a cut shape were a great advance from her cutting skills earlier in the year.

Up to this point Kathy and Pat had discussed the aspects of Shawna's development seen in her portfolio and through anecdotal records that reflected Shawna's progress in "age-appropriate development." Shawna's development of such concepts as one-to-one correspondence, the use of letters to represent spoken language, and spatial representation with blocks are aspects of development Kathy focused on in her observations. Skills such as counting in conventional order, using scissors, and writing her name also fell within the range of accomplishments Kathy expects of kindergarten children. More importantly, Shawna's records indicated growth in all areas from September to March.

Kathy's anecdotal records and samples of Shawna's writing also document the development of Shawna's friendship with Emily. Although Shawna still chooses to spend part of each day in solitary play, Kathy was pleased to see the development of a "best" friendship with Emily, since she believes most kindergarten children should have at least one friend.

Kathy felt that Shawna's ability to negotiate with other children seemed to have been bolstered by the bond she formed with Emily. For example, Kathy believed that part of the reason Shawna was able to confront the boys over the block building was because she felt she was speaking for her friend as well as herself. Kathy also showed Pat samples of notes with pictures and Emily's name on them that Shawna had written. She recalled that Shawna had proudly spelled out Emily's house number when she drew a picture of Emily's house after visiting one day after school.

ASSESSING INDIVIDUAL DEVELOPMENT

The second aspect of assessment that is equally important is that of individually appropriate development (Bredekamp & Copple, 1997). This aspect of development takes into account each child's cultural, linguistic and family background as well as personality qualities such as temperament and interests. Teachers often intuitively assess children's development with regard to these factors, but because they do not appear on report cards or find their way into "developmental norms" charts, individual factors in development may go by the wayside in favor of more "academic" goals. In her assessment, Kathy makes a point of including children's "dispositions" to learn such as taking initiative, curiosity, and cooperation (Katz & Chard, 1989). She also looks for ways in which children's play reflects their experiences at home, their styles of expressing themselves, and their social and emotional development.

Kathy's observations and portfolio samples for Shawna give her information about this aspect of development.

&- "Shawna comes from a family where she has two teenage brothers. She is the child of her father's second marriage. Some of her interests in block building and her ability to assert herself with the boys in the classroom may come from this experience with her brothers," speculates Kathy. "As a much younger sibling, her situa-

A teacher may assess dispositions to learn such as taking initiative, curiousity, and cooperation.

tion is somewhat similar to that of an only child in the family—Shawna seems to need a lot of time to play by herself. Although she has Emily and one other blossoming good friendship in the room, she often will go to the library corner or the table toys and prefer to play alone. I also think her home situation has fostered her ability to assert herself with adults and talk easily with them. She often includes parents who visit the classroom in her play, just as she did with you today." ❧

Intelligence Is Multifaceted

Another aspect of individual development that is essential for teachers to include in assessment is the interests and aptitudes observed in children's play in the classroom. Gardner (1983) extended the notion of "intelligence" beyond the paper and pencil language and math evaluations traditionally seen in school settings.

In his writing, Gardner (1983) discusses how abilities in music, spatial reasoning, and other aspects of personal expression are more often seen as special "gifts," but not integral to adapting to the world in an intelligent manner. Gardner reminds us that all these intelligences are present to some degree in everyone. Most of us have strengths in two or three intelligences that shape the way in which we see the world and express ourselves. Gardner believes that educators need to pay serious attention to avenues of expression other than the traditional linguistic and logical-mathematical ones emphasized in schools and assessed on standardized tests.

Gardner proposed five other intelligences that operate in people's daily lives. One of these is musical intelligence. Musical intelligence is expressed as children hum and sing to themselves. They often find patterns of sounds in literature, such as alliteration, and are interested in musical instruments, dance, and singing in the classroom.

Another intelligence is bodily kinesthetic intelligence. Children who readily express this intelligence are very active, expressing their thoughts and feelings through bodily movement. They may dance or leap across the room, exhibit coordination beyond their years in large motor activities and be particularly interested in and skilled at the mechanics of objects. They may build complex block structures or enjoy taking apart and exploring parts of simple machines such as adding machines or motors available in the classroom. Children who commonly express themselves through bodily kinesthetic intelligence may be interested in careers as dancers and choreographers, mechanics, athletes, or physicians.

Visual-spatial intelligence may be seen in children who are very interested and skilled in constructive play. Their block structures are very sophisticated in terms of design elements such as symmetry, color, and form, and their dramatic play is often characterized by elaborate use of objects to represent settings for their play. They may be very interested in art, using several different media to convey their ideas, or may focus on the similarities and differences in the shapes of letters and numbers as they begin to use written symbols. In the example above, Shawna exhibits many of the qualities associated with spatial intelligence.

Gardner (1983) also mentions the "personal" intelligences that teachers see in young children. Children who express themselves through *inter*personal intelligence are very interested and savvy about other people's thoughts, feelings, and perspectives. They are often very social and well liked by other children and adults. Others may exhibit more *intra*personal intelligence. These children are very introspective, reflecting on their own thoughts and feelings and are often able to discuss just how they solved a particular problem or how they felt in a certain situation.

Careful observation of children's play, in terms of both the process and content of their activities, offers teachers important clues as to the individual development of each child within this framework of seven intelligences. Current assessment efforts at local, state, and national levels are moving away from total reliance on linguistic and logical-mathematical modes of thinking (Boyd, Potter, & Carlson, 1989; Kamii, 1990; Leavitt & Eheart, 1991; Maeroff, 1991). Educators are beginning to recognize that schools need to support a variety of modes of expression and understanding in order for us to acknowledge the potential of each individual.

PLAY INFORMS ASSESSMENT STRATEGIES

First of all, play is the ultimate "integrated curriculum." It offers teachers windows to view all aspects of children's development. And these aspects of development, such as classification concepts or cooperative behavior, inform teachers about how to orchestrate more complex play.

Play occupies a privileged role in constructivist theories of learning and development. Therefore, it is the natural vehicle for assessing children's understanding of their experiences. In their play, children naturally emphasize concepts or broad patterns of thinking and problem solving rather than isolated skills. Play also offers a multi-dimensional look at concepts that are valued by teachers. It helps teachers to see a myriad of different avenues for developing and expressing understanding of these concepts among individual children.

For example, one of Kathy's goals is that all of her kindergartners learn to count objects using one-to-one-correspondence. But each child approaches this concept in a slightly different way. Jonathan develops his understanding by counting the number of blocks he needs to make the fence around his "lion cage" exactly the same on each side. Shawna sets the table in the housekeeping corner, and Emily arranges the paintbrushes and the cups in correspondence to one another, as she mixes colors for the day's easel painting.

A play-centered curriculum provides an atmosphere for assessment that is both comfortable and challenging. Children have many opportunities to make choices regarding their modes of expression and their playmates. In a classroom well equipped for play, children will find familiar objects and means of expression that scaffold their performances and allow them to create and problem solve in ways most comfortable to them.

Play enhances reliability of assessment by assuring that the results of an assessment are based on many opportunities for observing children at play with familiar materials and playmates. In this way, play-based assessment differs from assessment that occurs only once or twice during a school year in which children are confronted with unfamiliar materials and intimidating contexts and are expected to perform to a standard of achievement.

Play also enhances the validity of assessment. Children are best assessed by their performances in real contexts. For example, it makes sense to evaluate children's spatial reasoning while they are constructing with blocks or collage materials instead of administering a paper and pencil task.

ASCERTAINING THE CHILD'S VIEWPOINT

A major challenge for the teacher in implementing play-based assessment is the development of observation strategies and questioning strategies that will illuminate children's progress, while at the same time respecting children's right to control their own play. When Pat discovered Shawna could not yet count to fifty, she might have asked Shawna how high she could count. Pat decided, however, that interrupting the flow of Shawna's play in order to do direct teaching or to ask her to perform a task was not appropriate in that context. Kathy's anecdotal record in which she questioned Shawna about the numbers of spoons, cups, and napkins demonstrated a situation in which questioning was not disruptive to the play. Shawna seemed pleased to show off the setting, "Four and four and four—for my four friends" to her teacher.

This judgment call on the part of teachers is one that requires sensitivity, thoughtfulness, and a repertoire of strategies for determining when to assess by careful observation and when to guide or directly question a child. As teachers use their careful observations of children's play, they grow in their understanding of how children think and feel and develop a deeper insight into children's purposes and conceptions concerning the world, as well as an appreciation of how the peer culture in the classroom influences learning.

As teachers gain an understanding of children's worlds, they become better able to plan curriculum that is relevant and appropriate to children's development. In guided play experiences, teachers have specific goals in mind. They may use these guided play contexts to assess children's progress in ways that pinpoint the questions they have about the development and learning of individual children and the group.

Selma Wasserman (1990) developed principles for assessing and guiding children's play through questioning strategies and the introduction of new materials. Her model involves setting up materials for children to investigate concepts through their play, and asking questions that encourage children to communicate their thoughts and to elaborate their thinking.

Principles for Framing Play Questions

According to Wasserman (1990), the first rule of thumb in formulating questions for children regarding their play is to carefully attend to the child's behavior and/or verbalization. This may involve making eye contact with the child and certainly listening to children with full attention and interest. It may mean getting down to the child's level or moving close enough so the soft-spoken child may be heard. Attention also means looking for nuances of feeling in the child's behavior, voice pitch or tone. For example, many young children sing as they play with objects, sometimes creating a running monologue about what they are doing.

A second principle emphasized by Wasserman (1990) is respect of the child's intentions and autonomy. This means, in the most basic way, not passing judgment on the child's play behavior or on the product of that play. Respect may take the form of the teacher's decision not to ask a question, but instead to subtly and quietly put forth a new object or material the child might choose to use, and see what he or she does with it. This is part of the Artist Apprentice strategy for orchestrating play that we discussed in chapter 4.

If the teacher does decide to ask a question after determining that it will not be too intrusive, then a third consideration arises: Does the adult's question empower the child or does it foster dependence on adult judgment?

For example, if Pat had offered to teach Shawna to count to fifty, rather than accept the alternative of ten dollars offered by Shawna, she might have conveyed that her adult knowledge was the only alternative in this situation. On the other hand, Pat might have felt that Shawna was eager to perform her counting skills and asked "How high can you count?" In this way she would have invited Shawna to show off her knowledge. Instead, Pat chose to accept Shawna's suggestion of ten dollars, believing that to do otherwise would have interrupted the flow of the play.

Challenge Children's Thinking in Play

Other questioning strategies challenge children to analyze or to generate hypotheses about their play (Copple, Sigel, & Saunders, 1984; Sigel & Saunders, 1979). Asking children to predict, to verbalize or draw their plans for play, or to explain how their ideas might be tested are all examples of questions that challenge children to stretch their thinking. Ask, for example: I wonder if there's another way to do that? What do you suppose the lion would do if you allowed him out of his cage? Do you think you could make that same color again with paints?

Ask authentic questions.   Vivian Paley (1981) notes that she tries never to ask a question to which she already knows the answer. Along with others such as Duckworth (1996), Paley suggests that teachers' questions need to represent an authentic curiosity about how children are thinking about their experiences. This is qualitatively quite different from finding out if the child knows what the teacher knows. The challenge is not to impart the teacher's knowledge to the child, but to objectively and without judgment observe the process the child uses to interpret his or her environment. In addition, Heath (1983) and Tizard and Hughes (1984) point out that children who do not come from middle class homes are frequently bewildered by teachers asking questions to which there are obvious answers, such as "What color is the grass?" Genuine interest in children's own thoughts and perspectives is a more respectful and more meaningful approach to questioning.

Successful assessment of children's development in their play depends largely on keeping these principles in mind. Our viewpoints as teachers are constantly transformed as we listen to children while putting aside our preconceptions in order to open ourselves to children's purposes and meanings. As teachers, from both our pedagogical and adult perspectives, we often presume to know what is going on in children's hearts and minds. We sometimes neglect to take the time or marshall the attention needed to check our assumptions. While we may have certain goals in mind for children's development in their play, the children themselves know best what they are doing and we must observe their natural wisdom expressed through their play.

STRATEGIES FOR COLLECTING AND ORGANIZING INFORMATION

In Kathy's classroom, several strategies for systematically collecting information about children's progress are evident. The first and most essential strategy is anecdotal observation. Kathy says that she targets one or two children each day to observe during free play time. She records her thoughts on Post-it Notes or on sticky mailing labels and then completes her notes after school. She says she finds that keeping observations to a maximum of three children a day makes the task easier to accomplish and that she can put together her notes on each child rather quickly. The dated observation then goes on the form with the context noted in the upper right-hand corner (see Figure 12.1). Kathy says she adapted this form from the Primary Language Record (Barrs, Ellis, Hester, & Thomas, 1988), but uses it to record all aspects of development as well as language and literacy.

Other teachers simply place their notes taken on Post-it Notes or mailing labels on a paper in the child's folder, but Kathy says she prefers to "log" the observations as she takes them. "Then I can see where a child is spending most of her time. I can also see if I am really getting a good picture of the child's activities or if all my observations are too narrowly focused. For example, I looked at Mario's chart a few days ago and realized that nearly all my observations of him were taken when he was playing with the same group of boys. I have to make an effort to find him on his own and record his play."

Another strategy for collecting information about children's development is through their play in guided play experiences that teachers set up. For example, in her first grade classroom, Anita frequently sets up a store as one of the centers. She is often a participant as well as an observer, focusing on children's counting and understanding of money. A center where leaves and rocks are available for classifying, or one with a variety of objects and a tub of water, are setups that afford teachers opportunities to observe children's play and converse with them about their thinking.

Portfolios

Perhaps the most talked about strategy for gathering information on children's progress through play is the portfolio. Portfolio assessment at all levels of education is currently widely discussed (Strickland & Morrow, 1989; Tierney, Carter & Desai, 1991). Historically, teachers have gathered samples of children's "work" and collected them in files. But too often this work represents only a child's efforts to copy a set of sentences from the board, a teacher-modeled art project, or a set of math workbook computations. Contemporary children's portfolios reflect much more of children's processes. For example, Tierney (1991) and his colleagues recommend that children select their own samples for a language and literacy portfolio and include drafts as well as their final writing and drawing projects.

A preschool teacher holds a monthly art show in which children display their work. She asks children each month to pick out a piece of their artwork that they would like to be included in their portfolios.

One four-year-old's file included his efforts to write in Japanese. Tommy's family is part Chinese and he has recently become interested in the written forms of both the Chinese and Japanese languages. The family hosted a Japanese exchange student in their home for the summer. Tommy was impressed by the Japanese writing on the boxes of Japanese monster toys he was given as gifts, and by the student's translation of the symbols for him. Tommy's pretend writing "in Japanese" is clearly marked from the pretend writing he has also done "in English." His teacher has a short audiotape of him "reading" his writing to her. For the Japanese symbols, he makes sounds that he thinks are like the language he has heard. Then he translates it into English for his teacher.

Teachers can also take photographs of projects in process. For example, in Greta's fourth grade classroom, open choice playtime was the context for group projects that extended over several days or weeks. One group designed a whole series of robots, starting with the "X-100 model" that could serve soft drinks, extending to the "X-500 model" that could clean the whole house.

The children created a collection of promotional brochures for their robot series and Greta helped them videotape their pretend television commercial showcasing their products. She kept records of their constructions as they developed and the drafts of their brochures and scripts for the television commercial. She marked the development of their thinking as a group as well as their individual contributions to the project. Over time, it became clear that Sonia was the budding engineer of the group, suggesting additional functions and parts for the robots each day. Mauricio carefully wrote their scripts and illustrated the brochures. Lila, a child who recently moved to the area from Mexico, and who had been reluctant to speak English, starred in their commercial, which was presented in both English and Spanish.

Videotape

Richard teaches a kindergarten–first grade combination class in a rural area. Many of the children in his classroom speak English as a second language and their parents work in the nearby electronics industry. The parent group at Richard's school purchased a camcorder a year ago. Richard signs up to use it for an hour two days a week in his classroom, where he videotapes children's open-choice playtime and occasionally large group time discussions. He finds it to be less costly than the slide and film processing that he's done in the past.

Sometimes Richard sets the camera on a tripod in a given area of the classroom and lets it run. In this way he sees what goes on over time with a play project. He recalls two boys who came into his kindergarten without preschool experiences or much contact with other children. Both boys were limited in their social negotiation strategies, and both chose to play in the block corner nearly every day. Richard videotaped their play periodically over two months, documenting on videotape their progress from grabbing blocks and shouting "Mine!" to cooperative constructive play projects.

He often tapes play in the housekeeping area as well. Because Richard does not speak Korean, he is frequently at a loss to discover the content of some of the children's dramatic play sequences. With videotape as a tool, he is able to record sequences of play and then show them to a colleague who speaks Korean. She helps him to determine both the content and developmental level of the play he has taped.

"Letting the tape run" is also a strategy that Richard uses to assess what happens "on the periphery" of his classroom, and to plan curriculum accordingly. He observes and reflects on what the camera picks up. He often invites the children to watch some of the tapes and solve the problems they reveal. For example, Richard noted that some of the block and manipulative accessories were not being used much by the children. Through the videotape, it was revealed that the children seemed to have difficulty taking out the materials and putting them away. The class watched the tape together and some of the children explained their frustrations as they watched. They brainstormed a new way of storing the materials in the future.

Another technique that Richard developed is interviewing children about their play during playtime. He circulates through the room with the camera, and children explain their constructive play projects, science experiments, or dramatic play.

For example, during one play period, Juan described the three-story house he built of Cuisenaire rods while he and Richard conversed in Spanish. In the housekeeping area, a group of children had opened a restaurant and took Richard's order for spaghetti, writing his order on a clipboard and using invented spelling.

Richard checks in with children at various stages of their play. Richard's tape showed that Amanda and Jerry persisted for 45 minutes in making "magic potions," proudly reciting their newest ingredients each time they were interviewed.

He recorded Juan and Marty arguing over their block play early in the hour, then returned much later to two smiling boys peeping out of a structure. "You wanted to build a firehouse and *you* wanted to build an office. What did you finally decide?" asked Richard. "A police" announced Marty and they proudly showed off their telephone for "when people call 911" on the desk they built.

Checklists

Yet another useful strategy in assessing development through play is a checklist. Checklists might include stages of block play (Figure 12.2) or stages of sociodramatic play drawn from Smilansky's work (Figure 12.3). Other checklists include strategies observed in children's problem solving (Heath & Mangiola, 1991) or cooperative group play. A comprehensive checklist for assessment of young children on many dimensions of development is Project Construct, developed by the Missouri Department of Elementary and Secondary Education (1989).

Checklists have the advantage of giving the teacher "quick glance" feedback regarding the stages of development of both individuals and the group. For example, if in looking at a class checklist for stages of block play, a kindergarten teacher notes that many of the children are not yet constructing elaborated structures, she may want to consider some of the intervention strategies suggested in chapter 4. She may want to introduce some accessory boxes for new play themes that might stretch children's block representations to more complex levels. Checklists may also work to help summarize information from audiotaped or videotaped sequences of children's play, guiding the teacher to organize a large quantity of information into a succinct form.

Checklists have the disadvantage of giving the teacher little information about the context or detail of children's play when the observations are made. Just marking the stage and date of the observation is useful as a broad measure of development but may lack the richness of detail provided by anecdotal observations, videotapes, audiotapes, and portfolios.

Some teachers combine checklists with portfolios and observations. In a primary classroom, Mark takes observations and materials from portfolios every three months and summarizes the stages of development they represent on a checklist. This way he gives himself a picture of individual children's progress as well as the progress of the whole group, and ensures that he has collected a representative sampling of each child's experiences in his classroom.

Interpreting Play as Play

One of the major points of this book is that there is a reciprocal relationship between the development of play and the development of other aspects of cognitive and social-emotional functioning in childhood. Therefore, although play serves as a context for assessing the development of such qualities as representational thinking, emerging literacy, problem-solving strategies, and mathematical concepts, the development of play as play in a variety of contexts also concerns teachers of young children.

Class **Kgn – K. Andrews**

Year **1993**

Stages in Block building

Stage 1   Blocks are carried and arranged, but not used for construction

Stage 2   Children begin to build, constructing rows. Rows may be horizontal on the floor or table top or vertical (stacked). Much repetition.

Stage 3   Bridging—Two blocks set apart are connected by a third block

Stage 4   Enclosures—blocks enclose a space

Stage 5   Decorative patterns, often with symmetry

Stage 6   Structures are labeled for the purposes of dramatic play

Stage 7   Dramatic play is incorporated into the building and use of structures

* emerging

✓ mastery

Child's name	Stages 1	2	3	4	5	6	7
Alicia	✓	✓	✓	*			
Brandon	✓	✓	✓	✓			
Betsy	✓	✓	✓	✓	*		
Clark	✓	✓	✓	*			
Cami	✓	*	*	*			
Francisco	✓	✓	✓	✓			*
Gigi	✓	✓	✓	✓			*
Hsu	✓	*	*				
Ian	✓	✓	✓	✓		*	
Josh P.	✓	✓	✓	✓			
Josh T	✓	✓	✓	✓			

Figure 12.2
Source: Adapted from *The Block Book* by E. Hirsch, 1984, Washington, DC, NAEYC.

Smilansky (1968) developed a system for viewing children's sociodramatic play that is widely used for assessing young children. Dodge and Colker (1992) have interpreted Smilansky's work and created a chart that teachers may use as a tool for assessment (Figure 12.3). Sociodramatic play might appear in several contexts, such as the housekeeping area, around the climbing structure, in the sandbox, or with the blocks. In all contexts the features of sociodramatic play that mark social, linguistic, and cognitive complexity are the focus of assessment.

Smilansky's six components for assessing the quality of group dramatic play include:

1. Role play. Children declare their roles ("I'm the firefighter.") and engage in behavior consistent with that role (hosing down a pretend fire).

2. Using make-believe props. Children use objects to represent other objects (a block for a walkie-talkie); gestures or words to represent pretend action ("Whoosh! Whoosh!" while pretending to hose a fire), and/or verbalize a pretend situation ("Pretend the baby was trapped in the house").

3. Make-believe episodes. Make-believe play is coordinated into an elaborated episode ("Call the ambulance. This baby is *really* hurt bad.") rather than simple imitation of action with little integration into the story line of the play (picking up a phone and holding it to the ear).

4. Persistence. Children sustain their dramatic play over time. Smilansky recommends that teachers are likely to observe a minimum of five minutes of sustained play for preschoolers and kindergartners. First and second graders might frequently sustain play for 20 minutes or more and even continue story lines over several days' time.

5. Social interaction. Two or more children are engaged in enacting a play episode. Although solitary play may include many of the elements of pretend play we have discussed, the addition of another player or players to dramatic play increases the cognitive and social complexity of the play.

6. Verbal communication. Children use words to communicate make-believe transformations in play and to "direct" the play, by assigning roles or planning story sequences ("I'll be the ambulance driver, and you give me the baby").

Sophisticated sociodramatic play of preschool and primary grade children includes all of these elements in good measure. Children's developing complexity in their play may be traced through anecdotal observations or videotaping of dramatic play episodes.

For example, in Kathy's kindergarten class, two children, Amanda and Curt, spent much of their time in the housekeeping area arguing over who would use objects such as the toy telephone or the teapot. Both children's capacities to perform make-believe transformations were unsophisticated according to Smilanksy's scale. In story-play activities that Kathy offered three times a week, Amanda and Curt watched as others used gestures to represent imaginary

CRITERIA	BEGINNING LEVEL	ADVANCED LEVEL
Role Play		
Role chosen	Role relates to child's attempts to understand the familiar world (e.g., mommy, daddy, baby, animals)	Role relates to child's attempts to understand the outside world (e.g., firefighter, police officer, doctor)
How child plays role	Child imitates one or two aspects of role (e.g., child announces, "I'm the mommy," rocks the baby, and then leaves the house corner)	Child expands concepts of the role (e.g., child announces, "I'm the mommy," feeds the baby, goes to a meeting, prepares dinner, reads the newspaper, goes to work, talks on the phone, etc.)
Use of Props		
Type of prop needed	Child uses real objects or replica of object (e.g., real or toy phone)	Child uses any object as prop (e.g., block for phone) or a pretend prop (e.g., holds hands to ears and pretends to dial a telephone)
How child uses prop	Child enjoys physically playing with objects (e.g., banging receiver of phone, dialing)	Prop is used as part of play episode (e.g., child calls a doctor on phone because baby is sick)
Make-Believe	Child imitates simple actions of adult (e.g., child moves iron back and forth on ironing board, holds phone receiver to ear)	Child's actions are part of a play episode of make-believe (e.g., "I'm ironing this dress now so I can wear it for the party tonight")
Time	Fleeting involvement (e.g., child enters area, plays with doll, puts on hat, and leaves area)	Child stays in area more than 10 minutes (e.g., child is really involved in play episode and carries through on theme)
Interaction	Solitary play (e.g., child acts out role alone with no apparent awareness of others)	Functional cooperation (e.g., child interacts with others at various times when the need arises to share props or have a partner in play) Cooperative effort (e.g., child acts out role cooperatively with others, recognizing the benefits of working together)
Verbal Communication	Verbalization centers around the use of toys (e.g., "Bring me that phone" or "I had the carriage first")	Dialogue about play theme—constant chatter about roles children are playing (e.g., restaurant scene: "What do you want to eat?" "Do you have hamburgers?" "Yup. We have hamburgers, french fries, and cokes.")

Figure 12.3   Levels of Ability in Sociodramatic Play.

Source: Reprinted with permission from Diane T. Dodge and Laura J. Colker, *The Creative Curriculum for Early Childhood,* 3rd edition, Washington, DC: Teaching Strategies, Inc., 1992, pp. 122–123.

objects, and tried it themselves as actors in story-play productions. Kathy modeled for them the use of blocks for a variety of pretend objects, as she guided the resolution of their play disputes. After six weeks, Kathy repeated her play observations using the Smilansky scale and determined that both children had made progress in their use of make-believe props for play.

Although the Smilansky scale is the most concise assessment of symbolic play that we have found, teachers who care to look in more detail at the kind of play children engage in and its relationship to language might also wish to use the play complexity instrument described by Sylva, Roy, and Painter in their 1980 study *Child Watching at Playgroup and Nursery School*.

DEFINING THE PURPOSES OF ASSESSMENT

Assessment of children's progress is a complicated and multifaceted issue in early childhood education. While most teachers agree that the primary purpose of assessment is to inform their professional judgment about curriculum, other purposes of assessment frequently cloud this goal.

Teachers, administrators, and policymakers use assessment to evaluate programs and to come to decisions about groups of children. These assessments are by their nature designed to be cost- and time-efficient. The assessment instruments selected frequently reduce complex capabilities to a single score that may be interpreted readily by those who are not educators (Shepard, 1989).

In contrast to this is classroom-based or "performance-based" assessment which is designed to be more sensitive to the development of individual children. This kind of assessment involves complex and ongoing measures that focus on individual styles and paces of learning. In addition, performance-based assessment serves as a means of learning and reflection for the student as well as the teacher. If children are to develop the ability to reflect on their own developing concepts and take responsibility for their own learning, their participation in their own assessment process is critical.

Until quite recently, the accepted means for policy level group assessment has been standardized testing. This testing tradition has steadily supplanted the more informal and authentic means of assessing children that teachers design and use. However, recent research seriously questions the appropriateness of using standardized tests for either group or individual purposes in young children's programs. Critics of standardized testing cite the lack of validity and reliability as well as the more serious concern of the damage to children's self-esteem and dispositions to learn as a side effect of these measures (Meisels, 1987; National Association of State Boards of Education, 1988; NAEYC & NAECS, 1991; Perrone, 1990).

Currently, educators throughout the country are grappling with the question "If we throw out standardized tests as measures of student achievement, what will we use instead?" Our answer to this question is to turn to children's play. Play is the natural and spontaneous avenue for young children's learning. Children demonstrate through play the application and integration of skills and concepts learned in school. Therefore, it makes sense that observational records of children's processes in their play and examples of children's products in their play should serve as a primary means of assessing the progress of young learners in their classrooms.

Another feature of play as a means of assessment is its integrated quality. In play, many facets of children's development are revealed. Educators increasingly call for a refocusing of our goals for young children's programs based on what we know from child development theory and research. Standardized tests have targeted attention to surface skills such as memorizing the alphabet or numbers, and away from deeper concepts such as classification or the nature of narrative. We need to use assessment that recognizes the value of easily observable skills as well as the more subtle concepts children construct during their early years of education. Play assessment allows us to observe both.

We also need to observe and measure the long-term dispositions about learning and thinking developed during children's early years: How does the way that a skill such as identifying short and long vowel sounds is learned relate to children's enjoyment of reading and their interest in making literacy a part of their daily lives? Play allows us to see the cognitive as well as the emotional aspects of children's development and the ways in which they are connected.

Teachers are also expanding their notions of assessment to include social-moral development in addition to the more traditional questions of cognition and attitudes toward learning (Kamii, 1990; Leavitt & Eheart, 1991). In a society that is increasingly diverse in its values and perspectives, the development of children's abilities to negotiate, to understand the perspectives of others, and to communicate effectively becomes essential. Play-based assessment helps teachers shift their thinking to see social-moral development as a priority on a par with cognition and motivation, and offers a window to document progress and plan curriculum in these areas.

Play is the window to view both age-appropriate development and individual development. In play, teachers may discern whether children's understandings of concepts such as correspondence or classification fall within a range expected of a given age group. They may determine how many children in their group exhibit complex sociodramatic play according to Smilansky's guidelines, or how many need particular orchestration strategies to enhance their development of symbolic thought.

Play also illuminates the development of individual children. It allows teachers to notice and appreciate the interests and values a child brings from home, and the special kind of intelligence he or she may use to express thoughts and feelings. For example, in one second grade classroom, Juan Pablo, a recent arrival from Costa Rica, spends his playtime drawing detailed soccer games on paper, talking to himself in Spanish, and animating the imaginary soccer games with sounds and comments made by the players. His teacher can see that Juan Pablo's understanding of the game of soccer is a special window through which she can communicate with him.

Play and Assessments of Children with Special Needs

As a result of the passage of P.L. 99-457, the Individuals with Disabilities Education Act (IDEA), Federal law mandates assessment and intervention for young children with disabilities (Eisert & Lamorey, 1996). Myers, McBride and Peterson (1996) report that transdisciplinary, play-based assessments are being incorporated in some early childhood special education programs. There is growing awareness among researchers, teachers, and parents of children with special needs that play-based assessments provide valuable information regarding all children's development, and that traditional standardized assessment tools present a limited picture of children's abilities. For example, many standardized tests do not allow the examiner to change items or item presentation which may prove difficult for children with disabilities.

A number of researchers have developed several play-based scales that are appropriate for determining eligibility for special education services and making program decisions. For example, Eisert and Lamorey (1996) report on research using their Play Assessment Scale (PAS) that includes 45 items that measure play development in infants and preschool children. Both spontaneous and elicited play can be scored. Eisert and Lamorey emphasize that play-based assessments allow us to observe children with special needs using their skills functionally in natural environments.

Van der Kooij (1989a) developed two scales appropriate for use with school-age children. His Play Intensity Scale differentiated learning among disabled, school-age children. The scale consists of three concepts related to play: intrinsic motivation, internal locus of control, and suspension of reality. Van der Kooij's Mental Activity Scale provides information about a child's cognitive functioning during play.

Myers, McBride and Peterson (1996) point out that practitioners have been adopting transdisciplinary, play-based assessments because parents and educational professionals rate them highly, even though there has been relatively little research in this area. Myers et al. report that studies show that their assessments had a high rate of agreement with developmental ratings, and were highly time efficient, taking fewer days to complete. In addition, they indicate that professionals found that play-based assessments provided more information than standardized assessments on communication, social skills, and motor skills. Consequently, they recommend play-based assessments for use in planning instructional goals that take into consideration appropriate adaptations for individual children.

COMMUNICATING WITH PARENTS
ABOUT PLAY AND ASSESSMENT

Play is a valuable tool teachers can use in communicating with parents about their children's progress. It illustrates for parents the individual flavor of their child's expression. Play anecdotes also offer an opportunity for the teacher to explain what is being learned in the play-based curriculum as examples of the child's progress are cited. Brandon, the child in the opening anecdote in chapter 1, spends part of his 26th day in kindergarten building a maze for Fluffy, the pet rat, and then represents his play with a map. He gets carried away with fire-fighting fantasies, and some of the aggressive behavior his preschool teacher saw comes out in his play with others. Brandon's parents will appreciate hearing of his progress in map making, and of the complexity of his maze. They will enjoy hearing about his nurturing concern for Fluffy. They may be able to help the teacher understand his aggressive outbursts of behavior at school by comparing his behavior at home and at school.

The study by Myers et al. (1996), discussed above, found that play-based assessment may increase parent involvement. Parents are an integral part of some assessments, and may physically support a child or help elicit responses. This study also demonstrated that parents felt more comfortable in seeking information from professionals during play-based assessments and perceived the identified goals as important.

In Richard's K–1 combination class, videotape became useful in giving parents an opportunity to observe their children in particular and the whole curriculum in general. Twice a year he prepares a videotape with edited segments of children's activities and progress. At "Back to School Night" in the fall, he shows parents scenes from a typical day in his classroom and examples of play projects children have done in previous years. At "Open House" in the spring,

Play-based assessment may increase parent involvement.

Richard shows video clips of children's block constructions, dramatic play sequences, story plays, science experiments and other events and projects that he has captured on tape. He creates a video "yearbook" for children and their families from clips of classroom life throughout the year so that children may keep a permanent record of their kindergarten experience. Richard has found that video records of children's behavior also have been very helpful in communicating with parents whose children have special educational needs.

In one instance, the parents of Maureen, a child whom Richard believed needed special help, refused to believe that their daughter needed to be referred for special education. Richard documented Maureen's behavior at group time where her need to be touching Richard at all times was evident. He documented Maureen's play with other children in which she would frequently lash out and hit others. Because Maureen was an only child and their home was at the outskirts of this rural community, she had had few playmates. Consequently, her parents had little opportunity to compare their daughter's behavior with that of other children her age. The videotape helped Richard and Maureen's parents agree on special needs assessment for Maureen and helped them to plan some strategies together that would smooth Maureen's relationships with others.

SUMMARY AND CONCLUSION

In this chapter we have looked at some of the ways that play episodes inform teachers in their efforts to assess children's progress. Teachers' anecdotal observations of children's play and portfolios of the products of play offer an ongoing record of children's development in cognitive, linguistic, and social-emotional domains.

Play-based assessment paints a portrait of the "whole child," as individuals express their unique views of the world through play. Play-based assessment is a means for teachers to evaluate the success of their curriculum planning, to see if children replay the concepts and skills embedded in the curriculum and use them in their own play. Play-based assessment is appropriate for use with all children, and may have special advantages for assessing the development of children with special needs. Play provides information that informs teachers' future designs for curriculum and serves as a means of evaluating the progress of groups of children as well as the progress of individuals.

We have discussed multiple means of collecting information on children's play, including forms for organizing anecdotal observations, checklists of age-appropriate development, and audiotaping and videotaping techniques. We have looked at ways to assess how play contributes to development in traditional academic areas such as literacy and problem solving. We have also looked at ways to assess play as play, to highlight the reciprocal relationship of play to other aspects of early childhood development.

In this chapter we have addressed some of the major issues surrounding the use of standardized tests for young children and contrasted these methods with the more spontaneous, contextualized assessment that play provides in classrooms for young children.

Finally, we have discussed some of the ways that teachers use play-based assessment to communicate with parents. Using observational records, photographs, and audiotaped or videotaped samples of children's experiences in the classroom helps parents understand what their children are learning through their play as well as appreciate their children's unique styles of development and expression.

FOCUSING OUR THINKING

1. Collect slides, photographs, audiotapes, or videotapes of children's block play over a three-week period. What stages of block play are represented? (See Figure 12.3.) How do you think block play and dramatic play are connected?

2. Collect at least six 5-to-10 minute handwritten anecdotal records of children's sociodramatic play. Using Smilanksy's six factors of play complexity, evaluate the sophistication of the play episodes you collect.

3. Role-play a parent-teacher conference in which the teacher uses play-based assessment to inform the parents of their child's progress.

4. Add to your annotated bibliography of children's books. Select two or three books that you have included. Reread them and analyze how the child's play informs your assessment of his or her development.

SUGGESTED RESOURCES

1. Almy, M., & Genishi, C. (1982). *Ways of studying children* (rev. ed.). New York: Teachers College Press.

This books offers a multitude of strategies for looking at all aspects of children's development and progress in school. The authors illustrate their ideas with rich examples of children's play and suggest formats for recordkeeping for teachers of preschool and primary grade children.

2. Cohen, M. (1980). *First grade takes a test*. New York: Dell.

This is a children's book about the issue of assessing children through the use of standardized tests. It is short, poignant, and provides an excellent basis for discussing assessment of young children with children, parents, and colleagues.

3. Genishi, C., & Dyson, A. H. (1984). *Language assessment in the early years*. Norwood, NJ: Ablex.

This book outlines the development of oral language and emergent literacy in a variety of settings for young children. It offers strategies for observing and interpreting language development in play, including strategies for second language learners.

4. Barrs, M., Ellis, S., Hester, H., & Thomas, A. (1988). *The primary language record* and (1991) *Patterns of learning*. London: ILEA.

Both of these manuals for assessment created by London early childhood educators are gems. *The Primary Language Record i*s a detailed manual of observation and interviewing techniques for assessing children's developing literacy. There are excellent recordkeeping forms and suggestions for addressing the needs of children from diverse linguistic backgrounds. A concise and practical videotape is available to use along with the manual. *Patterns of Learning* extends the observation and recordkeeping techniques to other subject areas, and offers suggestions for classroom environments and scheduling that facilitate naturalistic assessment.

5. Kamii, C. (Ed.). (1990). *No achievement testing in the early grades.* Washington, DC: NAEYC.

This book offers numerous perspectives on the assessment of young children. It considers the viewpoints of educators, from teachers to state departments of education, offering arguments against standardized testing and suggesting strategies for authentic assessments in language and mathematics.

6. Genishi, C. (Ed). (1992). *Ways of assessing children and curriculum.* New York: Teachers College Press.

This book presents numerous classroom examples that illustrate how teachers can use alternative assessments to document children's development. Many illustrations demonstrate assessment techniques for play-centered curriculum. The authors also consider multiple, often novel, methods of assessing children from diverse backgrounds and with varied special needs.

CHAPTER **13**

Conclusion: Integrating Play, Development, and Practice

Two boys and a girl are walking up a hill. Four-year-old Charlie shudders and throws his arms up in quick staccato movements, making explosive sounds interrupted with calls for help. "I need your help, the Klingons are surrounding me." Jerry, wearing an Oakland A's baseball cap, shouts acknowledgment and comes to the rescue. "It's O.K., they're gone. Let's go." They link arms and descend. Sheila follows. "I have to go to the bathroom." The two boys look around. "The bathroom's over there," one says and points to a concrete building buried in the shadow of trees. "Come with me." Her request is ignored and the boys commence another episode. "I'll be Zelda," she says as she joins the play, but her body reminds her of other needs, and she descends toward the picnic tables. She later returns, holding her father's hand. They head towards the bathroom. Having addressed her own and her parent's concern for safety in unfamiliar places, she returns and re-enters the play with an assertion of her competence. "I was right. That is the bathroom."

A few hours later, the children chase Jerry's father across the field. He turns, and gently tosses his son to the ground. The chase continues, out past the concrete bathrooms, down to the beach, back up the hill. The two boys temporarily drop behind and plan their attack. "Listen, all we have to do is. . . . "

As the chase ends, they huddle and plot the afternoon's play. Sheila is excluded. Some distance away she sits down on the hillside, pulling at weeds. Shortly afterwards, she and Jerry begin walking together. She has a long face. "You weren't nice to me," she says. Charlie comes toward them, yelling, "Jerry, wait up! Wait up! There isn't a bee in it. I got it out (of the Coke can)." Sheila and Jerry wait for Charlie to catch up. The three old friends are again one.

Look at all that is occurring in this simple vignette. These four-year-olds are cooperating, collaborating on common themes which are agreed to and adhered to. They are vocal, imitating and reproducing elements of their culture. They are using language to guide their play and to provide its content. They display practical knowledge, as in recognizing the bathroom as well as understanding when parental protection is needed. Sheila is able to express her feelings of exclusion and to reinstate herself in the triad after her temporary absence. And, lastly, Charlie figured out how to get a bee out of a Coke can.

We see in play the expression of intelligence, the management of needs and emotions, the elaboration of common themes and efforts, the reproduction of culture. We see the give and take of cooperation. We see the evolution of social consciousness and of sexual identity. The world of childhood and the world of play are inseparable. Play is evident from infancy through adulthood and unquestionably occupies a central role in human development. It is our purpose to put play at the center of classroom curriculum. In this concluding chapter we revisit in somewhat broader terms the theoretical basis for our faith in the value of play as a focal point in curriculum planning and classroom management.

CONSTRUCTIVISM AND DEVELOPMENT

The term "constructivism" is used to express the belief that development is not simply maturation or biological unfolding, nor is it the result of the environment or experience imprinting itself on the developing mind, through, for example, reinforcement. The term is derived from the word "construct" and is meant to suggest that the child plays an active role in constructing that which is developed.

What Is Developed?

Each of the main theorists who have written about child development could tell us something different about what is going on in the above vignette. Piaget could help us understand the representational methods and the concepts expressed in the play. What are Klingons and how do they act? Why are they dangerous? What can be done about them? G. H. Mead could help us understand the way in which this play affects the sense of self developing in these three children. Vygotsky could show us how the collective activity of the children is creating a context for their own understanding. This context is a micro culture developing among the children with its own history. Their play also relates to the broader culture and history that the children share. Freud could help us understand how the play addresses deeper emotional themes associated with the control of instinctive forces. Erikson could help us see the development of trust and autonomy represented in the play. Notice how Sheila asks the boys to escort her to the bathroom and how she comfortably tells Jerry he wasn't nice to her. Dewey might help us see the competence and industry represented here.

Even in the simplest scenes of spontaneous and unguided play, development is occurring in all areas of human growth. For the sake of summary, we identify these areas as intelligence, personality, competence and, lastly, social-consciousness and sense of self. We believe that each of these is developed by the child through spontaneous and self-directed activity within social, cultural and historical contexts. This is the meaning of the "constructivist" view of development. Development does not result from the unfolding of genetically predetermined potentials, nor as the direct result of social experience in the form of education or selective reinforcement. Intelligence, personality, competence, and sense of self are constructed by the child through self-regulated activity imbedded in social, historical and cultural contexts. We maintain that this view is consistent with the above theorists, and believe that, without play, there would be no development.

Our position can be summarized with five points:

1. Play is the primary context in which *intelligence, personality, competencies,* and *social-consciousness* are developed and integrated. (This will be explored in depth later in this chapter.)

2. These four domains are inseparable from social experience within cultural/historical contexts.

3. Self-directed activity is necessary for development in these domains and is closely aligned with play.

4. These four domains are functionally interdependent and are each involved in all play.

5. Each domain is constructed through "means-ends coordinations."

Means-Ends Coordinations and Development

Another way to view constructivism is to think about the ways in which the child constructs the means of achieving desired goals. This is called "means-ends coordinations," which, for example, concern how a reorganization of old means can be used to achieve new ends or, conversely, how new means can be constructed to reach old ends. This is similar to evolutionary biology, which was

Emotions, intellect, and social life are drawn together in play.

Piaget's first professional calling, where evolution can be viewed, in part, as the transformation of old structures to serve new functions. For example, a bone formerly part of the gill structure of fish has evolved in mammals to become an inner ear bone used in hearing. The fact that intelligence develops through the dynamics of means-ends coordinations establishes the common tie between intelligence and constructivism.

Intelligence is the area of development most closely associated with Piaget's work. In Piaget's view, intelligence is not a trait that is capable of being measured, such as I.Q., nor does it relate to "smartness" or even factual knowledge. For Piaget, intelligence implies what we call "human reason" or "adaptive understanding." Piaget perceived the development of reason to be an evolution in the child's adaptation to the environment that subsequently leads to understanding. This evolution occurs because early understandings are ultimately challenged by the environment. When new experiences are inconsistent or incompatible with earlier ways of understanding, change ultimately results. For example, the idea that quantity relates to how things look is less satisfactory than understanding that quantity is a composition of units. The evolution of this understanding is universal, occurring in all cultures, but takes most of early childhood to evolve. Is this evolution a result of learning, of genetic unfolding, of social imitation and instruction, or of construction? Piaget's answer is "construction." We've discussed constructivism at some length in chapters 2 and 3 and again in chapter 8.

Personality also entails means-ends relations. Personality might be thought of as our unique means of maintaining acceptable emotional states while, at the same time, satisfying goals. A personality evolves as a specific way of satisfying physical and emotional needs. Personality begets emotional stability and, hopefully, satisfaction while its owner is carrying out daily-goal directed activity. Everyday acts, such as doing one's work, going to school, talking to one's children, or negotiating with one's insurance company are examples of ways in which personality manifests itself.

Those who have been around young children are often impressed with the range of differences between them. Even at birth some children are calm, some are agitated, some accept changes in routines, some do not. It is, therefore, easy to think of personality as fixed at birth. However, while such dispositions occur early and sometimes remain into adulthood, the issue of personality is more complex and tied in both direct and subtle ways to a child's experiences. Personality, like intelligence, is constructed.

Competencies are the things that we can reliably accomplish—the abilities that allow us to function in the world. Competencies are largely fashioned through intelligence, but, as indicated in the five points above, cannot be separated from other areas of development. Like intelligence and personality, competencies are also tied to means-ends relationships because they are either the means of reaching goals or the goals themselves. Thus, a competency can be instrumental in achieving a goal, such as when social competencies allow one to play effectively with others, or a competency can be a goal itself as when one struggles to learn how to play with others.

Social-consciousness is a term we use to understand the child's evolving sense of self and how the self is related to the other "selves" it comes in contact with in the course of daily life. Social-consciousness is inseparable from intelligence, personality and competency and, like these other areas, evolves through the coordination of means-end relations and, hence, is constructed. Here, however, the means-end coordinations are related to causality, or how people affect one another. Causality can also be thought of in terms of means-ends relationships. The means are the "causes" and the ends are the "effects." The sense of self is fashioned through an understanding of two types of causality. One is linked to an objective understanding of ourselves, and the other is linked to understanding how we affect others and how social conditions, in turn, affect us. For example, a stable understanding of ourselves must take into account how others see us or how others affect us. We are affected by the actions and perceptions of others, and, in turn, we create the same conditions for others. Understanding this requires a reflection on the means-end relationships that occur in social causality. That is, how am I affecting others and how do others affect me?

CONSTRUCTIVISM AND SOCIAL-CULTURAL THEORIES OF PLAY

Two major developmental psychologists are Jean Piaget and Lev Vygotsky, whose theories were introduced in chapter 2. While Piaget and Vygotsky were both constructivists, they had differing views of childhood development, and many feel that their theories are incompatible. It's important that we understand some of the issues that divide and unite these important thinkers.

Jean Piaget (1896–1980)

Asking what it means to be human is a question that has been posed since the beginning of human understanding. Historically, this question has been left to theology and philosophy, but in the twentieth century it has increasingly become the province of developmental psychology. Jean Piaget, the Swiss biologist, is probably the most recognized person in developmental psychology. His work spans most of the twentieth century and is responsible for transforming our understanding of human rationality.

Piaget, born in 1896, was a biologist interested in evolution. He made the startling discovery that even the most basic knowledge or understanding is not necessarily obtained or learned by the child through cultural transmission or even by direct physical experience. The construction of knowledge, according to Piaget, occurs as a series of predictable and universal stages unfolding as a function of a slowly elaborated form of internal mental consistency. His theory assumes that this sequence of stages is universal, occurring in a similar way for all humans who are healthy and active. Piaget's famous conservation experiments provide examples of predictable stages of understanding. The child first conserves number, understanding that rearranging a set of objects does not change the quantity of the set. It is years later before the child understands that changing the shape of something does not change its weight (i.e., the conservation of weight). It is later still that the child can conserve volume, understanding that changing the shape of a substance does not change its volume.

Development can be viewed as a movement towards internal consistency. It is the child who is subjectively aware of contradictions in his or her understanding, and it is the child, through self-regulated means, who resolves those internal contradictions. Hence, development in the constructivism of Piaget is autonomous and self-directed. This view gave a completely new twist to the nature/nurture controversy. Neither nature (genetic predisposition) nor nurture (the effects of the environment) was seen by Piaget as the source of development. Furthermore, the specific course of development was viewed as common to all people. It is Piaget's position that the developing child is not solely the passive recipient of a gene pool nor a product of environmental influences, but, rather, is the active constructor of his or her own nature. In addition, for Piaget, the child's development follows laws in the same way that thermodynamics or the movement of objects follows laws.

Teachers, however, may find it difficult to derive practical curriculum models from Piaget's theory because of his focus on autonomy and self-directed activity and because his theory says little about how social interactions affect development. In fact, Piaget did not address in depth the problems of education and curriculum. In spite of this, pedagogical theory throughout the United States, and much of the world in general, has been influenced by Piaget. The theories of Vygotsky, however, prompt us to think about what Piaget has left out of his formulations, and many educators today look to him for direction on how to structure the social elements of the classroom to achieve curriculum goals (Bodrova & Leong, 1996; Nicolopoulou, 1991).

Lev Vygotsky (1896–1934)

Vygotsky was born in Russia in 1896, the same year Piaget was born in Switzerland. Both were part of the new modernism that was influencing continental thought. Darwin's theory of evolution, Freud's theory of the unconscious, and Einstein's theory of relativity were all part of the modernism of the late nineteenth and early twentieth centuries. It was a time of great intellectual fervor. Karl Marx's theory of economics and social institutions, in fact, provided a foundation for the emergence of communism.

As discussed in chapter 2, Vygotsky was largely influenced by the social theory of his time and by the changes accompanying the Russian revolution. He was very interested in how social interactions affect individuals and how individuals and society are influenced by history and culture. Vygotsky greatly influenced Russian psychology and argued that conceptual activity cannot be separated from social experience. Further, this experience unfolds within a cultural-historical context. This was an extension of his belief that the regulation of conscious activity can only take place within a social context (Davydov, 1995).

Whereas Piaget believed that the child develops first on the individual plane and then coordinates with others, according to Vygotsky, all activity happens in a social context and begins as social experience which is later internalized (Piaget, 1962a). Since Vygotsky died in 1934, before Piaget published his most significant works, it would have been impossible for him to know how Piaget ultimately handled the issue of individual development and social experience.

Connecting Piaget's and Vygotsky's Theories

Attempts to understand the relationship between development and education will benefit from understanding both Piaget and Vygotsky. One obstacle to seeing how Piaget and Vygotsky complement each other is the mistaken assumption that Piaget was an individualist, believing that development can occur independent of social experience. A number of writers have addressed this misunderstanding and have pointed out how these two theorists complement one another (Alward, 1997b; DeVries, 1997; Nicolopoulou, 1996).

It is important to understand that while Piaget did not make it his focus, he firmly believed that conceptual knowledge was fundamentally tied to social processes. He felt that true conceptual activity, by which he meant rational thought, could not proceed without the use of a referential system that was tied to and dependent upon social agreement. Without language, words and mathematical symbols embedded in social contexts, where people must coordinate their points of view with those of others, agreeing and disagreeing, the world can be understood only from one point of view, making rationality impossible (Piaget, 1954, 1962, 1995).

This position is critical and necessary to the whole thrust of Piaget's work. He was primarily concerned with how humans establish logically necessary and objectively verifiable knowledge. That is, he was not concerned with the arts (graphic, performance or literary) or with the practical knowledge reflected in our daily work. Objective knowledge concerns our ability to think logically about spatial relationships, time, relationships between time, motion and distance, geometric relationships, quantitative relationships, such as number, volume, length and weight, laws of causality and chance. His theory holds that the attainment of objective knowledge is the result of a very gradual "decentering" process (Piaget, 1962b). This process involves a gradual development from a state where the child's ability to represent is limited to what is immediately available to the senses, to a later period in which presentation is still tied to the child's own experiences and, finally, to a representation that is entirely freed from specific sensation and experience and is socially coordinated with others through the use of arbitrary signs such as words.

A CLOSER LOOK AT PIAGET AND CONSTRUCTIVIST THEORY

Piaget is the primary architect of constructivist theory. In the following we take a closer look at his ideas, expanding upon and reviewing those introduced in chapter 2.

Schemes: Assimilation and Accommodation and Play

The concept of "scheme" is important to Piaget's view of intelligence. A scheme is a pattern for action that can be repeated, like a program in a computer. The reflexes of the newborn are the first schemes. Blinking, grasping, sucking, turning the head, moving the tongue, opening and closing the mouth are examples. By three years of age, more elaborate schemes, such as catching a ball or putting on a shirt, have evolved out of a coordination of simpler schemes. This elaboration of schemes continues throughout development and yields at each stage the possibility of more complex and adaptive activity (Piaget, 1963a).

Human development is driven by adaptation to the environment and consists of the twin processes of *assimilation* and *accommodation*. Assimilation is an incorporation of the environment into the child's own patterns of action or schemes. In a sense, the child uses already developed competencies to understand new events. Accommodation takes place when schemes or competencies are inadequate and create contradictory results. Accommodation is a change in schemes as they are modified to fit new circumstances and occurs as a result of interactions with the environment. For example, an amount can be changed by adding or subtracting substance. At some point in a child's development, he or she will sense the contradiction between this understanding and the belief that an amount can change even when there have been no additions or subtractions. This feeling of contradiction will contribute to the child's developing an understanding of conservation of quantities.

Assimilation distorts and changes things because it modifies the world according to the child's schemes. Thus, the world becomes what the child can make of it. This is called "egocentrism." Accommodation, on the other hand, is a process of bending to the pressure of reality. Piaget identifies "play" with assimilation (Piaget, 1962b). This reflects the link between assimilation and the distorting quality of play, where pretense and fantasy make the world what the child wishes. When the child turns the living room furniture into a space ship, the nature of the furniture has been distorted in the child's mind and turned, for the moment, into components of the rocket ship.

Piaget identifies accommodation with imitation. The link between imitation and accommodation reflects the reproduction of reality, which characterizes imitation. When a child makes the sounds of a horse in pretending to be a horse, the child is accommodating to the sounds made by horses.

While Piaget associates pure assimilation with play, in fact, assimilation and accommodation can never be entirely separated. Children's play entails complex coordinations and develops from both assimilative and accommodative activity. As children develop, so does their play: play themes become more elaborate; symbols become more evolved; social coordinations become more complex and cooperative. These developments are only possible because play involves both assimilation and accommodation. Thus, while Piaget is often thought to believe that play is an expression of assimilation, it is more accurate to say that play and assimilation share the subjugation of the world to the child's immediate interests.

How Do We Know Intelligence Is Constructed and Lawful?

As we've discussed, Piaget saw development as a lawful construction and not merely an effect of social imitation, direct experience, or learning. In this constructive activity the child uses existing action schemes to achieve goals and interpret events. If reality cannot be assimilated to the child's schemes, the schemes tend to undergo lawful change. These schemes are always "action schemes." They are either a coordination of actual sensorimotor actions or internal representations of actions, for example, the image of combining two elements to form a third. The change in schemes follows a lawful developmental path (Piaget, 1963b). The central premise of Piaget's work is that knowledge is constructed out of a coordination of sensorimotor actions and/or out of a coordination of internal images of possible actions. If the capacity to coordinate certain relationships has not yet developed, no amount of exposure, answers, and lessons will impart that knowledge.

The universal ways that children interpret experience are evidence that the construction of reality reflects developmental laws rather than learning. For example, all children at some point over-generalize language rules for marking time and number ("I *played* and I *goed* to the store," or "I put the *shoes* on my *foots*"). Or, as another example, all children at some point in their development reason that a "part" is larger than the "whole," that, for example, there are more roses in the vase than flowers, even though only some of the flowers are roses. All children at some point believe that a quantity changes even if only its appearance has changed. They believe that pouring a liquid into a different shaped container will change its amount, or that rearranging a pile of blocks will change the number of blocks. These ways of interpreting events are constructed and not copied from experience. It is the universal and "illogical" form of young children's thinking that points to the fact that knowledge is constructed and not simply learned or copied.

Stages of Development and Play

Because play is inseparable from all facets of development, play itself must develop. This was our focus in chapter 2. The first two years of life are called the *sensorimotor period*, because during this phase the child's understanding of the world is tied to direct physical, rather than mental, assimilations and accommodations. During this period the child lacks the ability to mentally represent the world. The ability to imagine, dream, pretend, talk, and imitate are being developed during this period. This development entails six distinct stages, beginning with birth and the exercise of sensorimotor reflexes and ending with the beginning of representational functions, such as imitation, pretense, and language, which emerge around two years of age.

Sensorimotor play lacks the symbolic or pretend quality of later play because pretense requires representation, which is achieved only at the end of this period. During the early stages of this development infants cannot construct the symbolism and imagery which are needed to support pretend activity, like picking up a piece of grass and pretending to eat it. During this period, play consists

Because play is inseparable from all facets of development, play itself must develop.

of physical actions combined and repeated for the simple pleasure of mastering new combinations.

The second major developmental period, the *pre-operational period*, begins with the onset of representation or the ability to form images of objects or events that are not immediately available to the senses. The emergence of representational thought is the result of an advance in the coordination of assimilation and accommodation. Assimilation and play are now capable of giving meaning to symbols produced by accommodations and imitation (Alward, 1996; Piaget, 1962). The ability to create symbols has a profound effect on children's play in terms of its themes, the symbols used to support the play, and the means of communicating the purpose and manner of the play. The play of this period does not replace sensorimotor play but, rather, joins sensorimotor play to create a more diverse palette of possible action.

During the pre-operational period, children are incapable of formulating or understanding true concepts, concepts that are reliable and stable. Comprehension of everything, from the concrete and familiar (e.g., mommies and daddies, brother and sister) to the abstract (e.g., number, time, movement, measurement), is unstable and in constant risk of contradiction because *young children reason from particular to particular rather than understanding how particular cases relate to the whole set of possible cases* (Alward, 1996; Piaget, 1966). For example, at one moment "mommies" may be people who help you, even though not all who help you are mommies and not all mommies help. At another moment a mommy may be anyone with a baby, even if the relationship is not maternal.

A third period, the *concrete-operational period*, begins at about the age of six or seven and is characterized by the emergence of consistent concepts. The emergence of true conceptual reasoning is brought about through a combining of the assimilative and accommodative dynamics with social experience made possible through language. These integrations allow the child to decenter from direct sensory data, such as imagery, perception, emotion, and practical behaviors. This decentering allows the formation of concepts that have a generalization and application that goes beyond individual experience and idiosyncratic symbols (Alward, 1996, 1997a, 1997b; Piaget, 1962, 1995). Chapter 8 looks at how the coordination of classes and relations contributes to conceptual understanding.

Play is still necessary to development but, because of the achievements during this period, the play of six- and seven-year-olds is increasingly directed towards social coordinations and successful reproductions of reality. This might be seen in formal games or a beginning interest in constructing models.

A fourth major period, the *formal-operational period*, begins with the elaboration of hypothetical or theoretically possible interpretations and the elaboration of scientific or logical means of deciding between competing hypothetical propositions. All the earlier forms of play remain a part of the young adolescent's life, but during the formal operational period, play also incorporates the complex refinements that characterize work. Youth group activities, where real tasks of working with others, or making things "that really work," are examples of play-related activity at this stage.

The Construction of Reality

The construction of reality entails gradual progress in the reliable and logical interpretation of experiences. This allows the prediction of unexperienced outcomes. For example, we know that pouring a liquid from one container into another does not change its amount. We know, *without carrying out the activity*, that if we were to pour the liquid back into the original container, it would occupy the same amount of space.

As noted earlier, Piaget was interested in how we construct an objective or rational understanding of *time* (the temporal succession of events), *objects* (the differentiation of sensation into discrete entities), *space* (the relative movements and positions of objects), and *causality* (the attribution of necessary links between events). In each of these areas, human intelligence eventually fashions an objective understanding. Moreover, these understandings successively deepen from those of the infant to those of the most advanced moments in science. Modern science is, after all, a continuing quest to understand the nature of objects, time, space, and causality. This quest will never be finished because each new understanding sets the conditions for further accommodations.

By two years of age, most children have constructed a limited, yet reliable, understanding that objects can be permanent entities, organized in space and time, and linked in causal relationships. Even this seemingly simple understanding is constructed gradually. Imagine a child of fourteen months sitting on the floor. His mother, whom he's been watching, approaches on his right and passes behind him. The infant turns to his left, anticipating seeing his mother reappear. This behavior suggests that objects, time, and space are becoming organized into a whole where objects continue to exist even though they appear and disappear over time; that they exist in a space where, for example, the same target can be reached by different routes. He anticipated his mother's trajectory in space and intersected that point not by visually following her, but by taking an alternative route.

This simple understanding takes many months to develop and is a precursor to a more complex mental organization, characterized by logical-mathematical coordinations. Finding objects hidden within or under other objects, finding one's way around the house, knowing that throwing the ball over the fence will be an obstacle to the dog with whom he's playing "go-and-fetch," being able to reach the same place by different routes, all speak to a spatial understanding in which *placements* (position or where something is in space) are coordinated with *displacements* (changes in position or the movement of an object from one position to another). The ability to coordinate positions with changes in position is an early form of logical-mathematical thought. It makes possible the problem solving in near-space, which we observe in children toward the end of the sensorimotor period. Understanding that objects continue to exist as they appear and disappear marks the first *conservations* where, in the context of changing sensations, something remains unchanged. It is the reversible coordinations of sensorimotor action that make the constructions of space, time, causality, and objects possible (Piaget, 1954).

During the early school years, we see advances in the child's understanding of reality. Children begin to understand that reality can be ordered in a variety of ways; for example, things can be ordered in a series from least to most. This shows up in many ways, including the understanding of time and numbers (e.g., history, age, the calendar). There is a beginning coordination of part-whole relations, where the child understands that wholes are composed of parts, that a whole can be broken into parts, and the parts can be reassembled into wholes. This also shows up in many ways, including the child's understanding of words ("There are more children in the classroom than there are boys") and beginning arithmetic ("Seven is bigger than four because if you take four from seven, you have three left over").

As understanding advances, we refer to the child's thinking as "operational," meaning that the internal mental coordinations carried out by the child are organized in a system of reversible operations that allow concepts to remain stable and, further, to obtain the status of objective reasoning. An example of operations is seen in the reversible coordination of part-whole relations and in order relations. For example, two parts can be combined to yield a third $(A + B = C)$ and a whole (C) can be divided into its parts $(A$ and $B)$. The fact that development tends towards these operational organizations shows that it is lawful and universal. See chapter 8 for a more in-depth treatment of this topic.

SOCIAL EXPERIENCE AND RATIONALITY

As discussed above, Piaget endeavored to show that rationality, expressed in what we've called "objective knowledge," is constructed through the internal regulations of the child. Since the laws of these internal regulations are assumed to be universal, there is a communality of knowledge among people. But we've seen that Vygotsky believed that all conceptual knowledge is first encountered in social interactions. If development is dependent upon social experience, one might expect people from different cultures and different social experiences to develop differently. Is it possible, as we believe, that Piaget and Vygotsky complement rather than contradict one another?

Piaget believed that there are two developmental themes, each consisting of coordinations that eventually lead to stable concepts. One is the internal regulations of the child, and the other is cooperation with others. Social coordinations are essentially the conditions that allow us to agree or disagree with another or to cooperate with others. Piaget asserts that these two processes are inseparable and are simply different sides of assimilation and accommodation and, further, that both aspects of development follow a lawful course. Social actions, like mental actions, tend to become organized in logical-operational systems. Social experience provides the possibility of differing points of view—agreeing and disagreeing, understanding and not understanding. Each of these affects the accommodations of our thinking. The corresponding and, at times, conflicting intelligence of others participates in the development of our own intelligence (Alward, 1997a; Piaget, 1995).

The child's evolving ability to think rationally is tied to social life. The child's capacity for reason must eventually detach from the child's own perspective and incorporate the perspective of others. This process of agreeing and disagreeing with others depends upon a means of representing reality that is free of the individual means of representation (practical knowledge, images, sensations, perceptions, dreams, unconscious symbols). It depends on a socially agreed upon system of representation such as that provided by language (Piaget, 1962b).

While a child may have developed certain mental operations, it does not follow, however, that this same child is necessarily competent in the particular cultural forms of knowledge that require these operations. For example, most eight-year-olds throughout the world have developed the operations necessary for understanding simple addition. But only some of these children know how to respond to the equation $14 + 79 =$ __. For an individual's intelligence to be applied or expressed in particular cultural forms, the individual must have experience in those forms. This is the job of schooling and other informal mechanisms of social transmission. The untutored mind may develop the intelligence to understand something, but without an encounter with the cultural form, the child may not be able to demonstrate or express the understanding.

Intellectual experience cannot be isolated from cultural experience. While Piaget believes that what we learn cannot be derived directly from social or

The child's evolving ability to think is tied to social life.

physical experience (because learning is constructed and also limited by the stage of development), it is also true that what we learn cannot be separated from social experience. Experience occurs only within the embrace of a particular historical-cultural moment, within the envelope of particular values and patterns for work and play. So while intelligence may proceed by a lawful unfolding coordination of schemes, what are coordinated are actions and representations, and these are inseparable from social experience. Thus, people in differing cultural and historical settings may develop through the same basic developmental stages and yet have very different ways of expressing their intelligence in daily life. This is because the demands of daily life differ across culture, societies and periods in history. Furthermore, much of human knowledge is not easily subjected to the rigors of logically-mathematically governed discourse and is, therefore, subject to complex disagreements. Science, for example, is an attempt to bring common interests into such a discourse setting.

PLAY AND DEVELOPMENT

We've emphasized throughout the book that play is a central source of children's development. In the following sections we summarize the relationship between play and four domains of development.

Play and the Development of Intelligence

The natural activity of the child feeds the self-regulated development of intelligence. *Natural activities* in the early years are almost exclusively play-bound because the character of non-play activity requires a way of understanding and a way of directing one's activity that have not yet developed in the young child. During the early childhood years, the child's intelligence is marked by a lack of coordination between the two functions of intelligence: assimilation and accommodation. The child is constantly understanding the world in ways which engender contradictions and fluctuations. The resulting modifications in understanding and behaviors are never complete enough to ward off continued vacillations and contradictions. The ongoing and constant modification of the child's intellectual structures is marked by a progressive coordination or equilibrium between assimilation, accommodation and social coordinations, but it is not until the end of middle childhood that this equilibrium is stable enough to yield a conceptually consistent and logically ordered world. Prior to this, the child is constantly processing contradictory information. A big block cannot fit into a small hole, but a big Santa Claus can fit down a small chimney. The examples are as numerous as the beliefs of children.

Until this equilibrium is achieved, the child's intellectual activity is always bound within the larger domain of play because, not being able to form an objective, reliable, and stable view of the world, there is always a subordination of the world to the child's immediate view. In a sense, because the child makes of the world what he wishes, we say that the child is bound by play, where work and practice are tied to pretense, fantasy, and imitation.

In short, intelligence develops through the child's self-directed and natural activities, which are always play-bound because all of a young child's activity tends toward the subordination of reality to the ego. Lacking the means of true work, where assimilation and accommodation are reliably coordinated, and where the child's intelligence is coordinated with others, the child is forced into a playful mode. In this mode, goal-directed activity slips into fantasy, attempts to grasp reality give way to pretense, and attempts to reconcile diverse perspectives slip into a subordination of reality to the child's immediate interests or perspectives. Hence, it is a truth about intelligence that the child, of necessity, must play in order to one day be able to do intelligent work. It is practice at play and not work that will one day produce the intelligent worker.

Play and the Development of Personality

The entire range of children's needs and emotions is arranged and expressed in play. Their play themes deal with abandonment, death, power, acceptance, and rejection. Emotions are practiced and linked to needs, but with pretense as a buffer between the real fear of abandonment, for example, and the fantasy expressed in the play, "let's say our mothers died and we're all alone."

Personality and intelligence, play and intelligence, and play and personality all support each other and are inseparable. Play is not simply one of the possible activities in which a child might engage; it is more accurate to say that play is an expression of the child's personality and intelligence.

There are also ways in which personality and intelligence are similar, and it is here that we find the powerful relationship between the development of a healthy personality and the healthy expression of play. One of the tenets of constructivism is that as the child attempts to understand the world, intelligence becomes more structured and more consistent, better organized, and more powerful. However, sometimes a personality may remain undeveloped, poorly formed, and maladaptive. For some the process of living results in the development of adaptive, well-structured, healthy personalities. For others, the early and incomplete personality of childhood, or parts of this personality, remain throughout life.

There is a process called "reflective abstraction," which is inevitable and necessary in the case of intelligence but not inevitable in the case of personality. Piaget created the concept of *reflective abstraction* to describe the way in which intelligence boot-straps itself up the developmental ladder. In *reflective abstraction*, the child brings into recognized forms, through representational activity, the unrealized or unrecognized relationships that make practical behaviors possible. That is, there is a natural, regulative process that advances intelligence simply through the activity of bringing unrealized ideas into representational focus (Piaget, 1977).

As adults we experience the power of reflective abstraction when, for example, we teach others. Teaching requires us to find a way of representing to others what we already know. The regulations underlying our practical knowledge are abstracted when we transform them into a representational form. In development, we might see a child who, for example, is on the verge of recognizing the conservation of liquid. We can imagine a developmental leap to understanding conservation through spontaneously counting (representing) the marbles in a jar. Counting the marbles may represent that a quantity (the jar full of marbles) is composed of smaller quantities (the marbles), the number of which does not change unless it is added to or subtracted from. The numerical representation of the marbles is not in itself knowledge of their conservation. Rather, representation assists the shift from the disequilibrium of an earlier stage to the relative equilibrium of a later stage.

A process similar to reflective abstraction is necessary to the development of personality. A child's personality develops towards an equilibrium between psycho-emotional needs and possible interactions within the world. This process is furthered when the child can consciously represent latent needs and emotions. In the case of intelligence, reflective abstraction is inevitable because the child attempts to formulate goals and orchestrate means to reach those goals. It forces the child to represent goals and the links between possible actions and the realization of goals.

For example, in trying to put a necklace of beads into a paper cup, an 18-month-old child might imagine (represent) what is happening when the necklace, draped over the edge of the cup, knocks the cup over. The child might succeed by bunching the necklace into a ball and dropping it into the cup. In doing so, the child represents to himself the goal (getting the necklace into the cup), the obstacle (the necklace knocks the cup over) and the solution (bunching the necklace into a ball). In the case of personality, on the other hand, the inner psycho-emotional self can remain unconscious, repressed, and fixated in patterns of action that can remain unreflected throughout life. For example, a child may develop a certain personality as a way of fitting into or solving certain problems within the family. While this development may be a coping mechanism, its origins can be repressed and unavailable to the child for reflection.

The parallel between intelligence and personality is established by the common process of means-ends coordination and reflective abstraction. For personality to continue to develop, it needs to be constantly embedded in reflective activity. Symbolic play is the way the child represents needs and concerns as well as how these needs and concerns are being dealt with. Adults may depend upon therapy, analysis, ritual, art, or work, but the child depends upon play for the development of personality. This process points to the critical and necessary role that play occupies in the lives of children. Through the free and unconstrained process of play, unrestrained because it is freed from inhibition and bends the world to immediate needs and interests, the child brings into represented forms the unconscious and inner psycho-emotional self.

Play and the Development of Competencies

During the early childhood years, children develop an astonishing array of intellectual, physical, social, and psycho-emotional competencies. The infant at birth is helpless, lacking in all but the most rudimentary reflexive sensorimotor competencies, such as sucking, grasping, or looking at objects. The simplest of human competencies, such as removing a blanket from the face or purposefully grasping an object, are not present at birth.

By the time they reach preschool, children have acquired control over their bodily functions, can feed themselves, can dress themselves, can jump, crawl, and run, and have acquired a language and a wide range of representational skills. They can initiate social interactions, have learned how acceptably to express some needs and feelings, have learned something about what is acceptable and unacceptable behavior, and have developed a problem-solving intelligence. In short, the preschool child has developed the unmistakable qualities of being human. And, of course, children continue to develop. Older children are more competent in how they feed and dress themselves. They can skip as well as jump. They can use language not only to initiate, but also to sustain interactions with others. The origins and the continued development of these competencies are closely tied to play.

Many competencies are sensorimotor schemes, integrating the senses with the use of muscles. Obvious examples might be eating, controlling the excretory functions, dressing, running and skipping, or even talking, which is a complex sensorimotor activity. Other competencies are not sensorimotor, but instead involve internal representations of possible actions, and are representational and abstract. The ability of children to think, problem solve, and coordinate their play with others are examples. Whether the competencies are sensorimotor or representational, their development is dependent upon play in a number of ways, the most obvious of which is *functional practice*. All acquired schemes, whether sensorimotor or not, are repeated. There is pleasure in the repetition of newly acquired skills. Children play at making the sounds of their native language, at large and small motor activities such as skipping or dressing, and at exploring and practicing new intellectual powers.

Play, in addition to providing the functional practice for competencies, provides their *contextualization* and meanings. Children embed emerging competencies in play activity, often with others, thereby refining not only their articulation, but also their meaning. For example, doll play may contain maternal and family themes, or house play may contain themes of "dressing up." Outdoor play may contain games that define conditions for running, jumping, and skipping. Much of this contextualized "meaning making" involves the fantasy and pretend elements of play and, therefore, might be thought of as *symbolic play*. In play, the child is either creating a symbol by, for example, using a plate of sand to stand for a plate of food, or creating a tapestry of meaning in which a variety of symbols are woven into a meaningful whole.

A third role of play concerns the *socialization* of competencies. In some cases, they are themselves social, as in the ability to initiate and maintain interactions or a dramatic play theme. In other cases, the competencies are not in themselves social, but can be brought together to meet social needs. For example, competencies for large motor activity, language, problem solving, and considering the needs of others might be brought together in a playground chase game with hero figures taken from the culture.

The ability to form social relationships in which common goals can be established and activities between members of the group are coordinated to achieve these goals is an exceedingly complex competency and slow to unfold. It begins with children playing together in proximity only, to eventually playing with each other, but without common themes or purposes. Then it proceeds to attempts to establish and sustain common purposes, but with constant changes in direction, manner, and roles. Finally, social relationships develop into sustained and coordinated play with agreed upon purpose, direction, manner and roles. This broad competency is almost synonymous with socialization and is at its core an evolution of the child's play.

In summary, competencies are the manifestations of intelligence and personality. They represent the child's ability to control means-ends relationships within the complex of needs and emotions, and to develop the means of participation within his or her culture. Their development is from the beginning tied to play, which provides (a) functional practice, (b) contextualization and meaning, and (c) socialization.

Play and the Development of Social-Consciousness

We are individuals from birth, if not from conception, and yet our identity, our sense of self, must be constructed, developing gradually and passing through many stages. During the first few months, infants cannot distinguish themselves from their surroundings because they lack the intentional ability to interact with the world. For example, infants are limited in their ability purposely to cause effects on objects or others because they cannot distinguish between what they are causing and what others are causing (Piaget, 1954). Without an awareness of what one causes, there is no real sense of self. So it is that the child will pass through the stages of intelligence, slowly moving from an undifferentiated beginning to a gradual recognition of the self as both the cause of effects and the effect of causes.

Because the awareness of self is, by necessity, tied to this reciprocal causality, the self being both a *cause and an effect*, its development takes two paths, each with its own ends, and yet, due to their common origin, ends which are insepa- rable. On the one hand, there is the developing sense of what one can do or who one is (that is, an awareness of one's intelligence, personality, and compe- tence). On the other hand, there is the gradual understanding of how the actions of others affect us and how we affect others. In the first, the end point of development is the *objective self*, a sense of self that progresses through a gradual shedding of its egocentric cloak, approaching an undistorted and objective stance where one's sense of self increasingly corresponds to how others see us. It is in the context of play that children learn to incorporate the viewpoint of oth- ers into their own sense of self. In the second, the end point of development is the *generalized self*, a sense of self as one social object among others, where the reciprocities between "self" and "other" are understood such that what is true for one must be true for others, and vice versa (Mead, 1934).

The sense of self is perhaps the most interesting and profound aspect of human development because its end is not just the *self*, but rather a social-con- sciousness capable of generating the ethical, moral, and even spiritual conditions that make the human experience possible. It is because of the sense of self and its inexorable tie to the development of a social conscience that we come to understand the necessary links between social experience and the conditions that foster healthy development and a healthy social order. The development of a sense of self is, from its inception, bound to play, where one's own efficacy is explored, where one's own view is coordinated with that of others, and where problems of social coordination are encountered and resolved every day. Play is at the foundation of humankind's most profound and necessary ability, the weaving of the individual spirit into a social fabric.

THE MEANING OF PLAY IN CHILDHOOD AND SOCIETY

How does play relate to the necessity of children eventually becoming part of their society? In the following we make some conclusions about the role of play in children's lives as they face the task of learning and responsibility.

The Adult World as a Condition in the Child's Life

We began by stating that the world of childhood and the world of play are insep- arable. We elaborated this view to emphasize the critical role of play in social, emotional, and intellectual development. At the same time we are aware that, left to their own devices, children would not develop the essential capacity to operate within the adult world. There is in this an apparent contradiction between our unhesitating belief that play is the foundation of healthy development and the acknowledgment that there is the correspondingly serious business of conforming to adult expectations. The confusion arises from viewing adult influences as the *cause* rather than one of the many *conditions* in human development.

As educators we must recognize that we cannot directly cause the child to learn. Our responsibility is to set the conditions for learning and development. We've emphasized the importance of play as one of the conditions for development. In the chapters on orchestrating play and in the content chapters, we endeavored to show that by supporting play in the classroom we create a condition for children to learn the school content in a way that honors their development.

When we insist, for example, that a child share his toys with a playmate, we are not causing the development of "sharing." The act of sharing is a complex social coordination that entails competencies which must be developed by the child. The imposition of our will is simply a condition, a quality of the environment in which certain competencies are implicit or explicit goals. As adults we create an environment which the child attempts to understand and in which the child must eventually adjust needs and emotions to possible actions.

Society impresses itself on children through the work it assigns or requires, through the models it provides, and through the authority it commands. In schools we must determine the work we expect of children. As educators and adults we model what it means to function in our society and we impose, however gently, our authority. However, work, modeling and authority are less important to development than is spontaneous play. How is it that play rather than work, that play rather than conformity to adult models, and that play rather than compliance with authority, is the major force in child development?

Play and the Work of Society

We distinguish between the *work of childhood* and the *work of society*. The first includes the many instances where the child formulates ends and means, such as when an infant works at finding and nursing the nipple, when a toddler works at chasing and catching a cat, or when a school-age child works at creating a play space. The second consists of the many instances where the purpose and desired ends, as well as the means and even the success of the work, are determined from outside.

While both forms of work are important and often merge, they have very different status in the child's development. Because we view "children's work" as self-directed activity, it is by definition *autotelic*, or containing within it its own direction and purpose. The "work of society," which must also be faced by the child, is *heterotelic*, having a direction and purpose imposed from outside. However, while the child may engage in both forms of work, autotelic activity is essential to development because the dynamics of development involve accommodations or modifications brought about by resistances which the world presents to the child's understanding. In a sense, the child treats the world according to what he or she knows; and with that being often inadequate, what the child knows must be modified. This is assimilation and accommodation. When, for example, a child finds his or her goal thwarted, it is within the child's inner experience that the goal, the obstacle, and the possible means of overcoming the obstacle are synthesized.

The dynamic interplay between the child's assimilations of the world and the corresponding accommodations is, by its very nature, autotelic because the understandings, the perceived sense of their inadequacy, and the willingness to make the necessary modifications are all *intrapersonal* (within the child) rather than *interpersonal* (outside the child). So it is that we assert the primacy of play over work as a source of development because the development follows from the autotelic work of childhood, which, in the early childhood years, is bound to and subordinate to play. We take this stand with full recognition that children often do not have the apparent luxury of play and, in fact, may lead lives where work is a common and everyday experience. Nor do we forget that many of the world's children live in trying and sometimes traumatic conditions of war, poverty, pestilence, and famine. In the face of these hard realities, and possibly more so because of them, we believe that play is the proper work of childhood.

In the schooling of children we must seek a blend between the work of childhood and the work of society. We must find that delicate balance that allows children to fully experience the inner tensions between what they presently know and the challenges of new experiences. We use the term "play" to characterize the context in which this balance is best achieved. This does not mean that we should not define the expected learning outcomes for the children in our care. It does, however, mean that in doing so we must never lose sight of the developmentally driven energies and interests of the child.

Adult Models as Content for Development

There is no question that adulthood impresses itself on the developing child by its models and examples. We illustrate how to be an adult within our culture by our very being as well as by our lessons and answers. What role, then, does play have in children's acquisition of the knowledge and skills that will shuttle them into adulthood?

If left to develop outside of culture, the child would certainly fail to develop the means of functioning within the culture. And yet it is equally true that the child cannot copy or imitate the models of adulthood, because these models contain a latent knowledge which the child is incapable of understanding. This is because the child lacks the means of constructing adult knowledge. In short, the child cannot behave or think as an adult simply by imitating adult behaviors or speech. So again, as in the case of work, we have an apparent contradiction. The child must be influenced by the models of adult society and yet cannot extract from those models the means of being an adult.

The resolution of this apparent contradiction lies in understanding the true value of models. Models are the content in development and not its cause. Children are interested in and constantly imitate the adult world in an attempt to understand and participate in it. However, the meaning of what is imitated develops out of the purposes and contexts in which the imitation takes place. The child imitates for a certain reason and in particular situations. The meaning of the imitation derives from these conditions. Hence, the adult social order serves as the content of development as well as the conditions in which that development will take place, but it does not in itself create understanding or competency.

In educating children we provide the content or the problems for children to address. Our own competencies as adults, our ability to cooperate with and understand others, our ability to read and write, do arithmetic, to talk about our lives and interests all serve as models and content for children. When we articulate the classroom curriculum, we refine these models in terms that we hope children can better understand. In early childhood education, integrating play into the curriculum provides an optimal refinement of the adult content that children strive to understand.

Autonomy as the Context for Development

The child lives in two inseparable, yet irreconcilable, social worlds: the world of adults and the world of peers. The adult society imposes itself on youth, creating a *heterotonomous* rather than *autonomous* condition where codes of behavior are sanctioned by adults and derived by forces totally outside of the child's control or comprehension. For example, a teacher may tell a child to "play fairly," but this does not mean that the child necessarily understands why being fair is important or why being fair should take a particular form.

The social world of peers, on the other hand, constitutes a condition of *autonomy* rather than heteronomy. Here children elaborate their own rules and codes for behavior, deciding among themselves what is fair, just, and appropriate to the immediate setting. Here they test the extension of their own wills, and here they orchestrate their campaigns against adult constraint.

Piaget made a strong argument that it is autonomy rather than heteronomy that creates the context for social, moral, and ethical development that is developed through social coordinations, that is, the coordinations of one's own activities and needs with those of others (Piaget, 1965d). Such coordinations require a reciprocity in which members of the social group are on an equal footing, addressing shared needs and shared frames of reference. The relationships between children and adults achieve this reciprocity only partially because children can never be on a truly equal footing with adults. Here, again, we face a seeming contradiction. We must wonder how it is that children, through their autonomous pursuits, will eventually obtain the adult traits that now separate them from this world. We can offer three answers that support the belief that autonomy among children, even in educational settings, has an important place in curriculum.

First, children work and play at accomplishing what they believe they will (or must) become. The classroom constitutes a micro culture that exemplifies a blend between the child's present level of development and the expectations of the adult world. There is nothing more important to children than participating in the adult world, of having its interest, attention, protection, and acceptance. Therefore, even when left to explore their own interests, children in large measure pursue the interests that correspond with our expectations.

Secondly, autonomy is necessary to development because social coordinations (and all shared knowledge is a social coordination) are, in fact, dependent upon autonomy. Each party of the coordination must take the other party into account. They must operate under "rules" that are particular to their own purpose and not imposed from without.

Lastly, social autonomy creates the *zone of proximal development*. We presented Vygotsky's concept of the ZPD in chapter 2. Vygotsky used the concept of the ZPD to characterize the social space where the disequilibrating perpetrations of the world are close enough to the child's level of development that the child can developmentally profit from these disturbances. It is in the *zone of proximal development* that both formal and informal teaching take place since it is only within this zone that what takes place "out there" can affect what takes place "in here" (Vygotsky, 1967). *Autonomy in social relations is a zone of proximal development.* Peers share a common level of development, focus, and interest and, therefore, feed one another's development. The perpetrations that originate in peer relationships fit into the zone of proximal development where problems and tasks that arise in activity between peers present appropriate stimuli to development.

SUMMARY AND CONCLUSION

Play is a dominant activity from birth through early adolescence. It participates in all areas of social, emotional, and intellectual growth. Play is a way of understanding the world and of comforting the self. It takes its material from the social world of the child as well as from the child's inner emotional needs. When we acknowledge the primacy of play, we recognize the primary vehicle in the child's early development.

We believe there is a privileged relationship between autonomous activity and development. Self-directed activity, as opposed to other-directed activity, is essential to development because the dynamics of development involve modifying existing ways of behaving or interpreting in order to adapt to new challenges. This process of assimilating experience to already established patterns and modifying these to accommodate surprises cannot take place outside the felt needs and tensions and the intuitively directed groping of the child. Hence, activity that is directed by the child is primary in development.

The issue of social autonomy is similar. The social conditions and regulations that children establish outside of adult authority are the necessary and primary conditions for social development. This, too, follows from the constructivists' position that social development is an evolution of social coordinations where children are increasingly able to align their respective goals to become partners in joint activity. This coordination and the ensuing reciprocities (how you treat me, I treat you) require autonomy rather than heteronomy (authority imposed from without) because reciprocity requires that the players be on an equal footing.

Piaget's work makes it clear that if children were not self-directed and engaged in autonomous social alliances, they would not develop. This does not mean, however, that adult guidance is not critical to the intellectual, emotional, and social development of the child. As we come to understand the constructivist point of view, we recognize that the guidance we provide must be a condition for growth, and growth in the early childhood years is indistinguishable from play itself.

In our view it is meaningless to talk about a developmentally based curriculum without implying a curriculum based on play. It is equally meaningless to talk about a play-centered curriculum that is not based on development. Teaching in a play-based and developmentally based curriculum requires knowing what the child knows, where the child's interests and energy lie, and where the child is going. It requires knowing how to engage the child so that the teacher's understanding of both the child and the curriculum is developed along with the child's progress in understanding and acquiring skills. Entering into the child's play, by direct or indirect means, allows the teacher to see what the child knows and where the child is headed. Orchestrating play allows the teacher to support the child's progress through further manipulations of the play and non-play environments. The teacher, rather than being the guardian and administrator of the curriculum, becomes the gardener and architect of the environment, using play as its nutrient and structure.

FOCUSING OUR THINKING

1. Intelligence, personality, competency, and social consciousness are integrated and developed in play. Re-read the play episode at the beginning of this chapter. What evidence do you see for this integration? Think about or discuss the goal-directed activities in the play, the emotional needs of the players, the competency of the children, and the social consciousness issues (i.e., children's awareness of how they affect each other and how they "see" each other).

2. Imagine a discussion with a parent who is concerned that his four-year-old daughter is spending a lot of time playing and not doing the kind of work that will prepare her for elementary school. What do you know about play that would address this father's concerns?

3. In your own words, tell why self-directed and socially autonomous activity is critical to a child's development.

4. After reading this chapter, how would you describe the role of social experience in child development?

5. Review your annotated bibliography. What have you learned about the relationship between play and development by reading these books? Which books would you recommend to others, and why?

6. An activity included in chapter 5 consisted of writing a brochure for parents describing the play-centered philosophy of your school. If you completed this

activity, revise it now, based upon your current understandings. If you did not, take time now to write a brochure that is informative and interesting.

SUGGESTED RESOURCES

1. DeVries, R., & Kohlberg, L. (1987). *Constructive early education: Overview and comparison with other programs*. Washington, DC: National Association for the Education of Young Children.

    This is a good sourcebook that provides a comprehensive overview of Piagetian approaches to education with a comparison of other approaches.

2. Flavell, J. H. (1963). *The developmental psychology of Jean Piaget*. Princeton, NJ: Van Nostrand.

    Flavell's book is a classic American interpretation of Piaget's general theory that is probably more useful to the advanced student.

3. Bodrova, E., & Leong, D. J. (1996) *Tools of the mind*. Upper Saddle River, NJ: Prentice Hall.

    This book presents a recent look at the Vygotskian approach to early childhood education.

References

Adams, J. (1976). *Conceptual blockbusting: A plea-surable guide to better problem solving.* New York: W. W. Norton.

Ainsworth, M. D., Bell, S. M., & Stayton, D. J. (1974). Infant-mother attachment and social development: "Socialization" as a product of reciprocal responsiveness to signals. In M. M. Richards (Ed.), *The integration of a child into a social world.* London: Cambridge University Press.

Aldis, O. (1975). *Play fighting.* New York: Academic Press.

Alkon, A., Genevo, J. L., Kaiser, J., Tschann, J. M., Chesney, M. A., & Boyce, W. T. (1994). Injuries in child care centers: Rates, severity, and etiology. *Pediatrics, 94*(16), 1043–1046.

Almy, M. (1984). *Applying Piaget's theory in the early childhood classroom: Resource report.* Chicago, IL: WorldBook-Childcraft.

Almy, M., & Genishi, C. (1982). *Ways of studying children* (rev. ed.). New York: Teachers College Press.

Alper, C. D. (1987). Early childhood music education. In C. Seefeldt (Ed.), *The early childhood curriculum: A review of current research* (pp. 211–236). New York: Teacher's College Press.

Althouse, R. (1988). *Investigating science with young children.* New York: Teachers College Press.

Alward, K. R. (1995, June). *Play as a primary context for development: The integration of intelligence, personality, competencies, and social consciousness.* Poster presentation at the Annual Meeting of the Jean Piaget Society, Berkeley, CA.

Alward, K. R. (1996). *Piaget's implicit social theory; play dreams and imitation revisited.* Paper for the Association for the Study of Play (TASP), Austin, Texas.

Alward, K. R. (1997a). *Piaget, rationality and play.* Paper for the Association for the Study of Play (TASP), Washington, DC.

Alward, K. R. (1997b). *Top down/bottom up play-based curriculum: An informal look at Piaget and Vygotsky.* Paper for the Jean Piaget Society, Santa Monica, California.

American Association for the Advancement of Science, Project 2061. (1993). *Benchmarks for science literacy.* New York: Oxford University Press.

Ashton-Warner, S. (1963). *Teacher.* New York: Simon & Schuster.

Athey, I. (1988). The relationship of play to cognitive, language, and moral development. In D. Bergen (Ed.), *Play as a medium for learning and development: A handbook of theory and practice* (pp. 81–102). Portsmouth, NH: Heinemann.

Bailey's book house. [Computer software]. (1992). Berkeley Learning Technologies. Redmond, WA: Edmark.

Balaban, N. (1985). *Starting school: From separation to independence.* New York: Teachers College Press.

Bandich, J. (1987). *Get ready for dramatic play: Twenty-four kit ideas to assemble for role-playing.* Cypress, CA: Creative Teaching Press.

Barnes, B. J., & Hill, S. (1983). Should young children work with computers: Logo before Lego? *The Computing Teacher, 10*(9), 11–14.

Baroody, A. J. (1987). *Children's mathematical thinking: A developmental framework for preschool, primary and special education teachers.* New York: Teachers College Press.

Barrs, M., Ellis, S., Hester, H., & Thomas, A. (1988). *The primary language record.* London, England: Centre for Language and Primary Education.

Barrs, M., Ellis, S., Hester, H., & Thomas, A. (1991). *Patterns of learning.* London, England: Centre for Language and Primary Education.

Bateson, G. A. (1976). A theory of play and fantasy. In J. S. Bruner, A. Jolly, & K. Sylva (Eds.), *Play: Its role in development and evolution* (pp. 119–129). New York: Basic Books.

Batteries and bulbs. (1995). Full Option Science System Unit. Chicago: Encyclopedia Britannica.

Beardsley, L. (1991). *Good day, bad day: The child's experience of child care.* New York: Teachers College Press.

Bergen, D. (Ed.). (1988). *Play as a medium for learning and development: A handbook of theory and practice.* Portsmouth, NH: Heinemann.

Berk, L. E., & Winsler, A. (1995). *Scaffolding children's learning: Vygotsky and early childhood education.* Washington, DC: National Association for the Education of Young Children.

Bernhardt, V. L. (1997). *Second Annual Evaluation Report of Education First Demonstration Schools, Pacific Bell and Pacific Bell Foundation.* (Unpublished).

Bettelheim, B. (1989). *The uses of enchantment.* New York: Random House.

Black, B. (1989). Interactive pretense: Social and symbolic skills in preschool play groups. *Merrill Palmer Quarterly, 35*(4), 379–397.

Blurton-Jones, N. G. (1972). Categories of child-child interaction. In N. G. Blurton-Jones (Ed.), *Ethnological studies of child behavior* (pp. 97–129). New York: Cambridge University Press.

Bodrova, E. & Leong, D. J. (1996). *Tools of the mind.* Upper Saddle River, NJ: Prentice Hall.

Bohm, D. (1978). A conversation with David Bohm—The enfolding-unfolding universe, conducted by Renee Weber. *ReVision, 1,* 3–4.

Bolton, G. (1985, Summer). Changes in thinking about drama in education. *Theory Into Practice, 24*(3), 151–157. Columbus, OH: Ohio State University.

Boyd, P. A., Potter, L. D., & Carlson, R. E. (1989). *Early childhood education: Current trends in instruction and assessment.*

Bredekamp, S. (1987). *Developmentally appropriate practice in early childhood programs serving young children birth through age 8.* Washington, DC: National Association for the Education of Young Children.

Bredekamp, S., & Copple, C. (Eds.). (1997). *Developmentally appropriate practice in early childhood programs* (rev. ed.). Washington, DC: National Association for the Education of Young Children.

Bretherton, I. (1984). *Symbolic play: The development of social understanding.* New York: Academic Press.

Bronson, W. (1995). *The right stuff for children from birth to 8: Selecting play materials to support development.* Washington, DC: National Association for the Education of Young Children.

Brown, L. K. (1986). *Taking advantage of media: A manual for parents and teachers.* Boston: Routledge & Kegan Paul.

Browne, N. (Ed.). (1991). *Science and technology in the early years: An equal opportunities approach.* Open University Press.

Bruner, J. S. (1963). *The process of education.* Cambridge, MA: Harvard University Press.

Bruner, J. S. (1976). The nature and uses of immaturity. In J. S. Bruner, A. Jolly, & K. Sylva (Eds.), *Play: Its role in development and evolution* (pp. 28–64). New York: Basic Books.

Bruner, J. S. (1980). *Under five in Britain.* Ypsilanti, MI: High Scope Press.

Bruner, J. S. (1986). *Actual minds, possible worlds.* Cambridge, MA: Harvard University Press.

Bruner, J. S. (1990). *Acts of meaning.* Cambridge, MA: Harvard University Press.

Bruner, J. S., Jolly, A., & Sylva, K. (Eds.). (1976). *Play: Its role in development and evolution.* New York: Basic Books.

California Instructional Technology Clearinghouse (online). (1997). Stanislaus County Office of Education, http://clearinghouse.k12.ca.us.

Campbell, F., & Fein, G. (1986). *Young children and microcomputers.* Upper Saddle River, NJ: Prentice Hall.

Carlsson-Paige, N., & Levin, D. (1987). *The war play dilemma: Balancing needs and values in the early childhood classroom.* New York: Teachers College Press.

Carlsson-Paige, N., & Levin, D. (1990). *Who's calling the shots?* Santa Cruz, CA: New Society Publishers.

Cazden, C. B. (1983). Adult assistance to language development: Scaffolds, models and direct instruction. In R. P. Parker & F. A. Davis (Eds.), *Developing literacy: Young children's use of language*. Newark, DE: International Reading Association.

Char, C. & Forman, G. (1994). Interactive technology and the young child: A look to the future. In J. L. Wright & D. D. Shade (Eds.), *Young children: Active learners in a technological age* (pp. 167–177). Washington, DC: National Association for the Education of Young Children.

Children's writing and publishing center [Computer software]. (1988). Menlo Park, CA: The Learning Company.

Christie, J. (1985). Training of symbolic play. *Early Child Development and Care, 19*, 42–46.

Christie, J. (1995). *Linking literacy and play*. Newark, NJ: International Reading Association.

Christie, J. F., & Johnsen, E. P. (1989). The constraints of settings on children's play. *Play and Culture, 2*, 317–327.

Clements, D. H. (1985). *Computers in early and primary education*. Upper Saddle River, NJ: Prentice Hall.

Clements, D. H. (1987). Computers and young children: A review of research. *Young Children, 34–44*.

Cliatt, M. J. P. and Shaw, J. M. (1992). *Helping children explore science: A sourcebook for teachers of young children*. Upper Saddle River, NJ: Merrill/Prentice Hall.

Cochran-Smith, M., Kahn, J., & Paris, C. (1990). Writing with a felicitous tool. *Theory Into Practice, 29*(4), 235–244.

Cochran-Smith, M. & Lytle, S. L. (1993). *Inside/outside: Teacher research and knowledge*. New York: Teachers College Press.

Cohen, M. (1980). *First grade takes a test*. New York: Dell.

Cole, M., & Cole, S. R. (1996). *The development of children* (3rd ed.). New York: W. H. Freeman.

Cook-Gumperz, J. (1977, November). *The natural history of an activity*. Unpublished manuscript.

Cook-Gumperz, J. (1986). *The social construction of literacy*. New York: Cambridge University Press.

Cook-Gumperz, J., & Corsaro, W. (1977). Social-ecological constraints on children's communication strategies. *Sociology, 11*, 412–434.

Cook-Gumperz, J., Corsaro, W., & Streeck, J. (Eds.). (1996). *Children's worlds and children's language*. Berlin: Mouton.

Cook-Gumperz, J., Gates, D., Scales, B., & Sanders, H. (1976). *Toward an understanding of angel's hair: Summary of a pilot study of a nursery play yard*. Unpublished manuscript. University of California, Berkeley.

Cook-Gumperz, J., & Gumperz, J. (1982). Introduction: Language and social identity. In J. Gumperz (Ed.), *Language and social identity* (Vol. 2, pp. 1–2). Cambridge, UK: Cambridge University Press.

Cook-Gumperz, J., & Scales, B. (1982). *Toward an understanding of angel's hair: Report on a study of children's communication in socio-dramatic play*. Unpublished manuscript.

Cook-Gumperz, J., & Scales, B. (1996). Girls, boys and just people: The interactional accomplishment of gender in the discourse of the nursery school. In D. Slobin, J. Gerhardt, A. Kyratzis & J. Guo (Eds.), *Social interaction, social context, and language*. Mahwah, NJ: Erlbaum.

Copple, C. E., Cocking, R. R., & Matthews, W. S. (1984). Objects, symbols and substitutes: The nature of the cognitive activity during symbolic play. In T. D. Yawkey & A. D. Pellegrini (Eds.), *Child's play: Developmental and applied* (pp. 105–123). Hillsdale, NJ: Erlbaum.

Copple, C. E., Sigel, I., & Saunders, R. (1984). *Educating the young thinker: Classroom strategies for cognitive growth*. Hillsdale, NJ: Erlbaum.

Corsaro, W. A. (1979). We're friends, right? Children's use of access rituals in a nursery school. *Language in Society, 8*, 315–336.

Corsaro, W. A. (1985). *Friendship and peer culture in the early years*. Norwood, NJ: Ablex.

Corsaro, W. A. (1997). *The sociology of childhood*. Thousand Oaks, CA: Pine Forge Press.

Corsaro, W. A., & Elder, D. (1990). Children's peer cultures. *Annual Review of Sociology, 16*, 197–220.

Corsaro, W., & Schwartz, K. (1991). Peer play and socialization in two cultures: Implications for research and practice. In B. Scales, M. Almy, A. Nicolopoulou, & S. Ervin-Tripp (Eds.), *Play and the social context of development in early care and education* (pp. 234–254). New York: Teacher's College Press.

Cowan, P. A. (1978). *Piaget with feeling: Cognitive, social and emotional dimensions.* New York: Holt, Rinehart & Winston.

Cuffaro, H. K. (1984). Microcomputers in education: Why is earlier better? *Teachers College Record, 85*(4), 559–568.

Cuffaro, H. K. (1995). *Experimenting with the world: John Dewey and the early childhood classroom.* New York: Teachers College Press.

Curry, N. E. (1971). Consideration of current basic issues on play. In N. Curry & S. Arnaud (Eds.), *Play: The child strives toward self-realization* (pp. 51–62). Washington, DC: National Association for the Education of Young Children.

Csikszentmihalyi, M. (1993). *The evolving self: A psychology for the third millenium.* New York: HarperCollins.

Davidson, J. (1995). *Emergent literacy and dramatic play in early education.* Albany, NY: Delmar Publishers.

Davydov, V. V. (1995). The influence of L. S. Vygotsky on education theory, research, and practice. *Educational Researcher, 24*(3), 12–21.

Derman-Sparks, L., & A.B.C. Task Force. (1989). *The antibias curriculum: Tools for empowering young children.* Washington, DC: National Association for the Education of Young Children.

de Uriarte, M., (1978). *The Berkeley child art studio.* Unpublished manuscript. Berkeley, CA.

DeVries, R. (1997). Piaget's social theory. *Educational Researcher, 26*(2), 4–17.

DeVries, R., & Kohlberg, L. (1987). *Constructivist early education: Overview and comparison with other programs.* Washington, DC: NAEYC.

DeVries, R., & Zan, B. (1994). *Moral classrooms, moral children: Creating a constructivist atmosphere in early education.* New York: Teachers College Press.

Dewey, J. (1971). *The child and the curriculum: The school and society.* Chicago: University of Chicago Press. (Originally published 1915)

Diaute, C. (1989). Play as thought: Thinking strategies of young writers. *Harvard Educational Review, 59,* 1–23.

Dodge, D. T., & Colker, L. J. (1992). *The creative curriculum for early education* (3rd ed.). Washington, DC: Teaching Strategies, Inc.

Dominick, A., & Clark, F. B. (1996). Using games to understand children's understanding. *Childhood Education, 72*(5), 286–288.

Doris, E. (1991). *Doing what scientists do: Children learn to investigate their world.* Portsmouth, NH: Heinemann Boynton/Cook.

Doyle, A. B., & Connolly, J. (1989). Negotiation and enactment in social pretend play: Relations to social acceptance and social cognition. *Early Childhood Research Quarterly, 4,* 289–302.

Duckworth, E. (1996). *"The having of wonderful ideas" and other essays on teaching and learning* (2nd ed.). New York: Teachers College Press.

Dyson, A. H. (1989). *Multiple worlds of child writers: Friends learning to write.* New York: Teachers College Press.

Dyson, A. H. (1990). Symbol makers, symbol weavers: How children link play, pictures and print. *Young Children, 45*(2), 50–57.

Dyson, A. H. (1993). *Social worlds of children learning to write in an urban primary school.* New York: Teachers College Press.

Dyson, A. H. (1994). *The ninjas, the X-men, and the ladies: Playing with power and identity in an urban primary school* (Technical Report No. 70). Berkeley, CA: University of California, National Center for the Study of Writing.

Dyson, A. H. (1995, April). *The courage to write: The ideological dimensions of child writing.* Paper presented at the Annual Meeting of the American Educational Research Association, San Francisco, CA.

Dyson, A. H. (1997). *Writing superheroes: Contemporary childhood, popular culture, and classroom literacy.* New York: Teachers College Press.

Dyson, A. H., & Genishi, C. (Eds.). (1994). *The need for story: Cultural diversity in classroom and community.* Urbana, IL: National Council of Teachers of English.

Edwards, C. (1993). Partner, nurturer, and guide: The roles of the Reggio teacher in action. In C. Edwards, L. Gandini, & G. Forman, (Eds.), *The hundred languages of children:*

The Reggio Emilia approach to early childhood education (pp. 151–169). Norwood, NJ: Ablex.

Edwards, C., Gandini, L., & Forman, G. (Eds.). (1993). *The hundred languages of children: The Reggio Emilia approach to early childhood education*. Norwood, NJ: Ablex.

Egan, K. (1988). *Primary understanding: Education in early childhood*. New York: Routledge.

Eisert, D., & Lamorey, S. (1996). Play as a window on child development: The relationship between play and other developmental domains. *Early Education and Development, 7*(3), 221–235.

Elgas, P., Klein, E., Kantor, R., & Fernie, D. (1988). Play and the peer culture: Play styles and object use. *Journal of Research in Childhood Education, 3*, 142–153.

Elkind, D. (1986, May). Formal education and early childhood education: An essential difference. *Phi Delta Kappan,* 631–636.

Elkind, D. (1990). Academic pressure—too much, too soon: The demise of play. In E. Klugman & S. Smilansky (Eds.), *Children's play and learning: Perspectives and policy implications* (pp. 3–17). New York: Teachers College Press.

Ellis, M. (1988). Play and the origin of species. In D. Bergen (Ed.), *Play as a medium for learning and development* (pp. 23–26). Portsmouth, NH: Heinemann.

Emihovich, C. (1990). Technocentrism revisited: Computer literacy as cultural capital. *Theory Into Practice, 29*(4), 227–234.

Erickson, F. (1993). Foreword. In M. Cochran-Smith & S. L. Lytle (Eds.), *Inside/Outside: Teacher research and knowledge*. New York & London: Teachers College Press.

Erikson, E. (1963). *Childhood and society* (2nd ed.). New York: Norton.

Erikson, E. (1977). *Toys and reasons.* New York: Norton.

Erwin, E. J. (1993). Social participation of young children with visual impairments in specialized and integrated environments. *Journal of Visual Impairment & Blindness, 87*(5), 138–142.

Facemaker. [Computer program]. (1986). Cambridge, MA: Spinnaker Software.

Fantavision. [Computer software]. (1985). Novato, CA: Broderbund Software.

Farver, J. (1992). Communicating shared meaning in social pretend play. *Early Childhood Research Quarterly, 7*(40), 501–516.

Fein, G. G. (1981). Pretend play in childhood: An integrative review. *Child Development, 52*, 1095–1118.

Fein, S. (1984). *Heidi's horse* (2nd ed.). Pleasant Hill, CA: Exelrod Press.

Fenson, L., & Ramsay, D. S. (1980). Decentration and integration of the child's play in the second year. *Child Development, 47*, 232–235.

Field, T. M. (1980). Preschool play: Effects of teacher/child ratios and organization of classroom space. *Child Study Journal, 10*, 191–205.

Flavell, J. H. (1963). *The developmental psychology of Jean Piaget*. Princeton, NJ: Van Nostrand.

Forman, G. (1992). The constructivist perspective in early education. In J. Roopnarine, & J. Johnson (Eds.), *Approaches to early childhood education* (2nd ed.). Upper Saddle River, NJ: Merrill/Prentice Hall.

Forman, G. (1994). Different media, different languages. In L. Katz, & B. Cesarone (Eds.), *Reflective essays on the Reggio approach* (pp. 41–54). Urbana, IL: ERIC Monograph Series #6.

Forman, G. (1996). A child constructs an understanding of a water wheel in five media. *Childhood Education, 72*(5), 269–273.

Forman, G. E., & Hill, F. (1984). *Constructive play: Applying Piaget in the preschool*. Menlo Park, CA: Addison-Wesley.

Forman, G. E., & Kaden, M. (1987). Research on science education for young children. In C. Seefeldt (Ed.), *The early childhood curriculum: A review of current research* (pp. 141–164). New York: Teachers College Press.

Forman, G. E., & Kuschner, D. S. (1977). *The child's construction of knowledge: Piaget for teaching children*. Belmont, CA: Wadsworth.

FOSS Newsletter. (Fall, 1995). Chicago: Encyclopedia Britannica.

Fromberg, D. (1992). A review of research on play. In C. Seefeldt (Ed.), *The early childhood curriculum: A review of current research* (2nd ed.), (pp. 42–84). New York: Teachers College Press.

Furth, H. G. (1970). *Piaget for teachers.* Upper Saddle River, NJ: Prentice Hall.

Gandini, L. (1993). Fundamentals of the Reggio Emilia approach to early childhood education. *Young Children, 49*(1), 4–8.

Gandini, L. (1997). The Reggio Emilia story: History and organization and foundations of the Reggio Emilia approach. In J. Hendrick (Ed.), *First steps toward teaching the Reggio way* (pp. 3–23). Upper Saddle River, NJ: Merrill/Prentice Hall.

Gardner, H. (1973). *The arts and human development: A psychological study of the artistic process.* New York: Wiley.

Gardner, H. (1983) *Frames of mind: The theory of multiple intelligences.* New York: Basic Books.

Garvey, C. (1977). *Play.* Cambridge, MA: Harvard University Press.

Garvey, C., & Berndt, R. (1977). *Organization of pretend play* (JSAS Catalogue of Selected Documents in Psychology, Manuscript 1589). Washington, DC: American Psychological Association.

Gaskins, S., Miller, P., & Corsaro, W. (1992). Theoretical and methodological perspectives in the interpretive study of children. *New Directions in Child Development, 58,* 5–23.

Genishi, C. (Ed.). (1992). *Ways of assessing children and curriculum.* New York: Teachers College Press

Genishi, C., & DiPaolo, M. (1982). Learning through argument in preschool. In L. C. Wilkonson (Ed.), *Communicating in the classroom* (pp. 49–68). New York: Academic Press.

Genishi, C., & Dyson, A. (1984). *Language assessment in the early years.* Norwood, NJ: Ablex.

Genishi, C., & Strand, E. (1990). Contextualizing logo: Lessons from a 5-year-old. *Theory Into Practice, 29*(4), 264–269.

Gentile, L. & Hoot, J. (1983). Kindergarten play: The foundation of reading. *The Reading Teacher, 36,* 436–439.

Gertrude's secrets. [Computer software]. (1988). Menlo Park, CA: The Learning Company.

Giffin, H. (1984). The coordination of meaning in the creation of a shared make-believe reality. In I. Bretherton (Ed.), *Symbolic play: The development of social understanding* (pp. 73–100). New York: Academic Press.

Ginsburg, H. P., Klein, A., Starkey, P. (1997). The development of children's mathematical thinking: Connecting research with practice. In I. Sigel & A. Renninger (Eds.), *Handbook of Child Psychology* (5th ed., Vol. 4), Child Psychology and Practice. New York: Wiley.

Goffman, E. (1974). *Frame analysis.* New York: Harper & Row.

Golomb, C., & Bonen, S. (1981). Playing games of make–believe: The effectiveness of symbolic play training with children who failed to benefit from early conservation training. *Genetic Psychology Monographs, 104,* 137–159.

Golomb, C., Gowing, E. D., & Friedman, L. (1982). Play and cognition: Studies of pretense play and conservation of quantity. *Journal of Experimental Child Psychology, 33,* 257–279.

Goncu, A. (1993). Development of intersubjectivity in the dyadic play of preschoolers. *Early Childhood Research Quarterly, 8,* 99–116.

Goncu, A., & Kessler, F. (1984). Children's play: A contextual-functional perspective. In F. Kessler, & A. Goncu (Eds.), *Analyzing children's play dialogues* (pp. 5–22). San Francisco: Jossey-Bass.

Goodnow, J. (1977). *Children drawing.* Cambridge, MA: Harvard University Press.

Goodwin, M. (1990). *He-said-she-said: Talk as social organization among black children.* Bloomington, IN: Indiana University Press.

Gould, R. (1972). *Child studies through fantasy.* New York: Quadrangle Books.

Greenberg, P. (1989). Ideas that work with young children: Learning self esteem and self discipline through play. *Young Children, 44*(2), 28–31.

Greenfield, P. M. (1984). *Mind and media: The effects of television, video games, and computers.* Cambridge, MA: Harvard University Press.

Greenman, J. (1988). *Caring spaces, learning places: Children's environments that work.* Redmond, WA: Exchange Press.

Griffin, E. (1982). *Island of Childhood: Education in the special world of the nursery school.* New York: Teachers College Press.

Gumperz, J. J., & Cook-Gumperz, J. (1982). Introduction: Language and the communication of social identity. In J. J. Gumperz & J. Cook-Gumperz (Eds.), *Language and social identity* (pp. 1–21). Cambridge, UK: Cambridge University Press.

Halliday, J., & McNaughton, S. (1982). Sex differences in play at kindergarten. *New Zealand Journal of Educational Studies, 17,* 161–170.

Hanline, M. F., & Fox, L. (1993). Learning within the context of play: Providing typical early childhood experiences for children with severe disabilities. *The Journal of the Association for Persons with Severe Handicaps, 18*(2), 21–129.

Harlan, J. D., & Rivkin, M. (1996). *Science experiences for the early childhood years* (6th ed.). Upper Saddle River, NJ: Merrill/Prentice Hall.

Harms, T. (1969). *My art is me.* Berkeley, CA: University of California Extension Media Center.

Harms, T., & Clifford, M. (1980). *The day care environment rating scale.* New York: Teachers College Press.

Hartmann, W., & Rollett, B. (1994). Play: Positive intervention in the elementary school curriculum. In J. Hellendoorn, R. van der Kooij, & B. Sutton-Smith (Eds.), *Play and intervention,* 195–202. Albany, NY: State University of New York Press.

Haugland, S. W. (1996). Enhancing children's sense of self and community through utilizing computers. *Early Childhood Education Journal, 23*(4), 227–230.

Haugland, S. W., & Shade, D. D. (1988). Developmentally appropriate software for young children. *Young Children, 43*(4), 37–43.

Hazen, N., & Black, B. (1984). Social acceptance: Strategies children use and how teachers can help children learn them. *Young Children, 39*(6), 26–60.

Heath, S. B. (1983). *Ways with words: Language, life and work in communities and classrooms.* New York: Cambridge University Press.

Heath, S. B. (1985). Narrative play in second language learning. In L. Galda & A. Pellegrini (Eds.), *Play language and stories: The development of children's literate behavior* (pp. 147–166). Norwood, NJ: Ablex.

Heath, S. B., & Mangiola, L. (1991). *Children of promise: Literate activity in linguistically and culturally diverse classrooms.* Washington, DC: National Education Association.

Heathcote, D., & Herbert, P. (1985, Summer). A drama of meaning: Mantle of the expert. *Theory Into Practice, 24*(3), 173–179. Columbus, OH: Ohio State University.

Hendrick, J. (1997). *First steps toward teaching the Reggio way.* Upper Saddle River, NJ: Merrill/Prentice Hall.

Hendrickson, J. M., Strain, P. S., Trembley, A., & Shores, R. E. (1981). Relationship between a material use and the occurrence of social interactive behaviors by normally developing preschool children. *Psychology in the Schools, 18,* 500–504.

Hewitt, K., & Roomet, L. (1979). *Educational toys in America: 1800 to the present.* Burlington, VT: The Robert Hill Fleming Museum.

Hill, D. M. (1977). *Mud, sand, and water.* Washington, DC: National Association for the Education of Young Children.

Hirsch, E. S. (Ed.). (1996). *The block book* (3rd ed.). Washington, DC: National Association for the Education of Young Children.

Ho, W. C. (Ed.). (1989). *Yani: The brush of innocence.* New York: Hudson Hills Press.

Holt, B. G. (1990). *Science with young children.* Washington, DC: National Association for the Education of Young Children.

Houck, P. (1997). Lessons from an exhibition: Reflections of an art educator. In J. Hendrick (Ed.), *First steps toward teaching the Reggio way* (pp. 26–41). Upper Saddle River, NJ: Merrill/Prentice Hall.

Howes, C., with Unger, O. & Matheson, C. (1992). *The collaborative construction of pretend: Social pretend play functions.* New York: State University of New York Press.

Hutt, C. (1971). Exploration and play in children. In R. E. Herron & B. Sutton-Smith (Eds.), *Child's Play* (pp. 231–251). New York: Wiley.

Inhelder, B., & Piaget, J. (1964). *The early growth of logic in the child.* New York: Norton.

Inigo's dream. [Computer software]. (1987). Santa Monica, CA: The Voyager Company.

Isaacs, S. (1966). *Intellectual growth in young children*. New York: Schocken Books. (Originally published in 1930.)

Isenberg, J., & Jacob, E. (1988). Literacy and symbolic play: A review of the literature. *Childhood Education, 59*(4), 272–276.

Isenberg, J., & Quisenberry, N. L. (1988). Play: A necessity for all children. *Childhood Education, 64*(3), 138–145.

Jackowitz, E. R., & Watson, M. W. (1980). Development of object transformations in early pretend play. *Developmental Psychology, 16,* 543–549.

Jaelitza. (1996). Insect love: A field journal. *Young Children, 51* (4), 31–32.

Jambor, T., & Palmer, S. D. (1991). *Playground safety manual*. Birmingham, AL: Injury Prevention Center, University of Alabama.

Johnson, J. E., Ershler, J., & Lawton, J. (1982). Intellective correlates of preschoolers' spontaneous play. *Journal of General Psychology, 106,* 115–122.

Johnson, J., Christie, J., & Yawkey, T. (1987). *Play and early childhood development*. Glenview, IL: Scott, Foresman.

Jones, E. (1973). *Dimensions of teaching-learning environments: Handbook for teachers*. Pasadena, CA: Pacific Oaks College.

Jones, E. & Reynolds, G. (1992). *The play's the thing: Teachers' roles in children's play*. New York: Teachers College Press.

Juggle's rainbow. [Computer software]. (1982). Menlo Park, CA: The Learning Company.

Jungck, S. (1990). Viewing computer literacy through a critical ethnographic lens. *Theory Into Practice, 29*(4), 283–289.

Kamii, C. (1982). *Number in preschool and kindergarten: Educational implications of Piaget's theory*. Washington, DC: National Association for the Education of Young Children.

Kamii, C. (Ed.). (1990). *No achievement testing in the early grades: The games grown-ups play*. Washington, DC: National Association for the Education of Young Children.

Kamii, C., with DeClark, G. (1985). *Young children reinvent arithmetic: Implications of Piaget's theory*. New York: Teachers College Press.

Kamii, C. & DeVries, R. (1980). *Group games in early education*. Washington, DC: National Association for the Education of Young Children.

Kamii, C., & DeVries, R. (1993). *Physical knowledge in preschool education*. New York: Teachers College Press. (Originally published 1978)

Katz, L. G., & Chard, S. (1989). *Engaging children's minds: The project approach*. Norwood, NJ: Ablex.

Katz, L., Evangelou, D., & Hartman, J. (1990). *The case for mixed age grouping in early education*. Washington, DC: National Association for the Education of Young Children.

Kellogg, R. (1969). *Analyzing children's art*. Palo Alto, CA: National Press.

Kellough, R. D. (1996). *Integrating mathematics and science for kindergarten and primary children*. Upper Saddle River, NJ: Merrill/Prentice Hall.

King, N. (1987). Elementary school play: Theory and research. In J. Block & N. King (Eds.), *School play: A source book* (pp. 143–166). New York: Garland.

King, N. (1992). The impact of context on the play of young children. In S. Kessler & B. Swadner (Eds.), *Reconceptualizing the early childhood curriculum* (pp. 43–61). New York: Teachers College Press.

Koons, K. (1991). A center for writers. *First Teacher, 12*(7), 23.

Kritchevsky, L., Prescott, E., & Walling, L. (1977). *Planning environments for young children: Physical space* (2nd ed.). Washington, DC: National Association for the Education of Young Children.

Kuczaj, S. A. (1985). Language play. *Early childhood development and care, 19,* 53–67.

Labov, W. (1972). *Language in the inner city: Studies in black English vernacular*. Philadelphia, PA: Pennsylvania University Press.

Leavitt, R. L., & Eheart, B. K. (1991). Assessment in early childhood programs. *Young Children, 46*(5), 4–9.

Lederman, J. (1992). *In full glory early childhood: To play's the thing*. Unpublished manuscript.

Levin, D. E. (1998). *Remote control childhood? Combating the hazards of media culture*. Washington, DC: National Association for the Education of Young Children.

Levin, D. E., & Carlsson-Paige, N. (1995). The mighty morphin power rangers: Teachers voice concern. *Young Children, 50*(6), 67–72.

Lewis, C. C. (1995). *Educating hearts and minds: Reflections on Japanese preschool and elementary education.* New York: Cambridge University Press.

Liss, M. B. (1986). Play of boys and girls. In G. Fein & M. Rivkin (Eds.), *The young child at play: Reviews of research* (Vol. 4, pp. 127–140), Washington DC: National Association for the Education of Young Children.

Loughlin, C. E., & Suina, J. H. (1982). *The learning environment: An instructional strategy.* New York: Teachers College Press.

Lowenfeld, V. (1947). *Creative and mental growth.* New York: Macmillan.

Lowery, L. F. (1985). *The everyday science sourcebook: Ideas for teaching in the elementary and middle school.* Palo Alto, CA: Dale Seymour Publications.

Lux, D. G. (Ed.). (1985, Summer). *Theory into Practice, 24*(3).

Maeroff, G. I. (1991). Assessing alternative assessment. *Phi Delta Kappan, 73*(4), 272–281.

Malone, T. W. (1983). Guidelines for designing educational computer programs. *Childhood Education, 59*(4), 241–247.

Manning, K., & Sharp, A. (1977). *Structuring play in the early years at school.* London: Ward Lock Educational.

McCune, L. (1985). Play-language relationships and symbolic development. In L. C. Brown & A. Gottfried (Eds.), *Play interactions* (pp. 38–45). Skillman, NY: Johnson & Johnson.

McEvoy, M., Shores, R., Wehby, J., Johnson, S., & Fox, J. (1990). Special education teachers' implementation of procedures to promote social interaction among children in integrated settings. *Education and Training in Mental Retardation, 25*(3), 267–276.

McLloyd, V. (1983). The effects of the structure of play objects on the pretend play of low-income preschool children. *Child Development, 54,* 626–635.

McLloyd, V. (1986). Scaffolds or shackles? The role of toys in preschool children's pretend play. In G. Fein & M. Rivkin (Eds.), *The young child at play: Review of the research* (Vol. 4, pp. 63–67). Washington, DC: National Association for the Education of Young Children.

Mead, G. H. (1934). *Mind, self and society.* Chicago: University of Chicago Press.

Meisels, S. (1987). *Developmental screening in early childhood: A guide.* Washington, DC: National Association for the Education of Young Children.

Meyers, C., Klein, E., & Genishi, C. (1994). Peer relationships among 4 preschool second language learners in "small group time." *Early Childhood Research Quarterly, 9,* 61–85.

Miller, P., & Garvey, G. (1984). Mother-baby role play: Its origins in social support. In I. Bretherton (Ed.), *Symbolic play: The development of social understanding* (pp. 101–130). New York: Academic Press.

Millie's math house. [Computer software]. (1992). Berkeley Learning Technologies. Redmond, WA: Edmark.

Missouri Department of Elementary and Secondary Education. (1989, May). *Project construct: Curriculum and assessment specifications.* St. Louis, MO.

Mitchell, P. A. (Ed.). (1991). *Child Health Alert.* Newton Highlands, MA: Child Health Alert.

Monighan-Nourot, P. (1990). The legacy of play in American early childhood education. In E. Klugman & S. Smilansky (Eds.), *Children's play and learning: Perspectives and policy implications* (pp. 59–85). New York: Teachers College Press.

Monighan-Nourot, P., Scales, B., Van Hoorn, J., with Almy, M. (1987). *Looking at children's play: A bridge between theory and practice.* New York: Teachers College Press.

Montessori, M. (1936). *The secret of childhood.* Bombay, India: Orient Longman.

Moore, G. T. (1985). State of the art in play environment. In J. L. Frost & S. Sunderlin (Eds.), *When children play: Proceedings of the International Conference on Play and Play Environments* (pp. 171–191). Wheaton, MD: Association for Childhood Education International.

Morrison, H. (1985). *Learning to see what I saw.* Unpublished report of a research project for the Bay Area Writing Project. Berkeley, CA: University of California.

Morrison, H. (1985). Workshop for the Bay Area Writing Center at the University of California, Berkeley, CA.

Morrison, H., & Grossman, H. (1985). *Beginnings*. Video produced for the Bay Area Writing Project. Berkeley, CA: University of California.

Morrow, L. M., & Rand, M. (1991). Preparing the classroom environment to promote literacy during play. In J. Christie (Ed.), *Play and early literacy development* (pp. 141–165). Albany, NY: State University of New York Press.

Myers, C., McBride, S., & Peterson, C. (1996). Transdisciplinary, play-based assessment in early childhood special education: An examination of social validity. *Topics in Early Childhood Special Education, 16*(1), 66–87.

Myhre, S. M. (1993). Enhancing your dramatic play area through the use of prop boxes. *Young Children, 48*(5), 6–11.

Nabhan, G. P., & Trimble, S. (1994). *The geography of childhood: Why children need wild places.* Boston: Beacon Press.

Nachmanovitch, S. (1990). *Free play: The power of improvisation in life and the arts.* New York: Putnam.

National Academy of Science. (1995). *National science education standards.* Washington, DC: National Academy Press.

National Association for the Education of Young Children & National Association of Early Childhood Specialists in State Department of Education. (1991). Guidelines for appropriate curriculum content and assessment in programs serving children ages 3 through 8. *Young Children, 46*(3), 21–38.

National Association for the Education of Young Children Position Statement: Technology and Young Children—Ages Three Through Eight. (1996). *Young Children, 5*(6), 11–16.

National Association of State Boards of Education. (1988). *Right from the start: The report of the NASBE task force on early childhood education.* Alexandria, VA: Author.

National Council of Teachers of Mathematics. (1989). *Curriculum and evaluation standards for school mathematics.* Reston, VA.

National Science Teachers Association. (1992). Outstanding science books for young children in 1991. *Young Children, 47*(4), 73–75.

Neuman, S. & Roskos, K. (1991). Peers as literacy informants: A description of young children's literacy conversations in play. *Early Childhood Research Quarterly, 6*(2), 233–248.

Newcomer, P. (1993). *Understanding and teaching emotionally disturbed children and adolescents.* Austin TX: Pro-Ed, Inc.

Newman, D., Griffin, P., & Cole, M. (1989). *The construction zone: Working for cognitive change in school.* Cambridge, MA, New Rochelle, NY, Melbourne, Sydney: Cambridge University Press.

Nickelsburg, J. (1976). *Nature activities for early childhood.* Menlo Park, CA: Addison-Wesley.

Nicolopoulou, A. (1991). Play, cognitive development and the social world: The research perspective. In B. Scales, M. Almy, A. Nicolopoulou & S. Ervin-Tripp (Eds.), *The social context of play and development in early care and education* (pp. 129–142). New York: Teachers College Press.

Nicolopoulou, A. (1996). *Individual and collective representations in a social context: The interplay of worldmaking, identity formation and group dynamics in narrative development.* Paper presented at the annual meeting of the Jean Piaget Society, Philadelphia, PA.

Nicolopoulou, A. (1996). *Narrative development in a social context.* In D. Slobin, J. Gearhart, A. Kyratzis, and J. Guo (Eds.), *Social interaction, social context, and language,* (pp. 369–390). Mahwah, NJ: Erlbaum.

Nicolopoulou, A. (1997). Worldmaking and identity formation in children's narrative play-acting. In B. D. Cox & C. Lightfoot (Eds.), *Sociogenetic perspectives on internalization* (pp. 157–187). Mahwah, NJ: Erlbaum.

Nicolopoulou, A., Scales, B. & Weintraub, J. (1994). Gender differences and symbolic imagination in the stories of four-year-olds. In A. H. Dyson & C. Genishi (Eds.), *The need for story: Cultural diversity in classroom and community* (pp. 102–123). Urbana, IL: NCTE.

Nicolopoulou, A., & Scales, B. (1990, March). *Teenage Mutant Ninja Turtles vs. the prince and the princess.* Paper presented at 11th Annual

Meeting of the Pennsylvania Ethnography and Research Forum, Philadelphia, PA.

Ninio, A., & Bruner, J. S. (1976). The achievement and antecedents of labeling. *Journal of Child Language, 5*, 1–15.

Nixon, W. (1997). How nature shapes childhood: Personality, play, and a sense of place. *The Amicus Journal, 19*(2), 31–35.

Nourot, P. M. (1997). Playing with play in four dimensions. In Isenberg, J., & Jalongo, M. (Eds.). *Major trends and issues in childhood education: Challenges, controversies, and insights.* New York: Teachers College Press.

Nourot, P. M. (1996). *First class: Guide to early primary education.* Manuscript submitted for publication. Sacramento, CA: California Department of Education.

Nourot, P. M. (1998). Pretending together: Sociodramatic play in early childhood. In D. Fromberg and D. Bergen (Eds.), *Play from birth to twelve and beyond: Conflicts, perspectives, and meaning.* New York: Garland Publishing.

Nourot, P. M., Henry, J., & Scales, B. (1990, April). *A naturalistic study of story play in preschool and kindergarten.* Paper presented at the Annual Meeting of the American Educational Research Association. Boston, MA.

Nourot, P. M., & Van Hoorn, J. (1991). Symbolic play in preschool and primary settings. *Young Children, 46*(6), 40–52.

Oaklander, V. (1978). *Windows to our children.* Moab, UT: Real People Press.

Once upon a time. [Computer software]. (1987). New Haven, CT: Compu-Teach.

Orellana, M. (1994). Appropriating the voice of the superheroes: Three preschoolers' bilingual language uses in play. *Early Childhood Research Quarterly, 9*(2), 171–193.

Ostrosky, M., Kaiser, A., & Odom, S. (1993). Facilitating children's social-communicative interactions through the use of peer-mediated interventions. In A. Kaiser & D. Gray (Eds.), *Enhancing Children's Communication* (pp. 159–185).

Paley, V. G. (1981). *Wally's stories.* Cambridge, MA: Harvard University Press.

Paley, V. G. (1984). *Boys and girls: Superheroes in the doll corner.* Chicago: University of Chicago Press.

Paley, V. G. (1986). *Mollie is three.* Chicago: University of Chicago Press.

Paley, V. G. (1988). *Bad guys don't have birthdays: Fantasy play at four.* Chicago: University of Chicago Press.

Paley, V. G. (1990). *The boy who would be a helicopter.* Cambridge, MA: Harvard University Press.

Paley, V. G. (1992). *You can't say you can't play.* Cambridge, MA: Harvard University Press.

Paley, V. G. (1994). Princess Annabella and the black girls. In A. H. Dyson and C. Genishi (Eds.), *The need for story: Cultural diversity in classrooms and community*, pp. 145–154. Urbana, IL: National Council of Teachers of English.

Paley, V. G. (1995). *Kwanzaa and me: A teacher's story.* Cambridge, MA: Harvard University Press.

Paley, V. G. (1997). *The girl with the brown crayon.* Cambridge, MA: Harvard University Press.

Papert, S. A. (1980). *Mindstorms: Children, computers and powerful ideas.* New York: Basic Books.

Papert, S. A. (1993). *The children's machine: Rethinking school in the age of the computer.* New York: Basic Books.

Parten, M. B. (1932). Social participation among preschool children. *Journal of Abnormal Psychology, 27*, 243–269.

Payne, J. N. (1990). *Mathematics for the young child.* Reston, VA: National Council of Teachers of Mathematics.

Pederson, D., Rook-Green, A., & Elder, J. (1981). The role of action in development of pretend play in young children. *Developmental Psychology, 17*, 756–759.

Pellegrini, A. D. (1982). Preschoolers' generation of cohesive text in two play contexts. *Discourse Processes, 5*, 101–107.

Pellegrini, A. D. (1984). The effects of exploration and play on young children's associative fluency: A review and extension in training studies. In T. D. Yawkey & A. D. Pellegrini (Eds.), *Child's play: Developmental and applied* (pp. 237–253). Hillsdale, NJ: Erlbaum.

Pellegrini, A., De Stefano, J. & Thompson, D. (1983). Saying what you mean: Using play to teach "literate language." *Language Arts, 60*(3), 380–384.

Pellegrini, A., & Galda, L. (1993). Ten years after: A reexamination of play and literacy research. *Reading Research Quarterly, 28*(2), 163–175.

Pellegrini, A., & Perlmutter, J. (1988). Rough and tumble play in the elementary school playground. *Young Children, 43*(2), 14–17.

Pepler, D. (1986). Play and creativity. In G. Fein & M. Rivkin (Eds.), *The young child at play: Reviews of research* (Vol. 4, pp. 143–154). Washington, DC: National Association for the Education of Young Children.

Pepler, D., & Ross, H. (1981). Effects of play on convergent and divergent problem solving. *Child Development, 52,* 1202–1210.

Perrone, V. (1990). How did we get here? In C. Kamii (Ed.), *No achievement testing in the early grades: The games grown-ups play* (pp. 1–14). Washington, DC: NAEYC.

Phyfe-Perkins, E. (1980). Children's behavior in preschool settings—A review of research concerning the influence of the physical environment. In L. G. Katz (Ed.), *Current topics in early childhood education* (Vol. 3, pp. 91–125). Norwood, NJ: Ablex.

Piaget, J. (1954). *The construction of reality in the child.* New York: Ballantine Books.

Piaget, J. (1962a). Comments. In L. S. Vygotsky, *Thought and language.* Cambridge, MA: MIT Press.

Piaget, J. (1962b). *Play, dreams and imitation in childhood.* New York: Norton.

Piaget, J. (1963a). *The origins of intelligence in children.* New York: Norton.

Piaget, J. (1963b). *The psychology of intelligence.* New Jersey: Littlefield, Adams.

Piaget, J. (1965a). *The child's conception of number.* New York: Norton.

Piaget, J. (1965b). *The child's conception of physical causality.* New Jersey: Littlefield, Adams.

Piaget, J. (1965c). *The child's conception of the world.* New Jersey: Littlefield, Adams.

Piaget, J. (1965d). *The moral judgment of the child.* New York: Free Press.

Piaget, J. (1966). *Judgment and reasoning in the child.* New Jersey: Littlefield, Adams.

Piaget, J. (1969a). *The child's conception of time.* New York: Basic Books.

Piaget, J. (1969b). *The language and thought of the child.* New York: World Publishing.

Piaget, J. (1971). *The child's conception of movement and speed.* New York: Ballantine.

Piaget, J. (1977). *The development of thought: Equilibration of cognitive structures.* New York: Viking.

Piaget, J. (1995). *Sociological studies.* New York: Routledge.

Piaget, J., & Inhelder, B. (1967). *The child's conception of space.* New York: Norton.

Piaget, J., & Inhelder, B. (1975). *The origin of the idea of chance in children.* New York: Norton.

Piaget, J., Inhelder, B., & Szeminska, A. (1960). *The child's conception of geometry.* London: Routledge & Kegan Paul.

Piaget, J., & Smith, L. (Eds.). (1995). *Sociological studies.* New York: Routledge.

Playroom. [Computer software]. (1989). Novato, CA: Broderbund.

Porter, R. (1991). Computers, children and teachers—Where are we headed? *Early Child Development and Care*, 73–83. (Originally published by Gordon Breach Science Publishers S.A., United Kingdom, 1991)

Pulaski, M. (1970). Play as a function of toy structure and fantasy predisposition. *Child Development, 41,* 531–537.

Ramsey, P., & Reid, R. (1988). Designing play environments for preschool and kindergarten children. In D. Bergen (Ed.), *Play as a medium for learning and development: A handbook of theory and practice* (pp. 213–240). Portsmouth, NH: Heinemann.

Reifel, S., & Yeatman, J. (1991). Action, talk and thought in block play. In B. Scales, M. Almy, A. Nicolopoulou, A., & S. Ervin-Tripp (Eds.), *The social context of play and development in early care and education* (pp. 156–172). New York: Teachers College Press.

Reynolds, G., & Jones, E. (1997). *Master players: Learning from children at play.* New York: Teachers College Press.

Rinaldi, C. (1993). The emergent curriculum and social constructivism. In C. Edwards, L. Gandini, & G. Forman (Eds.), *The hundred languages of children: The Reggio Emilia approach to early childhood education* (pp. 101–111). Norwood, NJ: Ablex.

Rivkin, M. S. (1995). *The great outdoors: Restoring children's right to play outside.* Washington, DC: National Association for the Education of Young Children.

Robinson, V. (1996). Cognitive development of children four through six years of age: Implications for practice. *Kindergarten Education: Theory, Research, and Practice, 1*(1), 11–27.

Rogers, D. L., & Ross, D. D. (1986). Encouraging positive social integration among young children. *Young Children, 41*(3), 12–17.

Roopnarine, J. L., & Johnson, J. E. (1983). Kindergarten play with preschool and school-aged children within a mixed age classroom. *The Elementary School Journal, 86*(5), 579–586.

Roopnarine, J. L., Johnson, J. E. & Hooper, F. H. (Eds.). (1994). *Children's play in diverse cultures.* Albany, NY: State of New York University Press.

Roskos, K. (1988). Literacy at work in play. *Reading Teacher, 41*(6), 562–567.

Roskos, K., & Neuman, S. B. (1993). Descriptive observations of adult facilitation of literacy in young children's play. *Early Childhood Research Quarterly, 8*, 77–97.

Rubin, K. H. (1980). Fantasy play: Its role in the development of social skills and social cognition. In K. H. Rubin (Ed.), *Children's play* (pp. 69–84). San Francisco: Jossey-Bass.

Rubin, K. H., Fein, G., & Vandenberg, B. (1983). Play. In E. M. Hetherington (Ed.) & P. H. Mussen (Series Ed.), *Handbook of child psychology: Vol. 4. Socialization, personality, and social development* (pp. 698–774). New York: Wiley.

Rubin, K. H., & Maioni, T. L. (1975). Play preference and its relationship to egocentrism, popularity, and classification skills in preschoolers. *Merrill-Palmer Quarterly, 21*, 171–179.

Rubin, K. H., Maioni, T. L., & Hornung, M. (1976). Free play behaviors in middle- and lower-class preschoolers: Parten & Piaget revisited. *Child Development, 47*, 414–419.

Sachs, J., Goldman, J., & Chaille, C. (1984). Narratives in preschool sociodramatic play: The role of knowledge and communicative competence. In L. Golden & A. Pellegrini (Eds.), *Play, language, and stories: The development of children's literate behavior* (pp. 45–62). Norwood, NJ: Ablex.

Saltz, E., & Johnson, J. (1974). Training for thematic fantasy play in culturally disadvantaged children: Preliminary results. *Journal of Educational Psychology, 66*, 623–630.

Scales, B. (1970, January). *Word and action: Creating a context for responsible autonomy.* Paper presented at a Drama in Education workshop at the University of Victoria, BC, Canada.

Scales, B. (1987). Play: The child's unseen curriculum. In P. Monighan-Nourot, B. Scales, J. Van Hoorn, with M. Almy, *Looking at children's play: A bridge between theory and practice,* pp. 89–103. New York: Teachers College Press.

Scales, B. (1989). Whoever gets to the bottom gets the soap, right? In *The Proceedings of the Annual Ethnography in Education Forum.* Philadelphia: University of Pennsylvania.

Scales, B. (1996). Researching the hidden curriculum. In S. Reifel (Ed.), J. Chafel & S. Reifel (Series Eds.), *Advances in early education and day care: Theory and practice in early childhood teaching* (Vol. 8, pp. 237–259). Greenwich, CT, London, England: JAI Press, Inc.

Scales, B. (1996, April). *Researching play and the hidden curriculum.* Paper presented at the annual meeting of TASP, Austin, TX.

Scales, B. (1997, April). *Play in the curriculum: A mirror of development and a catalyst for learning.* Paper presented at the Annual Meeting of TASP. Washington, DC.

Scales, B., Almy, M., Nicolopoulou, A., & Ervin-Tripp, S. (Eds.). (1991). *Play and the social context of development in early care and education. Part II: Language, literacy, and the social worlds of children* (pp. 75–126). New York: Teachers College Press.

Scales, B., & Cook-Gumperz, J. (1993). Gender in narrative and play: A view from the frontier. In S. Reifel (Ed.), *Advances in early education and day care: Perspectives on developmentally appropriate practice* (Vol. 5, pp. 167–195). Greenwich, CT: JAI Press.

Scales, B., & Webster, P. (1976). *Interactive cues in children's spontaneous play.* Unpublished manuscript.

Schrader, C. (1989). Written language use within the context of young children's symbolic play. *Early Childhood Research Quarterly, 4*, 225–244.

Schwartzman, H. B. (1976). Children's play: A sideways glance at make-believe. In D. F. Laney & B. A. Tindall (Eds.), *The anthropological study of play: Problems and prospects* (pp. 208–215). Cornwall, NY: Leisure Press.

Schwartzman, H. B. (1978). *Transformations: The anthropology of children's play.* New York: Plenum Press.

Schweinhart, L. J., Weikart, D. P., & Larner, M. B. (1986). Consequences of three preschool curriculum models through age 15. *Early Childhood Research Quarterly, I*(1), 15–45.

Shapiro, L. (1990, May 28). Guns and dolls. *Newsweek*, 56–65.

Sheldon, A. (1992). Conflict talk: Sociolinguistic challenges to self-assertion and how young girls meet them. *Merrill-Palmer Quarterly, 38*(1), 95–117.

Shepard, L. A. (1989). Why we need better assessments. *Educational Leadership, 46*(7), 4–8.

Sigel, I. E. (1993). Educating the young thinker: A distancing model of preschool education. In J. L. Roopnarine & J. E. Johnson (Eds.), *Approaches to early childhood education* (pp. 179–193, 237–252). Upper Saddle River, NJ: Merrill/Prentice Hall.

Sigel, I. E., & Saunders, R. (1979). An inquiry into inquiry: Question-asking as an instructional model. In L. G. Katz (Ed.), *Current topics in early childhood education* (Vol. 2, pp. 169–193). Norwood, NJ: Ablex.

Silvern, S. & Chaille, C. (1996). Understanding through play. *Childhood Education, 72*(5), 274–277.

Singer, J. L. (1973). *The child's world of make-believe: Experimental studies of imaginative play.* New York: Academic Press.

Singer, J. L., & Singer, D. G. (1980). The values of imagination. In B. Sutton-Smith (Ed.), *Play and learning* (pp. 195–218). New York: Gardner Press.

Singer, J. L., & Singer, D. G. (1985). *Make believe: Games and activities to foster imaginative play in young children.* Glenview, IL: Scott, Foresman.

Smilansky, S. (1968). *The effects of sociodramatic play on disadvantaged preschool children.* New York: Wiley.

Smilansky, S. (1990). Sociodramatic play: Its relevance to behavior and achievement in school. In E. Klugman & S. Smilansky (Eds.), *Children's play and learning: Perspectives and policy implications* (pp. 18–42). New York: Teachers College Press.

Smilansky, S., Hagan, J., & Lewis, H. (1989). *Clay in the classroom: Helping children develop cognitive and affective skills for learning.* New York: Teachers College Press.

Smilansky, S., & Shefatya, L. (1990). *Facilitating play: A medium for promoting cognitive, socio-emotional and academic development in young children.* Gaithersburg, MD: Psychosocial and Educational Publications.

Smith, P. (1994). *Play training: An overview.* In J. Hellendoom, R. van der Kooij, & B. Sutton-Smith (Eds.), *Play and intervention* (pp. 185–194). Albany, NY: State University of New York Press.

Smith, P. K., & Connolly, K. J. (1980). *The ecology of preschool behavior.* Cambridge, UK: Cambridge University Press.

Stewig, J. W., & Buege, C., (1994). *Dramatizing literature in whole language classrooms.* New York & London: Teachers College Press.

Stone, S. J. (1995). Wanted: Advocates for play in the primary grades. *Young Children, 50*(6), 45–54.

Stone, S. J., & Christie, J. F. (1996). Collaborative literacy during sociodramatic play in a multiage (K–2) primary classroom. *Journal of Research in Childhood Education, 10*(2), 123–133.

Strickland, D. S., & Morrow, L. M. (Eds.). (1989). *Emerging literacy: Young children learn to read and write.* Newark, DE: International Reading Association.

Sutton-Smith, B. (1968). Novel responses to toys. *Merrill-Palmer Quarterly, 14*, 151–158.

Sutton-Smith, B. (1988). The struggle between sacred play and festive play. In D. Bergen (Ed.), *Play as a medium for learning and development* (pp. 45–48. Portsmouth, NH: Heinemann.

Sutton-Smith, B., & Kelly-Byrne, D. (1984). The phenomenon of bipolarity in play theories. In T. D. Yawkey & A. D. Pellegrini (Eds.), *Child's play: Developmental and applied* (pp. 29–48). Hillsdale, NJ: Erlbaum.

Sutton-Smith, B., & Rosenberg, B. G. (1971). Sixty years of historical change in the game preferences of American children. In R. E. Herron & B. Sutton-Smith (Eds.), *Child's Play* (pp. 18–50). New York: Wiley.

Sylva, K., Roy, C., & Painter, M. (1980). *Child watching at play-groups and nursery school, Vol. 2: Oxford preschool research project.* Ypsilanti, MI: The High Scope Press.

Taylor, R. P. (Ed.). (1980). *The computer in the school: Tutor, tool, tutee.* New York: Teachers College Press.

Tierney, R., Carter, J., & Desai, L. E. (1991). *Portfolio assessment in the reading-writing classroom.* Norwood, MA: Christopher-Gordon.

Tizard, B., & Hughes, M. (1984). *Young children learning.* Cambridge, MA: Harvard University Press.

Trawick-Smith, J. (1988). Let's say you're the baby, ok? Play leaderships and following behavior of young children. *Young Children, 43*(5), 51–59.

Trawick-Smith, J. (1992). A descriptive study of persuasive preschool children: How they get others to do what they want. *Early Childhood Research Quarterly, 7*(1), 95–114.

Trawick-Smith, J. (1994). *Interactions in the classroom: Facilitating play in the early years.* Upper Saddle River, NJ: Merrill/Prentice Hall.

Tribble, C. (1996). *Individual differences in children's entrance strategies into preschool peer groups as a function of the quality of the mother-child attachment relationship.* Unpublished Dissertation. University of California, Berkeley.

Ungerer, J. A., & Sigman, M. (1984). The relation of play and sensorimotor behavior to language in the second year. *Child Development, 55,* 1448–1455.

Urberg, K., & Kaplan, M. (1986). Effects of classroom age composition on the play and social behaviors of preschool children. *Journal of Applied Developmental Psychology, 7*(4), 403–415.

van der Kooij, R. (1989a). Research on children's play. *Play and Culture, 2*(1), 20–34.

van der Kooij, R. (1989b). Play and behavioral disorders in schoolchildren. *Play and Culture, 2,* 328–339.

Veldhuis, H. A. (1982, May). *Spontaneous songs of preschool children.* Master's Thesis. San Francisco State University, San Francisco, CA.

Vergeront, J. (1987). *Places and spaces for preschool and primary (indoors).* Washington, DC: National Association for the Education of Young Children.

Vergeront, J. (1988). *Places and spaces for preschool and primary (outdoors).* Washington, DC: National Association for the Education of Young Children.

von Blanckensee, L. (1997). *Scale for choosing technology-based activities for young children, ages 3–7.* Unpublished manuscript.

Vukelich, C. (1990). Where's the paper? Literacy during dramatic play. *Childhood Education, 66*(4), 205–209.

Vygotsky, L. S. (1962). *Thought and language.* Cambridge, MA: MIT Press.

Vygotsky, L. S. (1967). Play and its role in the mental development of the child. *Soviet Psychology, 12,* 62–76.

Vygotsky, L. S. (1976). Play and its role in the mental development of the child. In J. S. Bruner, A. Jolly, & K. Sylva (Eds.), *Play: Its role in development and evolution* (pp. 537–544). New York: Basic Books.

Vygotsky, L. S. (1978). *Mind in Society: Development of higher psychological processes.* Cambridge, MA: Harvard University Press.

Wagner, B. J. (1976). *Dorothy Heathcote: Drama as a learning medium.* Washington, DC: National Education Association.

Wagner, B. J. (1990). Dramatic improvisation in the classroom. In S. J. Hynds & E. L. Robin (Eds.), *Perspectives on talk and learning* (pp. 195–211). Urbana, IL: National Council of Teachers of English.

Wassermann, S. (1990). *Serious players in the primary classroom: Empowering children through active learning experiences.* New York: Teachers College Press.

Weber, E. (1984). *Ideas influencing early childhood education: A theoretical analysis.* New York: Teachers College Press.

Wheeler, L., & Raebeck, L. (1985). *Orff and Kodaly adapted for the elementary school* (3rd ed.). Dubuque, IA: William C. Brown.

Where in the world is Carmen Sandiego? [Computer software]. (1982). Novato, CA: Broderbund.

White, T. H. (1958). *The once and future king.* New York: Berkeley.

Williamson, P., & Silvern, S. (1990). The effect of play training on the story comprehension of upper primary children. *Journal of Research in Child Education, 4*(2), 130–135.

Winn, M. (1977). *The plug-in drug*. New York: Bantam Books.

Wohlwill, J. F. (1984). Relationships between exploration and play. In T. Yawkey & A. Pellegrini (Eds.), *Child's play: Developmental and applied* (pp. 143–201). Hillsdale, NJ: Erlbaum.

Wolfgang, C., & Sanders, T. (1981). Defending young children's play as the ladder to literacy. *Theory Into Practice, 20*, 116–120.

Woods, J. & Scales, B. (1995, June). *The child's hidden curriculum*. Panel presentation at annual meeting of the Association of Constructivist Teaching. Berkeley, CA.

Wright, J. L. & Shade, D. D. (Eds.). (1994). *Young children: Active learners in a technological age*. Washington, DC: National Association for the Education of Young Children.

Zan, B. (1996). Interpersonal understanding among friends: A case study of two young boys playing checkers. *Journal of Research in Childhood Education, 10*, 114–122.

Index